Lecture Notes of the Institute for Computer Sciences, Social Informatics and Telecommunications Engineering   168

More information about this series at http://www.springer.com/series/8197

Phan Cong Vinh · Leonard Barolli (Eds.)

Nature of Computation and Communication

Second International Conference, ICTCC 2016
Rach Gia, Vietnam, March 17–18, 2016
Revised Selected Papers

 Springer

Editors
Phan Cong Vinh
Nguyen Tat Thanh University
Ho Chi Minh City
Vietnam

Leonard Barolli
Fukuoka Institute of Technology
Fukuoka
Japan

ISSN 1867-8211   ISSN 1867-822X (electronic)
Lecture Notes of the Institute for Computer Sciences, Social Informatics
and Telecommunications Engineering
ISBN 978-3-319-46908-9   ISBN 978-3-319-46909-6 (eBook)
DOI 10.1007/978-3-319-46909-6

Library of Congress Control Number: 2016954936

Printed on acid-free paper

This Springer imprint is published by Springer Nature
The registered company is Springer International Publishing AG
The registered company address is: Gewerbestrasse 11, 6330 Cham, Switzerland

Preface

The fourth edition of the International Conference on the Nature of Computation and Communication (ICTCC) ICTCC was held during March 17–18, 2016, in Rach Gia City, Vietnam. The aim of the conference is to provide an internationally respected forum for scientific research related to the natural aspects of computation and communication. This conference provides an excellent opportunity for researchers to discuss natural approaches and techniques for computation and communication. The proceedings of ICTCC 2016 are published by Springer in the series of *Lecture Notes of the Institute for Computer Sciences, Social Informatics and Telecommunications Engineering* (LNICST) (indexed by DBLP, EI, Google Scholar, Scopus, Thomson ISI).

For this edition, the Program Committee received over 100 submissions from 15 countries and each paper was reviewed by at least three expert reviewers. We chose 36 papers after intensive discussions held among the Program Committee members. We appreciate the excellent reviews and lively discussions of the Program Committee members and external reviewers in the review process. This year we chose three prominent invited speakers, Prof. Leonard Barolli from Fukuoka Institute of Technology (FIT) in Japan, Prof. Phan Cong Vinh from Nguyen Tat Thanh University (NTTU) in Vietnam, and Pandian Vasant from Universiti Teknologi PETRONAS in Malaysia.

ICTCC 2016 was jointly organized by The European Alliance for Innovation (EAI), Nguyen Tat Thanh University (NTTU), and Kien Giang University (KGU). This conference could not have been organized without the strong support from the staff members of these three organizations. We would especially like to thank Prof. Imrich Chlamtac (University of Trento and Create-NET), Barbara Fertaľova (EAI), and Ivana Allen (EAI) for their great help in organizing the conference. We also appreciate the gentle guidance and help from Prof. Nguyen Manh Hung, Chairman and Rector of NTTU.

March 2016

Phan Cong Vinh
Leonard Barolli

ICTCC 2016

Steering Committee

Imrich Chlamtac   Create-Net and University of Trento, Italy
Phan Cong Vinh   Nguyen Tat Thanh University, Vietnam

Organizing Committee

Honorary General Chairs

Thai Thanh Luom   Kien Giang University, Vietnam
Nguyen Manh Hung   Nguyen Tat Thanh University, Vietnam

General Chair

Phan Cong Vinh   Nguyen Tat Thanh University, Vietnam

Technical Program Committee Chairs

Truong My Dung   Ba Ria – Vung Tau University, Vietnam
Nguyen Thanh Tung   Hanoi Vietnam National University, Vietnam

Technical Program Committee Session or Track Leader

Huynh Nhat Phat   Hue University of Sciences, Vietnam

Workshops Committee Chair

Emil Vassev   University of Limerick, Ireland

Publications Committee Chair

Phan Cong Vinh   Nguyen Tat Thanh University, Vietnam

Marketing and Publicity Committee Chair

Vu Minh Loc   Ba Ria – Vung Tau University, Vietnam

Sponsorship and Exhibits Committee Chair

Le Diem   Kien Giang University, Vietnam

Panels and Keynotes Committee Chair

Vangalur Alagar   Concordia University, Canada

Demos and Tutorials Committee Chair

Nguyen Thanh Binh   Ho Chi Minh City University of Technology, Vietnam

Posters Committee Chair

Thai Thi Thanh Thao   Nguyen Tat Thanh University, Vietnam

Industry Forum Committee Chair

Le Huy Ba   Ho Chi Minh City University of Industry, Vietnam

Special Sessions Committee Chair

Nguyen Kim Quoc   Nguyen Tat Thanh University, Vietnam

Local Chair

Nguyen Tuong   Kien Giang University, Vietnam

Website Committee Chair

Tran Thi Nhu Thuy   Nguyen Tat Thanh University, Vietnam

Conference Manager

Barbara Fertalova   EAI (European Alliance for Innovation), Slovakia

Program Committee

Abdur Rakib	The University of Nottingham, UK
Aniruddha Bhattacharjya	Narasaraopeta Engineering College, India
Areerat Songsakulwattana	Rangsit University, Thailand
Ashad Kabir	Swinburne University of Technology, Australia
Ashish Khare	University of Allahabad, India
Athar Sethi	Universiti Teknologi PETRONAS, Malaysia
Chien-Chih Yu	National ChengChi University, Taiwan
Chintan Bhatt	Charotar University of Science and Technology, India
David Sundaram	The University of Auckland, New Zealand
Dinh Duc Anh Vu	University of Information Technology – HCMVNU, Vietnam
Duong Tuan Anh	Ho Chi Minh City University of Technology – HCMVNU, Vietnam
Gabrielle Peko	The University of Auckland, New Zealand
Giacomo Cabri	University of Modena and Reggio Emilia, Italy
Govardhan Aliseri	Jawaharlal Nehru Technological University Hyderabad, India
Hoang Huu Hanh	Hue University, Vietnam
Hoang Quang	Hue University of Sciences, Vietnam
Huynh Quyet-Thang	Hanoi University of Science and Technology, Vietnam

Huynh Trung Hieu	Ho Chi Minh City University of Industry, Vietnam
Huynh Xuan Hiep	Can Tho University, Vietnam
Kurt Geihs	University of Kassel, Germany
Le Hong Anh	Ha Noi University of Mining and Geology, Vietnam
Le Manh	Van Hien University, Vietnam
Le Ngoc Tran	Ba Ria-Vung Tau University, Vietnam
Le Van Quoc Anh	Ho Chi Minh City University of Transport, Vietnam
Ly Quoc Ngoc	Ho Chi Minh City University of Science – HCMVNU, Vietnam
Manik Sharma	DAV University, India
Manmeet Mahinderjit Singh	Universiti Sains Malaysia, Malaysia
Mubarak Mohammad	Concordia University, Canada
Muhammad Fahad Khan	Federal Urdu University of Arts, Science, and Technology, Pakistan
Naseem Ibrahim	Albany State University, USA
Nguyen Hung Cuong	Hanoi University of Science and Technology, Vietnam
Nguyen Quoc Huy	Saigon University, Vietnam
Nguyen Thanh Binh	Ho Chi Minh City University of Technology – HCMVNU, Vietnam
Nguyen Thanh Phuong	Polytechnic University of Bari, Italy
Nguyen Tuan Dang	University of Information Technology – HCMVNU, Vietnam
Ondrej Krejcar	University of Hradec Kralove, Czech Republic
Prasanalakshmi Balaji	Professional Group of Institutions, India
Pham The Bao	Ho Chi Minh City University of Science – HCMVNU, Vietnam
Shanmugam BalaMurugan	Kalaignar Karunanidhi Institute of Technology, India
Santi Phithakkitnukoon	Chiang Mai University, Thailand
Tran Dinh Que	Posts and Telecommunications Institute of Technology, Vietnam
Vangalur Alagar	Concordia University, Canada
Waralak V. Siricharoen	University of the Thai Chamber of Commerce, Thailand
Zhu Huibiao	East China Normal University, China

Contents

Currying Self-* Actions in Autonomic Systems

Phan Cong Vinh[1](✉) and Nguyen Thanh Tung[2]

[1] Faculty of IT, Nguyen Tat Thanh University (NTTU),
300A Nguyen Tat Thanh St., Ward 13, District 4, HCM City, Vietnam
pcvinh@ntt.edu.vn
[2] International School, Vietnam National University in Hanoi,
144 Xuan Thuy St., Cau Giay District, Hanoi, Vietnam
tungnt@isvnu.vn

Abstract. Self-* is regarded as a foundation for autonomic computing. The concepts of autonomic systems (ASs) and self-* action are considered as a basis for research on currying self-* actions. In this paper, we will specify ASs, self-* actions in ASs, product of ASs and universal properties, and then move on to consider curried self-* actions.

Keywords: Autonomic Computing · Autonomic Systems · Currying · Product · Self-*

1 Introduction

In our previous work [3], autonomic computing (AC) imitates and simulates the natural intelligence possessed by the human autonomic nervous system using generic computers. This indicates that the nature of software in AC is the simulation and embodiment of human behaviors, and the extension of human capability, reachability, persistency, memory, and information processing speed. AC was first proposed by IBM in 2001 where it is defined as

"*Autonomic computing is an approach to self-managed computing systems with a minimum of human interference. The term derives from the body's autonomic nervous system, which controls key functions without conscious awareness or involvement*" [1].

AC in our recent investigations [3–8,10,11] is generally described as self-*. Formally, let self-* be the set of self-_'s. Each self-_ to be an element in self-* is called a *self-* action*. That is,

$$\text{self-*} = \{\text{self-\_} \mid \text{self-\_ is a self-* action}\} \tag{1}$$

We see that self-CHOP is composed of four self-* actions of self-configuration, self-healing, self-optimization and self-protection. Hence, self-CHOP is a subset of self-*. That is, self-CHOP = {self-configuration, self-healing, self-optimization, self-protection} ⊂ self-*. Every self-* action must satisfy some certain criteria, so-called *self-* properties*.

© ICST Institute for Computer Sciences, Social Informatics and Telecommunications Engineering 2016
P.C. Vinh et al. (Eds.): ICTCC 2016, LNICST 168, pp. 1–10, 2016.
DOI: 10.1007/978-3-319-46909-6_1

In its AC manifesto, IBM proposed eight actions setting forth an AS known as *self-awareness, self-configuration, self-optimization, self-maintenance, self-protection (security and integrity), self-adaptation, self-resource- allocation* and *open-standard-based* [1]. In other words, consciousness (self-awareness) and non-imperative (goal-driven) behaviors are the main features of autonomic systems (ASs).

In this paper we will specify ASs and self-* and then move on to consider curried self-* actions in ASs. All of this material is taken as an investigation of our category, the category of ASs, which we call **AS**.

2   Outline

In the paper, we attempt to make the presentation as self-contained as possible, although familiarity with the notion of self-* in ASs is assumed. Acquaintance with the associated notion of algebraic language [2] is useful for recognizing the results, but is almost everywhere not strictly necessary.

The rest of this paper is organized as follows: Sect. 3 presents specification of autonomic systems (ASs). In Sect. 4, self-* actions in ASs are specified. In Sect. 5, products of ASs and some universal properties are considered. Curried self-* actions are investigated in Sect. 6. Finally, a short summary is given in Sect. 7.

3   Specification of Autonomic Systems (ASs)

From our previous publications [3–8, 10, 11], we can consider an *AS* as a collection of states $x \in AS$, each of which is recognizable as being in AS and such that for each pair of named states $x, y \in AS$ we can tell if $x = y$ or not. The symbol $\oslash$ denotes the AS with no states.

If AS_1 and AS_2 are ASs, we say that AS_1 is a sub-system of AS_2, and write $AS_1 \subseteq AS_2$, if every state of AS_1 is a state of AS_2. Checking the definition, we see that for any system AS, we have sub-systems $\oslash \subseteq AS$ and $AS \subseteq AS$.

We can use system-builder notation to denote sub-systems. For example the autonomic system can be written $\{x \in AS \mid x \text{ is a state of AS}\}$.

The symbol $\exists$ means "there exists". So we can write the autonomic system as $\{x \in AS \mid \exists y \text{ is a final state such that } self\text{-}*action(x) = y\}$

The symbol $\exists!$ means "there exists a unique". So the statement "$\exists! x \in AS$ is an initial state" means that there is one and only one state to be a start one, that is, the state of the autonomic system before any self-* action is processed.

Finally, the symbol $\forall$ means "for all". So the statement "$\forall x \in AS \ \exists y \in AS$ such that $self\text{-}* \ action(x) = y$" means that for every state of autonomic system there is the next one.

In the paper, we use the $\overset{def}{=}$ notation "$AS_1 \overset{def}{=} AS_2$" to mean something like "define AS_1 to be AS_2". That is, a $\overset{def}{=}$ declaration is not denoting a fact of nature (like $1 + 2 = 3$), but our formal notation. It just so happens that the notation above, such as Self-CHOP $\overset{def}{=}$ {self-configuration, self-healing, self-optimization, self-protection}, is a widely-held choice.

4 Specification of Self-* Actions in Autonomic Systems

From our previous investigations [3–8,10,11], self-* actions in autonomic systems can be specified as follows:

If AS and AS' are sets of autonomic system states, then a self-* action *self-*action* from AS to AS', denoted *self-*action*: $AS \to AS'$, is a mapping that sends each state $x \in AS$ to a state of AS', denoted *self-*action*$(x) \in AS'$. We call AS the domain of *self-*action* and we call AS' the codomain of *self-*action*.

Note that the symbol AS', read "AS-prime", has nothing to do with calculus or derivatives. It is simply notation that we use to name a symbol that is suggested as being somehow like AS. This suggestion of consanguinity between AS and AS' is meant only as an aid for human cognition, and not as part of the mathematics. For every state $x \in AS$, there is exactly one arrow emanating from x, but for a state $y \in AS'$, there can be several arrows pointing to y, or there can be no arrows pointing to y.

Suppose that $AS' \subseteq AS$ is a sub-system. Then we can consider the self-* action $AS' \to AS$ given by sending every state of AS' to "itself" as a state of AS. For example if $AS = \{a, b, c, d, e, f\}$ and $AS' = \{b, d, e\}$ then $AS' \subseteq AS$ and we turn that into the self-* action $AS' \to AS$ given by $b \mapsto b, d \mapsto d, e \mapsto e$. This kind of arrow, $\mapsto$, is read aloud as "maps to". A self-* action *self-*action*: $AS \to AS'$ means a rule for assigning to each state $x \in AS$ a state *self-*action*$(x) \in AS'$. We say that "x maps to *self-*action*(x)" and write $x \mapsto$ *self-*action*(x).

As a matter of notation, we can sometimes say something like the following: Let *self-*action*: $AS' \subseteq AS$ be a sub-system. Here we are making clear that AS' is a sub-system of AS, but that *self-*action* is the name of the associated self-* action.

Given a self-* action *self-*action*: $AS \to AS'$, the states of AS' that have at least one arrow pointing to them are said to be in the image of *self-*action*; that is we have $\mathrm{im}(\textit{self-*action}) \overset{def}{=} \{y \in AS' \mid \exists x \in AS$ such that *self-*action*$(x) = y\}$. Given *self-*action*: $AS \to AS'$ and *self-*action'* : $AS' \to AS''$, where the codomain of *self-*action* is the same set of autonomic system states as the domain of *self-*action'* (namely AS'), we say that *self-*action* and *self-*action'* are composable

$$AS \xrightarrow{\textit{self-*action}} AS' \xrightarrow{\textit{self-*action}'} AS''$$

The composition of *self-*action* and *self-*action'* is denoted by *self-*action'* $\circ$ *self-*action*: $AS \to AS''$.

We write $\mathrm{Hom_{AS}}(AS, AS')$ to denote the set of *self-*actions* $AS \to AS'$. Two self-* actions *self-*action*, *self-*action'* : $AS \to AS'$ are equal if and only if for every state $x \in AS$ we have *self-*action*$(x) =$ *self-*action'*(x).

We define the identity *self-*action* on AS, denoted $id_{AS} : AS \to AS$, to be the self-* action such that for all $x \in AS$ we have $id_{AS}(x) = x$.

A *self-*action*: $AS \to AS'$ is called an *isomorphism*, denoted *self-*action*: $AS \xrightarrow{\cong} AS'$, if there exists a self-* action *self-*action'* : $AS' \to AS$ such that *self-*action'* $\circ$ *self-*action* $= id_{AS}$ and *self-*action* $\circ$ *self-*action'* $= id_{AS'}$. We also say that *self-*action* is *invertible* and we say that *self-*action'* is the *inverse* of *self-*action*. If there exists an isomorphism $AS \xrightarrow{\cong} AS'$ we say that AS and AS' are isomorphic autonomic systems and may write $AS \cong AS'$.

Proposition 1. *The following facts hold about isomorphism.*

1. *Any autonomic system AS is isomorphic to itself; i.e. there exists an isomorphism $AS \xrightarrow{\cong} AS$.*
2. *For any autonomic systems AS and AS', if AS is isomorphic to AS' then AS' is isomorphic to AS.*
3. *For any autonomic systems AS, AS' and AS'', if AS is isomorphic to AS' and AS' is isomorphic to AS'' then AS is isomorphic to AS''.*

Proof:

1. The identity self-* action $id_{AS} : AS \to AS$ is invertible; its inverse is id_{AS} because $id_{AS} \circ id_{AS} = id_{AS}$.

2. If *self-*action*: $AS \to AS'$ is invertible with inverse *self-*action'* : $AS' \to AS$ then *self-*action'* is an isomorphism with inverse *self-*action*.

3. If *self-*action*: $AS \to AS'$ and $\widehat{self\text{-}*action} : AS' \to AS''$ are each invertible with inverses *self-*action'* : $AS' \to AS$ and $\widehat{self\text{-}*action}' : AS'' \to AS'$ then the following calculations show that $\widehat{self\text{-}*action} \circ self\text{-}*action$ is invertible with inverse $self\text{-}*action' \circ \widehat{self\text{-}*action}'$:

$$(\widehat{self\text{-}*action} \circ self\text{-}*action) \circ (self\text{-}*action' \circ \widehat{self\text{-}*action}') =$$
$$\widehat{self\text{-}*action} \circ (self\text{-}*action \circ self\text{-}*action') \circ \widehat{self\text{-}*action}' =$$
$$\widehat{self\text{-}*action} \circ id_{AS'} \circ \widehat{self\text{-}*action}' =$$
$$\widehat{self\text{-}*action} \circ \widehat{self\text{-}*action}' = id_{AS''}$$

and

$$(self\text{-}*action' \circ \widehat{self\text{-}*action}') \circ (\widehat{self\text{-}*action} \circ self\text{-}*action) =$$
$$self\text{-}*action' \circ (\widehat{self\text{-}*action}' \circ \widehat{self\text{-}*action}) \circ self\text{-}*action =$$
$$self\text{-}*action' \circ id_{AS'} \circ self\text{-}*action =$$
$$self\text{-}*action' \circ self\text{-}*action = id_{AS}$$

Q.E.D.

For any natural number $n \in \mathbb{N}$, define a set $\underline{n} = \{1, 2, \ldots, n\}$. So, in particular, $\underline{0} = \oslash$. A function $f : \underline{n} \to AS$ can be written as a sequence $f = (f(1), f(2), \ldots, f(n))$. We say that AS has cardinality n, denoted $| AS | = n$ if there exists an isomorphism $AS \cong \underline{n}$. If there exists some $n \in \mathbb{N}$ such that AS has cardinality n then we say that AS is finite. Otherwise, we say that AS is infinite and write $| AS | \geqslant \infty$.

Proposition 2. *Suppose that AS and AS' are finite. If there is an isomorphism of autonomic systems* $f : AS \to AS'$ *then the two autonomic systems have the same cardinality,* $\mid AS \mid = \mid AS' \mid$.

Proof: Suppose that $f : AS \to AS'$ is an isomorphism. If there exists natural numbers $m, n \in \mathbb{N}$ and isomorphisms $\alpha : \underline{m} \overset{\cong}{\to} AS$ and $\beta : \underline{n} \overset{\cong}{\to} AS'$ then

$$\underline{m} \overset{\alpha}{\to} AS \overset{f}{\to} AS' \overset{\beta^{-1}}{\to} \underline{n}$$

is an isomorphism. We can prove by induction that the sets $\underline{m}$ and $\underline{n}$ are isomorphic if and only if $m = n$. Q.E.D.

Consider the following diagram:

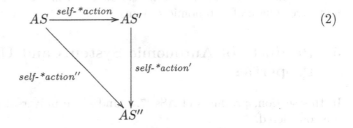 (2)

We say this is a diagram of autonomic systems if each of AS, AS', AS'' is an autonomic system and each of *self-*action, self-*action', self-*action''* is a self-* action. We say this diagram commutes if *self-*action' $\circ$ self-*action = self-*action''*. In this case we refer to it as a commutative triangle of autonomic systems. Diagram (2) is considered to be the same diagram as each of the following:

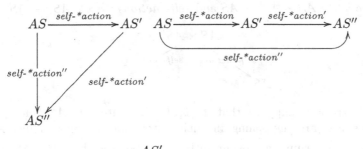

Consider the following picture:

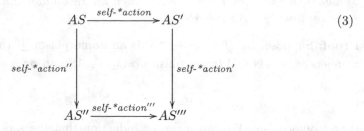

$$AS \xrightarrow{\;self\text{-}*action\;} AS' \tag{3}$$

We say this is a diagram of autonomic systems if each of AS, AS', AS'', AS''' is an autonomic system and each of $self\text{-}*action$, $self\text{-}*action'$, $self\text{-}*action''$, $self\text{-}*action'''$ is a self-* action. We say this diagram commutes if $self\text{-}*action' \circ self\text{-}*action = self\text{-}*action''' \circ self\text{-}*action''$. In this case we refer to it as a commutative square of autonomic systems.

5 Products of Autonomic Systems and Universal Properties

In this section, products of ASs [7,8] and some universal properties in ASs [9] are considered.

5.1 Products of Autonomic Systems

As considered in [7,8], let AS and AS' be autonomic systems. The product of AS and AS', denoted $AS \times AS'$, is defined as the autonomic system of ordered pairs (x, y) where states of $x \in AS$ and $y \in AS'$. Symbolically, $AS \times AS' = \{(x, y) | x \in AS, y \in AS'\}$. There are two natural projection actions of self-* to be $self\text{-}*action_1 : AS \times AS' \to AS$ and $self\text{-}*action_2 : AS \times AS' \to AS'$

$$AS \times AS' \tag{4}$$

For illustration, suppose that $\{a, b, c\}$ are states in AS and $\{d, e\}$ in AS', the states are happening in such autonomic systems. Thus, AS and AS', which are running concurrently, can be specified by $AS|AS' \overset{def}{=} \{(a|d), (a|e), (b|d), (b|e), (c|d), (c|e)\}$. Note that the symbol "|" is used to denote concurrency of states existing at the same time. We define self-* actions as $disable(d, e)$ and $disable(a, b, c)$ to be able to drop out relevant states.

$$\{(a|d), (a|e), (b|d), (b|e), (c|d), (c|e)\} \tag{5}$$

It is possible to take the product of more than two autonomic systems as well. For example, if AS_1, AS_2, and AS_3 are autonomic systems then $AS_1|AS_2|AS_3$ is the system of triples,

$$AS_1|AS_2|AS_3 \overset{def}{=} \{(a|b|c)|a \in AS_1, b \in AS_2, c \in AS_3\}$$

Proposition 3. *Let AS and AS' be autonomic systems. For any autonomic system AS'' and actions self-*$action_3 : AS'' \to AS$ and self-*$action_4 : AS'' \to AS'$, there exists a unique action $AS'' \to AS \times AS'$ such that the following diagram commutes*

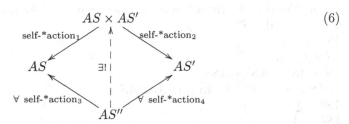

$$(6)$$

We might write the unique action as

$$\langle \text{self-*}action_3, \text{self-*}action_4 \rangle : AS'' \to AS \times AS'$$

Proof: Suppose given *self-*$action_3$* and *self-*$action_4$* as above. To provide an action $z : AS'' \to AS \times AS'$ is equivalent to providing a state $z(a) \in AS \times AS'$ for each $a \in AS''$. We need such an action for which *self-*$action_1 \circ z = $ self-*$action_3$* and *self-*$action_2 \circ z = $ self-*$action_4$*. A state of $AS \times AS'$ is an ordered pair (x, y), and we can use $z(a) = (x, y)$ if and only if $x = $ *self-*$action_1(x, y) = $ self-*$action_3(a)$* and $y = $ *self-*$action_2(x, y) = $ self-*$action_4(a)$*. So it is necessary and sufficient to define $\langle$*self-*$action_3$*, *self-*$action_4\rangle \overset{def}{=} ($self-*$action_3(a)$*, *self-*$action_4(a))$* for all $a \in AS''$. Q.E.D.

Given autonomic systems AS, AS', and AS'', and actions *self-*$action_3$* : $AS'' \to AS$ and *self-*$action_4$* : $AS'' \to AS'$, there is a unique action $AS'' \to AS \times AS'$ that commutes with *self-*$action_3$* and *self-*$action_4$*. We call it the *induced action* $AS'' \to AS \times AS'$, meaning the one that arises in light of *self-*$action_3$* and *self-*$action_4$*.

For example, as mentioned above autonomic systems $AS = \{a, b, c\}$, $AS' = \{d, e\}$ and $AS|AS' \overset{def}{=} \{(a|d), (a|e), (b|d), (b|e), (c|d), (c|e)\}$. For an autonomic system $AS'' = \varnothing$, which stops running, we define self-* actions as $enable(d, e)$ and $enable(a, b, c)$ to be able to add further relevant states. Then there exists a unique action

$$enable((a|d), (a|e), (b|d), (b|e), (c|d), (c|e))$$

such that the following diagram commutes

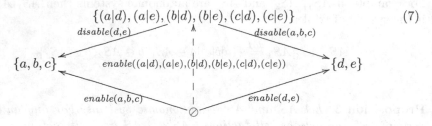

$$\{(a|d),(a|e),(b|d),(b|e),(c|d),(c|e)\} \qquad (7)$$

5.2 Universal Properties

As considered in [8], the following isomorphisms exist for any autonomic systems AS, AS', and AS''

$AS \times \underline{0} \cong \underline{0}$

$AS \times \underline{1} \cong AS$

$AS \times AS' \cong AS' \times AS$

$(AS \times AS') \times AS'' \cong AS \times (AS' \times AS'')$

$AS^{\underline{0}} \cong \underline{1}$

$AS^{\underline{1}} \cong AS$

$\underline{0}^{AS} \cong \underline{0}$

$\underline{1}^{AS} \cong \underline{1}$

$(AS^{AS'})^{AS''} \cong AS^{AS' \times AS''}$

If $n \in \mathbb{N}$ is a natural number and $\underline{n} = \{1, 2, \ldots n\}$, then AS^n is an abbreviation for $\prod_n AS$ and AS^n is an abbreviation for $AS^{\underline{n}}$. Thus, we have $AS^{\underline{n}} \cong \prod_n AS$

In the case of $\underline{0}^{\underline{0}}$, we get conflicting answers, because for any autonomic system AS, including $AS = \oslash = \underline{0}$, we have claimed both that $AS^{\underline{0}} \cong \underline{1}$ and that $\underline{0}^{AS} \cong \underline{0}$. Based on the definitions of $\underline{0}$, $\underline{1}$ and $AS^{AS'}$ given in Sect. 4, the correct answer for $\underline{0}^{\underline{0}}$ is $\underline{0}^{\underline{0}} \cong \underline{1}$. The universal properties, which are considered in this section, are in some sense about isomorphisms. It says that understanding isomorphisms of autonomic systems reduces to understanding natural numbers. But note that there is much more going on in the category of **AS** than isomorphisms; in particular there are self-* actions that are not invertible.

6 Currying Self-* Actions

Currying is the idea that when a self-* takes action on many ASs, we can let the self-* take action on one at a time or all at once. For example, consider self-* that takes action on AS and AS' and returns AS''. This is a self-* action $self\text{-}*action\colon AS \times AS' \to AS''$. This self-* takes action on two ASs at once, but it is convenient to curry the second AS. Currying transforms $self\text{-}*action$ into a self-* action

$$curry(self\text{-}*action)\colon AS \to \mathrm{Hom}_{\mathbf{AS}}(AS', AS'')$$

This is a good way to represent the same information in another fashion. For any AS', we can represent the self-* that takes action on AS and returns AS''. This is a self-* action

$$curry(self\text{-}*action)': AS' \to \mathrm{Hom}_{\mathbf{AS}}(AS, AS'')$$

Note that sometimes we denote the set of self-* actions from AS to AS' by

$$AS'^{AS} \overset{def}{=} \mathrm{Hom}_{\mathbf{AS}}(AS, AS')$$

If AS and AS' are both finite (so one or both are empty), then $|AS'^{AS}| = |AS'|^{|AS|}$. For any AS and AS', there is an isomorphism

$$\mathrm{Hom}_{\mathbf{AS}}(AS \times AS', AS'') \cong \mathrm{Hom}_{\mathbf{AS}}(AS, AS''^{AS'})$$

Let $AS = \{a, b\}$, $AS' = \{c, d\}$ and $AS'' = \{1, 0\}$. Suppose that we have the following self-* action $self\text{-}*action$: $AS \times AS' \to AS''$

$$self\text{-}*action : \begin{pmatrix} (a, c) \mapsto 1 \\ (a, d) \mapsto 0 \\ (b, c) \mapsto 0 \\ (b, d) \mapsto 1 \end{pmatrix}$$

Currying transforms $self\text{-}*action$ mentioned above into another self-* action with the same semantics

$$curry(self\text{-}*action) : \begin{pmatrix} a \mapsto \begin{pmatrix} c \mapsto 1 \\ d \mapsto 0 \end{pmatrix} \\ \\ b \mapsto \begin{pmatrix} c \mapsto 0 \\ d \mapsto 1 \end{pmatrix} \end{pmatrix}$$

7 Conclusions

The paper considers curried self-* actions using algebraic language. Currying is the idea that when a self-* takes action on many ASs, we can let the self-* take action on one at a time or all at once. Algebraic specification is presented in a simple way by a detailed discussion of the components required and only a brief mention to the more advanced components.

Acknowledgements. We would like to thank Vietnam National University, Hanoi to sponsor in the project QG.14.57 and NTTUFSTD (The NTTU foundation for Science and Technology Development) for Science and Technology Development) for the constant support of our work which culminated in the publication of this paper.

References

1. IBM. Autonomic Computing Manifesto (2001). Accessed http://www.research. ibm.com/autonomic/
2. Spivak, D.I.: Category Theory for the Sciences, 1st edn. The MIT Press, Cambridge (2014)
3. Vinh, P.C.: Formal aspects of self-* in autonomic networked computing systems. In: Zhang, Y., Yang, L.T., Denko, M.K. (eds.) Autonomic Computing and Networking, pp. 381–410. Springer, US (2009)
4. Vinh, P.C.: Toward formalized autonomic networking. Mob. Netw. Appl. **19**(5), 598–607 (2014). doi:10.1007/s11036-014-0521-z
5. Vinh, P.C.: Algebraically autonomic computing. Mob. Netw. Appl. **21**(1), 3–9 (2016). doi:10.1007/s11036-015-0615-2
6. Vinh, P.C.: Concurrency of self-* in autonomic systems. Future Gener. Comput. Syst. **56**, 140–152 (2016). doi:10.1016/j.future.2015.04.017
7. Vinh, P.C.: Products and Coproducts of Autonomic Systems. In: Vinh, P.C., Alagar, V. (eds.) ICCASA 2015. LNICSSITE, vol. 165, pp. 1–9. Springer, Heidelberg (2016). doi:10.1007/978-3-319-29236-6_1
8. Vinh, P.C.: Some universal constructions of autonomic systems. Mob. Netw. Appl. **21**(1), 89–97 (2016). doi:10.1007/s11036-015-0672-6
9. Vinh, P.C., Truong, N.M.: Products, coproducts and universal properties of autonomic systems. EAI Endorsed Trans. Context-aware Syst. Appl. **16**(7), 2 (2016)
10. Vinh, P.C., Tung, N.T.: Coalgebraic aspects of context-awareness. Mob. Netw. Appl. **18**(3), 391–397 (2013). doi:10.1007/s11036-012-0404-0
11. Vinh, P.C., Vassev, E.: Nature-inspired computation and communication: a formal approach. Future Gener. Comput. Syst. **56**, 121–123 (2016). doi:10.1016/j.future.2015.10.011

Towards User-Aware Service Composition

Giacomo Cabri$^{(\boxtimes)}$, Mauro Leoncini, Riccardo Martoglia,
and Franco Zambonelli

Università di Modena e Reggio Emilia, Modena, Italy
{giacomo.cabri,mauro.leoncini,riccardo.martoglia,
franco.zambonelli}@unimore.it

Abstract. Our everyday life is more and more supported by the information technology in general and by specific services provided by means of our electronic devices. The AMBIT project (Algorithms and Models for Building context-dependent Information delivery Tools) aims at providing a support to develop services that are automatically tailored based on the user profile. However, while the adaptation of the single services is the first step, the next step is to achieve adaptation in the *composition* of different services. In this paper, we explore how services can be composed in a user-aware way, in order to decide the composition that better meets users' requirements. That is, we exploit the user profile not only to provide her with customized services, but also to compose them in a suitable way.

Keywords: Services · User-awareness · Context

1 Introduction

We live in a device-supported world, where electronic devices provide us a lot of services in an ubiquitous way. Currently we have smartphones that enable us to perform requests and to get different kinds of information and services. In a not so far future, we will be surrounded by a multitude of different devices, from smart monitors that will provide us information in an adaptive way situational information to the surrounding public, to smart objects and wearables able to continuously interact with us.

All these interconnected devices will form an infrastructural substrate that could become possibly very useful to help users in performing different kinds of activities. However, the risk exists is that such potentially very large set of provided services will lead to confusion rather than helping users, who could eventually be overwhelmed by information and stimuli.

To overcome this problem, many researchers have proposed to develop applications with user-awareness capabilities [2,7,31]. A user-aware application recognizes the context in which the user is performing an activity by means of that application and exploits contextual information to adapt its behaviour.

In the literature we can find different approaches that address specific problems that arise in the development of user-aware applications (e.g., [1,6,24,26]).

© ICST Institute for Computer Sciences, Social Informatics and Telecommunications Engineering 2016
P.C. Vinh et al. (Eds.): ICTCC 2016, LNICST 168, pp. 11–21, 2016.
DOI: 10.1007/978-3-319-46909-6_2

The limitation of the existing approaches is that they are not global, being bounded to specific application fields or specific aspects of the context. So, in the frame of the AMBIT (Algorithms and Models for Building context-dependent Information delivery Tools) project[1] we have defined a model of user profile that aims at being more global than existing ones [8,13]; this model is composed of the following components: *Environment* parameters, which is a set of external conditions surrounding the user while performing activities (e.g., using an application); *Personal parameters*, which contain the essential data about the user's profile (e.g. name, gender, age, nationality), which are usually set by the user during the configuration of the application or the service; *History* parameters, which record past actions of the users, in order to have a more complete picture of the user itself.

This model of context is useful to enable a single application or a single service to adapt itself in order to provide more tailored functionalities.

In this paper we address the *composition* of different services. In fact, more and more often users requests are satisfied by a set of services that are composed to realize a higher-level service. In Sect. 4.1 readers can find an example. It happened for the web services [27], it is happening for the cloud services [16] and we can imagine that it will be the future for distributed systems [12].

Starting from these consideration, we propose to apply user-awareness to the composition of services, in order to meet the users' requests in a more customized way than the bare adaptation of single services. To this purpose, we rely on the SAPERE middleware infrastructure [9,32], which enables the dynamic and adaptive composition of services based on flexible nature-inspired rules, and extend its architecture in order to integrate adaptive and semantic composition of services, accounting in a semantic way for the current situation and context of users, accordingly to the models defined in the AMBIT project.

2   Related Work

Many challenging research problems in the area of user-awareness or more in general of context-awareness and context-dependent service delivery have been addressed in an already impressive body of work. These efforts are largely motivated by the astounding growth of the mobile device market and the need to support the evolution of the traditional Web into the so-called "Web of Things and Services". For some comprehensive surveys the reader is referred to [10,17,19,28] and the many references contained therein.

In the context of this huge active area, our research interests are primarily directed towards a general model of user profile and context, and its exploitation in order to provide better customized service compositions and services. First of all, it must be pointed out that the meaning associated to the word "context" is not unique and usually depends on the particular application(s) that researchers have in mind. For instance, in automotive applications context clearly refers to

---

[1] http://www.agentgroup.unimore.it/ambit/.

driving environment, while in health-care applications context is likely to refer to environmental, physiological and behavioral variables that apply to a specific patient. As another example, in online advertising the context is essentially the page (say, the page of an on-line newspaper) where the commercial is to be displayed, namely, its contents, the prevailing sentiment, etc.

Instead, we are interested in a general notion of user profile and context, that can possibly include all of the above and much more. There are a handful of research contributions that are relevant to this narrow area. Bettini et al. [4] take different types of context information into account (physical, computational, user context) and approach the problem of modeling and representation from within the perspective of automated reasoning. The rationale is that modeling real-life situations requires the ability to process basic context facts and reasoning makes it possible to attain pieces of information that are appropriate for use by context-aware applications. This highly cited survey is also important since it covers some prominent approaches to context modeling (object-role based, spatial models, ontology-based).

Han et al. [14] proposed a SOA-based approach to build automation systems with devices that are provided by a description that contains context information. This information is managed by a composition engine to coordinate appropriate devices/services based on the context, composition plan, and predefined policy rules. Another approach that is interesting because it takes into consideration different aspects is the one proposed by Peko et al. [25]. In fact, they start from the consideration that enterprises must be adaptable to the changes in the context they operate, but at the same time they must be sustainable in terms of economic, environmental, societal, and cultural concerns. Their approach considers the enterprises' context in terms of strategy, organization, process, and information. With respect to these works, our approach aims at exploiting a more general set of information (not only service/device enterprise-oriented) and is designed to address not only specific fields such as building automation or enterprise management, but a wider range of services.

The survey [5] covers various research works related to context modeling and awareness within the Context-ADDICT project of the Politecnico di Milano (see http://poseidon.ws.dei.polimi.it/ca/). They propose to design a context management system to be placed aside what they call the "operational system". While the latter is application dependent, the context management system is not, and exhibits a hierarchical structure in terms of observable (i.e., external) parameters that have a symbolic internal representation within a context schema. We will consider this separation of concerns also for building the bases of our user-aware service composer.

In [29] the authors propose a context-based approach for service discovery. The focus on services makes this work interesting for our purpose, even if we do not focus on the discovery. We will evaluate their formal definition of the context and possibly make it more general.

An approach that is interesting because it takes into consideration different aspects is the one proposed by Peko et al. [25]. In fact, they start from the consideration that enterprises must be adaptable to the changes in the context they operate, but at the same time they must be sustainable in terms of economic, environmental, societal, and cultural concerns. They approach consider the enterprises' context in terms of strategy, organization, process, and information. This global approach can influence our work and we could extend it to be more general.

Venkataram and Bharath [29] propose a context-based approach for service discovery. The focus on services makes this work interesting for our purpose, even if we do not focus on the discovery. We will evaluate their formal definition of the context and possibly make it more general.

3   The SAPERE Approach to Service Composition

3.1   The SAPERE Model

SAPERE starts from consideration that the large multitude of ubiquitous services that will soon enrich our lives, will make it suitable to model the ensemble of such services as a sort of distributed pervasive service *ecosystem* [32].

SAPERE conceptually models such pervasive ecosystem as a virtual *spatial environment* [30], laid above the actual network of devices infrastructure. The environment acts as a sort of shared space in which all service components situate, and the environment itself takes care of mediating all interactions. In other words, the spatial environment represents the ground on which services of different species indirectly interact and combine with each other. Such interactions take place in respect of a limited set of basic interaction laws (also called "eco-laws", due to their nature-inspired origins), and typically accounting on the spatial and contextual relationships between services.

For the *service components* populating in the ecosystem, SAPERE adopts a common modeling and a common treatment. Each of them has an associated semantic representation which we call "LSA" (*Live Semantic Annotations*, and describing a list of properties and characteristics for each services), to be injected in the spatial environment as it it were a sort of shared spatial memory. LSA support semantic and context-aware interactions both for service aggregation/composition and for data/knowledge management.

The *eco-laws* define the basic interaction policies among the LSAs of the various services of the ecosystem. The idea is to enforce on a spatial basis, and possibly relying on diffusive mechanisms, dynamic composition of data and services by composing their LSAs and exchanging data via them. Data and services (as represented by their associated LSAs) will be sort of chemical reagents, and interactions and compositions will occur via chemical reactions, relying on semantic pattern-matching between LSAs.

Without going into details about the specific of all the SAPERE eco-laws, we want to emphasize here that the advanced forms of adaptive pattern matching between LSAs that they enforce, can make it possible to dynamically compute, at any time and for every service of the ecosystem, the list of services potentially matching with which other services towards some forms of service composition.

Adaptivity in SAPERE is not in the capability of individual services, but in the overall self-organizing dynamics of the service ecosystem as a whole. In particular, adaptivity will be ensured by the fact that any change in the system (as well as any change in its services or in the context of such services, as reflected by dynamic changes in their LSAs) will reflect in the firing of new eco-laws, thus possibly leading to the establishment of new compositions or aggregations, and/or in the breaking of some existing service compositions.

3.2   The SAPERE Middleware

The execution of SAPERE applications is supported by a middleware infrastructure [9] which reifies the SAPERE environment in terms of a lightweight software support, enabling a SAPERE node to be installed in tablets and smartphones.

Each SAPERE node wishing to participate to the SAPERE ecosystem should host a local tuple space [11], to act as a local repository of LSAs for local services, and a local eco-laws engine. The LSA-space of each node is connected with a limited set of neighbor nodes based on spatial proximity relations. From the viewpoint of individual service, the middleware provides an API to access the local LSA space, to advertise themselves (via the injection of an LSA), and to support the services' need of continuously updating their LSAs. In addition, such API enables services to detect local events (as the modifications of some LSAs) or the enactment of some eco-laws on available LSAs.

Eco-laws are realized as a set of rules embedded in SAPERE nodes. For each node, the same set of eco-laws applies to rule the dynamics between local LSAs (in the form of bonding, aggregation, and decay) and those between non-locally-situated LSAs (via the spreading eco-law that can propagate LSAs from a node to another to support distributed service interactions and composition).

4   Towards Service Composition Based on User Profile

In this section we present the AMBIT service composer, relying on the SAPERE middleware, and our approach to user-aware service composition.

4.1   Case Study

A typical example of composition is an e-commerce transaction. Let us consider a user that aims at buying a good and requires the home delivery. She can exploit at least three services of different kind. The first one is the *shop* service, which enables the user to know which the goods on sale are, along with a set of further information such as the price, the availability, the size, and so on. The second service is related to the payment of the chosen good, for instance, a *credit card transaction* service. Finally, a *delivery agency* service is in charge of the actual delivery of the good to the users' home. Currently, these three services are provided by online e-commerce Web site as a whole, but in the future we envision that many services of each kind exist, and they can be composed to provide the higher-level service. In the latter case, the user preferences can influence the composition.

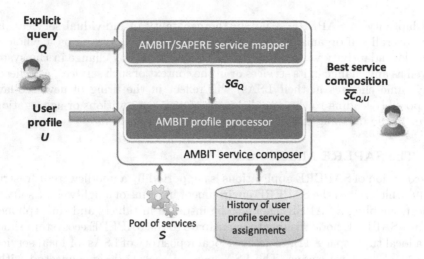

Fig. 1. High-level architecture of the AMBIT service composer

4.2 The AMBIT Architecture

The overall architecture of the AMBIT service composer includes two main modules: the AMBIT/SAPERE (which builds over SAPERE) and the AMBIT profile processor.

The AMBIT/SAPERE *service mapper* is basically an instance of that SAPERE middleware, embedding eco-laws and capable of digesting the LSAs of the different services of an ecosystem. In reaction to a user request that is translated into a query Q, which from within the SAPERE middleware takes the form of an LSA representing specific desirable features of a service, the eco-laws embedded within the SAPERE middleware react by determining – via pattern-matching – the set of possible service compositions SG_Q matching Q (Fig. 1).

The AMBIT *profile processor* has the goal of analyzing the set of possible service compositions SG_Q so as to find the best service composition $\overline{SC}_{Q,U}$ built upon the services available in pool S and matching at the best the user profile U (i.e., its preferences and context).

4.3 Service Mapper and Service Graphs

The AMBIT/SAPERE service mapper takes in input the query Q and determines a network (***service graph***) SG_Q of suitable service interactions, which represent the composition.

We assume a query Q to be characterized by a set of keywords, i.e., $Q = \{k_i^Q\}_{i=1,...,m}$. Similarly, the context is given by a user profile $U = \{k_i^U\}_{i=1,...,n}$; in this case, the keywords k_i^U can be determined using text analysis techniques, such as the ones described in [22], operating on the environment, user, and history data of the profile. Also, we consider a pool of available services S; each service $S \in \mathcal{S}$ is defined as $S = \{k_i^S\}_{i=1,\dots,l}$ a set of keywords k_i^S derived from the service description that characterize the service itself.

SG_Q is defined as a connected directed labeled graph $SG_Q = (\overline{\mathcal{S}}, I, w_Q)$ where $\overline{\mathcal{S}} \subseteq \mathcal{S}$ is a set of nodes (services), $I \subseteq \mathcal{S} \times \mathcal{S}$ is a set of directed arcs (service interactions) and $w_Q : I \to [0,1]$ is a function mapping directed arcs to their weights. SG_Q includes a source S_s and sink S_t corresponding to fictitious service nodes. The idea behind the weights $w_Q(S_1, S_2)$ is to quantify the relevance and suitability of a particular service interaction (S_1, S_2) w.r.t. Q. We do this by means of the following formula:

$$w_Q(S_1, S_2) = min(kwsim(S_1, Q), kwsim(S_2, Q)) \tag{1}$$

where $kwsim \in [0,1]$ is a similarity function that is computed between the keyword set Q and the sets S_1 and S_2, respectively. This can be, for instance, a Jaccard similarity [15] between the involved keyword sets. Note that we adopt a *semantic*, rather than a "syntactic" approach where keywords are matched on the basis of their semantic meaning (e.g. exploiting one or more thesauri such as WordNet [23] and taking synonyms and related terms into account [3,22]). The minimum in Eq. 1 captures the intuition that, if one of the two services $S1, S2$ is not particular relevant to Q, the relevance of the resulting interaction would presumably be equally low.

In Fig. 2 we report an example of service graph related to the case study previously introduced.

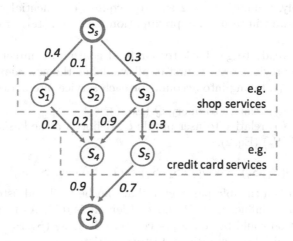

Fig. 2. An example of a service graph

4.4   Profile Processor and Best Service Composition

Given the service graph SG_Q computed on the basis of query Q, the goal of the AMBIT profile processor is to find, among all sequences $SC_{Q,U}$ of consecutive interaction arcs starting from S_s and ending in S_t, the "best" service composition(s) $\overline{SC}_{Q,U}$, also taking the user profile U into account. The obvious question now is how to define the concept of best service composition.

First of all, let's make a step back and elaborate on the concept of service composition as a *sequence* of interactions. The core idea of the profile processor is to store the *history* of service compositions assigned to users in past requests, in order to be able to statistically estimate the **probability** $P_U(S_y|S_x)$ that a given service interaction (S_x, S_y) is suitable for a given user profile U. Basically, given a service S_x, we want to find the most likely service S_y that could follow for user U. This can be done by working at the level of the single keywords composing profiles.

For a generic user $U = \{k_1, \ldots, k_n\}$ and any $I \subseteq \{1, \ldots, n\}$, let $count_I(S_x)$ and $count_I(S_x, S_y)$ denote the number of times users characterized (possibly among others) by the set of keywords $\{k_i\}_{i \in I}$ have been successfully serviced by service S_x and service interaction (S_x, S_y), respectively. The probability $P_U(S_y|S_x)$ of successful service interaction (S_x, S_y) for user U can then be estimated using the well-known principle of inclusion-exclusion[2]:

$$P_U(S_y|S_x) \approx \frac{\sum_{e=1}^{n}(-1)^{e-1} \sum_{I \subseteq \{1,\ldots,n\}, |I|=e} count_I(S_x, S_y)}{\sum_{e=1}^{n}(-1)^{e-1} \sum_{I \subseteq \{1,\ldots,n\}, |I|=e} count_I(S_x)} \qquad (2)$$

Unfortunately, computing Eq. 2 exactly requires exponential work so in our implementation we will recur to approximation (see, e.g., [18]) or even heuristic algorithms.

We are now ready to get back to our final goal and complete the picture. Building on the previous results, first of all we define the new **weights** w of the service graph SG_Q, taking into account for each service interaction (S_x, S_y):

(a) the weights w_Q relative to query Q (Eq. 1);
(b) the weights w_U relative to user profile U, defined on the basis of the *probability* $P_U(S_y|S_x)$ (Eq. 2).

$$w(S_x, S_y) = \alpha \cdot w_Q(S_x, S_y) + (1 - \alpha) \cdot w_U(S_x, S_y) \qquad (3)$$

where $\alpha \in (0, 1)$ is a tunable parameter that can be freely adjusted in order to change the relative influence of Q and U (default is 0.5). As to $w_U(S_x, S_y)$, a first approximation could be to simply compute it as $w_U(S_x, S_y) = P_U(S_y|S_x)$. However, in the initial computations, history statistics are not sufficient to compute a significant probability, thus we choose to initially base it on a similarity between S_x, S_y and U (similarly as Eq. 1 did for Q):

$$w_U(S_x, S_y) = \beta \cdot min(kwsim(S_x, U), kwsim(S_y, U)) + (1 - \beta) \cdot P_U(S_y|S_x) \quad (4)$$

---

[2] We adopt the well known Markov chain approximation: in our context, the probability of choosing the next service depends only on the preceding service and not on the whole sequence of services that preceded it.

where β is a time-dependent parameter decreasing from 1 to 0, gradually giving strength to the probability $P_U(S_y|S_x)$.

Finally, we define a **score** of a service composition $SC_{Q,U} = \{(S_s, S_x), (S_x, S_y), \ldots, (S_z, S_t)\}$ by composing the weights of its single interactions as defined in Eq. 3:

$$score(SC_{Q,U}) = \varphi(w(S_s, S_x), w(S_x, S_y), \ldots, w(S_z, S_t)) \tag{5}$$

where φ is a composition function that, at comparable weight, privileges the shortest sequences (eg. a composition of a very large number of suitable services is not expected to be equally suitable). A first level of approximation is the product: $score(SC_{Q,U}) = \prod_{a \in SC_{Q,U}} w(a) = w(S_s, S_x) \cdot w(S_x, S_y) \cdot \ldots \cdot w(S_z, S_t)$. In this way, finding the "best" service composition $\overline{SC}_{Q,U}$ becomes a matter of finding the sequence of service interactions maximizing the score in Eq. 5. Since the service graph is a DAG (Directed Acyclic Graph) and the "score" of service composition cannot but decrease when extending a path, this computation can be efficiently performed (in linear time) using a slightly modified version of Dijkstra algorithm.

For instance, for our example in Fig. 2, $\overline{SC}_{Q,U} = \{(S_s, S_3), (S_3, S_4), (S_4, S_t)\}$, $score(\overline{SC}_{Q,U}) = 0.3 \cdot 0.9 \cdot 0.9$.

5 Conclusions

In this paper we have proposed an approach to compose services taking into consideration the user profile, leading to *user-aware service composition*. To this purpose, we rely on the SAPERE infrastructure, which has been enhanced by adding a profile processor that takes the user profile as input and proposes the best composition among potential ones.

In future work we will consider the concept of "semantic path" from complementary research areas [20,21] for extending our semantic score computation method on a service graph; further, we aim at providing an effective implementation of our approach, and at evaluating it on some case studies.

Acknowledgement. This work was supported by the project "Algorithms and Models for Building context-dependent Information delivery Tools" (AMBIT) co-funded by Fondazione Cassa di Risparmio di Modena (SIME 2013.0660).

References

1. Abowd, G.D., et al.: Cyberguide: a mobile context-aware tour guide. Wirel. Netw. **3**, 421–433 (1997)
2. Baldauf, M., Dustdar, S., Rosenberg, F.: A survey on context-aware systems. Int. J. Ad Hoc Ubiquit. Comput. **2**, 263–277 (2007)

3. Bergamaschi, S., Martoglia, R., Sorrentino, S.: Exploiting semantics for filtering and searching knowledge in a software development context. Knowl. Inf. Syst. **45**(2), 295–318 (2015)
4. Bettini, C., et al.: A survey of context modelling, reasoning techniques. Pervasive Mob. Comput. **6**(2), 161–180 (2010). Context Modelling, Reasoning and Management
5. Bolchini, C., et al.: Context modeling and context awareness: steps forward in the context-addict project. Bull. Techn. Committee Data Eng. **34**, 47–54 (2011)
6. Burrell, J., Gay, G.K.: E-graffiti: evaluating real-world use of a context-aware system. Interact. Comput. **14**(4), 301–312 (2002)
7. Cabri, G., et al.: Location-dependent services for mobile users. IEEE Trans. Syst. Man, Cybern.-Part A: Syst. Hum. **33**(6), 667–681 (2003)
8. Cabri, G., Leoncini, M., Martoglia, R.: AMBIT: towards an architecture for the development of context-dependent applications and systems. In: Proceedings of the 3rd International Conference on Context-Aware Systems and Applications (ICCASA 2014), pp. 64–68. ICST, Brussels, October 2014
9. Castelli, G., et al.: Engineering pervasive service ecosystems: the sapere approach. ACM Transactions on Autonomous and Adaptive Systems (TAAS) **10**(1), 1 (2015)
10. de Prado, A.G., Ortiz, G.: Context-aware services: a survey on current proposals. In: The 3rd International Confernece on Advanced Service Computing, Service Computation 2011, pp. 104–109 (2011)
11. Gelernter, D.: Generative communication in linda. ACM Trans. Program. Lang. Syst. **7**(1), 80–112 (1985)
12. Gilmore, S., Hillston, J., Tribastone, M.: Service composition for collective adaptive systems. In: Nicola, R., Hennicker, R. (eds.) Software, Services, and Systems. LNCS, vol. 8950, pp. 490–505. Springer, Heidelberg (2015). doi:10.1007/978-3-319-15545-6_28
13. Grassi, D., Bouhtouch, A., Cabri, G.: Inbooki: context-aware adaptive e-books. In: Proceedings of the 2nd International Conference on Context-Aware Systems and Applications, November 2013
14. Han, S.N., Lee, G.M., Crespi, N.: Semantic context-aware service composition for building automation system. IEEE Trans. Ind. Inf. **10**(1), 752–761 (2014)
15. Jaccard, P.: Étude comparative de la distribution florale dans une portion des Alpes et des Jura. Bulletin del la Société Vaudoise des Sciences Naturelles **37**, 547–579 (1901)
16. Jula, A., Sundararajan, E., Othman, Z.: Cloud computing service composition: a systematic literature review. Expert Syst. Appl. **41**(8), 3809–3824 (2014)
17. Jun, J.H., Lee, D.W., Sim, K.B.: Realization of cooperative strategies and swarm behavior indistributed autonomous robotic systems using artificial immune system. In: Procedings of the IEEE International Conference on Systems, Man, and Cybernetics, IEEE SMC 1999, vol. 6, pp. 614–619 (1999)
18. Kahn, J., Linial, N., Samorodnitsky, A.: Inclusion-exclusion: exact and approximate. Combinatorica **16**(4), 465–477 (1996)
19. Kapitsaki, G.M., et al.: Context-aware service engineering: a survey. J. Syst. Softw. **82**(8), 1285–1297 (2009)
20. Mandreoli, F.: Sri@work.: Efficient and effective routing strategies in a PDMS. In: Proceedings of WISE Conference, pp. 285–297 (2007)
21. Mandreoli, F., et al.: Data-sharing P2P networks with semantic approximation capabilities. IEEE Internet Comput. (IEEE) **13**(5), 60–70 (2009)

22. Martoglia, R.: AMBIT: semantic engine foundations for knowledge management in context-dependent applications. In: The 27th International Conference on Software Engineering and Knowledge Engineering, SEKE 2015, Pittsburgh, PA, USA, 6–8 July 2015, pp. 146–151 (2015)
23. Miller, A.G.: Wordnet: a lexical database for english. Commun. ACM **38**(11), 39–41 (1995)
24. Munoz, M.A., et al.: Context-aware mobile communication in hospitals. Computer **36**(9), 38–46 (2003)
25. Peko, G., Dong, C.-S., Sundaram, D.: Adaptive sustainable enterprises: a framework, architecture and implementation. In: Vinh, P.C., Alagar, V., Vassev, E., Khare, A. (eds.) ICCASA 2013. LNICST, vol. 128, pp. 293–303. Springer, Heidelberg (2014). doi:10.1007/978-3-319-05939-6_29
26. Priyantha, N.B., Chakraborty, A., Balakrishnan, H.: The cricket location-support system. In: Proceedings of the 6th Annual International Conference on Mobile Computing and Networking, MobiCom 2000, pp. 32–43. ACM, New York (2000)
27. Rao, J., Su, X.: A survey of automated web service composition methods. In: Cardoso, J., Sheth, A. (eds.) SWSWPC 2004. LNCS, vol. 3387, pp. 43–54. Springer, Heidelberg (2005). doi:10.1007/978-3-540-30581-1_5
28. Truong, H.-L., Dustdar, S.: A survey on context-aware web service systems. Int. J. Web Inf. Syst. **5**, 5–31 (2009)
29. Venkataram, P., Bharath, M.: A method of context-based services discovery in ubiquitous environment. In: Vinh, P.C., Alagar, V., Vassev, E., Khare, A. (eds.) ICCASA 2013. lnicst, vol. 128, pp. 260–270. Springer, Heidelberg (2014). doi:10.1007/978-3-319-05939-6_26
30. Weyns, D., et al.: The agent environment in multi-agent systems: A middleware perspective. Multiagent Grid Syst. **5**(1), 93–108 (2009)
31. Zambonelli, F., Bicocchi, N., Fontana, D.: Towards a human-aware operating system. In: 9th International Conference on Body Area Networks, BODYNETS 2014, London, Great Britain, 29 September–1 October, 2014
32. Zambonelli, F., et al.: Developing pervasive multi-agent systems with nature-inspired coordination. Perv. Mob. Comput. **17**, 236–252 (2015)

Dense 3D Mapping Using Volume Registration

Luke Lincoln[(✉)] and Ruben Gonzalez

Information and Communication Technology, Griffith University,
Gold Coast, Australia
{l.lincoln,r.gonzalez}@griffithuni.edu.au

Abstract. In this paper, a novel closed form solution is presented for solving the simultaneous localization and mapping (SLAM) problem. Unlike existing methods which rely on iterative feature matching, the proposed method utilises 3D phase correlation. This method provides high noise robustness, even in the presence of moving objects within the scene which are problematic for SLAM systems. Quantitative and qualitative experimental results are presented, evaluating the noise sensitivity, reconstruction quality and robustness in the context of moving objects.

1 Introduction

Simultaneous localization and mapping (SLAM) has many applications in robotics, architecture and engineering, business and science. Its objective is to produce a map (2D birds-eye-view, or 3D) of an environment using image and other sensory data. This is typically performed by computing local features, iteratively matching them across frames and solving for the camera pose and location. This feature matching approach is dependent on finding a sufficient number of matches. When this is true the approach is able to cope with local matching disparities by treating them as outliers. This technique is not robust when features are not stable or when feature confusion occurs.

1.1 Monocular Camera Feature Based Systems

Monocular Feature based SLAM systems use feature matches to estimate camera pose and location changes across frames [4]. Variations of this method use different features including: corners and lines [13], image patches [24] and exemplar feature matching [3]. SIFT features are used most often in SLAM [1,7,12,21], in addition FAST features have been explored [15–18]. Beall et al. [1] made use of both SIFT and SURF features in their underwater SLAM system. Real-time monocular SLAM systems based on this approach have also been proposed [3,21]. RANSAC is often used in monocular SLAM [7,15–17,23] to remove outliers which cause incorrect camera parameter estimates. Bundle adjustment is also used as an additional step to refine camera parameter estimation [7].

© ICST Institute for Computer Sciences, Social Informatics and Telecommunications Engineering 2016
P.C. Vinh et al. (Eds.): ICTCC 2016, LNICST 168, pp. 22–32, 2016.
DOI: 10.1007/978-3-319-46909-6_3

1.2   Stereo Camera Feature Based Systems

Stereo based SLAM systems also use features to estimate camera parameters. However, stereo based systems are capable of generating dense depth data more easily using stereo algorithms. Miro et al. [19] proposed a stereo based method which uses SIFT and the extended Kalman filter. The method by Van Gool et al. [22] works with un-calibrated stereo pairs. It uses Harris corner features and a multi-view stereo algorithm. Sim et al. [25] and Gil et al. [8] both presented stereo based SLAM systems which use SIFT.

1.3   RGB-D Sensor Feature Based Systems

RGB-D SLAM systems use both depth and image data and are capable of generating dense 3D reconstructions. Many of these methods rely on feature matching techniques [5,6,10]. RANSAC is often used to filter outliers for the estimation of camera parameters [5,6,10]. Another method which has also been used extensively in the area is Iterative Closest Point (ICP) [2,6,10,11,20,26]. ICP iteratively registers point cloud data, and is used to refine camera parameter estimates. A method named KinectFusion was proposed by Newcombe et al. [20] which uses RANSAC and a GPU implementation of IPC. Whelan et al. [28] extended this method allowing it to map larger areas using Fast Odometry From Vision (FOVIS) over ICP. Bylow et al. [2] improved the ICP approach by registering data using a signed distance function.

1.4   Non-Feature Based Methods

Several RGB-D SLAM systems are also non-feature based [11,14,27]. Weikersdorfer et al. [27] presented a novel sensor system named D-eDVS along with an event based SLAM algorithm. The D-eDVS sensor combines depth and event driven contrast detection. Rather than using features, it uses all detected data for registration. Kerl et al. [14] proposed a dense RGB-D SLAM system which uses a probabilistic camera parameter estimation procedure. It uses the entire image rather than features to perform SLAM.

1.5   Summary

As is evident from the current literature, SLAM typically relies on feature matching and RANSAC. However, these approaches fail when there are too few features, when feature confusion occurs or, when features are non-stationary due to object motion. As the extent of random feature displacement becomes more global the effectiveness of these approaches diminishes. Feature matching also dominates in image registration. However, Fourier based methods have been shown to work well under larger rotations and scales [9] whilst being closed form, insensitive to object motion and scaling naturally to GPU implementations. Accordingly, we propose a novel, closed form Fourier based SLAM method.

2 Method

The proposed SLAM method consists of various steps. First each frame f_i that is captured, consisting of a colour and depth image pair is projected into 3D space, forming colour point cloud $points_i$ and re-sampled into a volume V_i. Then, the transform parameters between pairs of volumes V_i and V_{i+1} are estimated using $VolumeRegister_{\theta\varphi t_x t_y t_z}$ shortened to $VR_{\theta\varphi t_x t_y t_z}$. These parameters are used to update transformation matrix M. The points corresponding to f_2 ($points_1$) are then transformed using the updated M matrix and added to the cumulative $PointCloud$ database. Two lists, $Cameras$ and $Poses$, are also updated to track camera pose and location per frame. This basic procedure is given in Listing 1 and elaborated upon in subsequent subsections.

```
f₁ = ReadFrame();
PointCloud = project(f₁);
M = IdentityMatrix(),  Camera = [0,0,0]ᵀ,  Pose = [0,0,1]ᵀ;
Cameras = [Camera],  Poses = [Pose];
while(more frames){
    f₂ = ReadFrame();
    points₁ = project(f₂),  points₂ = project(f₁);
    V₁ = ResampleVolume(points₁),  V₂ = ResampleVolume(points₂);
    (θ,φ,tₓ,t_y,t_z) = VR_θφtₓt_yt_z(V₁,V₂);
    M = M× TransformMatrix((θ,φ,tₓ,t_y,t_z));
    points₁ = Transform(points₁, M);
    PointCloud = PointCloud ∪ points₁;
    Camera = M⁻¹ × Camera;
    Pose = M⁻¹ × Pose;
    Cameras.add(Camera);
    Poses.add ( (Pose−Camera)/|Pose−Camera| );
    f₁ = f₂;
}
```

Listing 1. Phase Correlation Based SLAM Algorithm

2.1 Sensor Input

The input to our method is a color and depth image pair, $f(u,v)$ and $g(u,v)$ obtained using an Asus Xtion PRO LIVE sensor at a resolution of 640×480. Each pixel is projected into 3D space using $X_{u,v} = \frac{(u-c_x)Z_{u,v}}{f}$, $Y_{u,v} = \frac{(v-c_y)Z_{u,v}}{f}$ and $Z_{u,v} = g(u,v)$. Here, $[c_x c_y]^T$ represent the center of the image whilst f represents the focal length, defined as 525.0. The point clouds generated by projecting these images are then quantized into image volumes. Results reported in this paper were obtained using volumes of 384^3 voxels in size.

2.2 Volume Registration

Figure 1 shows a functional block diagram of our method. The input data are two 3D volumes ($Volume_1$ and $Volume_2$) and the output is the transformation

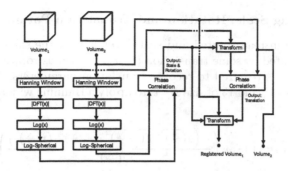

Fig. 1. System diagram for registration process

matrix required to register the two volumes. The volumes are first Hanning windowed. Next, a translation independent representation is obtained for each by taking the magnitude of their 3D FFTs. Then a log function is applied to the resulting magnitude values, improving scale and rotation estimation [9]. Following a log-spherical transformation, 3D phase correlation is performed to find the global rotation and scale relationship between $Volume_1$ and $Volume_2$. $Volume_1$ is then inversely transformed by the rotation and scale parameters, leaving only the translation to be resolved. This is found by applying phase correlation again between the transformed $Volume_1$ and $Volume_2$.

2.3   Phase Correlation

Given a volume V_1 and a spatially shifted version of it V_2, the offset can be recovered using *PhaseCorrelation* (Eq. 1). This function takes two volumes as input and returns the translation between them.

$$(x, y, z) = PhaseCorrelation(V_m, V_n) \tag{1}$$

The *PhaseCorrelation* function first applies 3D FFTs to volumes, V_1 and V_2, converting them into the frequency domain, i.e. $F_{1_{x,y,z}} = FFT(V_1)$ and $F_{2_{x,y,z}} = FFT(V_2)$. Taking the normalised cross power spectrum using Eq. 2 completes the Phase correlation function.

$$F_{3_{x,y,z}} = \frac{F_{1_{x,y,z}} \circ F^*_{2_{x,y,z}}}{|F_{1_{x,y,z}} \circ F^*_{2_{x,y,z}}|} \tag{2}$$

Here, $\circ$ is an element-wise multiplication and $|x|$ is the magnitude function. Taking the inverse FFT of F_3, gives the phase correlation volume V_3 ($V_3 = FFT^{-1}(F_3)$). The location of the peak value in V_3, (x_1, y_1, z_1) gives the shift between the V_1 and V_2. The phase correlation volume is typically noisy making the peak difficult to locate.

2.4   Recovering Scale, Rotation and Translation Parameters

If V_1 and V_2 are instead rotated and scaled versions of the same volume, such that they are related by some translation (t_x, t_y, t_z), y-axis rotation θ, and scale φ. Further action is required to recover translation parameters. The first step, given two volumes V_1 and V_2 of size N^3 is to apply a Hanning windowing function (Eq. 3).

$$HW_{x,y,z} = \frac{1}{2}\left(1 - cos\left(\frac{2\pi\left(\sqrt{\left(\frac{N}{2}\right)^3} - \sqrt{\left(x - \frac{N}{2}\right)^2 + \left(y - \frac{N}{2}\right)^2 + \left(z - \frac{N}{2}\right)^2}\right)}{2\sqrt{\left(\frac{N}{2}\right)^3} - 1}\right)\right) \quad (3)$$

The rotation and scale factors are recovered first using a translation independent representation of the volumes using the Fourier shift theory. For this, the magnitude of the FFT of the volumes is taken, $M_1 = |FFT(V_1)|$, $M_2 = |FFT(V_2)|$. The zero-frequency of both M_1 and M_2 is shifted to the center of the volume and the log of the result is taken $M_1' = Log(M_1)$, $M_2' = Log(M_2)$ which reduces noise on the phase correlation volume. A log-spherical transform is then used to turn rotation and scaling into translation for both M_1' and M_2'. Equation 4 shows the corresponding log-spherical space coordinate $(X_{log-spherical}, Y_{log-spherical}, Z_{log-spherical})$ for a given (x, y, z) euclidean space coordinate.

$$X_{log-spherical} = \frac{atan\left(\left(\frac{x - \frac{N}{2}}{\sqrt{x^2 + y^2 + z^2}}\right)\left(\frac{y - \frac{N}{2}}{\sqrt{x^2 + y^2 + z^2}}\right)^{-1}\right)N}{360}$$

$$Y_{log-spherical} = \frac{acos\left(\frac{y}{\sqrt{x^2 + y^2 + z^2}}\right)N}{180} \quad (4)$$

$$Z_{log-spherical} = \frac{log\left(\sqrt{x^2 + y^2 + z^2}\right)N}{log\left(\frac{N}{2.56}\right)}$$

The log-spherical transforms of M_1' and M_2' are then phase correlated to find the shift between them, $(x_{M'}, y_{M'}, z_{M'}) = PhaseCorrelation(M_1', M_2')$. The rotation θ and scale φ factors between V_1 and V_2 can then be found from the shift parameters using Eq. 5 .

$$\theta = \frac{-360x_{M'}}{N}$$

$$\varphi = e^{-\left(2.56^{-1}N\right)z_{M'}N^{-1}} \quad (5)$$

Using θ and φ, V_1 can now be inverse transformed (using $(\frac{N}{2}, \frac{N}{2}, \frac{N}{2})$ as the origin). This aligns V_1 and V_2 with respect to scale and y-axis rotation. The translation parameters (t_x, t_y, t_z) can then be found using phase correlation as given in Eq. 6.

$$(t_x, t_y, t_z) = PhaseCorrelation(scale(rotate(V_1, \theta), \varphi), V_2) \quad (6)$$

The complete function to recover translation, rotation and scaling, combining Eqs. 2–6 as is denoted in Listing 1 is 7.

$$(\theta, \varphi, t_x, t_y, t_z) = PhaseCorrelation_{\theta \varphi t_x t_y t_z}(V_m, V_n) \tag{7}$$

2.5 Performance Analysis

To assess the performance of our method, the size of the volumes being registered is defined as N^3 whilst each frame is sampled at a resolution of $W \times H$. The projection process requires $12WH$ operations whilst re-sampling the point cloud requires $2WH$ operations. The Volume Registration process, $VolumeRegister_{\theta \varphi t_x t_y t_z}(V_1, V_2)$ consists of $2 \times$ Hanning windowing processes, $2 \times$ 3D FFTs, $2 \times$ volume-logs, $2 \times$ log-spherical transforms, $2 \times$ phase correlation processes and $1 \times$ linear transformation and peak finding.

The Hanning windowing function requires 26 operations. The 3D FFT has complexity of $3N^3 \log N$, the log and log-spherical transform functions require 3 and 58 operations per voxel respectively. Multiplying two frequency spectra together and transforming a volume requires 15 and 30 operations per voxel respectively. Finding the peak value requires $2N^3$ operations. The complexity in terms of number of operations for the phase correlation process is given in Eq. 8 This process requires $2 \times$ 3D FFTs, $1 \times$ frequency spectra multiplication, and $1 \times$ peak finding operation.

$$6N^3 \log N + 2N^3 + 15 \tag{8}$$

The total complexity can then be found by taking into account the projection and re-sampling totals as well as the total for $VolumeRegister_{\theta \varphi t_x t_y t_z}(V_1, V_2)$. Tallying the number of operations for each process and multiplying them by number of times the process is performed gives us the number of operations as a function of W, H and N in Eq. 9.

$$6N^3 + 28WH + 18(N^3 \log N) + 230 \tag{9}$$

(a) Apartment   (b) Office   (c) Garden

Fig. 2. Reconstructed scenes.

3   Experiments

A number of experiments were undertaken to assess the reconstruction accuracy, noise sensitivity and robustness to object motion. Experiments were performed using an ASUS Zenbook UX303LN with an Intel i7 5500u Dual Core 2.4 GHz processor, 8 GB of RAM and an NVIDIA GE-FORCE 840 M GPU. For volumes of 384^3, 1 × registration per second was possible. To achieve real-time performance, 1 out of every 30th frames was processed.

3.1   Reconstruction Quality

To assess reconstruction accuracy, two indoor environments (Apartment and Office) as well as one outdoor environment (Garden) were used, these can be seen in Figs. 2a, b and c respectively. The Apartment reconstruction was recorded by moving through a room whilst rotating the camera. Some frames contained nothing but featureless walls, others had contrast shifts due to the camera's automatic contrast feature, yet, accurate reconstruction was achieved. The office reconstruction was generated by rotating the camera about the y-axis while moving backwards. Whilst our method is a closed form solution, its accuracy is still comparable to existing feature based SLAM methods. Typical feature based methods work well with indoor environments where local features are readily distinguishable and easy to match. They do not tend to work as well with complex outdoor scenes where feature confusion is likely. To assess performance in such outdoor scenes, a garden scene containing bushes, plants and a ground covering of bark and rocks was used. In the case of a feature matching approach this scene would likely result in feature confusion, making camera tracking difficult. The proposed method was able to produce a good quality reconstruction. Hence, our approach readily overcomes difficulties common to feature matching methods.

3.2   Noise Sensitivity

To assess robustness to noise, the estimated camera parameters are compared to ground truth data under different noise conditions. In each experiment, varying amounts of random noise were added per voxel prior to registration. This is expressed in decibels using the Signal to Noise Ratio (SNR). Each voxel value lies in the range [0–1]. Here, a noise value of 10 % means random noise was added in the range [−0.05, 0.05]. Tracking error is measured in centimetres and voxel error (the error in the phase correlation volume). The first experiment evaluated noise robustness whilst the camera was translated by varying amounts (5 cm, 10 cm and 15 cm). Results in Table 1 show that, for camera translations up to 15 cm and SNR values above 6.0 our method is robust to noise. At video rates, a displacement of 10 cm per frame equates to a camera velocity of 3 m/s (about twice the normal walking speed).

Table 2 shows the results for tracking camera rotations of 10, 20 and 30 degrees per frame. At video rates, 12 degrees per frame is almost a full rotation per second. In rotations of 10 degrees, the error was less than a degree for all

Table 1. Translation tracking

Translation (cm)	Noise range (%)	SNR	Error (cm)	Error (voxel)
5 cm	0	∞	0	0
5 cm	10	20 db	0	0
5 cm	25	12 db	0	0
5 cm	50	6 db	0	0
5 cm	75	2.5 db	112.28	89.83
10 cm	0	∞	0	0
10 cm	10	20 db	0	0
10 cm	25	12 db	0	0
10 cm	50	6 db	156.65	125.32
15 cm	0	∞	2.8	2.24
15 cm	10	20 db	2.8	2.24
15 cm	25	12 db	2.8	2.24
15 cm	50	6 db	198.55	158.84

Table 2. Rotation tracking

Rotation	Noise (%)	SNR	Error (θ)	Error (voxel)
10°	0	∞	0.31	0
10°	10	20 db	0.31	0
10°	25	12 db	0.63	1
10°	30	10.5 db	90.62	96
20°	0	∞	0.31	0
20°	10	20 db	0.63	1
20°	15	16.5 db	38.13	40
30°	0	∞	3.75	4
30°	10	20 db	3.28	3
30°	15	16.5 db	30	32

Table 3. Object motion test

Object size	Error (cm)	Error (voxel)
0.35	0	0
2.95	0	0
6.22	0	0
12.28	0	0
19.82	0	0
22.39	0	0
26.09	0	0
31.00	0	0
48.23	38.42	15
74.32	113.57	44

but a noise level of 30 % and above. This base line error is due to the sampling resolution of the volume, as voxel error was in fact zero. As with pure translation, the effect of noise increases with camera disparity. At 30 degrees, little matching information is available. However, for noise levels of 10 % or less, voxel distance error was as low as 4 with an angular error less than 3.8. Rotations of this magnitude are unlikely, moreover motion blur would occur.

3.3   Robustness to Object Motion

To assess robustness to object motion, experiments were conducted by moving the camera backwards along the z-axis by 5 cm per frame whilst moving objects in and out of the scene so that they only appear in one of the volumes being registered. Various sized objects including stacks of CDs, large boxes, people and several pieces of furniture were used and are measured by the percentage of the frame they occupy. Results from Table 3 show the proposed method was accurate upto an object size of 31 %, but failed for objects taking up over 48.23 %.

4   Conclusion

In this paper, we proposed a novel non-feature based approach to SLAM, which can generate accurate 3D color reconstructions of both indoor and outdoor environments. This method is a closed form solution, scales naturally to the GPU, and is shown to be robust to global noise and object motion. Future work in this area includes investigating a system to recover from misregistered frames.

References

1. Beall, C., Dellaert, F., Mahon, I., Williams, S.B.: Bundle adjustment in large-scale 3d reconstructions based on underwater robotic surveys. In: 2011 IEEE-Spain OCEANS, pp. 1–6. IEEE (2011)
2. Bylow, E., Sturm, J., Kerl, C., Kahl, F., Cremers, D.: Real-time camera tracking and 3d reconstruction using signed distance functions. In: Robotics: Science and Systems (RSS) Conference 2013, vol. 9 (2013)
3. Chekhlov, D., Pupilli, M., Mayol, W., Calway, A.: Robust real-time visual slam using scale prediction and exemplar based feature description. In: IEEE Conference on Computer Vision and Pattern Recognition, CVPR 2007, pp. 1–7. IEEE (2007)
4. Davison, A.J., Murray, D.W.: Simultaneous localization and map-building using active vision. IEEE Trans. Pattern Anal. Mach. Intell. **24**(7), 865–880 (2002)
5. Endres, F., Hess, J., Engelhard, N., Sturm, J., Cremers, D., Burgard, W.: An evaluation of the RGB-D slam system. In: 2012 IEEE International Conference on Robotics and Automation (ICRA), pp. 1691–1696. IEEE (2012)
6. Engelhard, N., Endres, F., Hess, J., Sturm, J., Burgard, W.: Real-time 3d visual slam with a hand-held RGB-D camera. In: Proceedings of the RGB-D Workshop on 3D Perception in Robotics at the European Robotics Forum, Vasteras, Sweden, vol. 180 (2011)
7. Eudes, A., Lhuillier, M., Naudet-Collette, S., Dhome, M.: Fast odometry integration in local bundle adjustment-based visual slam. In: 2010 20th International Conference on Pattern Recognition (ICPR), pp. 290–293. IEEE (2010)
8. Gil, A., Reinoso, O., Mozos, O.M., Stachniss, C., Burgard, W.: Improving data association in vision-based slam. In: 2006 IEEE/RSJ International Conference on Intelligent Robots and Systems, pp. 2076–2081. IEEE (2006)
9. Gonzalez, R.: Improving phase correlation for image registration. In: Image and Vision Computing New Zealand 2011 (IVCNZ 2011) (2011). http://ieeexplore.ieee.org/xpl/conhome.jsp?punumber=1002602

10. Henry, P., Krainin, M., Herbst, E., Ren, X., Fox, D.: RGB-D mapping: using depth cameras for dense 3d modeling of indoor environments. In: The 12th International Symposium on Experimental Robotics (ISER). Citeseer (2010)

11. Izadi, S., Kim, D., Hilliges, O., Molyneaux, D., Newcombe, R., Kohli, P., Shotton, J., Hodges, S., Freeman, D., Davison, A., et al.: Kinectfusion: real-time 3d reconstruction and interaction using a moving depth camera. In: Proceedings of the 24th Annual ACM Symposium on User Interface Software and Technology, pp. 559–568. ACM (2011)

12. Jensfelt, P., Kragic, D., Folkesson, J., Bjorkman, M.: A framework for vision based bearing only 3d slam. In: Proceedings of the 2006 IEEE International Conference on Robotics and Automation, ICRA 2006, pp. 1944–1950. IEEE (2006)

13. Jeong, W.Y., Lee, K.M.: Visual slam with line and corner features. In: 2006 IEEE/RSJ International Conference on Intelligent Robots and Systems, pp. 2570–2575. IEEE (2006)

14. Kerl, C., Sturm, J., Cremers, D.: Dense visual slam for RGB-D cameras. In: 2013 IEEE/RSJ International Conference on Intelligent Robots and Systems (IROS), pp. 2100–2106. IEEE (2013)

15. Konolige, K., Agrawal, M.: Frameslam: From bundle adjustment to real-time visual mapping. IEEE Trans. Robot. **24**(5), 1066–1077 (2008)

16. Konolige, K., Bowman, J., Chen, J., Mihelich, P., Calonder, M., Lepetit, V., Fua, P.: View-based maps. Int. J. Robot. Res. **29**(8), 941–957 (2010)

17. Kundu, A., Krishna, K.M., Jawahar, C.: Realtime motion segmentation based multibody visual slam. In: Proceedings of the Seventh Indian Conference on Computer Vision, Graphics and Image Processing, pp. 251–258. ACM (2010)

18. Leelasawassuk, T., Mayol-Cuevas, W.W.: 3d from looking: using wearable gaze tracking for hands-free and feedback-free object modelling. In: Proceedings of the 17th Annual International Symposium on Wearable Computers, pp. 105–112. ACM (2013)

19. Miro, J.V., Zhou, W., Dissanayake, G.: Towards vision based navigation in large indoor environments. In: 2006 IEEE/RSJ International Conference on Intelligent Robots and Systems, pp. 2096–2102. IEEE (2006)

20. Newcombe, R.A., Izadi, S., Hilliges, O., Molyneaux, D., Kim, D., Davison, A.J., Kohi, P., Shotton, J., Hodges, S., Fitzgibbon, A.: Kinectfusion: real-time dense surface mapping and tracking. In: 2011 10th IEEE International Symposium on Mixed and Augmented Reality (ISMAR), pp. 127–136. IEEE (2011)

21. Pollefeys, M., Nistér, D., Frahm, J.M., Akbarzadeh, A., Mordohai, P., Clipp, B., Engels, C., Gallup, D., Kim, S.J., Merrell, P., et al.: Detailed real-time urban 3d reconstruction from video. Int. J. Comput. Vis. **78**(2–3), 143–167 (2008)

22. Pollefeys, M., Van Gool, L., Vergauwen, M., Verbiest, F., Cornelis, K., Tops, J., Koch, R.: Visual modeling with a hand-held camera. Int. J. Comput. Vis. **59**(3), 207–232 (2004)

23. Pradeep, V., Rhemann, C., Izadi, S., Zach, C., Bleyer, M., Bathiche, S.: Monofusion: real-time 3d reconstruction of small scenes with a single web camera. In: 2013 IEEE International Symposium on Mixed and Augmented Reality (ISMAR), pp. 83–88. IEEE (2013)

24. Silveira, G., Malis, E., Rives, P.: An efficient direct approach to visual slam. IEEE Trans. Robot. **24**(5), 969–979 (2008)

25. Sim, R., Elinas, P., Griffin, M., Little, J.J., et al.: Vision-based slam using the rao-blackwellised particle filter. In: IJCAI Workshop on Reasoning with Uncertainty in Robotics, vol. 14, pp. 9–16 (2005)

26. Stückler, J., Behnke, S.: Robust real-time registration of RGB-D images using multi-resolution surfel representations. In: 7th German Conference on Robotics; Proceedings of ROBOTIK 2012, pp. 1–4. VDE (2012)
27. Weikersdorfer, D., Adrian, D.B., Cremers, D., Conradt, J.: Event-based 3d slam with a depth-augmented dynamic vision sensor. In: 2014 IEEE International Conference on Robotics and Automation (ICRA), pp. 359–364. IEEE (2014)
28. Whelan, T., Kaess, M., Fallon, M., Johannsson, H., Leonard, J., McDonald, J.: Kintinuous: spatially extended kinectfusion (2012)

Energy Efficient Spectrum Allocation in IP-over-EON with Traffic Grooming

Bingbing Li and Young-Chon Kim[✉]

Department of Information Technology, Chonbuk National University, Jeonju, Korea
{bingbingli,yckim}@jbnu.ac.kr

Abstract. Elastic optical network (EON) based on flexible grid and optical orthogonal frequency division modulation (OFDM) has emerged as an innovative approach to meet the ever-increasing demand. In EON, traffic grooming can improve the efficiency of spectrum by removing the guard band between two adjacent channels. Although network spectrum resource can be utilized more efficiently by traffic grooming, the operation leads to considerable power consumption due to the high data rate of transponder and electronic processing overhead at intermediate nodes. In this paper, we investigate the power consumption of IP-over-EON with traffic grooming. An efficient mixed integer linear programming (MILP) model is proposed to solve the spectrum allocation problem with the objective to minimize network power consumption in IP-over-EON with traffic grooming. The performance of the proposed model is evaluated in terms of spectrum allocation and energy consumption through a case study.

Keywords: Elastic Optical Network · MILP · Power consumption · Traffic grooming

1 Introduction

In recent years, the Elastic Optical Network (EON) has drawn a lot of attention as an innovative approach to utilize spectrum resource efficiently and flexibly. The widely-deployed Wavelength Division Multiplexing (WDM) networks adopt the ITU-T fixed-grid standard which divides the spectrum range of 1530-1565 nm (C-band) into fixed 50 GHz frequency slots (FSs). Data rate of 400 Gbps or higher for one wavelength channel cannot be achieved by the fixed grid and modulation format based on existing standard. Comparing to traditional WDM networks, OFDM-based EON can achieve sub-wavelength and super-wavelength accommodation for various traffic demand. By allocating enough bandwidth with appropriate modulation format, a spectrum path can be all-optically established between source and destination nodes. If two spectrum paths share one or more common physical links, these spectrum paths should be separated by guard band for filtering and recovering signal.

Traffic grooming is a technique to aggregate multiple low-data-rate traffic requests and groom them onto a high-speed wavelength channel in traditional WDM networks to improve wavelength utilization. In the context of EON, traffic grooming can be realized in either electrical layer or optical layer. Electrical traffic grooming follows the

© ICST Institute for Computer Sciences, Social Informatics and Telecommunications Engineering 2016
P.C. Vinh et al. (Eds.): ICTCC 2016, LNICST 168, pp. 33–42, 2016.
DOI: 10.1007/978-3-319-46909-6_4

same way with that in WDM networks, introducing additional electrical switching and optical-electrical-optical (OEO) conversion. Although lots of research work has been performed in traditional IP-over-WDM networks [1–6], there is little attention on the traffic grooming issue in EON. In EON, Bandwidth Variable Transponder (BVT) can support much larger capacity, 400 Gbps or beyond, compared to the transponder in WDM networks. This makes traffic grooming in EON obviously important. Reference [7] introduces the traffic grooming in EON for the first time and presents two MILP models based on with and without traffic grooming, both with the objective to minimize the average spectrum utilization. In the objective function, average spectrum utilization is a weighted value in terms of fiber lengths in network topology. The link-based models are based on "gridless" EON and electrical traffic grooming in order to reduce guard band overhead. Another MILP model related to electrical traffic grooming in IP-over-EON is proposed by [8]. In this model, k-shortest paths are pre-computed for each (s, d) pair. Different from [7], this work is based on the mini-grid scenario and considers allocating FSs to each traffic demand. In addition, the capacity of an optical fiber in terms of FSs, and the number of BVTs at each node are limited. With limited resources (spectrum, transponders), the objective is to maximize total amount of served traffic demand. The spectrum continuity and contiguity constraints and non-overlapping constraint are ensured. Reference [9] proposes an MILP model to design the spectrum sliced elastic optical path networks under traffic grooming. It extends the work in [7] by adding the constraint on total number of transceivers. The objective function is the same with that in [7]: to minimize the average spectrum utilization in network. But this work aims to efficiently utilize resources in terms of both transceivers and spectrum.

Although the original intention of traffic grooming in IP-over-EON was to improve spectrum utilization and reduce required BVTs, huge power consumption caused by traffic grooming is an unavoidable problem. Existing optimization models for IP-over-EON with traffic grooming aim to minimizing the average spectrum utilization [7], or maximizing the amount of served traffic demand under limited spectrum resource on each fiber link [8], while no or little attention has been paid to the power consumed by traffic grooming. In this paper, we study the bandwidth allocation in IP-over-EON with traffic grooming. A link-based MILP formulation is proposed to determine the routing and bandwidth allocation to each traffic demand. Different from existing models, our objective is to minimize the network power consumption to accommodate all traffic demands.

The rest of this paper is organized as follows: In Sect. 2, the network architecture and power consumption model are analyzed. The mathematical model is presented and explained in Sect. 3. In Sect. 4 the MILP model is evaluated and compared with traditional model by case study; and the numerical results will be analyzed. Finally, we conclude the paper in Sect. 5.

2   Problem Statement

The network models of an EON without and with traffic grooming are illustrated in Fig. 1. IP-over-EON consists of two layers: IP layer and optical layer. IP routers are deployed at network nodes and constitute the IP layer (electrical layer). Network traffic is aggregated into IP router from low-end routers in access networks. The functions of IP router is to generate (as a source node), process (as a grooming node) and drop (as a destination node) IP traffic. They are connected with Bandwidth Variable Optical Cross-Connect (BV-OXC) via BVTs, which are used to emit and terminate lightpaths. With the OEO processing capability of transponder, full wavelength conversion can be realized at switch node. Two adjacent BV-OXCs are interconnected by an optical fiber link and responsible for switching lightpaths optically. All the BV-OXCs and optical fibers construct the optical layer. For the long-distance transmission of optical signals, erbium doped fiber amplifiers (EDFA) are deployed on optical fibers. Without traffic grooming, an end-to-end all-optical lightpath is established for each connection request between source and destination node pair. The establishment of one lightpath needs a pair of BVTs. As shown in Fig. 1(a), three connection requests (A-C, C-D, A-D) consume six

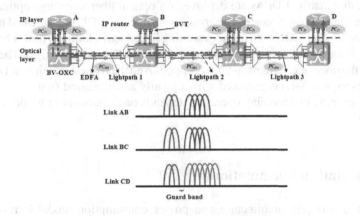

(a) IP-over-EON without traffic grooming

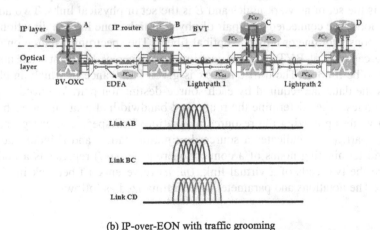

(b) IP-over-EON with traffic grooming

Fig. 1. Network architecture and spectrum allocation

BVTs to establish three lightpaths, each dedicated for a source-destination pair. If the demand for each request is low, the utilization of BVT is considerably low, compared with the allowable capacity of BVT. On the contrary, traffic grooming enables that multiple traffic flows can be groomed onto high-speed channel and transmitted together. As shown in Fig. 1(b), only two lightpaths (A-C, C-D) are established to serve three connection requests. IP traffic flow A-D can be consecutively carried by lightpaths A-C and C-D, resulting in saving of two BVTs. Moreover, the spectrum for guard band which is necessary to separate two lightpaths on their common links can be saved.

Based on the direct bypass IP-over-EON shown as Fig. 1(a), one end-to-end lightpath is established through two BVTs at source and destination nodes of a connection request. There is no electrical processing and the lightpath is switched optically by BV-OXCs at intermediate nodes. The power consumption of BVT (PC_{Tr}) is related to the actual transmission rate (TR). Note that the power consumption for adding/dropping traffic at source/destination nodes is not considered because this power contributor is constant for given traffic matrix. EDFAs are deployed on optical fiber to enlarge optical signal after transmitting certain distance. The power consumed by EDFA is indicated by PC_{OA}. However, the IP-over-EON with traffic grooming introduces additional power consumption for electrical processing at the IP routers of intermediate nodes (PC_{EP}). The request destined to the node (e.g. request A-C) is dropped. And the request which is not destined to the node (request A-D) is groomed with a locally added request (request C-D). The power consumption by grooming operation depends on the amount of traffic processed in IP routers.

3   Mathematical Formulation

Based on the networks architecture and power consumption model introduced in previous section, the MILP optimization model is presented and explained in this section. The physical topology of network is represented as a graph G (V, E), in which V is the set of network nodes and E is the set of physical links. Two adjacent network nodes are connected by a pair of physical links, one in each direction. Each link may consist of one or multiple optical fibers. The spectrum resource on optical fiber, the capacity of BVTs and the maximum number of BVTs at each node are assumed to be limited. The traffic matrix is given in advance in which an element indicates the data rate required by each source-destination pair. We need to provision all requests (i.e., determine the route, and bandwidth allocation for each traffic demand) while optimizing the resource utilization (i.e., spectrum, energy etc.). In following part: (s, d) indicates a source-destination pair, s and d index the originating and terminating nodes of a connection request; (i, j) represents a node pair which are the two ends of a virtual link; (m, n) represents a fiber link in physical topology. The notations and parameters are summarized as follows:

Given:

$G(V, E)$- Network physical topology consisting of node set V and edge set E

$TM = [\lambda^{sd}]$- Traffic Matrix, λ^{sd}- Traffic demand from s to d, $s, d \in V$ (in Gbps)

Parameters:

L_{mn}- Length of physical link (m, n) (in Km)

GB- Bandwidth for one filter guard band (in GHz)

C- Total bandwidth of one optical fiber (in GHz)

C_{Tr}- Maximum capacity of an OFDM-transponder (in Gbps)

Max_Tr- Maximum number of transponders at each node

PC_{Tr}- Power consumption of an OFDM-transponder, depending on the TR

PC_{EP}- Power consumption for electrical processing unit amount of traffic (Gbps)

PC_{OA}- Power consumption of an in-line optical amplifier

SP_{total}- Total spectrum allocated for provisioning all traffic demand

PC_{total}- Total power consumption of network

Decision Variables:

$f_{ij,k}^{sd}$- Traffic flow of λ^{sd} that is served by the kth transponder of virtual link (i, j)

N_{ij}- The number of lightpaths between node i and j

$V_{ij,k}$- The bandwidth of an elastic lightpath using the kth transponder on (i, j)

F_{mn}- The number of optical fibres on physical link (m, n)

$PL_{mn}^{ij,k}$- The bandwidth that a lightpath using the kth transponder on virtual link (i, j) uses on physical link (m, n)

$X_{mn}^{ij,k}$- (binary) equals 1 if lightpath using the kth transponder on virtual link (i, j) is routed on physical link (m, n); 0, otherwise

$Y_{ij,k}$- (binary) equals 1 if there is one lightpath using the kth transponder on virtual link (i, j); 0, otherwise

The objective function is to minimize the total power consumption of network to serve all traffic demands:

$$Minimize \; PC_{total}$$

Where

$$PC_{total} = PC_{EP} \times \sum_{i} \sum_{j} \sum_{k} \sum_{s,i \neq s} \sum_{d} f_{ij,k}^{sd}$$
$$+ \sum_{k} \sum_{i} \sum_{j} (V_{ij,k} \times PC_{Tr} + Y_{ij,k} \cdot PC_{Tr}^{0}) + \sum_{(m,n) \in E} A_{mn} \cdot F_{mn} \cdot PC_{OA}$$

The total power consumption of network consists of three parts: power consumption for electrical processing, power consumed by BVTs to establish lightpaths, and power consumed by amplifiers on optical fiber. To compare with traditional model, another objective function is presented to minimize the total allocated spectrum in network to serve all traffic demands:

$$Minimize \; SP_{total}$$

Where

$$SP_{total} = \sum_{(m,n)\in E} \sum_i \sum_j \sum_k (PL_{mn}^{ij,k} + GB \cdot X_{mn}^{ij})$$

Both objective functions are subject to following constraints:

$$\sum_j \sum_k f_{ij,k}^{sd} - \sum_j \sum_k f_{ji,k}^{sd} = \begin{cases} \lambda^{sd}, & if \ i = s \\ -\lambda^{sd}, & if \ i = d \\ 0, & otherwise \end{cases} \quad \forall(s,d), \forall i \in V \qquad (1)$$

$$\sum_n PL_{mn}^{ij,k} - \sum_n PL_{nm}^{ij,k} = \begin{cases} V_{ij,k}, & if \ m = i \\ -V_{ij,k}, & if \ m = j \\ 0, & otherwise \end{cases} \quad \forall m, i, j \in V, \forall k \qquad (2)$$

$$\sum_{(s,d)} f_{ij,k}^{sd} = V_{ij,k}, \forall i, j \in V, \forall k \qquad (3)$$

$$V_{ij,k} \leq Y_{ij,k} \cdot C_{Tr}, \forall i, j \in V, \forall k \qquad (4)$$

$$\sum_j (N_{ij} + N_{ji}) \leq Max\_Tr, \forall i \in V \qquad (5)$$

$$\sum_i \sum_j \sum_k (PL_{mn}^{ij,k} + GB \cdot X_{mn}^{ij,k}) \leq C \cdot F_{mn}, \forall m, n \in V \qquad (6)$$

$$\sum_k Y_{ij,k} = N_{ij}, \forall i, j \in V \qquad (7)$$

$$f_{ij,k}^{sd} \leq Y_{ij,k} \cdot \lambda^{sd}, \forall i, j \in V, \forall k \qquad (8)$$

$$X_{mn}^{ij,k} \leq Y_{ij,k}, \forall i, j, m, n \in V \qquad (9)$$

Constraint (1) is the flow conservation constraint for flows of (s, d) pairs in virtual topology. Constraint (2) is the flow conservation constraint for the routing of lightpaths in optical physical topology. Constraint (3) denotes that the bandwidth of a lightpath is allocated to aggregate sub-flows for all (s, d) pairs. Constraint (4) limits that: if the kth transponder on virtual link is not used ($Y_{ij,k} = 0$), there is no bandwidth allocated; else, the bandwidth allocated for the lightpath on virtual link (i, j) via the kth transponder, cannot be greater than the transponder capacity. Constraint (5) limits the number of lightpaths emitted or terminated on virtual link (i, j) cannot beyond the maximum number of transponders deployed at each node. Constraint (6) limits that the total allocated bandwidth on physical link (m, n), including for lightpaths and for guard bands, cannot be greater than the fiber capacity. Constraint (7) calculates the number of lightpaths on virtual link (i, j). Constraint (8) limits that: the amount of flow for (s, d) running on the lightpath, which is established on virtual link (i, j) via the kth transponder, cannot be greater than the demand of request (s, d). Constraint (9) limits that: if there is no lightpath is established by using the kth transponder on virtual link (i, j) ($Y_{ij,k} = 0$), then no lightpath using the kth transponder on virtual link (i, j) is routed on physical link (m, n).

4 Numerical Results

The numerical results will be shown and analyzed in this section. To evaluate the performance of the proposed model, we apply it to a case study. Our results are obtained via optimization software IBM ILOG CPLEX Optimization Studio Version12.6 on the computer with Intel Core (TM) i5-2500 CPU (3.30 GHz) and 8 GB RAM.

4.1 Network Topology and Parameters

The physical topology of the network used in case study is shown as Fig. 2. Adjacent nodes are connected by bi-directional links, one fiber on each direction. The value besides the link indicated physical distance in kilometer. The spectrum resource of each fiber is $C = 1000$ GHz. The filter guard band is $GB = 10$ GHz. The maximum capacity of an OFDM transponder is set to be $C_{Tr} = 400$ Gbps. The maximum number of transponders deployed at each node is $Max\_Tr = 16$. The traffic demands for each source-destination pair is randomly generated between 1 and D Gbps ($D = 100, 200, 300, ..., 500$). The modulation format considered is BPSK. The span of optical amplifier is 80 km. The power consumption of network devices considered in our study is summarized in Table 1, referring to some literatures [10, 11].

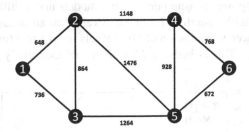

Fig. 2. Network physical topology

Table 1. Power consumption of devices

Devices	Power consumption (Watt)
Transponder	12.5*TR + 31.5
Optical Amplifier	8
Electrical Processing	25 (per Gbps)

4.2   Results and Analysis

Figure 3 presents the total spectrum allocated in network under different traffic load. Comparing to the *Min SP* scheme, *Min PC* model consumes 14.5 % to 93.7 % more spectrum resource according to different traffic load. When traffic load increases, the difference between two schemes becomes smaller. Under low traffic load, *Min PC* scheme tries to put network devices into inactive status to save energy, e.g., some optical fibers can be in sleep mode and the EDFAs on these fibers will not consume any energy. However, keeping less fibers activated means that less choices on routing and spectrum assignment. This may lead to longer routes for connection requests and more spectrums, consequently. While under high traffic load, all optical fibers are activated. The impact of sleep optical fibers on spectrum allocation does not exist. Then *Min PC* scheme can find shorter route and occupy less spectrum.

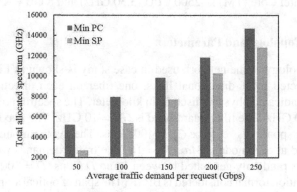

Fig. 3. Total allocated spectrum

The total network power consumption of two models under different traffic load is compared in Fig. 4. It is obvious that *Min PC* shows absolute advantage in term of power consumption. The power consumption of *Min SP* scheme is 6 to 7 times that of *Min PC* under all traffic loads. This is because *Min SP* model essentially aims to minimize

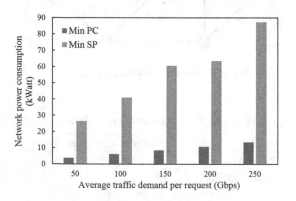

Fig. 4. Network power consumption

spectrum usage, without concerning about the power consumption is a heavy overhead introduced by traffic grooming. To achieve minimal spectrum usage, connection requests are groomed onto a common lightpath, removing the guard bands between adjacent connections and increasing the capacity of lighpath. However, at the same time, the power consumption from BVTs at source and destination nodes and electrical processing at intermediate nodes will be extremely enlarged.

Figure 5 presents the total number of lightpaths established in network under different traffic load. Under low load, *Min PC* needs slightly more lightpaths to support all traffic demand. With the traffic load increasing, the number of lightpaths obtained by *Min PC* becomes less than that by *Min SP*. Two schemes achieve similar performance in view of established lightpaths (i.e., necessary BVTs). Considering the increasing speed and huge amount of Internet traffic, *Min PC* may be more beneficial in future.

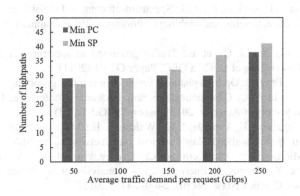

Fig. 5. Number of lightpaths

5   Conclusion

Traffic grooming is an efficient technique to improve the utilization of network spectrum resource in IP-over-EON. However, the grooming operation may introduce considerable power consumption due to the electrical processing in IP layer. In this paper, we investigated the potential to reduce network power consumption in IP-over-EON with traffic grooming. We proposed an MILP model to solve the routing and spectrum allocation problem with the objective to minimize network power consumption. The proposed model was evaluated and compared with traditional model via a case study. The numerical results showed that our proposed model could achieve power saving to a great extent at the cost of slightly more spectrum occupation. And the proposed model also showed advantage in term of BVTs which needed to be deployed in future.

Acknowledgments. This work was supported by Basic Research Program through the National Research Foundation of Korea (NRF) funded by the Ministry of Education (2014-055177).

References

1. Zhu, K., Mukherjee, B.: Traffic grooming in an optical WDM mesh network. IEEE J. Sel. Areas Commun. **20**(1), 122–133 (2002)
2. Dutta, R., Rouskas, G.: Traffic grooming in WDM networks: past and future. IEEE Netw. **16**(6), 46–56 (2002)
3. Chiu, A., Modiano, E.: Traffic grooming algorithms for reducing electronic multiplexing costs in WDM ring networks. IEEE J. Sel. Areas Commun. **18**(1), 2–12 (2000)
4. Konda, V., Chow, T.: Algorithm for traffic grooming in optical networks to minimize the number of transceivers. In: Proceedings of IEEE Workshop on High Performance Switching and Routing, pp. 218–221, 29–31 May 2001
5. Dutta, R., Rouskas, G.: On optimal traffic grooming in WDM rings. IEEE J. Sel. Areas Commun. **20**(1), 110–121 (2002)
6. Jinno, M., Takara, H., Kozicki, B., et al.: Spectrum-efficient and scalable elastic optical path network: architecture, benefits, and enabling technologies. IEEE Commun. Mag. **47**(11), 66–73 (2009)
7. Zhang, Y., Zheng, X., Li, Q., et al.: Traffic grooming in spectrum-elastic optical path networks. In: Proceedings of OFC/NFOEC, Paper OTu11 (2011)
8. Cai, A., Shen, G., Peng, L.: Optimal planning for electronic traffic grooming in IP over elastic optical networks. In: Asia Communications and Photonics Conference, OSA Technical Digest (Optical Society of America, 2013), paper AF4G.5 (2013)
9. Assis, K.D.R., Queiroz, I., Almeida, R.C., Waldman, H.: MILP formulation for resource optimization in spectrum-sliced elastic optical path networks. In: SBMO/IEEE MTT-S International Microwave & Optoelectronics Conference, vol. 1(4), 4–7 August 2013
10. Vizcaino, J., Ye, Y., Monroy, I.: Energy efficiency analysis for flexible-grid OFDM-based optical networks. Comput. Netw. **56**(10), 2400–2419 (2012)
11. El-Gorashi, T.E.H., Dong, X., Elmirghani, J.M.H.: Green optical orthogonal frequency-division multiplexing networks. IET Optoelectron. **8**(3), 137–148 (2014)

Comparison Between Parametric and Non-Parametric Approaches for Time-Varying Delay Estimation with Application to Electromyography Signals

Gia Thien Luu[✉] and Tran Trung Duy

Post and Telecommunication Institute of Technology, Ho Chi Minh City, Vietnam
{lgthien,trantrungduy}@ptithcm.edu.vn

Abstract. Muscle fiber conduction velocity (MFCV) is generally measured by the estimation of the time delay between electromyography recording channels. In this paper, we compare performances of two well-known approaches: parametric and non-parametric. The results indicate that the non-parametric approach can obtain better performance when the noise is strong (SNR = 10 dB). With the low noise level, the parametric approaches become more interesting.

Keywords: Muscle Fiber Conduction Velocity · EMG · Multi-channel acquisition · Fatigue · Time-varying delay estimation

1 Introduction

Due to the easy interpretability, Muscle Fibers Conduction Velocity (MFCV) becomes an useful physiological indicator of electromyography (EMG) activity. Specially, the MFCV is considered as an interesting indicator in many EMG fields, *e.g.* monitoring neuromuscular degenerative diseases [1] and the assessment of pain in the case of fibromyalgia [2]. Moreover, it is also applied in many fundamental studies on motor control whose applications include both the medical field and ergonomics.

As mentioned in [3], the MFCV can be estimated from intramuscular or surface electromyography recordings. However, the estimation of the MFCV from the surface EMG (sEMG) signals is complex because this task requires the advanced tools for processing signals. Ideally, it is required that the shape of the detected sEMG signals must not be changed over the entire length of the fiber. However, this condition is difficult to fulfill in practice due to the following reasons: first, the electrical activity cannot be characterized as a pure propagation because of the different conduction velocity of motors. In addition, as mentioned in [4], the tissues separating the muscle fibers and the recording electrodes are in-homogeneous along the direction of propagation, and hence they affect the shape of the sEMG signals during the propagation. Finally, the quality

© ICST Institute for Computer Sciences, Social Informatics and Telecommunications Engineering 2016
P.C. Vinh et al. (Eds.): ICTCC 2016, LNICST 168, pp. 43–51, 2016.
DOI: 10.1007/978-3-319-46909-6_5

of the signals also is affected from the noises caused from movements, contact between electrodes and skin.

From the reasons above, we provide several difficulties when estimating the MFCV as follow: first, the estimation procedure is based on data modeling. However, it is worthy noting that a method that too strongly depends on the model cannot adjust to reality. Second, the sEMG signals suffers from several limitations due to anatomical problems and changes in the action potential volume conductor that impact the conduction velocity estimation. There are three factors which affect the sEMG signal: the non-stationary property of the data [5], the change in conductivity properties of the tissues separating electrodes and muscle fibers, and the relative shift of the electrodes with respect to the origin of the action potential [4].

In order to extend the estimators to the multichannel case which would face to various local signal-to-noise ratios (SNRs), the SNR parameters should be taken into account in the time-delay estimator design. Hence, the multichannel scheme should be developed, follows the steps as follow: at first, we have to investigate the two-channel scheme with a constant time delay. In the next step, the best estimators which can be obtained from the previous study will be extended to the time-varying delay case. Finally, in the last step, we will specifically design methods for multi-channel recordings based on the study at the second step. Most recently, the authors in [6] proposed a method in which only the first step is presented. In [7], a parametric approach, i.e Maximum - Likelihood estimation (MLE) of time varying delay for two channels of sEMG signals, were investigated. In this approach, the delay with unknown model is cut into many slices and is tested via Monte-Carlo simulations. As presented in [7], the proposed method obtains the better performance as compared with the time-frequency one in [5, 8]. In [9], we used the best estimators of the generalized cross correlation that indicated in [6] by sliding the window through over the data in order to take into account the non-stationary of the data. In this paper, we will compare the performance of the best estimator of the parametric and non-parametric approaches to classify them and to determinate if their performance are sufficient for practical applications. Moreover, the Root Mean Square Error (RMSE) theoretical will be shown in order to compare with the performance experimental presented in [6]. Although this work is still limited in the case of two channels, we will extend the best estimators to the multi-channels case from the obtained results of this paper.

The paper is organized as follow: In Sect. 2, the models of signals and time varying delay will be defined. In Sect. 3, the generalized cross correlation and the Maximum likelihood estimation will be presented. Section 4 presents the simulation results with first synthetic sEMG data. In Sect. 5, we conclude the paper.

2 Model of Time-Varying Delay (TVD) and sEMG Synthetics Signals

2.1 Signal Model

Considering the sEMG signal $s(n)$ propagation between channel 1 and channel 2, a simple analytical model of two observed signals $x_1(n)$ and $x_2(n)$ in a discrete time domain, without shape differences, is the following:

$$
\begin{aligned}
x_1(n) &= s(n) + w_1(n), \\
x_2(n) &= s(n - \theta(n)) + w_2(n),
\end{aligned}
\tag{1}
$$

where $\theta(n)$ is the propagation delay between the two signals, and $w_1(n)$ and $w_2(n)$ are assumed to be independent, white, zero mean, additive Gaussian noises, of equal variance σ^2. Once $\theta(n)$ is estimated, the MFCV can simply be deduced by MFCV $(n) = \Delta e / \theta(n)$ where e stands for the inter-electrode distance, which is taken as 5 mm in the following. The digitization step is processed at the sampling frequency $F_s = 2048\,\text{Hz}$. We detail below the two models used for the time varying delay (TVD) function as well as the way for generating synthetic sEMG signals with predefined TVD functions.

2.2 Inverse Sinusoidal Model

In this study, we used the inverse sinusoidal model of TVD defined as follows:

$$
\theta(n) = F_s \frac{5.10^{-3}}{5 + 3\sin(0.2n2\pi/F_s)}
\tag{2}
$$

This model has been previously proposed in [5]. It takes into account reasonable physiological variations of MFCV that may be encountered during dynamical exercise situations. In particular, the minimum and maximum MFCV values are $2\,m.s^{-1}$ and $8\,m.s^{-1}$ respectively. The maximum acceleration value is $2.5\,m.s^{-2}$. One period of the sine wave is considered corresponding to 5 s observation duration or to equivalently 10000 data samples.

2.3 Delayed Signal Generation

The signals are synthetic ones and are generated according to the following analytic Power Spectral Density (PSD) shape proposed by Shwedyk et al. in [10] and written in the following equation as

$$
\text{PSD}(f) = \frac{k f_h^4 f^2}{(f^2 + f_l^2).(f^2 + f_l^2)^2}.
\tag{3}
$$

An example of sEMG PSD shape is given in [11], where the low and high frequency parameters are fixed as $f_l = 60\,\text{Hz}$ and $f_h = 120\,\text{Hz}$ respectively. The parameter k is a normalization factor. The first channel is generated by linear filtering a white Gaussian noise with the impulse response corresponding to this PSD (*i.e.* the inverse Fourier transform of the square root of the previous PSD shape. Once the first channel is generated, its delayed version is created thanks to the sinc-interpolator [12]:

$$s\left(n - \theta\left(n\right)\right) = \sum_{i=-p}^{p} \operatorname{sinc}\left(i - \theta\left(n\right)\right) s\left(n - i\right) \qquad (4)$$

The parameter p is the filter length and is fixed to p=40. Finally, both channels are distorted by adding White Gaussian noise at a given signal to noise ratio (SNR) level.

3   Methods

3.1   Fourier Phase Coherency Method (CohF)

This method was proposed in [5]. The local Fourier coherence of two signals $x_1\left(t\right), x_2\left(t\right)$ is

$$\operatorname{CohF}\left(t, f\right) = \frac{E_t\left\{P_{x_1 x_2}\left(t, f\right)\right\}}{\sqrt{E_t\left\{P_{x_1 x_1}\left(t, f\right) P_{x_2 x_2}\left(t, f\right)\right\}}}, \qquad (5)$$

where $P_{x_1 x_2}\left(t, f\right) = X_1\left(t, f\right) X^*_2\left(t, f\right) = \left|P_{x_1 x_2}\left(t, f\right)\right| e^{i\emptyset_{x_1 x_2}\left(t, f\right)}$ is the local cross spectrum, $X_1\left(t, f\right)$ and $X_2\left(t, f\right)$ are the local Fourier transform of the signals $x_1\left(t\right), x_2\left(t\right)$: and given as follow:

$$X_i\left(t, f\right) = \int_{-\infty}^{\infty} h\left(\tau - t\right) x_i\left(\right) e^{-i2\pi f\tau} d\tau, \qquad (6)$$

The function $h(t)$ is the Hanning weighting window function that restricts the Fourier transform around the time instant t. The asterisk refers to the conjugate of the signal. The expectations E_t are estimated by the Welch method. Each N-samples window is divided in three N/2 samples Hanning weighted windows with 50 % of overlapping. It can be shown that

$$P_{x_1 x_2}\left(t, f\right) \approx P_{ss}\left(t, f\right) e^{-2i\pi f\theta(t)} \qquad (7)$$

Since all the other terms in the coherence function are positive and real, the phase term in CohF(t,f) entirely contains at each time instant the delay (t).

3.2   The Generalized Cross-Correlation (GCC) Method

In [6], the GCC method proposed in [13] has been evaluated and tested with two synthetics sEMG signal in the case of time delay constant. The fractional part of the time delay(TD) was calculated by the parabolic interpolation [14]. In [9], we used the best estimator of GCC method which identified in [6] and slide the window over the data in order to take into account the non-stationarity of the data and the change over time of the delay.

3.3   Maximum Likelihood Estimation (MLE)

This method was derived in [7], the MLE method for a TVD which follow a polynomial model was detailed and applied to the TVD with unknown model (Inverse sinusoidal model) by cutting de TVD and sliding over the data. In this paper, we used this method as a reference to compare with the proposed methods and the "CohF" method in [5].

4   Results and Discussions

When the signals are continuous and duration T, the theoretical values for the mean square error (MSE) of the time delay estimators obtained by generalized cross-correlation were evaluated in [15] as

$$\text{MSE} = \text{E}\left\{\left(\hat{\theta} - \theta\right)^2\right\} = \frac{\int_{-\infty}^{\infty} A(f)_{x_1 x_2}(f)^2 df}{T.\left[\int_{-\infty}^{\infty} B(f)_{x_1 x_2}(f) df\right]^2} \tag{8}$$

where $w(f)$ is the weight function called the processor which were defined in [6] for each processor by

$$A(f) = (2\pi f)^2 \left[G_{w_1 w_1}(f).G_{ss}(f) + G_{w_2 w_2}(f).G_{ss}(f) + G_{w_1 w_1}(f).G_{w_2 w_2}(f)\right] \tag{9}$$

$$B(f) = (2\pi f)^2 G_{ss}(f). \tag{10}$$

Figure 1 shows the square root of these MSE values. These values theoretically in seconds were reduced to values in samples, for the sampling frequency of $F_s = 2048\,\text{Hz}$ previously considered. This allows us to understand the magnitude of these theoretical errors with regard to the experimentally calculated errors. We see that these theoretical curves deteriorate over shorter observation time as in the experimental case [6].

A Monte-Carlo simulation with 100 independent runs was performed for each signal to noise ratio (SNR) value in order to study the noise impact of these estimators. In this work, two synthetic sEMG signals have the same value of SNR $= 10, 20, 30, 40\,\text{dB}$ respectively. Duration of the signals is 5 s.

Figure 2 shows the evaluation results for an overlapping of 50 % of the slices for the parametric method. The statistical mean of the root mean square error (RMSE) between the expected time-varying delay and the estimated one is reported as a function of the signal-to-noise ratio (SNR). The graph shows no significant performance improvement with respect to the non overlapping case.

It is now interesting to compare the performance of two proposed improvements, namely the parametric approach (coefficients estimations of a low-order polynomial function over several successive short time slices) and non-parametric approach (sliding local estimations by GCC methods).

Figure 3 shows a comparison between the two tracks of proposed improvement compared with the reference method CohF. For a SNR $= 10\,\text{dB}$, the error obtained with the parametric method is two times greater than the non-parametric approaches (local GCC). However, the parametric method becomes

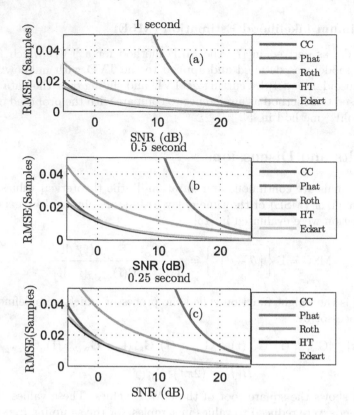

Fig. 1. Square root of the theoretical MSE based SNR for the 5 tested methods and three experimental periods 1 s (a) - 0.5 s (b) - 0.25 s (c). The reference method is the CC method. For comparative purposes, the errors calculated for continuous data were converted from second to sample, with $F_s = 2048\,Hz$

interesting in favorable noise condition (SNR = 40 dB). Note that the sliding CC method is relatively insensitive to the noise level. In the case of real data, this method is attractive because improvements displayed by the Eckart processor require knowledge of the shape of the PSD of the signal and the noise.

Figure 4 represents the mean value of the RMSE as a function of SNR for the methods Eckart and CC. The length of signals was set equal to 500 ms in the stationary case (1024 points), which corresponds to the length of the sliding time slide used for the non-stationary case. This allows to highlight the deterioration of errors of the delay estimation in the case non-stationary case compared with the stationary case. The processor Eckart in this study provides a significant improvement compared to the CC method. The impact time-varying delay compared to the case of time delay constant, resulting in an error of about 0.01 samples, regardless of the SNR.

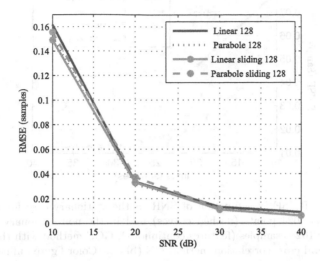

Fig. 2. Mean of RMSE as a function of SNR for parametric methods. Newton method with 128 points linear (solid line) or parabolic (dotted line) estimations; disjoint successive slices (blue) or successive overlapping slices of 50 % (green) (Color figure online)

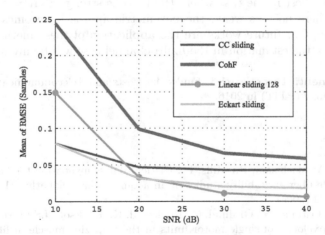

Fig. 3. Comparison of two proposed improvements (parametric and non-parametric methods). Mean of RMSE as a function of SNR. Non parametric methods: one point sliding processors Eckart (cyan) and CC (dotted blue) applied on 1024 points. windows; phase coherence method [5] (red); Parametric method: Newton method with 128 points linear slices estimation and 50 % overlapping (green). (Color figure online)

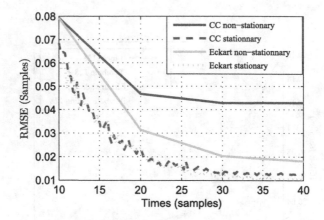

Fig. 4. Mean of RMSE as a function of SNR in the stationary case for a period of 500 ms, which is 1024 points (dashed curves) and in the non-stationary case, for a period of 5 s, or 10240 samples (features continuous). GCC method with the processor Eckart (cyan) and cross-correlation method-CC (blue). (Color figure online)

5 Conclusions

In this paper, we proposed to compare the best results of the parametric and non-parametric approach for the estimation of time-varying delay applied to MFCV evaluation of sEMG signals. The results indicate that the non-parametric approach is the best in the case where the noise is strong (SNR = 10 dB) but in the case where noise is weak, the parametric approach becomes the most interesting one. Our future works are the application of these methods to the real data. Also, the estimation in the multi-channel case will be investigated.

Acknowledgment. This research is funded by Posts and Telecommunications Institute of Technology (PTIT) in 2016.

References

1. Allen, D., Arunachalam, R., Mills, K.: Critical illness myopathy: further evidence from muscle-fiber excitability studies of an acquired channelopathy. Muscle Nerve **37**(1), 14–22 (2008)
2. Gerdle, B., Ostlund, N., Grnlund, C., Roeleveld, K., Karlsson, J.S.: Firing rate and conduction velocity of single motor units in the trapezius muscle in fibromyalgia patients and healthy controls. J. Electromyogr. Kinesiol. **18**(5), 707–716 (2008)
3. Merletti, R., Lo Conte, L.R.: Surface EMG signal processing during isometric contractions. J. Electromyogr. Kinesiol. **7**(4), 241–250 (1997)
4. Farina, D., Merletti, R.: Methods for estimating muscle fibre conduction velocity from surface electromyographic signals. Med. Biol. Eng. Comput. **42**(4), 432–445 (2004)

5. Leclerc, F., Ravier, P., Farina, D., Jouanin, J.-C., Buttelli, O.: Time-varying delay estimation with application to electromyography. In: Proceedings of EUSIPCO, Lausanne, Switzerland, August 2008
6. Ravier, P., Luu, G.-T., Jabloun, M., Buttelli, O.: Do the generalized correlation methods improve time delay estimation of the muscle fiber conduction velocity? In: Proceedings of the 4th International Symposium on Applied Sciences in Biomedical and Communication Technologies, Barcelona, Spain (2011)
7. Luu, G.-T., Ravier, P., Buttelli, O.: Comparison of maximum likelihood and time frequency approaches for time varying delay estimation in the case of electromyography signals. Int. J. Appl. Biomed. Eng. 6(1), 6–11 (2013)
8. Leclerc, F., Ravier, P., Buttelli, O., Jouanin, J.-C.: Comparison of three time-varying delay estimators with application to electromyography. In: Proceedings of EUSIPCO, Poznan, Poland, pp. 2499–2503, September 2007
9. Luu, G.-T., Ravier, P., Buttelli, O.: The non-parametric approach for time-varying delay estimation with application to the electromyographics signals. In: Proceedings International Conference on Green and Human Information Technology (ICGHIT), Ho Chi Minh city, VietNam, September 2014
10. Shwedyk, E., Balasubramanian, R., Scott, R.N.: A nonstationary model for the electromyogram. IEEE Trans. Biomed. Eng. BME–24(5), 417–424 (1977)
11. Farina, D., Merletti, R.: Comparison of algorithms for estimation of EMG variables during voluntary isometric contractions. J. Electromyogr. Kinesiol. 10(5), 337–349 (2000)
12. Chan, Y., Riley, J., Plant, J.: Modeling of time delay and its application to estimation of nonstationary delays. IEEE Trans. Acoust. Speech Sig. Process. [see also IEEE Transactions on Signal Processing] 29(3), 577–581 (1981)
13. Knapp, C., Carter, G.: The generalized correlation method for estimation of time delay. IEEE Trans. Acoust. Speech Sig. Process. 24(4), 320–327 (1976)
14. Blok, E.: Classification and evaluation of discrete subsample time delay estimation algorithms. In: Proceedings of the 14th International Conference on Microwaves, Radar and Wireless Communications, vol. 3, pp. 764–767 (2002)
15. Azaria, M., Hertz, D.: Time delay estimation by generalized cross correlation methods. IEEE Trans. Acoust. Speech Sig. Process. 32(2), 280–285 (1984)

An Approach to Detecting Brown Plant Hopper Based on Morphological Operations

An C. Tran[1(✉)], Nghi C. Tran[1], and Hiep X. Huynh[1,2]

[1] Can Tho University, Can Tho, Vietnam
tcan@cit.ctu.edu.vn
[2] DREAM-CTU/IRD, Can Tho, Vietnam

Abstract. Detecting brown plant hopper (BPH) population in images is recently concerned to support the insect monitoring application in agriculture. Combination of this research topic and the light trap systems may help to automate the counting of BPHs falling in the traps, which is currently done manually. In this paper, a new approach to detecting BPH in images based on morphological operations will be proposed. By applying these operations appropriately, shape structure and size of the BPH in images can be identified and the number of BPHs can be counted. This allows to detect BPH in images more effective and accurate, and reduce time and effort in doing this task. In addition, we also propose a method for removing noise (inserts other than BPH) in images based on the weight and color factors. The experimental results show that the proposed approach is suited for detecting and counting BPH in images.

Keywords: Brown plant hopper detection · Morphological operations · Image processing

1 Motivation and Related Work

Brown plant hopper (BPH) is one of the most dangerous insect for rice plants. It harms rice plants by directly feeding on them and transmitting many serious diseases such as ragged stunt virus and grassy stunt virus. This leads to serious losses of rice fields. As the result, BHP is causing serious damages on Vietnamese agriculture as well as other rice-growing countries [4, 8]. For example, in the Mekong Delta of Vietnam, the BPH outbreak caused the loss of around 1 million tons of rice in 2007, which resulted in a government freeze on the export of rice. The Office of Agricultural Economics in the Ministry of Agriculture and Cooperatives of Thailand reported that the outbreaks caused losses worth $52 million during the dry season of 2010 [4].

Monitoring BPH can help to identify appropriate time for starting crops to reduce the damage of brown plant hopper. Many approaches have been proposed to eliminate the damage of BPH on rice plants. One of them is to create new rice varieties that have the BPH resistance capability. Many rice varieties that are resistant to the brown plant hopper represent their life long history of breeding

© ICST Institute for Computer Sciences, Social Informatics and Telecommunications Engineering 2016
P.C. Vinh et al. (Eds.): ICTCC 2016, LNICST 168, pp. 52–61, 2016.
DOI: 10.1007/978-3-319-46909-6_6

and successful application in the field [7,8]. More than 20 resistance genes to BPH have been identified and they have been used to create rice varieties resistant to BPH such as Mugdo, ASD 7, etc. [7,8]. However, adaptation of BPH to resistance limits the effectiveness of resistant rice varieties. Therefore, it is necessary to find out more approaches to deal with this problem.

Another approach to detecting BPH infestation is based on SPAD reading and reflectance of the rice. The results in [5,14] show that SPAD reading and reflectance from rice are significantly effected by BPH infestation. The spectral reflectance from rice canopy significantly decreased in the near-infrared wavelength range as BPH infestations increased. The ratio indices of SPAD readings are also significantly related to BPH infestations. The main effects of BPH infestations on SPAD reading and reflectance are consistent regardless of nitrogen application rates. Therefore, these factors can be used to detect BPH infestation in rice fields. The results of these research show that this is a potential approach to detecting BPH infestation in rice fields. However, reflection and SPAD values from the leaves are not only effected by BPH infestation but also many other factors such as nitrogen-fertilizer and the kind of leaves.

On the other hand, Prasannakumar N.R. and Chander Subhash proposed a regression pest-weather model to describe the relation between BPH light trap catches and weather parameters [11]. The empirical results show that weather parameters such as maximum/minimum temperature, rainfall, humidity and sunshine hours are closely correlated with BPH light trap catches. Although empirical pest-weather model have significantly contributed in understanding pests population dynamics, it is influenced by local conditions and thus behaves in a location-specific manner. The pest population is thus shown to be affected by different factors at various locations.

Another approach to this problem is to apply the information techniques such as image processing [6,12] and digital signal processor [15]. In these studies, the authors proposed several approaches to detecting BPH in images based on machine learning (e.g. AdaBoots, SVN, etc.) and image processing techniques (e.g. single-threshold segmentation, wavelet transform) to detect BPH. In addition, in [15], the mathematical morphology de-noising operations were also used to remove noises from the images. Basically, these studies can detect BPH in the image automatically. However, they still have limitation: (i) some of them have not been well-investigated [15]; (ii) the preprocessing and de-noising step are still simple and ineffective that leads to the detection accuracy was only about 70 %–85 % [9,12]; (iii) some of them cannot count the BPH in images [6]. In addition, the morphological operations have not been used effectively. They were mainly used for de-noising and removing the redundant details in the images while their capability is beyond this task.

Therefore, in this paper, we propose an approach to counting BPH in images based on morphological operations. These operations are used to identify the morphological characteristics of BPH in images. The result of this task will be combined with the well-studied morphological characteristic of the BPH to detect and count them. In addition, we also use these operations in conjunction with the color and size of the BPH in the preprocessing step to remove noises in the images to increase detection accuracy.

This paper is organized as follows. The proposed approach to detecting and counting BPH in images based in morphological operations is described in Sect. 2. It is followed by the description of our method to removing noises in images in Sect. 2.3. We present the experimental results in Sect. 3 and conclusion in Sect. 4.

2   Detecting BPH Using Morphological Operations

In this section, we will propose a model for BPH detection based on morphological operations which are used to highlight the morphological characteristics of BPH. They are recognized based on the matching between their well-studied morphological characteristics and those are identified by the morphological operations.

2.1   Morphology of Brown Plant Hopper (BPH)

BPHs have yellowish brown body and their head overhangs towards the front. Their wings are transparent and the front wings have a black spot at the back side. The morphological characteristics of the BPH depend upon their stage. The BPH egg has crescent shape (about 0.3 to 0.4 mm) and whitish. In this stage, the BPH is not damage the rice. The BPH nymphs are small, have creamy white with pale brown tinge. Their color gradually turns into light brown when growing. The length of the adult BPHs body differ depending on their type. Adult male BPH body length is about 3.6 mm to 4.0 mm while female BPH body length is longer, about 4.0 mm to 5.0 mm. The whole body of the long-wing BPHs are covered by their wings while only a part of the short-wings BPHs body are covered by their wings. The BPH are most damaged at the nymph and adult stage. In our system, the detection is mainly based on the shape and size of the BPHs. Their color will be used to remove the insects other than BPHs.

2.2   Morphological Operations

Mathematical morphology is a theory and technique for analysing and processing geometrical structures based on set theory, lattice theory, topology, and random functions [13]. It contributes a wide range of operators to image processing that are particularly useful for the analysis of binary images. The common usages of these operators include edge detection, noise removal, image enhancement and segmentation.

Morphological operators often take a binary image and a structuring element as input and combine them using a set operator. They process objects in the input image based on characteristics of their shape, which are encoded in the *structuring element* (also known as *kernel*). The two most basic operators in mathematical morphology are *erosion* and *dilation*. Other morphological operators are defined based on these operators including the *opening* and *closing* operators. In this section, we will introduce these operators applying to binary images only. A binary image I can be considered as a set of *pixel location* in the foreground: $Q_I = \{p|I(p) = 1\}$, in which $p = (u, v)$ is a location in I.

Structuring Element. The structuring element consists of a pattern specified as the coordinates of a number of discrete points relative to some *origins*. For the binary image, a structuring element H is a small image in which each pixel has a value of 0 or 1: $H(i, j) \in 0, 1$. Some basic structuring elements are square, diamond, cross, diagonal cross, horizontal line, vertical line.

Erosion. The erosion of an binary image B by a structuring element S, denoted by $B \ominus S$, is a set of points x such that H is included in B when its origin is placed at x: $B \ominus S = \{x \mid H_x \subseteq B\}$. The basic effect of the operator on a binary image is to erode away the boundaries of regions of foreground pixels (i.e. white pixels, typically). Thus, area of foreground pixels shrink in size, and holes within those areas become larger.

Dilation. The dilation of an binary image B by a structuring element S, denoted by $B \oplus S$, is a set of points x such that H hits B when its origin coincides with x: $B \oplus S = \{x \mid S_x \cap B \neq \emptyset\}$. The basic effect of the operator on a binary image is to gradually enlarge the boundaries of regions of foreground pixels (i.e. white pixels, typically). Thus areas of foreground pixels grow in size while holes within those regions become smaller.

Opening. The opening operators of an binary image B by a structuring element S, denoted by $B \circ S$, is defined as the erosion of B by S followed by the dilation by S: $B \circ S = (B \ominus S) \oplus S$. This operator makes stray foreground structures that are smaller than the S structure element will disappear.

Closing. This operator is also derived by the erosion and dilation operators. The closing operator of an binary image B by a structuring element S, denoted by $B \bullet S$, is defined as the dilation followed by the erosion operators: $B \bullet S = (B \oplus S) \ominus S$. This operator preserves background regions that have a similar shape to the structuring element, or that can completely contain the structuring element, while eliminating all other regions of background pixels.

2.3 Brown Plant Hopper Detection Model

In this section, we will propose a model for detecting and counting BPHs in images based on morphological operations and the sequential region labeling algorithm. The model is shown in Fig. 1 which includes three steps: (i) preprocessing, (ii) identifying BPHs in image, and (iii) counting number of BPHs.

Fig. 1. A model for detecting and counting BPH in images. (Color figure online)

Preprocessing. The objective of this step is to increase the input image quality and convert it into binary image. Images taken by the light trap usually have unbalanced brightness and noise. Therefore, it is necessary to take the preprocessing step to reduce noise and increase quality of the input image to improve the accuracy of the proposed system. In addition, the input image will be converted into binary form so that we can use binary morphological operations in the image to improve performance of the system. This step includes 3 tasks:

1. Convert the input RGB image into gray image using the approach proposed in [3] as follow:

$$I(x, y) = 0.2989 \times R(x, y) + 0.587 \times G(x, y) + 0.114 \times B(x, y) \qquad (1)$$

in which, $R(X, y), G(x, y)$, and $B(x, y)$ are the red, green and blue level of the pixel at (x, y) in the RGB image; $I(x, y)$ is the gray level of the pixel at (x, y) in the output gray image.

2. Increase image contrast using the linear transform histogram algorithm [3]:

$$I'(x, y) = 255 \times \frac{I(x, y) - min}{max - min} \qquad (2)$$

in which, $I'(x, y)$ is the grey level of the pixel at (x, y) in the output image; $I(x, y)$ is the grey level of the pixel at (x, y) in the input image; max and min are the maximum and minimum gray level of the input image respectively.

3. Convert grey image into binary image using adaptive threshold method [1]:

$$B(x, y) = \begin{cases} 1, & \text{if } I'(x, y) > T(x, y) \\ 0, & \text{otherwise} \end{cases} \qquad (3)$$

in which, $B(x, y)$ is the binary value of the pixel at (x, y); $I'(x, y)$ is the grey value of the input image at (x, y); $T(x, y)$ is the local threshold value of $I'(x, y)$.

Identifying BPH. The objective of this step is to identify BPHs in image based on their morphological characteristics using the morphological operations. The input image, after preprocessed in the first step, will be applied the morphological two times to highlight the BPHs in the image based on their size.

Firstly, we use the opening operation on the input preprocessed image by the 3 × 3 diamond structuring element to reduce the small noisy pixel in the image. The structuring element used in this step was selected based on the size morphology of BPH and our experimental result on different type of structuring elements and BPH images.

Next, we apply the opening operation again on the image produced by the above step to remove the objects other than BPHs based on the BPH shape morphology. Several experiments had been conducted to find out an appropriate structuring element for the opening operation in this step. Due to the limitation on the paper's length, detail of the experiments are not presented. Our experimental result suggests the most suited structuring element is the square one. It was produced by combining the different shapes of BPH observed in the images. The opening operation in this step not only helps to remove the object other than BPHs but also helps to separate the remaining BPHs in the image.

Result of this step is demonstrated in Fig. 2.

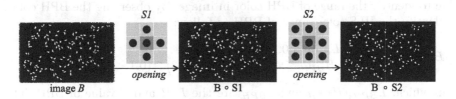

Fig. 2. Identifying BPHs using the opening operation.

Counting BPH. To count BPHs in the processed image, we use the sequential region labeling algorithm with the 4-connected neighborhood. The number of BPHs is the number of labeled areas. Figure 3 demonstrates the result of applying the sequential region labeling algorithm on the image produced by the above steps in Fig. 2.

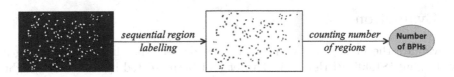

Fig. 3. Counting BPHs based on sequential region labelling algorithm.

Removing Other Insects in Image. Images taken in the field, particularly the light-trap images, usually contains other insects like whorl maggot, zigzag leafhopper, etc. To increase detection accuracy, we also propose an approach to removing insects other than BPH based on the size and color morphology of BPH.

Adult and nymph BPH size is from 3.6 mm to 5 mm. Support that the distance between camera and the base of light trap is 20 cm (a typical distance), size of the BPH in images will be about 9 to 40 pixels. Therefore, to remove the insects other than BPH, we will remove objects whose size is greater than 40 pixels.

Beside the size, we also consider the color of BPHs in removing the insects. The most used color system is the RGB. However, the RGB color system is not suitable for recognizing the BPH color in light trap images as the brightness condition when taking the images may be vary from image to image. Therefore, it is not apparent to identify the real color of BPHs in the image to compare with the color morphology of BPHs (which is the yellow-brown color). In addition, in the RBG system, a color is the combination of red (R), blue (B) and green (G). The yellow-brown color is the combination of non-continuous value of the R, G and B, that will cause difficulty in detecting the BPH color.

In this context, the HLS color system [10] is more suited as the hue value can describe the color of BPHs without the effect of brightness. We can use hue value to identify the range of BPH color in image. By observing the BPH color, we identify the HLS color range of BPH as follow:

$$BPH_{HLS} : \begin{cases} 0 \leq L_{BPH} \leq 0.1 \\ (0 < H_{BPH} \leq 40) \cap (S_{BPH} < 0.3) \cap (0.1 < L_{BPH} \leq 1) \end{cases} \quad (4)$$

in which, L_{BPH}, H_{BPH} and S_{BPH} are the L, H and S value of BPH. The algorithm for converting an RGB value to HLS value can be found in [2]. Based on the size and color morphology of BPHs as analysed above, we propose an algorithm for removing insects other than BPH as in Algorithm 1.

2.4 The Algorithm

Algorithm 2 implements our proposed approach to counting BPHs in image described in Sect. 2.3. This algorithm takes an RGB image as the input and returns a region-labeled image and the number of BPHs in the image.

3 Evaluation

To evaluate the proposed system, we used a dataset that includes 180 images (containing 181,405, BPHs). This dataset had been created by a simulated light trap system in which the BPHs were intentionally drop into a base. For each case, the images had been taken in different conditions (light and noise). The dataset can be divided into 8 groups: (1) balanced light, no other insect, no noise; (2) balanced light, other insect, no noise; (3) balanced light, no other insect, noise; (4) balanced light, other insect, noise; (5) unbalanced light, no other insect, no noise; (6) unbalanced light, other insect, no noise; (7) unbalanced light, no other insect, no noise; and (8) unbalanced light, other insect, noise.

The experimental result is shown in Table 1. The result shows that the average detection accuracy (F1) is about 93.4 % in which the best result was achieved

---

Algorithm 1. Other Insect Removal Algorithm – OINSTREMOVAL(I)

Input: A region-labeled image I.

Output: A region-labeled image I' with insects removed.

1 **begin**
2   const MAX_SIZE = 40   /* maximum size of a typical BPH */
3      $I' = I$
4   **foreach** *region* $r \in I'$ **do**
         /* calculate the average of R, G and B value in r */
5          $R_r = \frac{\sum (\text{R value in r})}{sizeof(r)}$; $G_r = \frac{\sum (\text{G value in r})}{sizeof(r)}$; $B_r = \frac{\sum (\text{B value in r})}{sizeof(r)}$
         /* remove region if it's bigger than usual BPH size */
6   **if** $sizeof(r) > MAX\_SIZE$ **then**
7   remove r from I'
         /* remove region if it isn't a BPH based on color */
8          $(H, L, S) = $ RGBTOHLS(R_r, G_r, B_r) /* convert RGB to HLS [2] */
9   **if** *(H, L, S) does not satisfy Eq. 4* **then**
10   remove r from I'
11   **return** I'

Algorithm 2. Morphological-Based BPH Detection Algorithm

Input: An RGB-image I.

Output: A region-labeled image L and the number of BPHs in the image L.

1 **begin**
     /* pre-processing step */
2      $G = $ CONVERTTOGRAY(I) /* convert I to gray using Eq. 1 */
3      $G' = $ LINEARTRANSFORM(B) /* increase contrast using Eq. 2 */
4      $B = $ TOBINARY(G') /* convert G' to binary using Eq. 3 */
     /* identifying BPHs */
5      $BI = $ invert of B /* get the invert image of B */
6   S1 = diamond structuring element size 3×3
7   S2 = square structuring element size 3×3
8      $O1 = BI \circ S1$ /* applying opening operation on BI by $S1$ */
9      $O2 = O1 \circ S2$ /* applying opening operation on $O1$ by $S2$ */
     /* removing other insets &counting BPHs */
10      $L = $ SEQREGIONLABELING$(O2)$ /* L: a region-labeled image */
11      $LR = $ OINSTREMOVAL(L) /* remove other insects, c.f. Alg. 1 */
12      $n = $ number of regions in LR /* n: number of regions or BPHs */
13   **return** (LR, n)

---

on group 1 (balanced light, no noise, no other insect) with 95.72 %. The detection accuracy reduce for the images with noise or unbalanced light. The worst case happens on group 8 (unbalanced light, noise, other insects) with the F1 is 90 %.

Table 1. Experimental result of the BPH detection algorithm.

Group	No of BPHs	BPH Detected	TP	FN	FP	Precision(%)	Recall(%)	F1(%)
1	4445	4191	4134	311	59	98.59	93	**95.72**
2	3514	3506	3263	251	243	93.07	92.86	**92.96**
3	4445	4295	4152	293	143	96.67	93.41	**95.01**
4	3514	3575	3264	250	311	91.3	92.89	**92.09**
5	4445	4180	4123	322	59	98.59	92.76	**95.58**
6	3514	3486	3245	269	241	93.09	92.34	**92.71**
7	4445	4395	4116	329	283	93.57	92.6	**93.08**
8	3514	3676	3238	276	438	88.08	92.15	**90.07**

Table 2. Evaluate the Other Insect Removal Algorithm.

Group	BPH Detected	TP	FN	FP	Precision (%)	Recall (%)	F1 (%)
2	3850	3263	251	587	84.75	92.86	**88.62**
4	4004	3264	250	740	81.52	92.89	**86.83**
6	3855	3245	269	610	84.18	92.34	**88.07**
8	4665	3238	276	1427	69.41	92.15	**79.18**

The experimental result also shows that the appearance of other insects effect on the detection accuracy stronger than the light condition (e.g. group 1 (95.72 %)–group 2 (92.96 %) vs. group 1 (95.72 %)–group 5 (95.58 %)). Other insects also effect on detection accuracy stronger than noise (e.g. group 1 (95.72 %)–group 2 (92.96 %) vs. groups 1 (95.72 %)–group 3 (95.01 %)).

We also conducted a further experiment to evaluate the effectiveness of the *Other Insect Removal Algorithm*. We used the images that contains other insects (group 2, 4, 6, 8) in the above dataset for this evaluation. We run the experiment without the removal algorithm and compare with the result in Table 1. The experimental result is shown in Table 2. The result shows that removal of other insect helps to increase detecting accuracy about 4 % in average.

4 Conclusion

In this paper, we proposed a model for detecting BPH in images, particularly the images from light trap systems which are usually effected by different lighting conditions, noise, etc. This model bases on the morphological operations combined with several image processing techniques for preprocessing the images. In addition, we also proposed an algorithm for removing insects other than BPHs to increase detection accuracy. This algorithm bases on size and color morphology of BPH. The experimental results show a promising result with the average detection accuracy (F1) is about 93.4 %, in which the algorithm for removing other insects helped to increase the accuracy more than 4 %.

To improve the proposed system, we suggest to find out an approach to dealing with the images containing overlapped BPHs. In fact, there are some studies that propose light trap systems with the capability to eliminate the overlapped BPHs. However, most of the in-use light trap systems do not have this feature. Therefore, it is worth to propose a solution for dealing this problem. In addition, the current model should be investigated with different parameters (e.g. the structuring elements, the preprocessing techniques, etc.) to gain more understanding in the system to propose further improvement on the model.

References

1. Bradley, D., Roth, G.: Adaptive thresholding using the integral image. J. Graph. GPU Game Tools **12**(2), 13–21 (2007)
2. Burger, W., Burge, M.J.: Principles of Digital Image Processing. Springer, London (2009)
3. Gonzalez, R.C., Woods, R.E., Eddins, S.L.: Digital image processing using MAT-LAB. Pearson Education India (2004)
4. Heong, K.L., Wong, L., Reyes, J.H.D.: Addressing planthopper threats to asian rice farming and food security: fixing insecticide misuse. In: Rice Planthoppers, pp. 65–76. Springer (2013)
5. Huang, J.-R., Sun, J.-Y., Liao, H.-J., Liu, X.-D.: Detection of brown planthopper infestation based on spad and spectral data from rice under different rates of nitrogen fertilizer. Precis. Agriculture **16**(2), 148–163 (2015)
6. Huynh, H.X.: Identifying the effects of brown plant hopper based on rice images. In: Statistics & its Interactions with Other Disciplines-2013 (2013)
7. Jena, K.K., Kim, S.-M.: Current status of brown planthopper (BPH) resistance and genetics. Rice **3**(2–3), 161–171 (2010)
8. Kobayashi, T., Yamamoto, K., Suetsugu, Y., Kuwazaki, S., Hattori, M., Jairin, J., Sanada-Morimura, S., Matsumura, M.: Genetic mapping of the rice resistance-breaking gene of the brown planthopper nilaparvata lugens. Proc. R. Soc. Lond. B Biol. Sci. **281**(1787), 20140726 (2014)
9. Mongkolchart, N., Ketcham, M.: The measurement of brown planthopper by image processing. In: International Conference on Advanced Computational Technologies & Creative Media (ICACTCM 2014) (2014)
10. Plataniotis, K.N., Venetsanopoulos, A.N.: Color image processing and applications. Springer Science & Business Media (2000)
11. Prasannakumar, N.R., Chander, S.: Weather-based brown planthopper prediction model at Mandya, Karnataka. J. Agrometeorol. **16**(1), 126–129 (2014)
12. Yao, Q., Xian, D., Liu, Q., Yang, B., Diao, G., Tang, J.: Automated counting of rice planthoppers in paddy fields based on image processing. J. Integr. Agriculture **13**(8), 1736–1745 (2014)
13. Spencer, A., Zwicky, A.M.: The Handbook of Morphology. Blackwell, Oxford (1998)
14. Yang, C.-M., Cheng, C.-H., Chen, R.-K.: Changes in spectral characteristics of rice canopy infested with brown planthopper and leaffolder. Crop Sci. **47**(1), 329–335 (2007)
15. Zou, X.: Design of recognition system for rice planthopper over digital signal processor. In: Zhong, Z. (ed.) Proceedings of the International Conference on Information Engineering and Applications (IEA) 2012, pp. 407–414. Springer, London (2013)

An Efficient Virtual Machine Migration Algorithm Based on Minimization of Migration in Cloud Computing

Nguyen Khac Chien[1(✉)], Vo Sy Giang Dong[2], Nguyen Hong Son[3], and Ho Dac Loc[4]

[1] The People's Police University, Ho Chi Minh City, Vietnam
nkchienster@gmail.com
[2] FPT Software, Ho Chi Minh City, Vietnam
giangdongptit@gmail.com
[3] Post and Telecommunication Institute of Technology,
Ho Chi Minh City, Vietnam
ngson@ptithcm.edu.vn
[4] Ho Chi Minh City University of Technology, Ho Chi Minh City, Vietnam
hdloc@hcmhutech.edu.vn

Abstract. Virtual machine (VM) migration in the cloud computing (CC) environment is an important issue to solve many problems, such as: Load Balancing, accomplished by migrating VMs out of overloaded/overheated servers, and Server Consolidation, where servers can be selectively brought down for maintenance after migrating their workload to other servers. In this paper, we propose an efficient VM migration algorithm based on minimization of migrations in CC to improve efficiency and response the requirements for user and restrict of service level agreements (SLA) violation. Experimental results showed the effectiveness of the proposed algorithm compared with existing algorithm.

Keywords: Virtual machine · Datacenter · Cloud computing · Live migration · Cloudsim

1 Introduction

In CC, storage, application, server and network devices can be virtualized. Virtualization can make many benefits, such as resource utilization, portability, and application isolation, reliability of system, higher performance, improved management ability and fault tolerance.

During operation of the datacenter in CC, many issues will arise, where energy issue plays an important role. Energy consumption in the datacenter will be very large, occupying a large part of operating costs. Greater power consumption leads to emit more CO_2 emissions, causing the greenhouse effect, the effect posed on the environment. The consolidation of VMs on a physical server that has light loads, use live migration, then state transition of idle servers into a state with low energy consumption (sleep, hibernate), which will help service providers optimize cloud resource usage and reduce energy consumption. However, it is very difficult to optimize the use of energy

© ICST Institute for Computer Sciences, Social Informatics and Telecommunications Engineering 2016
P.C. Vinh et al. (Eds.): ICTCC 2016, LNICST 168, pp. 62–71, 2016.
DOI: 10.1007/978-3-319-46909-6_7

as the programs' workload keeps changing all the time which requests for the supply of dynamic resources. Therefore, the consolidation of VMs may badly affect performance. If the resources required by an application that is not fully allocated, then the responses to the application of user may be slow, or not available.

In addition, overloading of the services on the VM leads to a fact that we need to migrate to the VM has greater processing capacity to ensure quality of services (QoS) of cloud computing provider with customer commitment through the SLAs.

Determining when to implement VM migration in the CC is a major challenge to researchers and providers of CC services. Making a decision on implementing VM migration effectively and ensuring the performance of the system as well as the most efficient system resources usage are the ultimate goals of CC. This paper proposes a method of improving VM algorithm based on minimization of migrations to improve utilization, as well as satisfying the requirements for users.

The rest of the paper is organized as follows: Sect. 2 discusses related work, in Sect. 3, we propose method to improve VM migration algorithm, the experiment is described in Sect. 4, and the conclusion is presented in Sect. 5.

2   Related Work

Live migration facilitates online maintenance, load balancing and energy management [12]: (1) Online maintenance: Improving system's reliability and availability a system must be connected with the clients and the upgradation and maintenance of the system is also a necessary task so for this all VMs are migrated away without disconnections. (2) Load Balancing: VMs can be migrated from heavy loaded host to light loaded host to avoid overloading of any one server. (3) Energy Management: VMs can be consolidated to save the energy. Some of the underutilized server VM's are switched down, and the consolidated servers ensure power efficient green cloud.

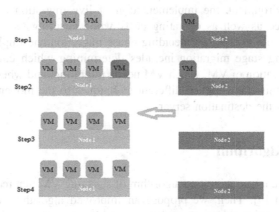

Fig. 1. An example of migrating VM [6].

Figure 1 shows the process of migrating VM. Initially, there are three VMs on a physical server Node 1 and one VM on a physical server Node 2. The migration process allows VM to run on Node 2 switched on Node 1.

The nature of the migration of a VM from one server to another server is that it transfers the whole system run-time state, including CPU state, memory data, and local disk storage, of the VM.

VM Migration methods are divided into two types [7]: Live migration and non-live migration. The status of the VM loses and user can notice the service interruption in cold migration. VM keeps running while migrating and does not lose its status. User doesn't feel any interruption in service during live migration. In live migration process, the state of a VM to migrate is transferred. The state consists of its memory contents and local file system. Local file system does not need to be transferred. First, VM is suspended, then its state is transferred, and lastly, VM is resumed at destination host. This migration method is applied to cloud computing environments.

Anton Beloglazov et al. [2] proposed migration techniques and VM consolidation for ultimate energy in a data center. The algorithms [2] were proposed: a general algorithm of migration decision-making and an algorithm to select VMs to migrate. Ts EpoMofolo et al. [8] proposed a prediction method based on the allocation of resources using VM migration. The authors proposed an algorithm to select the destination server. The goal of this algorithm is ensuring the servers to operate at an acceptable level to maximize available capacity of the system. Anton Beloglazov et al. [3] proposed two algorithms, the first: selecting the VM to migrate based on the criteria of the least of migration times; the second: Selecting the destination server to migrate with a goal to optimize the energy consumption of the system. Christopher Clark et al. [4] focus on the study of how to make "live migration", in [4] study Pre-copy migration method and its optimal solution. In addition, several other studies also study VMs migration on the CC environment [1, 5, 10, 11], the general characteristics of these researchs are aimed at achieving optimal use of energy of the system, also fully exploiting the processing power of the system.

In the CC environment, the implementation of live migration aimed at optimal system performance as well as operating costs while ensuring QoS. The migration process is divided into two phases: deciding phase migration and implementing phase migration. Deciding stage migration includes determining which conditions will be needed for the migration of VM, which VM needs migrating, and where to imgrate. In the second stage, this stage applied different techniques to the movement of the VM state is working to the destination server.

3   Proposed Algorithm

In this section, we analyze migration algorithm of selecting VM that requires minimum times of migration [3]. Then, we propose an improved algorithm with the goal of improving VM migration selection, so that it could have number of times at least and the remaining available CPU is minimal.

Algorithm [3] has the advantage that the number of times of migration is at least, leading to less occurrence of SLA violations while also minimizes consuming CPU performance as well as network bandwidth for migration process. Besides, the list of VMs is sorted before performing VM selection to migrate, in case of migrating only one VM, then the remaining available CPU after migration is smallest. That exploits thoroughly the resources.

However, in case you need to migrate more than one VM, the algorithm will not get the maximum exploitation of system resources. That is becaused during implemention process, if the algorithm does not find a VM to satisfy the condition in line 9 in Fig. 2, the algorithm will select a VM with the highest CPU usage to migrate, which will obviously ensure the selecting number of VMs at least leading to smallest of migration times, but the availability of the CPU of server after migration of VMs found was not the smallest. For example, assuming that a host has many VMs with CPU utilizations were 1, 3, 4, 5, 7 and it has the maximum CPU utilization threshold UT = 16. Thus, this server is overloaded, and has to migrate one or more VMs, so that total CPU utilization of the VMs migration is always greater than 8 to put the server operating within allowed threshold. If we apply above algorithm to choose the VM for migration, then two VMs with CPU utilization were 3 and 7 will be selected. The CPU utilization of server after migrating two selected VMs is $3 + 7 - 8 = 2$. But, we easily see that two VMs have CPU utilization 4, 5 as well as that make server not overloaded. Wherea, the CPU utilization after migrating two VMs is $4 + 5 - 8 = 1$. If these two VMs are selected, it will ensure miminum number of times, but still fully utilize system capacity.

From above limitation, we can improve the algorithm in [3] by Anton *et al.* so that the number of VMs, which are migrated, that is at least. At the same time achieving the purpose of maximizing the performance of the server. Meaning, the CPU utilization of

```
1  Input: hostList;    Output: MigrationList
2  foreach h in hostList do
3      vmList ← h.getVmlist()
4      vmList.sortDecreasingUtilization()
5      hUtil ← h.getUtil()
6      bestFitUtil ← MAX
7      while hUtil > THRESH_UP do
8          foreach vm in vmList do
9              if vm.getUtil() > hostUtil − THRESH_UP then
10                 t ← vm.getUtil() − hUtil + THRESH_UP
11             if t < bestFitUtil then
12                 bestFitUtil ← t
13                 bestFitVm ← vm
14             else
15                 if bestFitUtil = MAX then
16                 bestFitVm ← vm
17             break;
18         hUtil ← hUtil − bestFitVm.getUtil()
19         migrationList.add(bestFitVm)
20         vmList.remove(bestFitVm)
21     if (hUtil < THRESH_LOWER) then
22         migrationList.add(bestFitVm)
23         vmList.remove(bestFitVm)
24 return migrationList
```

Fig. 2. Pseudo-code for the Minimization of Migration (MM) Algorithm [3]

the server after performing the migration will reach the threshold of the most over-loaded. We suggest the improvements selecting VM in case you need to migrate multiple VMs. In the data center, there is a list of overloaded servers, each server has a list of VMs *vmList* that has to migrate the VM (*migrationList*) in oder to put server on an acceptable level within thresholds, CPU utilization of the server is *hostUtil* which are exceeded on the *UT, diffValue* is a real number representing the difference between current CPU utilization of the server and above threshold. Select the minimum number of VMs for migration, the total CPU utilization of the VMs, which are migrated, *vmsMigrateUtil* is larger than *diffValue* (bringing server utilization to be within threshold), while (*bestFitValue = vmsMigrateUtil − diffValue*) is minimal to maximize exploitation of system resources.

The proposed algorithm for multi VMs immigration are: Determine number of migrating VMs: *numbersVmMigrate*.

After determined number of VMs that going to be migrated, list out the migration plans based on VM's location in vmlist of the host. With each plans the algorithm will calculate *bestFitValue* and decide migration plan based on the value of *bestFitValue*, the plan with smallest *bestFitValue* will be chosen.

Listing out migration plans is actually matter of listing element *numbersVmMigrate=k* in array *listVm.size() =n*. This paper uses backtracking algorithm to accomplish. Optimal migration plan is determined through attempts. The result is represented by a vector *XOPT[]* including *numbersVmMigrate* elements. Also, each migration plan is represented by a vector *result* that consists of *numbersVmMigrate* element *result* = $(x_1, x_2, ..., x_k)$.

At each step i:

Built up elements $x_1, ..., x_{i-1}$

Creating components x_i by evaluating all the possibilities that x_i can be.

If there is an ability j that is appropriate to x_i, then x_i is determined according to j. If $i = numbersVmMigrate$, we identified a complete migration plan. Check if this migration plan is better than previous plan, then we proceed an update, if it is not better there wil be no update required. However, if i is smaller than *numbersVmMigrate* proceed step $i+1$ to determine x_i+1.

Backtracking algorithms can be written in the form of pseudo-code as follows:

Procedure In line 6 of Fig. 3 is used to update the migration plan. To clarify how the listing of this approach work, we describe an example that illustrate to select two elements of sequence {7, 5, 4, 3, 1} - the sequence has been shown in the example above (Fig. 4).

```
1  void Try(1, result,totalVms, numberVmMigrate, vmList) {
2     for (int j =result[i-1]+1; j<= totalVms −numberVmMigrate +i, j++)
3        {result[i] = j
4        if (i==k)
5        Process(result, numberVmMigrate, vmList)
6        else Try(i+1, result, n,k)
7     }
8  }
```

Fig. 3. Pseudo-code for the Backtracking Algorithm

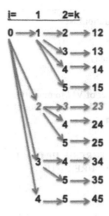

Fig. 4. Illustration of selected VM migration.

Using the backtracking technique to list out all of avaibility that are selected with two elements. Each result is the position of the two numbers that taken out from sequence. In each plan, the process will be executed to filter out the plan that is most fit to requirement. The improved algorithm is described in Fig. 5.

4 Experiment

In this section, we conducted experiments on heterogeneous cloud computing environment which has a data center with features such as Table 1. The algorithms are implemented through simulation package CloudSim based tool [9]. Java language is used for develop and implement the algorithms. Experiments will be conducted to compare the improved algorithm with the algorithm in [3] based on the following scenario:

Pair 1: Select migrated VM that has smallest times of migration according to the original algorithm and Select lowest energy consumption server

Pair 2: Select migrated VM that has smallest times of migration according to improved algorithm and Select lowest energy consumption server (Table 2)

In the simulation environment with a Broker's request of 2001 VMs, as follows (Table 3):

These VMs require same number of hard-drive and bandwidth. Assuming the VMs are running the game services, online services with parameters of cloudlet: 2500 Mips, outputFile = inputfile = 300 bytes.

The over-load and under-load threshold used in simulation programs are 70 % and 20 % respectively. Simulation time in scenarios is 1 day = 60 * 24 = 1440 min. The time for the system considering the migration is 350 s.

The simulation results are shown in Figs. 6 and 7: the blue line is the result of applying the original algorithm which has not been improved, the red line is the result of improved algorithm.

```
1  Input: hostList;      Output: MigrationList
2  foreach h in hostList do
3     vmList ← h.getVmlist()
4     vmList.sortDecreasingUtilization()
5     hUtil ← h.getUtil()
6     bestFitUtil ← MAX
7     numberVmMigrate =0 // Number of VM to migration
8     tongUtil =0 //Ulti is number of VM as needed migrating multiple VM
9     while hUtil > THRESH_UP do
10      foreach vm in vmList do
11        bestFitVm = Null
12        if vm.getUtil() > hostUtil – THRESH_UP then {
13          t ← vm.getUtil() – hUtil + THRESH_UP
14        if t < bestFitUtil then {
15          bestFitUtil ← t
16          bestFitVm ← vm
17        }}
18        else {
19          if bestFitUtil = MAX then {
20          numberVmMigrate++
21          tongUtil = tongUtil+vm.getUtil()
22          if (tongUtil> hostUtil-THRESH_UP) then
23            break;
24          } else
25          break;
26        }
27      if (bestFitVm !=NULL) then {
28        hUtil ← hUtil – bestFitVm.getUtil()
29        migrationList.add(bestFitVm)
30        vmList.remove(bestFitVm)
31      }
32      if (numberVmMigrate > 1) then {
33        int totalVms = vmList.size()
34        XOPT = new int[numberVmMigrate + 1]
35        int result[] = new int[numberVmMigrate + 1]
36        XOPT[i] =0
37        result[0] =0
38        Try(1, result, totalVms, nuberVmMigrate, vmList)
39        Get result from XOPT[]
40      }
41      if (hUtil < THRESH_LOWER) then
42        migrationList.add(bestFitVm)
43        vmList.remove(bestFitVm)
44 return migrationList
```

Fig. 5. Pseudo-code for the Improved MM Algorithm

Thus, Figs. 6 and 7 show that the improved algorithm is better than original algorithm in multiple evaluation criteria.

In theory, improved algorithm enables maximum server resource utilization, namely the CPU usage after migrating VMs get close to the upper limit, leading to higher Utilization index (Fig. 7, The Utilization is represented in red line). Sometimes, the utilization level of two algorithms are relatively balanced. This happens when the migration of just one VM server can provide acceptable threshold.

Table 1. Detail of the data center

OS	Linux
Architecture	X86
VMM	Xen
TimeZone	10
VM Migration	Enable
Cost per Second ($)	3
Cost per RAM ($)	0.05
Cost per Storage ($)	0.001
Cost per Bandwidth ($)	0

Table 2. The table in the simulation server

Type of server	HP Proliant G4
Number	220
Host Mips	1860
Number of PE	2
Ram	4 Gb
Bandwidth	10 Gbps
HDD	100000 Tbs

Table 3. Detail of VMs in simulations

Name of VM	Mips	Ram	Policy	Number lượng
low	500	500	Time Shared	2001

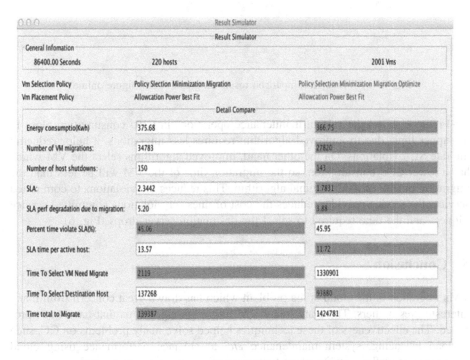

Fig. 6. Result implemented in the form (Color figure online)

In terms of energy consumption, improved algorithms also give better results that are shown in Fig. 6. In the improved algorithm, the number of active servers maintained at a lower level that are as shown in Fig. 7, therefore energy consumption of servers and cooling systems will be less.

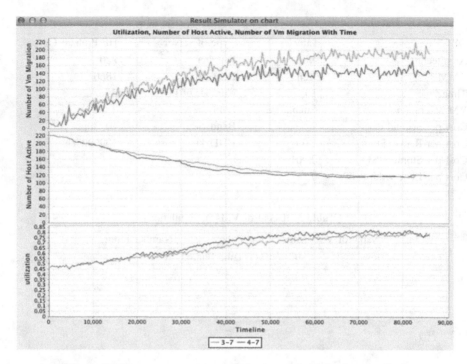

Fig. 7. Performance comparison results in graph (Color figure online)

Figure 6 shows the system maintenance operations in CPU consumption close to the upper limit, due to improved algorithm requires less migrations, it helps reducing the rate SLA violations. On the other hand, improved algorithms select the VM which has a lower CPU consumption, so the migration time of the VM will be less than the migration time of VMs of original algorithm. This reduces the violations to committed service, the service provider reduces the cost of fines for violations committed service triggers and the time required to select the destination server drops (Fig. 6).

5 Conclusion

VMs migration in the cloud is the problem which has drawn great concern from many interested researchers. There are many VM migration algorithms that have been proposed. The effectiveness of these techniques helped solve many problems on CC, such as load balancing, system maintenance *etc.* to enhance performance using cloud computing as well as quality of customer service.

This paper proposed an efficient VM migration decision-making algorithm on CC to solve the above problems. However, due to the fact that the new method was tested on simulated cloud environment using CloudSim tool, this method should be qualified on real environment in the future to clearly see its performance.

References

1. Ashima, A., Shangruff, R.: Live migration of virtual machines in cloud. Int. J. Scient. Res. Publ. **2**(6) (2012). ISSN 2250-3153
2. Anton, B., Rajkumar, B.: Optimal Online Deterministic Algorithms and Adaptive Heuristics for Energy and Performance Efficient Dynamic Consolidation of Virtual Machines in Cloud Data Centers. Published online in Wiley InterScience (2012). doi:10.1002/cpe.1867
3. Anton, B., Jemal, A., Rajkumar, B.: Energy-aware resource allocation heuristics for efficient management of datacenter for cloud computing (2011). doi:10.1016/j.future.2011.04.017
4. Christopher, C., Keir, F., Steven, H., Jacob, G.H., Eric, J., Christian, L., Ian, P., Andrew, W.: Live migration of virtual machines. In: Proceedings of the 2nd Conference on Symposium on Networked Systems Design & Implementation, NSDI 2005, vol. 2, pp. 273–286 (2005)
5. Michael, R.H., Kartik, G.: Post-copy based live virtual machine migration using adaptive pre-paging and dynamic self-ballooning. In: Proceedings of the 2009 ACM SIGPLAN/SIGOPS International Conference on Virtual Execution Environments, pp. 51–60 (2009). ISBN: 978-1-60558-375-4
6. Kakhi, K.R., Getzi, J.L.P.: Live virtual machine migration techniques-a survery. Int. J. Scient. Res. Publ. **1**(7) (2012). ISSN 2278-0181
7. Michael, R., Michael, H.: A new process migration algorithm (1996). ISBN-13: 978-1-86451-041-6
8. Ts`epoMofolo, Suchithra, R.: Heuristic based resource allowcation using virtual machine migration: a cloud computing perspective (2013). ISSN (online) 2319-183X, (Print) 2319-1821
9. Rodrigo, N.C., Rajiv R., Anton, B., Cesar, A.F.D.R., Rajkumar, B.: Cloudsim: a toolkit for modeling and simulation of cloud computing environments and evaluation of resource provisioning algorithms. Softw.: Pract. Exp. **41**(1), 23–50 (2011). ISSN: 0038-0644, Wiley Press, New York, USA
10. Richa, S., Nidhi, P., Hiteshi, D.: Power Aware Live Migration For Data Centers in Cloud using Dynamic Threshold (2012). ISSN 2229-6093
11. Xiaoying, W., Xiaojing, L., Lihua, F., Xuhan, J.: A decentralized virtual machine migration approach of data centers for cloud computing. Article ID 878542, 10 (2013)
12. Divya, K., Emmanuel, S.P., Ramesh, C.J.: Live Virtual Machine Migration Techniques: Survey and Research Challenges (2012). 978-1-4673-4529-3/12/$31.00⊕2012 IEEE

Fast Bilateral Symmetry Detection Using Inverted Gradient Hash Maps

R. Gonzalez[✉] and L. Lincoln

School of ICT, Griffith University, Parklands Drive, Southport, QLD, Australia
r.gonzalez@griffith.edu.au

Abstract. This paper presents a fast and novel algorithm for bilateral symmetry detection based on inverted gradient hash maps (IGHMs). A hash map is an associative array that stores image gradient magnitudes and orientations in the form of an inverted index. This mapping of image gradients to their locations permits points of interest to be located very rapidly without needing to search through the image. Unlike many symmetry operators it is able to detect large-scale symmetry. The method is described and experimentally evaluated against existing methods for bilateral symmetry detection.

Keywords: Symmetry detection · Reflective · Bilateral · Mirror

1 Introduction

The detection of symmetry has an important role in visual perception. It is also a fundamental process within many image-processing applications. It has a variety of uses such as an attentional operator in computer vision, as a detector of man made and natural objects such as human faces and also shape representation and characterization. While different kinds of symmetry can be detected, the most common are radial (rotational) and bilateral (reflective or mirror) symmetries.

Perhaps the best-known symmetry detector is Reisfeld's generalized symmetry transform [1]. This can detect bright and dark, isotropic or radial symmetries. It's main drawback is its computation complexity, having an order of NK^2, where N is the number of pixels in an image and K is the kernel size A variety of other bilateral and radial symmetry detectors have been proposed in the literature such as those utilizing the Hough transform [1–3] which have an order of KBN, where B is the number of angular steps. Faster algorithms have been proposed for detecting only radial symmetry such as that of Loy [5] that has an order of KN. While Reisfeld's algorithm requires 259 Mflops for a 30×30 kernel and a 521×512 pixel image, the Hough based methods require around 34 Mflops, and Loy's approach requires between 8–19 Mflops [6]. The main limitation with many of these methods is that they require multiple passes through the image to consider symmetry at multiple scales. Detecting bilateral symmetry across an entire image requires a kernel that is the same size as the image. In this case the required computing time becomes very large.

Typical symmetry detection operates by either searching for matching gradients within a kernel using the image's intrinsic Cartesian space or by using a one to many

© ICST Institute for Computer Sciences, Social Informatics and Telecommunications Engineering 2016
P.C. Vinh et al. (Eds.): ICTCC 2016, LNICST 168, pp. 72–81, 2016.
DOI: 10.1007/978-3-319-46909-6_8

voting scheme using an alternate parameterized 'Hough' accumulator space. In contrast, the method proposed in this paper operates purely in gradient space and avoids searching by using an inverted index. Until recently, inverted indices have only been used in for speeding up retrieval in databases [7]. Yet as described in [8] the concept of an inverted gradient space representation presents certain advantages for algorithms that exploit image gradients. Most importantly, by eliminating the need to search for matching gradients within a kernel, it can reduce processing time by up to two orders of magnitude.

In the following sections the inverted gradient space representation using hash maps is first described. Then fast bilateral symmetry detection using an IGHM is presented in Sect. 2.3. Experimental results for the performance of this algorithm relative to existing methods are presented in Sect. 3 and conclusions in Sect. 4.

2   Method Description

2.1   Inverted Gradient Hash Maps

A typical image f, is a mapping of image coordinates (x,y) to pixel intensity values i:

$$f: (x, y) \rightarrow i \text{ where } [x,y] \in \mathbb{N}^2 \tag{1}$$

The derivative of the image intensity at a given coordinate (x,y) gives rise to the local gradient and is defined by the magnitude and orientation $\{m, \theta\}$ at that coordinate:

$$m_{x,y} = \sqrt{\left(\frac{\partial}{\partial x} i_{x,y}\right)^2 + \left(\frac{\partial}{\partial y} i_{x,y}\right)^2} \text{ and } \theta_{x,y} = \arctan\left(\frac{\partial}{\partial x} i_{x,y}, \frac{\partial}{\partial y} i_{x,y}\right) \tag{2}$$

A mapping of image coordinates to their corresponding gradients is known as the gradient image g:

$$g: (x, y) \rightarrow \{m, \theta\} \tag{3}$$

A reverse mapping from the image gradients to image coordinates is known as an inverted gradient image h.

$$h: \{m, \theta\} \rightarrow (x, y) \tag{4}$$

While there is a single gradient for each image coordinate, there may be many image coordinates that have the same gradient. Thus, the inverted gradient image cannot be simply stored as a two dimensional array. Instead the inverted gradient image is best stored as a hash map where collisions in $\{m, \theta\}$ are resolved via chaining. This hash map is simply a two dimensional array of lists. These lists are indexed by the gradient magnitude and orientation and store the coordinates of the pixels having the indicated local gradient as depicted in Fig. 1.

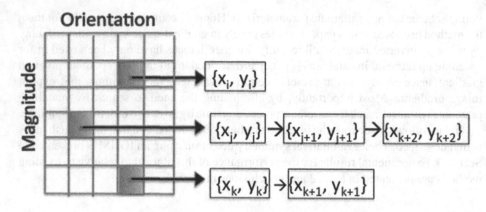

Fig. 1. Inverse Gradient Hash Map Data Structure

The size of the two-dimensional hash map is determined by the desired angular and scalar resolution used for the values (m, θ). Typically $m \rightarrow 0..255$ and $\theta \rightarrow 0..360$ in one degree increments.

2.2   Symmetry Detection

In Reisfeld's transform a full search of the image is required to find potentially contributing pairs of pixels within a given range defined by the kernel size. Each pixel is checked multiple times. This is avoided using an inverse gradient hash map. A single pass is made through the image visiting each pixel only once in order to populate the hash map. Once the hash map is formed all of the relevant pairs of gradients can be found via a simple lookup and their contribution assessed in a single pass.

The algorithm proceeds by simply looking up all the pairs of pixels having similar gradient magnitudes and opposing orientations (i.e. are rotated by approximately 180°). A margin of up to ±45° is used to include gradients that partially contribute to symmetry. This lookup results in two lists containing the coordinates of all the pixels matching the gradient criteria. The contribution of each pair of pixels in these two lists to the symmetry at the given orientation can then be calculated. Thus symmetry in specific directions can be readily determined or if desired, for all directions.

In the following pseudo code description of the basic algorithm, the outer two loops iterate over the entire hash table using indices a and m. Ideally magnitudes below some noise floor *thres* should be ignored. The next two inner loops using indices b and n only iterate respectively over the range of $(a + 45 + 180)$ and $(a - 45 + 180)$ degrees and also $(m - 5)$ to $(m + 5)$ to allow for noise in the gradient magnitude. For each pair of indices (a, m) and (b, n) two lists containing the relevant points are referenced using two pointer variables ptrA and ptrB. For each pair of coordinate points, i and j in these lists, the contribution to the symmetry is calculated (as further described below) and accumulated if it is within the target range of influence.

```
function symmetry(IGHM, output, maxdist, thres)
Begin
  //-- visit all gradients in hash map --
  Foreach a = gradient orientations from 0...360
    Foreach m = gradient magnitudes > thres
      //-- get contributing gradient points --
      For (b = a-45; b < a+45; b++)
        For (n = m-5; n < m+5; n++)
        Begin
          Var c = (b + 180) % 360
          var ptrA = &(IGHM[a][m])
          Var ptrB = &(IGHM[c][n])
          //-- walk coordinate lists --
          For (i=0; i< ptrA->len; i++)
            For (j=0; j< ptrB->len; j++)
            Begin
              Var Dij = Distance(ptrA[i], ptrB[j])
              Var Cij = Calc(a,b,ptrA[i], ptrB[j])
              Var x = (ptrA[i].x + ptrB[j].x) / 2
              Var y = (ptrA[i].y + ptrB[j].y) / 2
              If (Dij < maxdist) Output[x][y] += Cij
            End
        End
  End
End
```

The contribution C_{ij} of each pair of pixels p_i and p_j is a function of the magnitude of the nominated gradient m_i and m_j, the deviation of the gradient orientation to the suggested axis of symmetry and optionally, the distance between contributing pixels D_{ij}. This contribution is assigned to the halfway point q_{ij} between the contributing pixel pair. A two-dimensional accumulator C is used to store the contribution of each pair at the halfway points.

Given a pair of contributing pixels p_i and p_j, as depicted in Fig. 2, the first step is to determine the orientation of the suggested axis of symmetry φ_{ij}. This is calculated as the normal to the vector connecting p_i and p_j, thus:

$$\phi_{ij} = \arctan 2\left(\frac{p_i(y) - p_j(y)}{p_j(x) - p_i(x)}\right) \tag{5}$$

Next the angular difference between the orientation of the suggested axis of symmetry φ_{ij} and the orientation of the gradients θ_i and θ_j at each point is found, using a formulation that avoids costly transcendental functions.

$$\Delta_i = \left|\pi - \left|\left|\phi_{ij} - \theta_i\right| - \pi\right|\right| \; and \; \Delta_j = \left|\pi - \left|\left|\phi_{ij} - \theta_j\right| - \pi\right|\right| \tag{6}$$

The contribution of the gradients p_i and p_j becomes

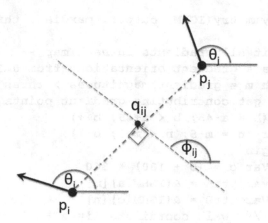

Fig. 2. The geometry associated with points contributing to symmetry.

$$C_{ij} = \frac{m_i \times m_j}{1 + |\Delta_i - \Delta_j|}$$ (7)

The Euclidean distance between contributing pixels D_{ij} can be used to limit the range of influence that gradients can have exert by ignoring the contributions of points beyond this range limit.

The symmetry can be calculated to consider all gradients or only those that pertain to bright objects on a dark background (bright symmetry) or dark object on a bright background (dark symmetry). To do this the orientation of the gradient relative to the halfway point needs to be determined. First the angle A_i from each point p_i to the halfway point q_{ij} is found and similarly for A_j.

$$A_i = \arctan\left(\frac{q_{ij}(y) - p_i(y)}{p_i(x) - q_{ij}(x)}\right) \quad and \quad A_j = \arctan\left(\frac{q_{ij}(y) - p_j(y)}{p_j(x) - q_{ij}(x)}\right)$$ (8)

These values are next compared to the gradient orientation θ_i and θ_j at p_i and p_j to see whether the gradients are aligned towards or away from A_i and A_j.

$$\varphi_i = |\theta_i - A_i| \quad and \quad \varphi_j = |\theta_j - A_j|$$ (9)

Depending on the value of ψ_i and ψ_j the contribution C_{ij} for that pair is retained or set to zero. For bright symmetry the following relationship holds:

$$C_{ij} = \begin{cases} 0 & (\varphi_i < 90 \vee \varphi_i > 270) \wedge (\varphi_j < 90 \vee \varphi_j > 270) \\ C_{ij} & otherwise \end{cases}$$ (10)

For dark symmetry the following relationship is used

$$C_{ij} = \begin{cases} 0 & (\varphi_i > 90 \land \varphi_i < 270) \land (\varphi_j > 90 \land \varphi_j < 270) \\ C_{ij} & otherwise \end{cases} \qquad (11)$$

2.3   Complexity Analysis

From the foregoing discussion one can observe that the computational complexity of this method, given the three sets of two loops in the basic algorithm is in the order of:

$$(A * M) * (A/4 * 10) * (La * Lb)$$
$$= k * A^2 * M * La * Lb \qquad (12)$$

Here A and M are respectively the number of orientation and magnitude bins used in the hash map and are a function of the angular and scalar resolution used for the values (m, θ). The constant k for a typical implementation equals 2.5, but could be reduced if desired. La and Lb are the lengths of the two coordinate lists and are related to the load factor of the hash map. The load factor will be a function A and M relative to the image size in pixels N. Typically the average load factor L_f is defined as:

$$L_f = N/(A * M) \qquad (13)$$

Since on average the lengths of the two lists La and Lb will be equal to the load factor the following substitutions can be made to simplify the calculation of (12):

$$A^2 * M * L_f * L_f = A^2 * M * N^2/(A * M)^2$$
$$= N^2/M \qquad (14)$$

Although the worst-case complexity of this algorithm will never be greater than N^2, in practice this upper bound will never be approached unless the hash map only a single bin for the gradient magnitude, which defeats the purpose of using a two dimensional hash map. The complexity using a 360×256 cell hash map is unlikely to ever exceed $N^{1.8}$ as can be seen from Table 1 for the different size images:

Table 1. Computational Complexity for various image sizes.

Image pixels	Complexity
256×256	$N^{1.5}$
512×512	$N^{1.56}$
1024×1024	$N^{1.6}$
2048×2048	$N^{1.65}$
4096×4096	$N^{1.67}$
8192×8192	$N^{1.69}$
$1,000,000 \times 1,000,000$	$N^{1.8}$

In addition to the symmetry calculation the cost of generating the hash map needs to be considered. As this is a linear operation with a complexity of N it has fairly small impact on the total complexity.

3 Experimental Results

Symmetry detection experiments were run using a variety of images. For ease of comparison, a version of the "Cards, keys and hand" image from Reisfeld's paper was used with the results shown in Fig. 3 for Reisfeld's method in the centre and the proposed one on the right.

Fig. 3. Bilateral symmetry with the original image on the left, symmetry detected Reisfeld's method using a kernel size of 16 in the middle and IGHM based method with a D_{ij} of 16.

While symmetry detection algorithms typically work well for simple, small-scale symmetry such as that in Fig. 3, the real challenge is for detecting image wide symmetry. For this experiment the well-known Lena image was first mirrored horizontally and then vertically around a central axis as shown in Fig. 4. In addition, other images of natural and man made objects as depicted in Fig. 5 were also evaluated. In both Figs. 4 and 5 the mirrored images are shown on the left, with the result of the proposed symmetry operator in the centre. The axis of symmetry is found by applying a line detector after non-maximal suppression to the resulting image.

To compare the ability of the proposed method to detect image wide symmetry relative to Reisfeld's method, his operator was applied with a kernel size of 256 to the mirrored Lena image used in Fig. 4. As the results in Fig. 6 show, the Reisfeld operator (on the right side) completely fails to identify the symmetry in the image.

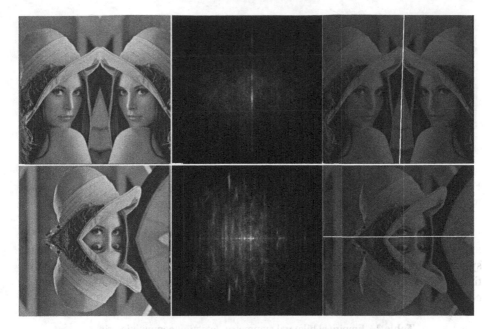

Fig. 4. Symmetry of mirrored images with the originals on the left, detected symmetry in the centre and the resulting axes of symmetry superimposed over the original on the right.

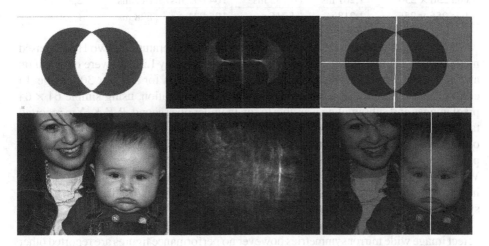

Fig. 5. Bilateral symmetry with the original images on the left, output of the symmetry detector in the centre and the resulting axes of symmetry superimposed over the original on the right.

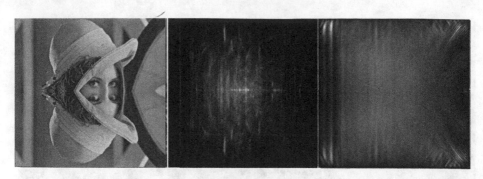

Fig. 6. Comparison of large field symmetry detection. The original is on the left, the proposed method in the centre and Reisfeld's on the right side.

The time performance of the proposed method was evaluated on a MacBookPro with a 2.6 GHz Intel i7 with 16 GB of memory. The running time of Reisfeld's general symmetry transform was measured for kernel sizes of 8, 16 and 256 as well as the running time for the proposed method with corresponding maximum gradient influence distance constraints (Table 2).

Table 2. Empirical bilateral symmetry detection computation time.

Image	Reisfeld-8	Reisfeld-16	Reisfeld-256	IGMH-16	IGHM-256
Card, keys and hand	1,173 ms	4,322 ms	100,222 ms	152 ms	624 ms
Lena 256 × 256	1,207 ms	4,535 ms	104,097 ms	811 ms	2,527 ms
Elvis 256 × 256	1,218 ms	4,716 ms	105,931 ms	898 ms	1,750 ms

These results were compared to those reported in the literature for two Hough based methods by Li et al. [2] and Yip [4]. The results reported by Li et al. were obtained on a 2.2 GHz Pentium using Matlab and took from 10 to 20 s for a 300 × 300 image. Li et al. further reported that a native C language implementation, using simple 64 × 64 pixel images and subsampling was able to run in under one second. R.K.K. Yip reported taking between 20–50 s results using a 500 MHz Pentium 2 for simple 256 × 256 images of polygons, and about 50 min for more complex synthetic images. In comparison the proposed IGMH based method processes simple 256 × 256 images in about 150 ms. While it is half an order of magnitude faster when using small kernel sizes on complex images, the processing time is orders of magnitude less when considering image wide symmetry, as is predicted from the complexity analysis.

Like the proposed method, Patraucean's Hough voting based approach [3] is able to detect image wide mirror symmetries however no performance figures are reported other than that the validation time alone, for each symmetry candidate on an 800 × 600 image requires 2 s on an 2.53 GHz, Intel i5 based computer. Since typically between five to ten candidates need to be validated, the total time for the validation alone amounts to 10 to 20 s. This however does not include the time required for the selection of the symmetry candidates themselves. In contrast, for similar sized images the proposed IGHM based method completes the task in about 10 s.

4   Conclusions

Detection of symmetry is a fundamental task in image processing but it has traditionally been computationally expensive. While efficient algorithms have been developed for calculating radial symmetry, algorithms for the detection of bilateral symmetry are still relatively slow. This paper has presented a fast and novel approach to finding bilateral symmetry based on inverted gradient hash maps. Not only is it significantly faster than other methods for detecting bilateral symmetry but it can successfully detect such symmetry on large scales. Future work will consider methods for automatic selection of D_{ij} the maximum distance between contributing pixels.

References

1. Reisfeld, D., Wolfson, H., Yeshurun, Y.: Context-free attentional operators: the generalized symmetry transform. Int. J. Comput. Vision **14**(2), 119–130 (1995)
2. Li, W.H., Zhang, A.M., Kleeman, L.: Fast global reflectional symmetry detection for robotic grasping and visual tracking. In: Proceedings of Australasian Conference on Robotics and Automation, December 2005
3. Patraucean, V., von Gioi, R.G., Ovsjanikov, M.: Detection of mirror-symmetric image patches. In: 2013 IEEE Conference on Computer Vision and Pattern Recognition Workshops (CVPRW), pp. 211–216, 23–28 June 2013
4. Yip, R.K.K.: A Hough transform technique for the detection of reflectional symmetry and skew-symmetry. In: Pattern Recognition Letters, Vol. 21, Issue 2, pp. 117–130, Feb 2000
5. Loy, G., Zelinsky, A.: A fast radial symmetry transform for detecting points of interest. IEEE Trans. Pattern Anal. Mach. Intell. **25**(8), 959–973 (2003)
6. Loy, G.: Computer Vision to See People: a basis for enhanced human computer interaction. Ph.D. Thesis, Australian National University, January 2003
7. Zobel, J., Moffat, A.: Inverted files for text search engines. ACM Comput. Surv. **38**(2), 6 (2006)
8. Gonzalez, R.: Fast line and circle detection using inverted gradient hash maps. In: The 40th International Conference on Acoustics, Speech and Signal Processing, Proceedings of (ICASSP2014), Brisbane, Australia, 19–24 April 2015. IEEE (2015)

A Review of Two Approaches for Joining 3D Meshes

Anh-Cang Phan[1]([⊠]), Romain Raffin[2], and Marc Daniel[2]

[1] VinhLong College of Economics and Finance, Vinh Long , Vietnam
`pacang@vcef.edu.vn`
[2] Aix-Marseille University, CNRS, LSIS UMR 7296, 13009 Marseille, France

Abstract. The construction of smooth surfaces of 3D complex objects
is an important problem in many graphical applications. Unfortunately,
cracks or holes may appear on their surfaces caused by the limitation of
scanners or the difference in resolution levels and subdivision schemes
between adjacent faces. In this paper, we introduce two approaches for
joining 3D meshes of different resolutions to remove the cracks or holes.
These approaches use a wavelet transform and a RBF local interpolation
or a tangent plane local approximation. They guarantee that the discrete
continuity between meshes is preserved and the connecting mesh can
change gradually in resolution between coarse and fine mesh areas.

Keywords: Triangular meshes · Mesh connection · Smoothness · Local
approximation · RBF local interpolation · B-spline wavelets

1 Introduction

3D object models with complex shapes are usually generated by a set of assembled patches or separate meshes which may be at different resolutions, even with
different subdivision schemes. A generic problem arising from subdividing two
meshes initially connected along a common boundary is the occurrence of cracks
or holes if they are separately subdivided by different schemes (i.e. Butterfly [1],
Loop [2], etc.). In order to deal with these drawbacks and particularly cracks,
we propose two new approaches joining two selected meshes of a 3D model so
that the "continuity" between these meshes can be preserved. It means that
the curvatures must be "continuous" on the boundaries, which must be studied
in terms of discrete curvatures, the latter being not presented here. We aim at
constructing a high quality connecting mesh linking two meshes of different resolutions. The connecting mesh is constructed by adding triangle strips to each
boundaries up to the time they are close enough to be linked.

2 Previous Work

Some research [3–5] are related to the incremental subdivision method with Butterfly and Loop schemes. The main goal of these methods is to generate a smooth

© ICST Institute for Computer Sciences, Social Informatics and Telecommunications Engineering 2016
P.C. Vinh et al. (Eds.): ICTCC 2016, LNICST 168, pp. 82–96, 2016.
DOI: 10.1007/978-3-319-46909-6_9

surface by refining only some selected areas of a mesh and remove cracks by simple triangulation. However, this simple triangulation changes the connectivity, the valence of vertices, and produces high valence vertices leading to long faces. This not only alters the limit subdivision surface, but also creates ripple effects on the subdivision surface and therefore reduces its smoothness. In addition, several research [6,7] relevant to joining meshes along boundary curves are of immediate practical interest. These methods consist in connecting the meshes of a surface at the same resolution level which adopt various criteria to compute the planar shape from a 3D surface patch by minimizing their differences. In general, they are computationally expensive and memory consuming. Besides, the algorithms do not mention the continuity and the progressive change in resolution between meshes after joining. Meanwhile, the main challenge in designing a mesh connection algorithm is to guarantee these features. From the above motivation, we propose in this paper two new methods based on mesh connection approaches to overcome these drawbacks and particularly cracks and holes.

3 Background

3.1 Wavelet-Based Multiresolution Representation of Curves and Surfaces

Wavelets has been applied successfully in the areas of computer graphics [8,9]. The combination of B-splines and wavelets leads to the idea of B-spline wavelets [10]. Taking advantage of the lifting scheme [12], the Lifted B-spline wavelet [11] is a fast computational tool for multiresolution of a given B-spline curve with a computational complexity linear in the number of control points. The Lifted B-spline wavelet transform includes the forward and backward B-spline wavelet transforms. From a fine curve at the resolution level J, C^J, the forward wavelet transform decomposes C^J into a coarser approximation of the curve, C^{J-1}, and detail (error) vectors. The detail vectors are a set of wavelet coefficients containing the geometric differences with respect to the finer levels. The backward transform synthesizes C^{J-1} and the detail vectors into a finer curve, C^J. In our approach, we apply the Lifted B-spline wavelet transform for multiresolution of discrete boundary curves of a connecting mesh.

3.2 Radial Basis Function (RBF) Local Interpolation

In order to extrapolate local frames (tangents, curvatures) between two meshes, we need a local interpolation method on the points that will be projected. In this section, we choose the RBF local interpolation [13,14] to construct an expected surface in crack removal and hole filling from subsets of nearest neighboring points because it provides local details of the interpolated surface and exploits the characteristics of flexibility and accuracy. The basic idea of the RBF local interpolation is to find a local interpolation function which implicitly defines a surface (denoted CM) using a set of local control points. The signed distance function $f(x)$ is represented as the signed distance from x to the closest point on CM. If point x lies on CM, $f(x)$ vanishes ($f(x) = 0$). Point x is called "on-surface point". In contrast, it is called "off-surface point" and $f(x)$ is not zero. Given a set of N data points $X = \{x_k = (a_k^x, a_k^y, a_k^z)\}_{k=1}^N \subset \mathbb{R}^3$. For each $x_k \in X, k = 1, ..., N$, we determine:

- A set of local control points: $X_k = \{x_k\} \cup \{x_i \in \mathbb{R}^3; x_i \in Neighbors(x_k)\}$ corresponding to a set of the signed distance function values F_k, where $Neighbors(x_k)$ is the nearest neighboring points of x_k. For each point of X_k, we compute one off-surface point to specify a set of the local control points in X_k so that the number of points in X_k is multiplied by 2.
- Distance function values: $F_k = \{f_i = f(x_i), i \in I_k\} \subset \mathbb{R}$, where I_k is the set of indexes of X_k and $N_k = |X_k|$ is the number of the local control points in X_k. The signed distance function f is defined by equation:

$$\begin{cases} f(x_i) = 0, \text{ if } x_i \text{ are on-surface points} \\ f(x_i) = d \in \mathbb{R}, \text{ if } x_i \text{ are off-surface points} \end{cases} \quad (1)$$

with d is a parameter predefined by the user.

A RBF local interpolation function $s_k \colon \mathbb{R}^3 \to \mathbb{R}$ on X_k is expressed:

$$s_k(x) = \sum_{c \in I_k} \lambda_c \phi(\|x - x_c\|) \quad (2)$$

where $\phi(\|x - x_c\|)$ are the radial basis functions (RBFs); x_c are the control points and are also the nearest neighboring points of x_k; λ_c are the RBF weights; $\|x\|$ is the Euclidean norm. The user needs to find $s_k(x)$ such that it satisfies the constraints:

$$s_k(x_i) = f_i = \sum_{c \in I_k} \lambda_c \phi(\|x_i - x_c\|), i \in I_k \quad (3)$$

The basis function is normally chosen from the family of spline functions. Typically, the Gaussian function $\phi(r) = e^{-\left(\frac{r}{h}\right)^2}$ is suggested in our method because we want that the RBF local interpolation function $s_k(x)$ provides a local approximation of data points x. The user should choose h as the average distance between x and control points x_c [15]. Combining (2) and (3) leads to the linear system expressed in a matrix form:

$$\begin{pmatrix} \phi_{1,1} & \cdots & \phi_{1,N_k} \\ \vdots & \ddots & \vdots \\ \phi_{N_k,1} & \cdots & \phi_{N_k,N_k} \end{pmatrix} \begin{pmatrix} \lambda_1 \\ \vdots \\ \lambda_{N_k} \end{pmatrix} = \begin{pmatrix} f_1 \\ \vdots \\ f_{N_k} \end{pmatrix} \quad (4)$$

Equation (4) may be re-written in simplified matrix form:

$$\Phi_{X_k} \Lambda_{X_k} = F_{X_k} \quad (5)$$

where $\phi_{i,c} = \phi(\|x_i - x_c\|)$, $\Phi_{X_k} = (\phi_{i,c})$ with $i, c \in I_k$, $\Lambda_{X_k} = (\lambda_1, \lambda_2, ..., \lambda_{N_k})^T$, $F_{X_k} = (f_1, ..., f_{N_k})^T$. After solving the linear system (5) to compute Λ, a set of data points on CM is simply reconstructed by computing $s_k(x)$ at $x \in X_k$ using (2). The RBF local interpolation give good results for surface reconstruction but it is not adequate for data points with abrupt and large changes within small distances. In addition, it requires much more estimations of the shape parameter (h), off-surface constraints. Therefore, we need to find other feasible and reliable methods such as an implicit surface fitting with tangent planes [17] that produces high quality surfaces in our work.

3.3 Tangent Plane Local Approximation for Implicit Surface Reconstruction

We describe here a tangent plane local approximation proposed by Hoppe et al. [16] for implicit surface reconstruction from 3D point cloud. Given a set of data points $P = \{p_i\} \in \mathbb{R}^3$ of a surface CM, to determine data points p_{new} on CM, the authors estimate a set of local tangent planes $Tp(p_i)$ represented as local linear approximations of CM, and then find the projection p_{new} of an arbitrary point $p \in \mathbb{R}^3$ onto CM. The estimation of $Tp(p_i)$ and the projection of p onto CM are described as follows:

Estimation of a tangent plane: Let $Tp(p_i)$ be the tangent plane corresponding to point p_i and passing through a centroid point o_i. An arbitrary point p is projected onto tangent plane $Tp(p_i)$ which has point o_i closest to point p. Tangent plane $Tp(p_i)$ is determined by passing through point o_i with unit surface normal n_i as follows:

– Find local neighbors of each data point:
  For each point $p_i \in \mathbb{R}^3$, the user finds a set of nearest neighbors of p_i denoted $Neighbors(p_i)$.
– Compute a centroid point on a tangent plane: For each point $p_i \in \mathbb{R}^3$, the user computes the centroid point o_i based on all nearest neighbors of p_i:

$$o_i = \frac{\sum_{p_j \in Neighbors(p_i)} p_j}{N} \tag{6}$$

where N is the number of the neighbors of p_i.
– Estimate a normal vector of a tangent plane: The principal component analysis (PCA) method is used to estimate normal n_i of $Tp(p_i)$. The point covariance matrix $CV_i \in \mathbb{R}^{3\times3}$ from the neighbors of p_i is first computed:

$$CV_i = \sum_{p_j \in Neighbors(p_i)} (p_j - o_i) \otimes (p_j - o_i) \tag{7}$$

where $\otimes$ denotes the outer product vector operator: if x and y have components x_i and y_j respectively, the matrix $x \otimes y$ has $x_i y_j$ as its ij-th element. Eigenvalues $\lambda_{i,1} \geq \lambda_{i,2} \geq \lambda_{i,3}$ of CV_i are then determined corresponding to unit eigenvectors $v_{i,1}, v_{i,2}, v_{i,3}$. Since normal n_i is the eigenvector corresponding to the smallest eigenvalue, the user chooses to be either $v_{i,3}$ or $-v_{i,3}$. The choice determines the tangent plane orientation [16].

Projection of p onto $Tp(p_i)$: The projected point p_{new} is the orthogonal projection of point p onto $Tp(p_i)$. Let $f(p)$ be a signed distance from an arbitrary $p \in \mathbb{R}^3$ to CM:

$$f(p) = dist(p, p_{new}) = (p - o_i).n_i \qquad (8)$$

Then, the projected point p_{new} is computed by:

$$p_{new} = p - (f(p)\, n_i) \qquad (9)$$

4   Overview of Two Methods for Joining Meshes

4.1   Notation

In order to lighten notations, we decide not to use vectorial notations for all the notations or equations having vectorial relations. Moreover, we denote the position vector $\overrightarrow{Op}$ of a vertex p by p, where O is the frame origin. Each multiplication of a scalar value and a vector is understood as the vector components multiplied by the scalar value.

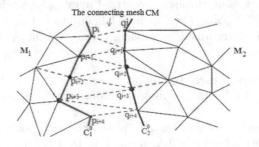

Fig. 1. Topology representation of the algorithm.

Let M_1 and M_2 be two meshes of different resolutions, and p_i, q_k their vertices. An edge connecting p_i to q_k is denoted e_i or p_iq_k. An edge is usually shared by two faces. If it is shared by only one, it corresponds to a boundary edge and its end vertices are called boundary vertices. We need to construct a connecting mesh CM between M_1 and M_2 so that the continuity between them can be preserved as illustrated in Fig. 1. First we will introduce the notations used in the algorithms:

– s: number of newly created boundary curves of CM created between M_1 and M_2. It is a user parameter computed based on the distance between two original boundaries of M_1 and M_2 and it controls the resolution of CM.
– j: order number of the decomposition step to create intermediate discrete curves, also called the level. Since two boundary curves between M_1 and M_2 will be created at each level j, j is in $[1, \frac{s}{2}]$.

- C_1^j and C_2^j: two boundary curves of CM at level j. C_1^0 and C_2^0 are the two original boundary curves of meshes M_1 and M_2.
- $N(C_1^j)$: number of vertices of boundary curve C_1^j at level j. It corresponds to the density of vertices of boundary curve C_1^j.
- p_i^j, q_i^j: vertices i on boundary curves C_1^j and C_2^j. ($p_i^0 = p_i$ and $q_i^0 = q_i$)
- L_1^j: list of the boundary vertex pairs (p_i^{j-1}, q_k^{j-1}); L_2^j: list of the pairs (q_k^{j-1}, p_i^{j-1}).

4.2 Our General Algorithm for Joining Meshes

The idea is to generate the connecting mesh CM consisting of newly created boundary curves using the Lifted B-spline wavelet transform and the local RBF interpolation (for CM2D-RBFW method) or the tangent plane local approximation (for CM2D-TPW method). The general algorithm of our proposed methods consists of the following main steps detailed in the next sections.

A General Algorithm for Joining Meshes
Input: a crack between two meshes of different resolutions and schemes.
Output: a high quality connecting mesh CM and a smooth connection surface.

- **Step 1**. Boundary detection: read the input model of two meshes M_1 and M_2. Detect and mark boundary vertices of the two boundaries C_1^0 and C_2^0 of M_1 and M_2.
- **Step 2**. Boundary vertex pairs and boundary curve creation: for each level j, we pair the boundary vertices of C_1^{j-1} and C_2^{j-1} based on the distance between them. If this distance is too narrow (smaller than a certain threshold), we go to Step 3 to connect the boundary curve pair (C_1^{j-1}, C_2^{j-1}). In contrast, we create two new boundary curves C_1^j, C_2^j from the paired boundary vertices by a linear interpolation and a RBF local interpolation (CM2D-RBFW method) or a tangent plane local approximation (CM2D-TPW method). It finally refines or coarsens these new boundary curves applying wavelet transforms and operations of vertex insertion or deletion.
- **Step 3**. Boundary curve connection: perform a boundary triangulation for each boundary curve pair (C_1^{j-1}, C_1^j) and (C_2^{j-1}, C_2^j).
- **Step 4**. Repeat steps 2 and 3 until both mesh areas M_1 and M_2 have been connected or patched by all newly created triangles.

5 Boundary Curve Creation and Connection

5.1 Boundary Vertex Pairs

This work is to find all vertices of a boundary curve closest to vertices of a remaining boundary curve to pair. In order to create boundary curves between two meshes M_1 and M_2 by interpolating previously created boundary curves, we pair the boundary vertices $p_i^{j-1} \in C_1^{j-1}$ with $q_k^{j-1} \in C_2^{j-1}$ and vice versa based on the distances between them. Since the densities of vertices of both boundary curves are different, we need to create two lists of the closest boundary vertex pairs L_1^j and L_2^j. Assume that j is the current level, for each boundary vertex $p_i^{j-1} \in C_1^{j-1}$, we search for and insert into L_1^j the corresponding paired vertex $q_k^{j-1} \in C_2^{j-1}$ such that:

$\left(\forall q \in C_2^{j-1}, dist(p_i^{j-1}, q_k^{j-1}) \leq dist(p_i^{j-1}, q) \right)$, where the notation $dist(p_i^{j-1}, q_k^{j-1}) = ||p_i^{j-1} - q_k^{j-1}||$ is the Euclidean distance between p_i^{j-1} and q_k^{j-1}. The list of boundary vertex pairs L_2^j is created similarly.

5.2   Boundary Curve Creation

5.2.1   CM2D-RBFW Algorithm

The idea of our algorithm is to create the discrete boundary curves C_1^j and C_2^j between M_1 and M_2 from the paired vertices of two previously created boundary curves C_1^{j-1} and C_2^{j-1} using the RBF local interpolation and the Lifted B-spline wavelet transform. Then, we connect each new curve C_1^j to C_1^{j-1}, and C_2^j to C_2^{j-1}. Therefore, it is called the algorithm of **connecting mesh in two directions based on the RBF local interpolation and the Wavelet transform** (CM2D-RBFW). Details of the algorithm are introduced as follows:

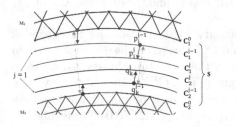
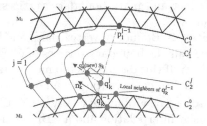

Fig. 2. Creation of new boundary curves.   **Fig. 3.** Projection of the vertices onto CM.

We assume $N(C_1^0) \leq N(C_2^0)$ and let the density of vertices of the two boundary curves C_1^j and C_2^j be two functions $N(C_1^j)$ and $N(C_2^j)$ defined by:

$$N(C_1^j) = N(C_1^0) + \frac{j}{s+1}[N(C_2^0) - N(C_1^0)]$$
$$N(C_2^j) = N(C_2^0) - \frac{j}{s+1}[N(C_2^0) - N(C_1^0)]$$

(10)

The boundary curve creation is computed in three phases:

Phase 1: Create vertices of two new boundary curves by a linear interpolation.

– Create new vertices $p_i^j \in C_1^j$ at each level j (see Fig. 2): for each boundary vertex pair $(p_i^{j-1}, q_k^{j-1}) \in L_1^j$, we apply the linear interpolation equation (11) to create new boundary vertices $p_i^j \in C_1^j$.

$$p_i^j = p_i^{j-1} + \frac{j}{s+1}(q_k^{j-1} - p_i^{j-1}) \tag{11}$$

where i are the subscripts of boundary vertices of C_1^j, $1 \leq i \leq N(C_1^{j-1})$, and k are the subscripts of boundary vertices of C_2^{j-1}, $1 \leq k \leq N(C_2^{j-1})$.

– In the same way, we create new vertices $q_k^j \in C_2^j$ at each level j: for each boundary vertex pair $(q_k^{j-1}, p_i^{j-1}) \in L_2^j$, we apply the linear interpolation equation (12) to create new boundary vertices $q_k^j \in C_2^j$.

$$q_k^j = q_k^{j-1} + \frac{j}{s+1}(p_i^{j-1} - q_k^{j-1}) \tag{12}$$

where k are the subscripts of boundary vertices of C_2^j, $1 \leq k \leq N(C_2^{j-1})$, and i are the subscripts of boundary vertices of C_1^{j-1}, $1 \leq i \leq N(C_1^{j-1})$.

Equations (11) and (12) have been chosen with a local linear expansion classically used in marching methods. Starting from C_1^0 and C_2^0 when $j = 1$, we recursively compute (11) and (12) based on vertices of the curves C_1^{j-1} and C_2^{j-1} but not C_1^0 and C_2^0. In addition, since C_1^{j-1} and C_2^{j-1} are then refined or coarsened by wavelet transforms, their resolutions are increased or reduced respectively.

Phase 2: Project created boundary vertices onto CM using the RBF local interpolation.

The goal of phase 2 is to improve the resulting surface CM after applying phase 1. Since new boundary vertices p_i^j and q_k^j of curves C_1^j and C_2^j are created by a linear interpolation in phase 1, they lie on a line through two vertices p_i^{j-1} and q_k^{j-1} but not on the expected surface CM. As a result, the boundary curves are produced without respect to local curvatures when CM is a complex curved surface. Therefore, the generated connecting mesh CM will not respect the expected continuity between the meshes. This problem is overcome by an implicit surface reconstruction with a RBF local interpolation. We project new vertices $p_i^j \in C_1^j$ and $q_k^j \in C_2^j$ created in phase 1 onto CM by a RBF local interpolation as shown in Fig. 3. Projecting the created vertices $q_k^j \in C_2^j$ onto CM is performed as follows: first, for each vertex q_k^j, we find the closest vertex $q_k^{j-1} \in C_2^{j-1}$ and its neighbors to choose as a set of the local control vertices of q_k^j. Then, we compute the weights of the RBFs (using (4)) and the local interpolation function values s_k for q_k^j (using (2)). Next, we project them onto CM with the projection distances s_k along normals at the vertices q_k^{j-1} (see Fig. 3). The normals at the vertices q_k^{j-1} are estimated via the principal component analysis (PCA) method. Finally, we update the vertices q_k^j as their projections. Similarly, we also perform the same for the created vertices $p_i^j \in C_1^j$.

A problem shows that if we only use on-surface vertices directly to solve for the weights of the radial basis functions, the system Eq. (4) becomes trivial. This problem can be overcome by creating additional off-surface vertices to construct the RBF local interpolation function. Typically, for each vertex q_k^j, we choose a set of local control vertices Q_k^j corresponding to the signed distance function values $f(q) = 0$ for $q \in Q1_k^j$ and $f(q) = d$ for $q \in Q2_k^j$ to construct the RBF local interpolation function, where $Q_k^j = Q1_k^j \cup Q2_k^j$. $Q1_k^j$ and $Q2_k^j$ are computed by:

- $Q1_k^j$ is referred to as a set of on-surface vertices. It is defined by:
  $Q1_k^j = \{q_k^{j-1} \in C_2^{j-1}\} \cup \{q_1 \in \mathbb{R}^3; q_1 \in Neighbors(q_k^{j-1})\}$, where $Neighbors(q_k^{j-1})$ is a set of the local neighbors of q_k^{j-1} which have edges connecting to q_k^{j-1}.
- $Q2_k^j$ is referred to as a set of off-surface vertices. It is defined in form:
  $Q2_k^j = \{q_2 \in \mathbb{R}^3; q_2 = q_1 + d\ n(q_1), \forall q_1 \in Q1_k^j\}$, where d is the estimate of the signed distance to the surface (also called the signed projection distance) defined by the user. However, d can't be too small, otherwise, the matrix of the linear system in Eq. (4) will be ill-conditioned. On the other hand, if d is too large, wrong off-surface points could be created. This can result in an incorrect surface; $n(q_1)$ is the normal vector at the vertex q_1.

When the curves C_1^{j-1} and C_2^{j-1} are close together, the neighbors are chosen from both sides of model to make a set of on-surface vertices. That means, for each vertex $q_{l_k}^j$, we take the two closest vertices $p_i^{j-1} \in C_1^{j-1}$ and $q_k^{j-1} \in C_2^{j-1}$ along with their local neighbors to specify a set of on-surface vertices of q_k^j. This implies that we take into account the local curvatures on both sides to finish CM and have a nice join.

Phase 3: Refine or coarsen new boundary curves with the wavelet transforms. Since the densities of vertices of C_1^j and C_2^j are now $N(C_1^{j-1})$ and $N(C_2^{j-1})$, we need to increase and reduce their densities to be $N(C_1^j)$ and $N(C_2^j)$. Taking advantage of the Lifted B-spline wavelet transform presented in Sect. 3.1, we apply this transform for the multiresolution analysis of the curves C_1^j and C_2^j to refine the curve C_1^j, coarsen the curve C_2^j. Then, we perform operations of the vertex insertion or deletion to control the densities of vertices of C_1^j and C_2^j. Thus, the created curves C_1^j, C_2^j, and the associated connecting mesh CM are changed gradually in resolution between both mesh areas.

CM2D-RBFW method requires too much estimation consisting of the off-surface constraints, the choice of the user parameter values d and h, and the solution of linear systems for an interpolation problem. Thus, in the next section we propose a more reliable method for mesh connection called CM2D-TPW method which allows us to construct a high quality connecting mesh CM and a continuous surface. The goal is to gain in both time of computation and surface quality.

5.2.2   CM2D-TPW Algorithm

Similar to CM2D-RBFW method, we create new curves C_1^j and C_2^j from the paired vertices in each level j based on a tangent plane local approximation and a wavelet transform as shown in Fig. 4. We also assume $N(C_1^0) \leq N(C_2^0)$ and the density of vertices of the two boundary curves C_1^j and C_2^j are two functions $N(C_1^j)$ and $N(C_2^j)$ defined by Eq. (10). The boundary curve creation is produced in three phases.

Phase 1: Create vertices of two new boundary curves by a linear interpolation.

This phase is similar to phase 1 of CM2D-RBFW method. We recursively compute (11) and (12) based on vertices of the curves C_1^{j-1} and C_2^{j-1} starting from C_1^0 and C_2^0 when $j = 1$.

Phase 2: Project created boundary vertices onto CM using a local approximation.

When CM is a complex curved surface, the newly created vertices p_i^j and q_k^j can not lie on CM because we do not consider the curvature information in phase 1. As a result, the produced connecting mesh will not ensure the expected continuity between two meshes. To solve this problem, we need a tangent plane local approximation [16, 17] on which points will be projected as provided in Sect. 3.3 to extrapolate local frames (tangents, curvatures) between two meshes. We first apply phase 1 (linear interpolation) to create new boundary vertices, and then project these vertices onto local tangent planes corresponding to a C^1 or C^2 continuous surface as shown in Fig. 4. As a result, the new vertices are positioned on the expected surface CM with respect to the variation of the tangent planes. It implies that we take into account the local curvatures to have a nice join and a smooth transition with at least C^1 continuity (tangent continuity). Projecting the created vertices $q_k^j \in C_2^j$ onto surface CM is performed as follows: First, for each vertex q_k^j, we find the closest vertex $q_k^{j-1} \in C_2^{j-1}$ and its local neighbors $Neighbors(q_k^{j-1})$ which have edges connected to q_k^{j-1} to determine the local control vertices of q_k^j (see Fig. 4). Next, we estimate the local tangent plane $Tp(q_k^{j-1})$ which is a local linear approximation of surface CM. The plane $Tp(q_k^{j-1})$ passes through the centroid vertex o_k^{j-1} (using (6)) with unit normal vector n_k^{j-1} (using (7)). From that, we compute $f(q_k^j)$ using (8) whose value is referred to as the signed projection distance between q_k^j and $Tp(q_k^{j-1})$. Then, we use (9) to project them onto CM with the projection distances $f(q_k^j)$ along normals of the local tangent planes represented as surface normals (see Fig. 4).

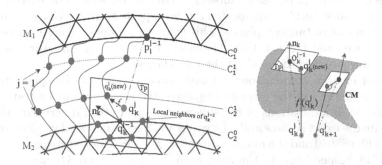

Fig. 4. Projection of the vertices onto CM with a tangent plane local approximation.

Finally, we update vertices q_k^j by their projections. Similarly, we perform the same operation for vertices $p_i^j \in C_1^j$.

When the two curves C_1^{j-1} and C_2^{j-1} are close together, we take the neighboring vertices from both curves to define the set of local neighboring vertices. For each vertex q_k^j, we keep the two closest vertices $p_i^{j-1} \in C_1^{j-1}$ and $q_k^{j-1} \in C_2^{j-1}$ with their neighbors. It permits us to take into account the local curvatures on both sides.

Phase 3: Refine or coarsen the new boundary curves with wavelet transforms. This phase is similar to phase 3 of CM2D-RBFW method.

5.3   Boundary Curve Connection

After creating two boundary curves C_1^j and C_2^j, we connect each new boundary curve to each previously created boundary curve, C_1^{j-1} to C_1^j and C_2^{j-1} to C_2^j, based on the method of stitching the matching borders proposed by G. Barequet et al. [6].

6   Results and Comparisons

We first provide experimental results of CM2D-TPW and CM2D-RBFW methods and then compare these methods with various types of 3D objects. Both methods have been implemented in Matlab on a PC 2.27 GHz CPU Core i5 with 3 GB Ram to make possible their comparisons. To understand the quality of the results, we plot the images of the connecting mesh, surface and Gaussian curvature map.

In Fig. 5, CM2D-TPW method produces a smooth connecting mesh CM with the progressive change in resolution between M_1 and M_2 defined by subdivision schemes (Loop and Butterfly), each mesh being at a different level of subdivision. Based on a set of tests, $s = 4$ is an empirical good value to apply this method for joining M_1 and M_2.

As we seen, Gaussian curvatures in Fig. 6c is respected better than these in Fig. 6b because CM2D-TPW method is possible to constrain the surface to have specified tangent planes at subsets of control vertices to be extrapolated. The newly created vertices are located on the expected surface CM with respect to the variations of tangent planes. This leads to a smooth transition between boundary faces and faces of CM. Therefore, the Gaussian curvatures are well respected and are "continuous" on the boundaries.

In order to draw comparisons, we have chosen examples of a sphere to have accurate evaluations of the error and runtime. We have developed a test on four density-based discretizations of the sphere, since analytical description permits to compute the exact surface and relative errors. The numbers of vertices are 240, 3840, 61440, 983040 and the numbers of vertices of the removed strips are 66, 720, 5982, 70743, respectively. In this way, both meshes M_1 and M_2 have the same density of vertices for each given discretization level, and the process to obtain

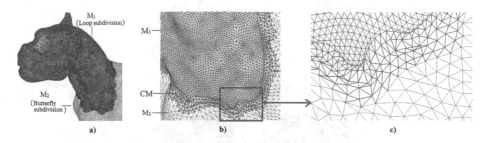

Fig. 5. The Tiger model with CM2D-TPW algorithm: (a) The connecting mesh CM produced with $s = 4$; (b) Zoom of CM; (c) Zoom of one of the interesting parts of CM.

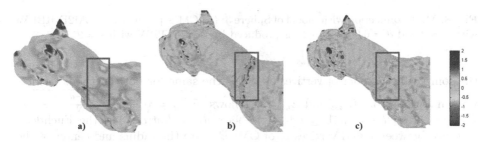

Fig. 6. Gaussian curvature map of the Tiger model: (a) Before crack; (b) After removing crack by CM2D-RBFW algorithm; (c) After removing crack by CM2D-TPW algorithm.

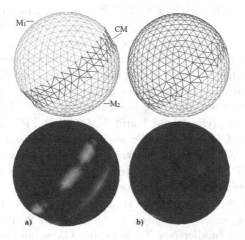

Fig. 7. Mesh connection with model of Sphere 2: (a) CM is produced by CM2D-RBFW with $s = 2$ and $d = 0.004$; (b) CM is produced by CM2D-TPW with $s = 2$.

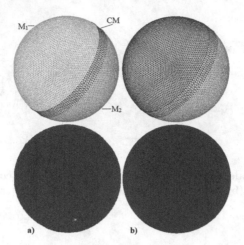

Fig. 8. Mesh connection with model of Sphere 3: (a) CM is produced by CM2D-RBFW with $s = 2$ and $d = 0.004$; (b) CM is produced by CM2D-TPW with $s = 2$.

the compatible number of vertices of CM is the same for both methods. Hence, we define the errors E_{dist} and E_{max} as follows: $E_{dist} = \sqrt{\frac{\sum_{p_i \in CM}(R - dist(c, p_i))^2}{N}}$; $E_{max} = sup(|R - d_i|)$, $1 \leq i \leq N$; where: $d_i = dist(c, p_i)$ is the Euclidean distance between c and vertices p_i of CM; R, c are the radius and center of the sphere, respectively (in our tests, $c = (0, 0, 0)$ and $R = 10$). N is the number of vertices of CM.

Figures 7, 8 and Table 1 summarize the results. First, we use CM2D-RBFW method for the discretization models of the sphere with $s = 2$ as illustrated in Figs. 7a and 8a. Then, we also apply CM2D-TPW method on these models (see Figs. 7b and 8b). Obviously, CM2D-TPW method can position the newly inserted vertices on the expected surface with respect to the variation of tangent planes (phase 2) without destroying the Gaussian curvature and altering the original meshes. As a result, it gives the high quality connecting meshes and smooth surfaces. Figure 8b shows the sphere with a nice join between meshes since Gaussian curvature maps of meshes are virtually the same.

Figures 9a–b show the connecting mesh and surface CM produced with linear interpolation by applying phase 1 and 3 of CM2D-TPW algorithm without phase 2. As a result, CM is hyperbolic and the surface continuity is not guaranteed. While Figs. 9c–d present CM after applying all phases of the algorithm. Obviously, CM2D-TPW method generates a smooth surface with natural shape where continuity between meshes is preserved.

According to these experimental results, we can see that CM2D-TPW method gives better results compared to CM2D-RBFW method since errors to the real surface are smaller (see Table 1) and Gaussian curvatures are much better respected (see Figs. 6, 7 and 8). In addition, a well-known drawback of RBF based reconstruction methods is the difficulty to provide abrupt changes

Table 1. Comparison of errors and runtimes of CM2D-RBFW and CM2D-TPW algorithms for spheres with center $c = (0, 0, 0)$, and radius $R = 10$; the numbers of vertices and faces of CM are in columns V and F.

Model	CM		E_{dist}		E_{max}		Runtime (secs)	
	V	F	RBFW	TPW	RBFW	TPW	RBFW	TPW
Sphere 1	38	40	0.927	0.758	2.366	2.048	0.406	0.316
Sphere 2	159	240	0.202	0.065	0.486	0.222	0.459	0.376
Sphere 3	639	960	0.034	0.015	0.058	0.029	1.386	0.917
Sphere 4	2641	3963	0.063	0.033	0.145	0.076	14.496	9.022

Fig. 9. The surface continuity of Sphere preserved after applying CM2D-TPW method with $s = 2$: (a)–(b) CM produced by linear interpolation; (c)–(d) CM produced by CM2D-TPW method.

in a small distance. It requires much more estimation which includes estimating the linear constraints on the control vertices as well as the off-surface constraints to construct and solve a linear system for each interpolated vertex. Therefore, the time of computation will be inevitably longer or the memory requirements may exceed the capacity of the computer. As a consequence, the runtime of this algorithm is rapidly increasing when the vertex numbers of the models increase as illustrated in Table 1. We have applied the algorithm to various 3D objects with complex shapes. The runtime increases quadratically. Moreover, the most critical disadvantage is that it is very important for the user to make a decision on the choice of the basis functions and the user parameter values, i.e. d-the signed distance and h-the shape parameter. This leads to the fact that the user chooses them by a rather costly trial and performs their numerical experiments over and over again until they end up with a satisfactory result consisting of the well-chosen values and a surface with a natural shape. In order to overcome these disadvantages, we have proposed a more reliable method, CM2D-TPW method. It produces surfaces of good approximation, computationally more efficient and occupied less memory compared to the C2MD-RBFW method.

7   Conclusion

We have introduced new simple and efficient mesh connection methods which join two meshes of different resolutions while maintaining the surface continuity and not destroying local curvatures. The wavelet transform and the methods of local approximation or interpolation are applied to position newly inserted vertices on the expected surface. Additionally, our methods keep the original boundaries of the meshes and the closest faces around these boundaries while connecting them. The connecting mesh is changed gradually in resolution between coarse and fine areas. CM2D-TPW method gives better results compared to CM2D-RBFW method since it improves the reconstruction capability of the connecting surface as illustrated by Gaussian curvatures and error evaluations. The advantages of CM2D-TPW method are: (1) It is simple, efficient, and local; (2) It generates smooth connecting surfaces; (3) There is no need to solve a system of linear equations. As a consequence, our algorithm is then numerically stable.

References

1. Dyn, N., Levin, D., Gregory, J.A.: A butterfly subdivision scheme for surface interpolation with tension control. ACM Trans. Graph. **9**, 160–169 (1990)
2. Loop, C.: Smooth Subdivision Surfaces Based on Triangles. Master's thesis (1987)
3. Husain, N.A., Bade, A., Kumoi, R., Rahim, M.S.M.: Iterative selection criteria to improve simple adaptive subdivision surfaces method in handling cracks for triangular meshes. In: Proceedings of the VRCAI 2010, pp. 207–210. ACM, USA (2010)
4. Husain, N.A., Rahim, M.S.M., Bade, A.: Iterative process to improve simple adaptive subdivision surfaces method with Butterfly scheme. World Acad. Sci. Eng. Tech. **79**, 622–626 (2011)
5. Pakdel, H., Samavati, F.F.: Incremental subdivision for triangle meshes. J. Comput. Sci. Eng. **3**(1), 80–92 (2007)
6. Barequet, G., Sharir, M.: Filling gaps in the boundary of a polyhedron. Comp. Aided Geometric Des. **12**(2), 207–229 (1995)
7. Hongbo, F., Tai, C.-L., Zhang, H.: Topology free cut and paste editing over meshes. In: GMP, pp. 173–184 (2004)
8. Stollnitz, E.J., DeRose, T.D., Salesin, D.H.: Wavelets for Computer Graphics: Theory and Applications. Morgan Kaufmann Publishers, San Francisco (1996)
9. Mallat, S.G.: A Wavelet Tour of Signal Processing. Academic Press (1998)
10. Bertram, M., Duchaineau, M.A., Hamann, B., Joy, K.I.: Generalized B-spline subdivision-surface wavelets for geometry compression. IEEE **10**, 326–338 (2004)
11. Bertram, M.: Biorthogonal wavelets for subdivision volumes. In: Proceedings of the SMA 2002, pp. 72–82. ACM, New York (2002)
12. Sweldens, W.: The lifting scheme: a construction of second generation wavelets. SIAM J. Math. Anal. **29**, 511–546 (1998)
13. Casciola, G., Lazzaro, D., Monte-fusco, L.B., Morigi, S.: Fast surface reconstruction and hole filling using radial basis functions. In: Numerical Algorithms (2005)
14. Branch, J., Prieto, F., Boulanger, P.: Automatic hole-filling of triangular meshes using local Radial Basis Function. In: 3DPVT, pp. 727–734 (2006)
15. Alexa, M., Behr, J., Cohen-Or, D., Fleishman, S., Levin, D., Silva, C.T.: Computing and rendering point set surfaces. IEEE Trans. Vis. Comp. Grap. **9**(1), 3–15 (2003)
16. Hoppe, H., DeRose, T., Duchamp, T., McDonald, J., Stuetzle, W.: Surface reconstruction from unorganized points. SIGGRAPH Comput. Graph. **26**, 71–78 (1992)
17. Alexa, M., Rusinkiewicz, S., Adamson, A.: On normals and projection operators for surfaces defined by point sets. In: Eurograph Symposium on Point-Based Graph, pp. 149–155 (2004)

A Synchronous Network for Brown Planthopper Surveillance Based on Hexagonal Cellular Automata

Bao Hoai Lam[1(✉)], Huu-Hung Huynh[2], Hiep Xuan Huynh[3],
and Bernard Pottier[1]

[1] Université de Bretagne Occidentale, LAB-STICC, UMR CNRS 6285, Brest, France
{bao-hoai.lam,pottier}@univ-brest.fr
[2] Danang University, Danang, Vietnam
hhhung@dut.udn.vn
[3] DREAM Team/UMI 209 UMMISCO-IRD, Cantho University, Cantho, Vietnam
hxhiep@ctu.edu.vn

Abstract. The paper proposes a new approach to model the Brown Planthopper surveillance as a synchronous network, network consists of components running simultaneously, based on hexagonal cellular automata. In the surveillance network, working space of hoppers is divided as a hexagonal cell system of which cell is a node of a graph G and two neighborhood cells compose an edge of the graph. Sensor nodes are deployed at some cells to measure surrounding conditions as well as hopper density. Simulation results of the hopper surveillance network model with data collection in Cantho, Mekong Delta may provide some useful information in managing pest insects as well as in sensing and collecting data from observation wireless sensor network.

Keywords: Synchronous network · Hexagonal cellular automata · Brown Planthopper · BPHSYN

1 Introduction

Light trap network is considered as an useful tool in pest management. For instance, in Britain, Rothamsted light trap networks [1] have been established since the early 1960 s in order to understand the population change when pest insects occur and to measure as well as analyze biodiversity [2]. In addition, to confront with Brown Planthopper (BPH) invasion, a light trap network [7] with more than 340 traps have been constructed in Mekong Delta since 2006 so that people can know situations of their fields better and make decision if possible.

The Wireless Sensor Network approach applied to a light trap network (as proposed solutions in [3,4]), may help calculating Brown Planthopper (BPH) densities and measure environmental factors automatically. This kind of solution uses sensors, new automatic light traps, to measure environments and hopper behaviors. These sensed values from sensors will be sent via a wireless network to

© ICST Institute for Computer Sciences, Social Informatics and Telecommunications Engineering 2016
P.C. Vinh et al. (Eds.): ICTCC 2016, LNICST 168, pp. 97–112, 2016.
DOI: 10.1007/978-3-319-46909-6_10

a data center periodically. Next, a back-end system will manipulate these values and propose solutions relating to situations of collected data. Such application is called BPH surveillance network.

Factors influencing BPH behaviors occur continuously and concurrently. Continuous occurrence means these factors compose an unbroken whole, without interruption. Concurrency implies that they can happen at the same time. For example, some factors such as temperature, wind causing hoppers invasion from one place to another. These conditions are continual. Besides, they are concurrent because the motivation to propagate from a source to a destination comes from surrounding conditions of the source and its neighbors. These conditions from such different places must be simultaneous executions.

In this paper, we propose a new approach to model BPH surveillance network as a synchronous network [13] to illustrate the concurrency and continuousness of these influencing conditions. Topology of the synchronous network is based on hexagonal cellular automata [22], a parallel structure.

The structure of this paper is as follows. Section 2 depicts some previous work relating to wireless sensor network as well as insect surveillance modeling. Definition of synchronous network is depicted in the next section. This section also depicts the synchronous BPH surveillance network based on hexagonal cellular automata. Implementations of the above model is described in Sect. 4. Next section illustrates some simulation results of BPH surveillance network with data collection in Cantho, Mekong Delta. The last section is our conclusion and future plans.

2   Related Work

Light trap method is one of solutions to prevent high densities of spruce budworm in Canadian forests [8,9]. This method allows people to participate insect trapping by giving light traps to them and track their traps from June to end of August every year. Periodically, people only report estimated densities of insects via a website, an application or even with a paper and a pen. Finally, trap samples are collected and counted in a lab environment. Applications of data collections from these light traps are variant, for example, thanks to wing wear and body size measurements of adult spruce budworms captured at light traps in some previous years, some useful inference on seasonal patterns related to reproduction can be archived [10]. However, these light traps seem not to compose a network, instead, they create a combination of traps to collect data for post processing. Therefore, there are few information about the model of the light trap network.

An insect surveillance network is modeled based on Unit Disk Graph [7]. In this model, a sensing device is a node where an edge between two nodes is established if the distance between them is at most the disk radius r. The weight of that edge is the ability insects move from the start node to the end node. This weight is calculated based on historical and current data at these nodes.

A BPH surveillance network is considered as a graph $\mathbf{G} = (V, E)$ [3,4] where each sensing device is modeled as a node and an edge is created between 2 nodes based on the communication ranges them. Some basic algorithms of WSN such as diameter, routing table are implemented using the data collection in provincial level in the Mekong Delta. Nevertheless, factors influencing hopper behaviors are not examined in these work.

There are not many investigations of synchronous network in modeling insects surveillance, especially synchronous network based on hexagonal cellular automata.

3   Brownplant Hopper Synchronous Network

3.1   Synchronous Network

Synchronous network [13] is a network describing synchronized rounds of message exchange and computation. It consists of pieces of processes which may send and receive messages simultaneously.

Mathematically, a synchronous network can be considered as a graph G where processes are located at the nodes and they communicate together via the edges using message sending.

Each node in a synchronous network is termed as a process which consists of the following components:

- $states_i$: a collection of states at process i.
- $msgs_i$: a message-generation function specifies that the process i sends to the indicated neighbor, starting from the given state.
- $trans_i$: a state-transition function specifies the new state to which the process i moves from the current state and messages from incomming neighbors.

In practice, both message-generation and state-transition functions can be shortly called as "transition rules", rules allowing the process i to send messages to neighbors in order to compose its new state.

3.2   Wireless Sensor Network

A Wireless Sensor Network (WSN) [16] consists of n wireless sensor nodes distributed in a two dimensional planes (Fig. 1). As in this figure, data collected from sensor nodes of the physical world is transmitted to a gateway which these pieces of data are manipulated by an application to make decisions.

Figure 1 shows the star topology [24] of WSN where sensor nodes use single-hop to communicate with the gateway. In the star topology, if a sensor node fails, it does not effect the whole network, except that the gateway does.

Gateway plays an important role as a data center to collect sensed data from sensor nodes. Commonly, it is connected to Internet and/or to an application for post processing.

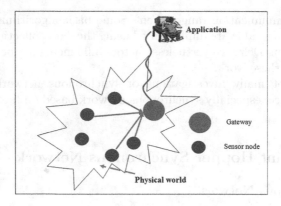

Fig. 1. Sensor nodes in WSN.

3.3   Brownplant Hopper Surveillance Network

A Brownplant hopper (BPH) surveillance network is a network to monitor BPH behaviors due to environmental factors based on WSN approach [3,4,7]. In this network, working space or working environment of hoppers such as rice fields and meteoric conditions, is divided as a grid of hexagonal cells (a hexagonal cellular automaton) (Fig. 2). Some cells of the grid contain automatic light trap sensor nodes to sampling measure surrounding conditions and hopper densities. These sensor nodes compose a WSN which has a star topology for minimizing communications.

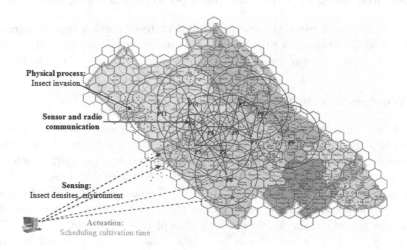

Fig. 2. The hexagonal automaton of the BPH surveillance network. It is composed by dividing the map into hexagonal cells, next some sensor nodes (centers of circles) are distributed to these cells.

The above grid of hexagonal cells represents a hexagonal cellular automaton which is depicted by a triple (S, n, f) where:

1. A finite state set S. A state of a cell describes the hopper status of that cell. This status is calculated thanks to the density of hoppers at that cell. In practice, people use following table [5] (Fig. 3) to depict hopper statuses in their fields:

BPH density (BPH/m²)	Color	Meaning
< 500	Background	Normal
500 -< 1500	rgb[0,255,0]	Light infection
1500 -< 3000	rgb[255,255,0]	Medium infection
3000 -≤ 10000	rgb[251,153,234]	Heavy infection
> 10000	rgb[255,0,0]	Hopper burn

Fig. 3. Ascending levels of infested BPHs in rice fields.

Therefore, at the time t, a cell in the hexagonal CA can be valued as an element of the set {*Normal*, *Light*, *Medium*, *Heavy*, *Burn*}.

In addition, a cell may locate an automatic light trap sensor node. This trap can catch hoppers and the density of hoppers in the trap may indicate the real infected situation at that cell. The following table [27] (Fig. 4) is used for describing hopper statuses in a sensor node:

BPH density	Color	Level of hoppers
< 1000	Background	1
1000 -< 2500	rgb[0,255,0]	2
2500 -< 5000	rgb[255,255,0]	3
5000 -<10000	rgb[251,153,234]	4
≥ 10000	rgb[255,0,0]	5

Fig. 4. Ascending levels of infested BPHs in light traps.

2. Distance n identifying neighbor cells, *normally n=1*. When $n=1$, a cell has at most 6 surrounding cells.
3. Transition rule f: $S^n \rightarrow S$ depict the change of a cell's state at a specific time based on the current state of the cell and its neighbors. For example, if the center cell and its neighbors have the state **N**ormal at the time t, then the state of that cell at the time t+1 is **N**ormal: f(NNNNNNN) = N.
   At the time t, the state of a cell depends on the state at time t−1 of its neighbors. The cell itself can be integrated in its neighborhoods. Updating cells are done by a transition rule. All cells have the same transition rule and the transition rule is applied to all cells at the same time. Whenever the rule are applied to the entire system, they could change the entire system synchronously.

In fact, the transition rule f is a function depending on some variables such as: density of hoppers in a cell as well as its neighbors, rice age, wind, hopper velocity and other environmental factors.

- Rice age: The young rice is a very good food for hoppers, therefore, they tend to locate at the young rice fields [5,6,14]. On the other hands, hoppers can not suck ripe rice so they will propagate to other fields due to wind if their rice in their current fields become mature or ripe. In addition, young rice is the first condition for hoppers landing. The green color of young rices mapped into the water is a very attractive color source for hoppers, therefore, they tend to take landing to the young ones. On the other hands, ripe rice color does not attract hoppers because they are not sensitive with this color.
- Wind: the wind velocity, calculated in cells/time step. It illustrates the maximum distance that adult hoppers can propagate in a time step. For example, 5 cells/t means that hoppers can propagate to another cell with the distance 5 from the current cell under the wind direction. To be simple, in this model, there are 6 wind directions according to 6 neighbor directions. If there is no wind, hopper can transmit to 6 neighbor cells. Only a part of adult one can propagate to other fields. In this paper, it is an predetermined constant.
- Hopper velocity. Without wind, hoppers can propagate to near rice fields by this their velocities, approximate 0.4 m/s [15].
- Hopper age. Totally, the life circle of BPHs is 26–30 days [14] depending on environmental factors and it spreads in 3 phases: eggs, nymphs and adults. The growth time lapse of each phase is as followed: eggs 6–8 days, nymph 12–15 days, adults 19 days. Some experiments show that a female adult BPH can lay 100–300 eggs during its life circle [14].
- Density of hoppers in a cell and its surroundings. The relation between the density of a cell and its state depicted in Fig. 3.

Mathematically, the above hexagonal cellular automaton is a topology of **a synchronous network** which is modeled as a directed graph $\mathbf{G} = (V, E)$ where V is the collection of nodes and E is the set of edges.

Nodes. Each hexagon in Fig. 2 represents a node in the graph $\mathbf{G} = (V, E)$. By the time passing, each node (or process) i composes a collection of states $states_i$ of which a state holds values of rice age, wind, and BPH density at the time t.

Each node may consist a sensor node to sense above factors of a state. When the sensor node senses environment, it transmits the collected data to a gateway for storing and post processing.

Edges. Edges in the graph G are composed by links between a hexagon node and its neighbors (6 neighbors). Because G is a directed graph, there are 2 edges between the node and a neighbor of it (2 directions).

Example. Figure 5 is an example of a graph of the BPH surveillance network in Phongdien district, Cantho, Vietnam. In this example, the map of this district is divided as cells, each cell is almost a commune of the district. For example, if Phongdien and Nhonai communes are considered as a hexagonal center (**Center cell** in the figure), following communes such as Truonglong, Tanthoi, Giaixuan, Mykhanh, Nhannghia (hexagons 1, 2, 3, 4, 5) become neighbors of the hexagonal center approximately. The hexagon 0 is another neighbor of the center, however, it seems to occupy few area of Phongdien district.

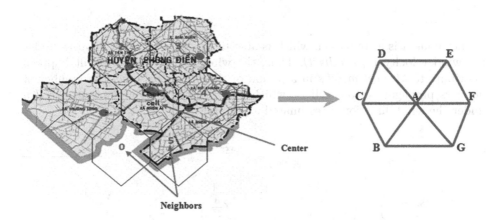

Fig. 5. The graph of Phong Dien district, Cantho when it is divided as hexagonal cells.

The graph of the BPH surveillance network of this district is illustrated in the right of Fig. 5. In this graph, each hexagonal cell becomes a node and 2 cells in a neighborhood compose an edge. The **Center cell** is illustrated as a node A which has 6 neighbors named B, C, D, E, G, F (corresponding to cells 0, 1, 2, 3, 4, 5 respectively). However, each of B, C, D, E, G, F only has 3 neighbors.

Behaviors. Behaviors at node i are expressed by transition rules of states *transitions$_i$*. Normally, these rules are functions mapping a collection of states at a cell and its neighbors at the time t to create the new state of that cell at the time t+1. These transition rules are applied simultaneously at every cell.

The following pseudo code depicts the transition rule of a node n:

```
Calculate the insect density at node n using reproduction model
Update current state of n
if (node n has BPH density >= THRESHOLD or rice IS NOT young){
  if (no wind)
    for (j in neighbors of n){
      Calculate the number of adult BPHs migrating to j
      Update the state of j
      Update current state of n
```

```
        }
    else
        for (j in neighbors of n)
            if (j is in leeward of n){
                Calculate the number of adult BPHs migrating to j
                    according to the wind velocity
                Update the state of j
                Update current state of n
            }
    }
}
}
```

Let node n is a source cell which is able to propagate d *adult hoppers* under the wind velocity v *(m cells/t)*. Thus, the wind velocity causes adult hoppers distribute to *at most m cells* in a period of time t. In this case, the number of hoppers propagating to a cell n_k which has *distance k* from the *source cell n* under the wind direction, is estimated as $\frac{d}{2^k}$ (Fig. 6).

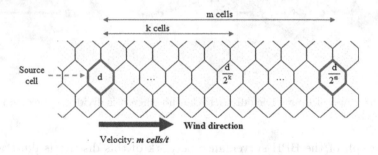

Fig. 6. Estimation of propagated adult hoppers due to wind

Wireless Sensor Network. WSN is applied by distributing sensors in some cells to sampling measure environmental factors and hopper density. Data collections from the WSN can be considered as indications for the operating of the whole BPH surveillance network as well as for post processing. To be simple, in this paper the WSN is supposed to have the star topology to transmit data.

3.4   BPHSYN

The above synchronous network for BPH surveillance based on hexagonal CA can be shortly called the BPH Surveillance sYnchronous Network (BPHSYN).

4   BPHSYN Implementation

4.1   Workflow

The implementation of a surveillance model contains 3 important parts: data structure, states and behaviors. Firstly, data structure (cells in Fig. 2) is generated from geographic data. Next, states and behaviors are implemented in CUDA [18] to illustrate the synchronous characteristic in the model.

CUDA is chosen for implementing BPHSYN since the parallel programming paradigm of CUDA is well-suited for the synchronous network model's concurrency.

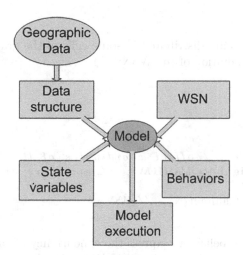

Fig. 7. Work flow for modeling insect physical and WSN system.

4.2   The Hexagonal CA Based Synchronous Network

Graph.   The following CUDA code is the definition of the graph described in Sect. 3.3:

```
typedef struct{
    int x, y;
}Point2D;
typedef struct{
    int xPos, yPos; //offset coordinates
    Point2D Corners [6]; // 6 corners
    int Neighbors [6]; // 6 neighbors numbered from 0 to 5
}Hexagon;
typedef Hexagrid Hexagon[N]; // Honeycomb structure
```

State.   Each node in the graph represents a process in a synchronous network. This process maintains a structure to store its states by the time passing. The following code is the definition of a state in the case study BPH surveillance network:

```
typedef struct{
  int xPos, yPos; //position
  float        riceAges;      // rice ages
  InsectDensity densityBPH;
  float        windVelocity;
  Direction        windDirection;
}State;
```

WSN. Sensor nodes are distributed in some cells of the graph. The following code describes the definition of the WSN:

```
typedef struct{
    int node;
    float distance;
}Neighbor;
typedef struct{
    int xPos, yPos; //offset coordinates of the hexa cell
    Neighbor Neighbors[MAXFLOW]; // neighbors of sensor node
}Channel;
typedef Network Channel[N]; // WSN
```

Behaviors. Because behaviors express the concurrency of the model, they are implemented as device codes run in GPU [19]. The skeleton of the behaviors code is as followed:

```
extern __global__ void compute(State *now, int node_number){
  int idx=threadIdx.x+blockIdx.x*blockDim.x;
  if (idx < node_number){
    Calculate behaviors of node idx
  }
}
```

5   Experiment

5.1   Data Used

The simulation of the BPH synchronous network uses data collections in Cantho city (Fig. 2), a typical rice city in the Mekong Delta. Current light traps (8 traps till 2015) are considered as sensor nodes in the simulation (circles in Fig. 2). The area of Cantho is divided as hexagonal cells with approximately $0.18\,km^2$ each.

5.2   Tools Used

HexGen, a tool written in C++ is used to generate the synchronous network code in Cuda. Besides, the map of Cantho city is processed by the tool PickCell in the framework NetGen [17]. Behaviors of the BPHSYN are implemented in CUDA to run the simulation on the NVIDIA card GeForce GTX 680 1.15 GHz with 1536 CUDA Cores (8 Multiprocessors × 192 CUDA Cores/MP).

5.3   Scenario 1: Observing Hoppers at a Location

This scenario allows observing the reproduction phase of hoppers at a location. In this scenario, some communes in Cantho suffer lightly from hoppers (light infection color of rice fields and warning level of sensor nodes in Fig. 8) while the rest do not cultivate yet. The wind direction is 2 (the direction from the **Center cell** to **cell 5** in Fig. 5 with the velocity is 5 km/h (approximately 10 hexagonal cells/h). That means BPHs can transmit to the cell distance 10 from the source cell in one hour.

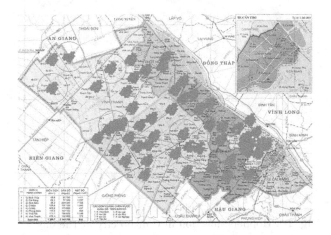

Fig. 8. Light infections at some communes in Cantho city.

Figure 9 describes the hoppers infection in Cantho city at the day 3, 4, 5, 7. At the day 3, most of the experimental communes suffer from heavy infection of BPHs. Hoppers density reaches the peak point at the day 4 and starts decreasing a few days later. At the day 7, normal infections appear in some communes although other are still light, medium or even heavy (warning level of sensor nodes in Fig. 10). However until the day 9, hoppers seem not to appear in Cantho city.

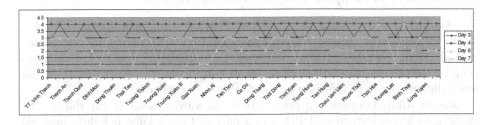

Fig. 9. Hoppers infection in Cantho city at the day 3, 4, 6, 7.

This scenario depicts the reproduction of hoppers in Cantho city. Initially, experimental communes are infested lightly due to hoppers. By the time passing, hoppers are growing and become adults. At adult phase, hoppers can propagate to other places due to wind, however, these places do not contain rice, therefore, propagated hoppers die because of lack of food. Densities of hoppers at experimental communes decline gradually and return normal infestation after the peak day of hoppers 6 to 7 days.

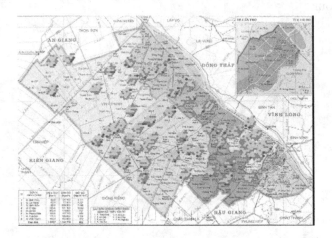

Fig. 10. Hoppers infection in Cantho city at the day 7.

The scenario illustrates the 'Escape Strategy' or 'Chien Luoc Ne Ray' in Vietnamese to confront with hoppers [23]. This strategy can be done by monitoring the historical light traps data through several years to recognize the trend of hoppers migrations. Next, crops are sown after the peak season of BPHs. If crops are sown after that peak day very soon, when the next generation of hoppers comes (around 28 days later), the rice is strong enough to resist with hoppers. In this case the WSN can help to sense the surrounding conditions data and maintain these pieces of data so that the peak point of hoppers can be identified later.

5.4   Scenario 2: Hoppers Propagation Due to Wind

This scenario assumes that the Thoi Lai district is an infection source with lightly infestation in almost its communes (Fig. 11). A current unique sensor at Dinh Mon, Thoi Lai provides following meteorological data: wind velocity: 5 km/h (10 cells/h), wind direction: 2 (from Dinh Mon toward Phong Dien and also indicates the light infection at the rice field in this commune.

Due to wind, hoppers can propagate to leeward fields. At the day 3, the whole Thoi Lai is burned by BPHs and a part of Phong Dien is lightly infected (Figs. 11, 12). At the day 7, the light trap at Dinh Mon sensor node still gives burn warning although other communes in this district become normal.

Day/Commune	THOI LAI DISTRICT													PHONG DIEN DISTRICT			
	Thoi Lai	Dinh Mon	Dong Binh	Dong Thuan	Tan Thanh	Thoi Tan	Thoi Thanh	Truong Thanh	Truong Thang	Truong Xuan	Truong Xuan A	Truong Xuan B	Xuan Thang	Truong Long	Tan Thoi	Nhon Ai	Nhon Nghia
0	L	L	L	L	L	L	L	L	L	L	L	L	L	*	*	*	*
2	B	B	B	H	B	B	B	H	H	H	H	H	B	N	N	*	*
4	B	B	B	B	B	B	B	B	B	B	B	B	B	L	N	N	N
7	B	N	N	N	N	B	N	B	N	N	B	B	N	H	L	N	N

*: No Infected   N: Normal   L: Light   M: Medium   H: Heavy   B: Burn

Fig. 11. Hoppers infestation in Thoi Lai and Phong Dien in 7 days.

However, the area of infestation in Phong Dien district is broaden from Truong Long, Tan Thoi, to Nhon Ai, Nhan Nghia. BPHs spread over these communes from heavy infection in Truong Long to light ones (almost normal) in Nhon Ai, Nhon Nghia (Fig. 13). Indeed, under the wind direction 2, the commune Truong Long, Phong Dien is the leeward of the commune Truong Thanh, Thoi Lai. Similarly, the commune Tan Thoi, Phong Dien is the leeward of the commune Dinh Mon, Thoi Lai. Inside the district Phong Dien itself, the commune Nhon Ai is the leeward of Tan Thoi and is the windward of Nhon Nghia. Therefore, due to wind, hoppers can transmit to Nhon Nghia as well.

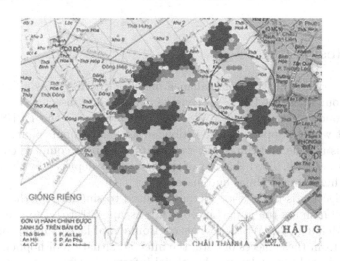

Fig. 12. Hoppers infection in Thoi Lai and Phong Dien at the day 3.

In this scenario, the sensor node at Dinh Mon plays as the indication for the hoppers infestation and the hoppers propagate according to the transition rules mentioned in the Sect. 4.2. However, this only one sensor node in Thoi Lai (with 20,345.16 ha rice field[1]) may not provide enough information relating to hoppers and the surrounding environment. Indeed, although the wind direction collected at Dinh Mon is toward the direction 2 of this hexagon, the wind direction at

[1] http://cantho.gov.vn/wps/portal/thoilai.

Wind
direction

Fig. 13. Leeward communes in Phong Dien district.

other communes in Thoi Lai may be different. It could be better if each commune has a sensor node to sense surrounding conditions more details because these conditions can provide useful information for the direction of propagation of hoppers.

6   Conclusion

We have described the BPH surveillance network BPHSYN as a synchronous network. In our work, the BPHSYN consists of a physical insect process modeled as a synchronous network and a WSN as indications for the BPHSYN. The environment where hoppers behave is divided as a hexagonal cellular system of which each is a node and the cell as well as its neighbors compose edges of the synchronous network. The behaviors of the network is depicted by the transition rules of the hexagonal cellular automata.

Data collection is in Cantho, Vietnam is used to simulate for the BPHSYN. The simulation shows the importance of the 'Escape Strategy' to confront with hoppers in Mekong. The WSN provides environmental factors input for the simulation and from these pieces of data, the infected situation of hoppers could be predicted and could provide some beneficial information for pest management.

The simulation also figures out that it is necessary to have more sensor node to sense environmental factors in order to better provide these values as inputs for the model execution. An alternative could be to use external data sources to provide meteoric data for the model so that the these pieces of data can be embedded to the BPHSYN as well.

The topology of the WSN system in the surveillance network could be mesh network to have a better communications (instead of star topology in the paper). In this case, the distance between 2 sensor nodes is quite far, therefore, LORA [25] technology could be considered as an alternative to transmit data to a distant destination.

Acknowledgments. The work of this paper was in the scope of the "OBSNET - Optimizing the Brown Planthopper surveillance network using automatic light traps in the Mekong Delta region" project of the Ministry of Education and Training, Vietnam. The first author was funded by the program 911 of Ministry of Education and Training, Vietnam.

References

1. Conrad, K.F., Fox, R., Woiwod, I.P.: Monitoring biodiversity: measuring long-term changes in insect abundance, Insect conservation biology, pp. 203–225, ISBN 9781845932541. Cabi Publisher (2007)
2. Woiwod, I.P., Harrington, R.: Flying in the face of change: The Rothamsted Insect Survey. In: Leigh, R.A., Johnston, A.E. (eds.) Long-term Experiments in Agricultural and Ecological Sciences, pp. 321–342. CAB International, Wallingford (1994)
3. Lam, H.B., Phan, T.T., Vuong, L.H., Huynh, H.X., Pottier, B.: Designing a brown planthoppers surveillance network based on wireless sensor network approach. In: ISCRAM (Information Systems for Crisis Response and Management) Vietnam 2013 Conference (2013)
4. Lam, B.H., Huynh, H.X., Traoré, M., Lucas, P.Y., Pottier, B.: Monitoring environmental factors in Mekong Delta of Vietnam using Wireless Sensor Network approach. In: 8th International conference on Simulation and Modelling in the Food and Bio-Industry FoodSim 2014, pp. 71–78, ISBN 978-90-77381-84-7 (2014)
5. Cuong, H., Phan, H.X.H., Drogoul, A.: An agent-based approach to the simulation of brown plant hopper (BPH) invasions in the mekong delta. In: 2010 IEEE RIVF International Conference on Computing & Communication Technologies. Research, Innovation, and Vision for the Future (RIVF), Hanoi, Vietnam, pp. 1–6. IEEE, Heidelberg (2010)
6. Nguyen, V.G., Nhi, H., Xuan, H., Vo, T.T., Drogoul, A.: On weather affecting to brown plant hopper invasion using an agent-based model. In: Proceedings of the International Conference on Management of Emergent Digital EcoSystems, MEDES 2011, pp. 150–157, ISBN 978-1-4503-1047-5. ACM, New York (2011)
7. Truong, V.X., Huynh, H.X., Le, M.N., Drogoul, A.: Modeling a surveillance network based on unit disk graph technique – application for monitoring the invasion of insects in mekong delta region. In: Rahwan, I., Wobcke, W., Sen, S., Sugawara, T. (eds.) PRIMA 2012. LNCS (LNAI), vol. 7455, pp. 228–242. Springer, Heidelberg (2012). doi:10.1007/978-3-642-32729-2_16
8. http://www.healthyforestpartnership.ca/
9. Rhainds, M., Heard, S.B.: Sampling procedures and adult sex ratios in spruce budworm. Entomol. Exp. Appl. **154**, 91–101 (2014)
10. Rhainds, M.: Wing wear and body size measurements of adult spruce budworms captured at light traps: inference on seasonal patterns related to reproduction. Appl. Entomol. Zool. **50**(4), 477–485 (2015). Springer, Japan, ISBN 0003-6862
11. Heong, K.L., Hardy, B.: Planthoppers: new threats to the sustainability of intensive rice production systems in Asia, ISBN 978-90-77381-84-7. International Rice Research Institute, Asian Development Bank, Australian Government, Australian Centre for International Agricultural Research (2009)
12. Lee, E.A.: CPS foundations. In: Proceedings of the 47th Design Automation Conference (DAC), pp. 737–742. ACM (2010)
13. Lynch, N.A.: Distributed Algorithms. Morgan Kaufmann Publishers Inc., San Francisco (1996). ISBN 155860348

14. Reissig, W.H., Heinrichs, E.A., Litsinger, J.A., Moody, K., Fiedler, L., Mew, W., Barrion, A.T.: Illustrated Guide to Integrated Pest Management in Rice in Tropical Asia. IRRI, Philippines (1986)
15. Cheng, S., Chen, J., Si, H., Yan, L., Chu, T., Wu, C., Chien, J., Yan, C.: Studies on the migrations of brown planthoppers. Nilaparvata Lugens Std. Acta Entomol. Sinica **22**, 1–21 (1979). (Chinese, English summary)
16. Li, Y., Thai, M.T., Wu, W.: Wireless Sensor Networks and Applications. Springer (2008)
17. Pottier, B., Lucas, P.-Y.: Dynamic networks "NetGen: objectives, installation, use, and programming". Université de Bretagne Occidentale (2015). https://github.com/NetGenProject
18. NVDIA. https://developer.nvidia.com/cuda-zone
19. GPU. http://www.nvidia.com/object/what-is-gpu-computing.html
20. IEEE Standard for Modeling and Simulation (M&S) High Level Architecture (HLA) Federate Interface Specification. IEEE Std 1516.1-2010, pp. 1–378 (2010)
21. Dufay, C.: Contribution a l'Etude du phototropisme des Lépidopteres noctuides. Annales des Sciences Naturelles Zoologie, Paris **12**(6), 81–406 (1964)
22. Wolfram, S.: Cellular Automata and Complexity, ISBN: 0-201-62716-7. Westwiew Press, Perseus Books Group (1994)
23. Chien, H.V., Huan, N.H., Cuong, L.Q.: Escape Strategy can successfully manage BPH and virus disease in the Mekong (2012). http://ricehoppers.net/2012/09/escape-strategy-can-successfully-manage-bph-and-virus-disease-in-the-mekong
24. Cecílio, J., Pedro, F.: Wireless sensor networks: concepts and components. In: Wireless Sensors in Heterogeneous Networked System, Computer Communications and Networks, pp. 5–25. Springer International Publishing (2014)
25. LORA technology. http://www.semtech.com/wireless-rf/rf-transceivers/sx1276/
26. Lasnier, G., Cardoso, J., Siron, P., Pagetti, C., Derler, P.: Distributed simulation of heterogeneous and real-time systems. In: 2013 IEEE/ACM 17th International Symposium on Distributed Simulation and Real Time Applications (DS-RT), pp. 55–62 (2013)
27. Quang, T.C., Minh, V.Q., Nguyen, T.H., Chien, H.V.: Managing the Brown Planthopper caught by light traps for supporting of rice cultivation in the Mekong Delta. In National GIS application conference (in Vietnamese) (2013)

Optimizing Energy Consumption with Delay Constraint in Wireless Sensor Networks

Trong-Thua Huynh[1,2(✉)], Bui Cong Giao[4], Cong-Hung Tran[2], and Anh-Vu Dinh-Duc[3]

[1] HCM City University of Technology, Ho Chi Minh City, Vietnam
[2] Posts and Telecommunications Institute of Technology, Ho Chi Minh City, Vietnam
{htthua,conghung}@ptithcm.edu.vn
[3] University of Information Technology, Ho Chi Minh City, Vietnam
vudda@uit.edu.vn
[4] Sai Gon University, Ho Chi Minh City, Vietnam
giao.bc@cb.sgu.edu.vn

Abstract. Many existing energy efficiency protocols are proposed to address energy optimization for wireless sensor networks. However, most of them have weaken to take into account the factor of end-to-end delay. This paper investigates to find the best trade-off between two objectives: minimizing the energy consumption and end-to-end delay in wireless sensor network. We first propose a new energy-cost function for the inter-cluster routing algorithm. Next, we provide a k-least routes algorithm which is used to disseminate sensing data from cluster-heads to sink with minimum energy consumption subject to an end-to-end delay constraint. We evaluate the effectiveness of the energy balance between cost functions by simulation. In addtion, the extended simulations show that our proposal performs much better than similar protocols in terms of energy consumption and end-to-end delay.

Keywords: Energy consumption · End-to-end delay · Trade-off · Multi-hop

1 Introduction

Energy is the most crucial resource for wireless sensors, particularly in certain environments where replacing or recharging sensors' batteries is impossible. How to design an energy efficient routing protocol becomes the main objective for wireless sensor network (WSN). However, in many current applications of WSN like forest fire detection, data should be transmitted from sources to sink within a limited time. If it exceeds this limitation, data will not be useful anymore. Thus, a trade-off existing between energy consumption and end-to-end delay is extremely necessary.

The trade-off between energy consumption and delay in WSN have proposed by several recent works [1–3]. None of them obtain the optimum balance. The common network scheme of these protocols implements multi-hop approach. The advantage of this architecture is that it allows sensor nodes transmit data to the remote destination which is not in their transmission range by relaying on the other adjacent sensor nodes. This reduces energy consumption significantly and extends the lifetime of the network, but increases the end-to-end delay. However, the multi-hop communication from sensor

© ICST Institute for Computer Sciences, Social Informatics and Telecommunications Engineering 2016
P.C. Vinh et al. (Eds.): ICTCC 2016, LNICST 168, pp. 113–123, 2016.
DOI: 10.1007/978-3-319-46909-6_11

nodes to sink does not take advantage of ability of data aggregation in network that reduces duplication of data between the adjacent sensor nodes whereas the data aggregation in the network is done very effectively by clustering method [4]. Therefore, in this study, we employ multi-hop routing approach for the clusterhead nodes that receive the sensed data from member nodes and then forward to sink through other clusterhead nodes. The clustering algorithm used in this study is what has been proposed by us in the most recent research [5]. Based on this model, we propose a new approach called DCEM (Delay Constrained Energy Efficient Multi-hop) to optimizing energy consumption with delay constraint in WSNs. Whereas the routing algorithm proposed in [5] is based on the aggregation cost function between energy consumption and end-to-end delay, the routing algorithm proposed in this study is based on the optimization method which finds the least energy-cost route satisfying end-to-end delay constraint. The major contributions of this reseach are followings:

- We propose a new energy-cost function to determine the most energy-efficient cost route for data dissemination from clusterheads to sink subject to an end-to-end delay constraint.
- We also provide a inter-cluster k-least routes algorithm which take into consideration both energy consumption and end-to-end delay.
- We present the simulation results to compare with other similar protocols.

The rest of the paper is organized as follows. In Sect. 2, we discuss related works for the same problem. Section 3 presents network and energy models. Section 4 describes our proposal in detail. We show simulation results in Sect. 5. Finally, Sect. 6 concludes this paper.

2   Related Works

In recent years, several works have proposed to figuring out the problem of energy efficient, delay-constrained routing in WSN.

In HEED [6], clusterheads are chosen out periodically based on a hybrid of the node residual energy and a secondary parameter, such as node proximity to its neighbors or node degree. HEED can achieve uniform clusterhead distribution across the network, but it needs many times of iterations to incur high overhead.

Akkaya and Younis proposed an energy-efficient protocol for delay-constrained data in [7]. This protocol allows packets relaying on multi-hop paths to minimizing energy consumption. Authors employ an packet scheduling method to guarantee the data delivery in real-time. Their approach, however, does not take into the delays that can occur in other layers.

Yingshu Li et al. studied the Minimum-Latency Aggregation Schedule problem in [8] to propose a collision-free transmission schedule of data aggregation for all sensors such that the delay for aggregated data to reach the sink is minimized. By constructing a Cluster-based Data Aggregation Tree, this protocol permits the packet transmissions among different clusters are concurrent and collision free. However, constructing distributed trees using broadcasting technique generates more overhead.

T.T Huynh et al. proposed an energy efficient delay-aware routing algorithm on the multi-layer WSN in [9], which sensors (clusterhead role) at each layer interconnected as de Bruijn graph model to improve network delay, energy consumption, and system relia-bility. Experimental results show outperformance of the delay and energy consumption.

Shi Bai et al. proposed an energy-constrained routing algorithm satisfying the bounded delay in [10]. This protocol allows packets are continuously distributed between the multiple paths with different delay constraints. It balances the diferential delay between the different paths by providing a polynomial-time algorithm. In addition, authors also proposed an approximation algorithm to solve the problem in general case. However, this algorithm requires quite a large buffer memory, which limits its potential application.

In [11], authors proposed a partial aggregation algorithm which can balance energy consumption and end-to-end delay using Markovian chain. This algorithm is designed to increase the rate of transmission and avoid from long delay. In [12], authors proposed a data forwarding protocol to finding the optimum trade-off between energy consumption and end-to-end delay by slicing communication range of sensors into concentric circles. Authors proved the proposed algorithm achieve near optimal on the *energy x delay* metric.

3 Network and Energy Model

3.1 Network Model

We employ the hierarchical network model for our proposal in Fig. 1. In this hierarchical network model, sensor nodes are distributed in local clusters. Each cluster itself elects

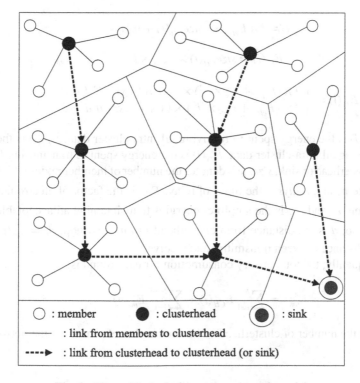

Fig. 1. Hierarchical wireless sensor network model.

a clusterhead that aggregates data from its members and sends fused data to the sink in the multi-hop manner. In addition, the clusterhead nodes also act as relays which forward packets to sink from the other clusterheads.

3.2   Energy Model

We verify a simplified model for the radio hardware energy dissipation in [13] to calculating energy costs for our enery model.

The energy consumption of each sensor member to sending l-bit data to its clusterhead is given by following equation:

$$E_{mem}(j) = l \times E_{elec} + l \times \varepsilon_{fs} \times d(j)^2 \tag{1}$$

where E_{elec} is the factor of electronics energy consumption, ε_{fs} is the amplifier energy to maintain an acceptable signal-to-noise ratio, $d(j)$ is distance from member j to its clusterhead.

The energy consumption of each clusterhead to fusing the all intra-cluster data from its members and transmitting data to other clusterheads is given by Eq. (2):

$$E_{CH}(i) = E_{Rx}(i) + E_{Fx}(i) + E_{Tx}(i) \tag{2}$$

where:

$$E_{Rx}(i) = l \times E_{elec} \times \left(size_{CH}(i) + relays \right) \tag{3}$$

$$E_{Fx}(i) = size_{CH}(i) \times E_{fuse} \times l \tag{4}$$

$$E_{Tx}(i) = \begin{cases} l \times (E_{elec} + \varepsilon_{fs} \times d^2) \times (1 + relays) & \text{if } d < d_0 \\ l \times \left(E_{elec} + \varepsilon_{mp} \times d^4 \right) \times (1 + relays) & \text{if } d \geq d_0 \end{cases} \tag{5}$$

where $E_{Rx}(i)$ is the energy spent to receiving all intra-cluster data, $E_{Fx}(i)$ is the energy spent to fusing all intra-cluster data, $E_{Tx}(i)$ is the energy spent to transmitting l-bit data to other clusterhead or sink, $size_{CH}(i)$ denotes the number of member nodes which belong to the clusterhead i, $relays$ is the times of relay, E_{elec} is the factor of electronics energy consumption, ε_{fs} and ε_{mp} is the amplifier energies to maintaining an acceptable signal-to-noise ratio, d is the distance from clusterhead i to its next hop, $d_0 = \varepsilon_{fs}/\varepsilon_{mp}$ is the reference distance between transmitter and receiver.

Consequently, the total energy consumption for each round is:

$$E_{total} = \sum_{i=1}^{K} E_{CH}(i) + \sum_{j=1}^{N-K} E_{mem}(j) \tag{6}$$

where K is the number of clusterheads, N is the number of sensors in the network.

4   Delay Constrained Energy Efficient Multi-hop Routing

In this section, we describe DCEM protocol in detail. Operation of DCEM is divided into consecutive rounds. Each round starts with network construction phase consisting of establishment of clusters and designation the delay-constrained energy-efficient route from clusterheads to the sink, followed by data transmission phase from sensor nodes to sink based on findings from previous phase.

To establishing clusters, we use the algorithm was proposed in our recent study. This algorithm is described in [5]. In the following section, we propose the cost function and the routing algorithm to balance the energy consumption and guarantee end-to-end delay in WSN.

4.1   Link and Route Cost Functions

We define the following cost function for a link between clusterhead nodes i and j.

$$cost_{ij} = \left(E^i_{Rx} + E^i_{Fx} + E^i_{Tx}\right) \times cost\left(E^i_{Re}\right) \tag{7}$$

where E^i_{Rx} is the energy that clusterhead i spent for receiving l-bit data from member nodes, given by Eq. (3). E^i_{Fx} is the energy that clusterhead i spent for fusing l-bit data from m member nodes, given by Eq. (4). E^i_{Tx} is energy spent for transmission of a l-bit data from clusterhead i to clusterhead j over distance d, given by Eq. (5).

And $cost(E^i_{Re})$ is cost function which takes into consideration the remaining energy of sensors for the energy balance among sensors. Therefore, the function $cost(E^i_{Re})$ is based on the principle in which small changes in remaining energy of sensors can result in large changes in value of cost function. Exponential function $f(x) = e^{(1/x^2)}$ is the kind of function that can satisfy the this principle [14]. Replacing x by E^i_{Re}(the remaining energy of sensor i), we have the following cost function:

$$cost(E^i_{Re}) = exp^{\left(1/\left(E^i_{Re}\right)^2\right)} \tag{8}$$

To calculating the cost function for a route from clusterhead node x to sink s, we define the following equation:

$$Cost(x, s) = \sum_{i,j \in \{x,U,s\}} cost_{ij} \tag{9}$$

where U is set of intermedia nodes from clusterhead x to sink s.

4.2   Inter-Cluster Multi-hop Routing Algorithm

Our optimization problem is finding the least-cost route (most energy-efficient route) from a clusterhead node x to the sink s such that the end-to-end delay along that route does not exceed a delay constraint Δ. The constrained minimization problem is:

$$\min_{R_k \in R'(x,s)} Cost(R_k) \tag{10}$$

where R_k is the kth route, $R'(x,s)$ is the set of routes from clusterhead node x to the sink s for which the end-to-end delay is bounded by Δ, given by:

$$D_{ete}(R_k) \leq \Delta, R_i \in R'(x,s) \tag{11}$$

where $D_{ete}(R_k)$ is the time elapsed between the departure of a data packet from a source x of the kth route and its arrival to a sink s. We defined this delay in [5] by following equation:

$$D_{ete}(x,s) = \sum_{i,j \in \{x,U,s\}} \left(\left(\frac{1}{\mu - \lambda} \right) + \frac{1}{\psi} + \frac{d_{ij}}{\gamma} \right) \tag{12}$$

where μ, λ, ψ, and γ are constants with assumption that they are same for all clusterheads, l is the packet size (bits), ψ is the link bandwidth (bps), d_{ij} is the length of physical link from clusterhead i to clusterhead j, and γ is the propagation speed in medium (m/sec), U is set of intermediate nodes from clusterhead x to the sink s.

Input: clusterhead nodes x, sink s, energy and postion of x, position of s.

Output: the best route with minimum energy consumption and match the end-to-end delay.

1. SeR = $\varnothing$; //The selected route to disseminate data from clusterhead x to the sink s.

2. NoSa = $\varnothing$; //Set of routes that is not satisfy the delay bound Δ.

3. Calculate $cost_{ij}$, $\forall i, j \in C$; //C is set of clusterhead nodes, j can be sink.

4. Calculate K(x,s); //Number of probable routes from clusterhead node x to the sink s.

5. while(k $\neq$ K(x,s)) // initial k =1

    {

6.   Find k-least cost routes kSR(x,s,k);

7. R_k = kSR(x,s,k) \ NoSa; //R_k is the kth least-cost route

8.   Calculate $D_{ete}(R_k)$ from equation (7);

9.   If $D_{ete}(R_k) \leq \Delta$ Then SeR = R_k;

10. Else {

11.   NoSa = NoSa $\cup$ R_k;

12.   k = k +1;

        }

    }

13. Return SeR;

Fig. 2. Pseudo code for DCEM algorithm.

By considering the optimization problem above, we propose the algorithm shown in Fig. 2 to find k-least cost routes that meet the end-to-end delay constraint.

The algorithm calculates the $cost_{ij}$ (line 3) for each link from clusterhead i to clusterhead or sink j based on the cost function defined in Eq. (7). Then, it calculates the number of probable routes from clusterhead node x to the sink s (line 4) using Depth-first search (DFS) algorithm in [15]. In line 6, the algorithm uses the k-shortest path in [16] to find k-least cost route (initial $k = 1$) based on Eqs. (7), (8) and (9). After determining the least-cost route, R_k, the algorithm calculates the end-to-end delay $D_{ete}(R_k)$ for that route using Eq. (12). Then, it checks whether this end-to-end delay satisfy the specified threshold value Δ or not. If so, R_k is chosen (SeR, line 9), if not, R_k will be removed and added to the NoSa (line 11). Line 7 will remove least-cost routes that are not satisfy the delay bound Δ.

5   Simulation Results

We use MATLAB 8.1 to evaluating the effectiveness of our proposal. The simulation parameters are summizied in Table 1.

Table 1. Simulation parameters.

Parameter	Value
Network size	100 m x 100 m
Number of sensor nodes	100 nodes
Sink location	(50, 50)
Size of data packet	30 bytes
λ	3
μ	6
Initial energy of each node	1 J
E_{elec}	50 nJ/bit
ε_{fs}	10 pJ/bit/m^2
ε_{mp}	0.0013 pJ/bit/m^4
E_{fuse}	5 nJ/bit
ψ	40 bps
γ	50 m/s.

In Sect. 4, we have proposed an new energy-cost function to determine the least-cost route for data dissemination from clusterheads to sink. In the first simulation, we want to show the primacy of the cost function that we have proposed in Eqs. (7), (8) and (9) as compared with the previous cost functions. In [17], instead of using the consumed energy e_{ij} as the cost function presented in [18], when a packet is transmitted between node i and node j, the link cost is essentially equivalent to function $cost_{ij} = \dfrac{e_{ij}}{E_i}$ where E_i

is the remaining energy of node i. We compare the network lifetime using different cost functions which are $cost_{ij} = e_{ij}$ [18], $cost_{ij} = \dfrac{e_{ij}}{E_i}$ [17] and $cost_{ij}$ proposed in Eqs. (7), (8).

In Fig. 3, we evaluate the number of dead nodes through each round. As can be seen in Fig. 3, the line represented by the equation $cost_{ij} = e_{ij} + exp(1/E_i^2)$ shows that the number of dead nodes increases slowly in the first rounds but increases rapidly in the last rounds. Whereas, number of dead nodes in lines represented by equations $cost_{ij} = e_{ij}$ and $cost_{ij} = e_{ij}/E_i$ increases steadily over time.

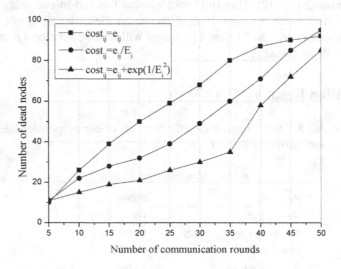

Fig. 3. Compare the energy balance of different cost functions in terms of number of dead nodes over time.

In Fig. 4, the line represented by the equation $cost_{ij} = e_{ij} + exp(1/E_i^2)$ shows that the total consumed energy increases rapidly increases slowly in the first rounds but increases slowly in the last rounds. Whereas, total consumed energy in lines represented by equations $cost_{ij} = e_{ij}$ and $cost_{ij} = e_{ij}/E_i$ increases steadily over time. These results are explained by the exponential function of the remaining energy that we applied in cost function. This function, $cost(E_{Re}^i)$ in Eq. (8), makes the large change in value of cost function as remaining energy of sensors changes a few. Thus, it balances the energy consumption among clusterhead nodes and maximizes network lifetime.

In the second simulation, we evaluate the performance of the DCEM protocol comparing with LEACH in [13] and HEED in [6]. We run 5 experiments which was performed in 20 rounds (each round is 1 s). Each experiment is assigned a distinctive end-to-end delay constraint (we set the bounded delay Δ from 10(ms) to 50(ms) for experiments respectively). The results are shown via Figs. 5 and 6.

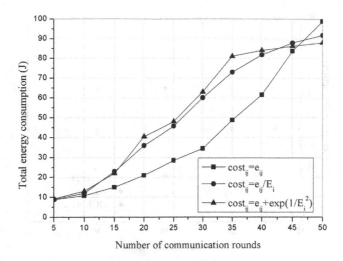

Fig. 4. Compare the energy balance of different cost functions in terms of total energy consumption over time.

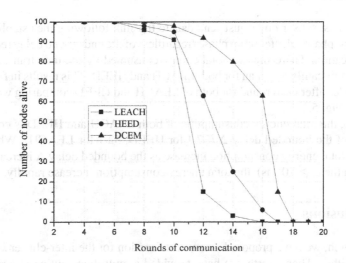

Fig. 5. Performance of LEACH, HEED, and DCEM on number of nodes alive with respect to given delay constraint.

In Fig. 5, the result is the average value of 5 experiments. For LEACH, each node i elects itself to become a clusterhead with probability $CH_{prob}(i) = \left(\dfrac{E_i}{E_{total}} \times k, 1 \right)$, where E_i is the remaining energy of node i, and $E_{total} = \sum_{i=1}^{N} E_i$. For HEED, the optimal number of clusterheads k_{opt} is computed to using as an initial percentage of clusterheads. This may result in slower death of sensor nodes. LEACH and HEED are organized for multihop networks, however, neither of them take interest in the end-to-end delay

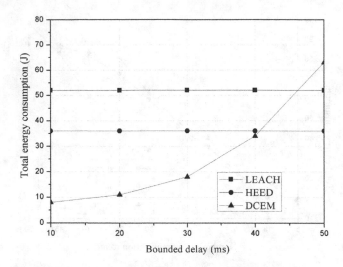

Fig. 6. Performance of LEACH, HEED, and DCEM on Total Energy Consumption with respect to different delay constraints.

constraint. Thus, sensor nodes just send data to the sink following the established time slot in the first phase (cluster setup phase) regardless of the end-to-end delay requirement of the application. Therefore, the total energy consumed by the data transmission for DCEM is significantly less than for both LEACH and HEED. This results in faster death of sensor nodes after each round for both of LEACH and HEED comparing with DCEM as shown in Fig. 5.

In Fig. 6, the total energy consumption of both LEACH and HEED is constant for any values of the bounded delay Δ (37 J for HEED, 52 J for LEACH). Whereas, for DCEM, the total energy consumption increase as the bounded delay Δ increases. Especially, when the $\Delta \geq 70$(ms), the total energy consumption increase rapidly.

6   Conclusions

In this research, we have proposed a new cost function for the inter-cluster k-least cost routes algorithm. Thenceforth, we have provided a multi-hop routing algorithm from clusterheads to sink with minimum energy consumption subject to an end-to-end delay constraint. By simulation, we have evaluated our cost function compared with other functions in terms of energy balance. In the expansion work, we have shown the outstanding performance of our proposal by comparing with other protocols in terms of network lifetime and energy consumption respect to different delay constraints.

References

1. Oh, H., Chae, K.: An energy-efficient sensor routing with low latency, scalability in wireless sensor networks. In: IEEE International Conference on Multimedia and Ubiquitous Engineering (2007)
2. Allirani, A., Suganthi, M.: An energy sorting protocol with reduced energy and latency for wireless sensor networks. In: IEEE International Conference on Advance Computing (2009)
3. Zhang, X., Zhang, L.: Optimizing energy-latency trade-off in wireless sensor networks with mobile element. In: IEEE 16th International Conference on Parallel and Distributed Systems (2010)
4. Boyinbode, O., et al.: A survey on clustering algorithms for wireless sensor networks. In: IEEE 13th International Conference on Network-Based Information Systems (2010)
5. Huynh, T.T., et al.: Delay-energy aware clustering multi-hop routing in wireless sensor networks. In: International Conference on Information Science and Applications 2016, Hochiminh, vol. 376, pp. 31–40 (2016)
6. Younis, O., Fahmy, S.: Heed: a hybrid, energy-efficient, distributed clustering approach for ad-hoc sensor networks. IEEE Trans. Mobile Comput. 3(4), 660–669 (2004)
7. Akkaya, K., Younis, M.: Energy-aware routing of time-constrained traffic in wireless sensor networks. J. Commun. Syst., Special Issue Serv. Diff. QoS Ad Hoc Netw. 17(6), 663–687 (2004)
8. Li, Y., et al.: An energy efficient distributed algorithm for minimum latency aggregation scheduling in wireless sensor networks. In: IEEE 30th International Conference on Distributed Computing Systems (2010)
9. Huynh, T.T., et al.: Energy efficient delay-aware routing in multi-tier. In: The IEEE International Conference on Advanced Technologies for Communications, pp. 439–444 (2013)
10. Bai, S., et al.: DEAR: Delay-bounded Energy-constrained Adaptive Routing in wireless sensor networks. In: IEEE International Conference on Computer Communications (2012)
11. Wuyungerile, L., et al.: Tradeoff between delay and energy consumption of partial data aggregation in wireless sensor networks. In: The Fifth International Conference on Mobile Computing and Ubiquitous Networking (2010)
12. Ammari, H.M.: On the energy-delay trade-off in geographic forwarding in always-on wireless sensor networks: A multi-objective optimization problem. Comput. Netw. 57(9), 1913–1935 (2013)
13. Heinzelman, W.B., et al.: An application specific protocol architecture for wireless sensor network. IEEE Trans. Wirel. Commun. 4, 660–670 (2002)
14. Liu, A., et al.: Design principles and improvement of cost function based energy aware routing algorithms for wireless sensor networks. Elsevier Comput. Netw. 5(7), 1951–1967 (2012)
15. Sedgewick, R.: Algorithms in C ++: Graph Algorithms, 3rd edn. Pearson Education (2002)
16. de Queiros Vieira Martins, E., et al.: The K shortest paths problem. CISUC, Research Report (1998)
17. Ok, C.-S., et al.: Distributed energy balanced routing for wireless sensor networks. Comput. Ind. Eng. 57(1), 125–135 (2009)
18. Ettus, M.: System capacity, latency, and power consumption in multihop-routed SS-CDMA wireless networks. In: IEEE Radio and Wireless Conference, Colorado Springs, CO, pp. 55–58 (1998)

Construction of Vietnamese Argument Annotated Dataset for Why-Question Answering Method

Chinh Trong Nguyen and Dang Tuan Nguyen[(✉)]

Faculty of Computer Science, University of Information Technology, VNU-HCM,
Ho Chi Minh City, Vietnam
{chinhnt,dangnt}@uit.edu.vn

Abstract. In this paper, the method of building a Vietnamese Argument Annotated Dataset (VAAD) is presented. This dataset contains argumentative data
which can be used to answer the why-questions. Therefore, it is important to
discover the characteristics of the answers of why-questions to develop why-
question answering method by using causal relations between texts. In addition,
this dataset can be used to generate the testing dataset for evaluation of answering
method. In order to build the dataset, a process of four steps is proposed after
studying relevant problems. To briefly evaluate the method, an experiment is
conducted to show the applicability of the method in practice.

Keywords: Discourse analysis · Why-question answering · Vietnamese
Argument Annotated Dataset

1 Introduction

At present, the development of question answering systems for Vietnamese language
can be founded on researched solutions of answering the factoid questions [13–16].
These solutions are mostly based on knowledge mining techniques therefore they need
a large annotated corpus to train, to evaluate and to develop.

Although why-questions are rarely asked, 5 % of all questions asked according to
the observation of Hovy [1], they seem to be the important type of question because
their answers, found by causal relations in discourse structures instead of the bag of
words in texts, provide the reasons about problems. Therefore, building a why-question
answering (why-QA) system for Vietnamese language has been conducted. However,
the Vietnamese corpus for researching why-question answering methods is lacked.
Although TREC has developed testing datasets for question answering systems for many
years, the datasets mostly contain factoid questions and they are written in English. At
present, it is important to build a large Vietnamese annotated dataset for researching and
testing why-QA.

For the above reasons, a Vietnamese Argument Annotated Dataset (VAAD) for why-
questions should be built to develop why-QA answering methods. The dataset should
be suitable for developing many answering methods and evaluation. In this paper, the
process of building VAAD for why-questions is presented in five sections. Section 1
introduces the exigence of developing VAAD. Section 2 explores some problems related

© ICST Institute for Computer Sciences, Social Informatics and Telecommunications Engineering 2016
P.C. Vinh et al. (Eds.): ICTCC 2016, LNICST 168, pp. 124–132, 2016.
DOI: 10.1007/978-3-319-46909-6_12

to building the dataset. According to these problems, the annotation format of Vietnamese VAAD and the building process is presented Sect. 3. Then, the experiment of building the dataset is presented in Sect. 4. At the end, some conclusions are drawn in Sect. 5.

2 Related Works

The methods of question answering can be divided into two approaches that are knowledge mining, as in [13–16], and knowledge annotation, as in [17]. The methods based on knowledge mining techniques have the advantage of information redundancy from the internet. The redundancy of information can be utilized to propose question answering methods which do not need to use complex natural language processing techniques. Therefore, many researches in question answering have focused on this approach.

According to the knowledge mining approach, developing question answering methods need large datasets to discover the patterns which are used to find the candidate answers. These datasets are also used to test the question answering methods. These datasets should be not only collected but also annotated into a specific format. The format of a dataset depends on the feature analyzed by the researching methods. For example, Saint-Dizier's dataset in [12] is annotated by using Rhetorical Structure Theory (RST) [7] because the question answering method is based on the argumentation which is identified in discourse structure of the document.

In why-QA, the question answering method can be divided into two types: cue-based method and discourse-based method. The cue-based methods are developed with clues as in [11] or with cue words and paragraph retrieval techniques as in [2]. They have the simplicity in analysis but the results are quite low because the semantic features have not been analyzed yet. In contrast, the discourse-based methods are developed with discourse structure of the document as in [4–6, 12]. In this type, the methods have to use the context of the sentences in a document to build the relations between them. These relations express the intention of the writer. Among these relations, the causal relations between sentences form the writer's argument structures. The discourse-based methods need more complicated analysis but their results are more relevant to the questions than the cue-based ones. Despite of the differences, these types of answering method need why-QA datasets for training and testing. These datasets have to be built for each research project because there are no appropriate dataset for all purposes.

In discourse structure of document, there are two approaches of representation. In the RST representation [7], a document is a "tree of spans". Each span, which can be a clause, a sentence or a paragraph, links to another span following rhetorical relations to form a larger span. These spans are still presented in text therefore they are easy to search. In the Discourse Representation Theory (DRT) [18], a document is a set of Discourse Representation Structure (DRS) which is a group of first-order logic expressions. These representations can be used to reason in order to find new information, however it is complex to build a set of DRS from a document in natural language.

In other aspect of discourse structure, the visual structure of a document also affects its discourse structure as Power shown in [8].

3   Building VAAD for Developing Why-QA Method

The purpose of building the VAAD is to develop why-QA methods. These methods can be cue-based or discourse-based approaches therefore the dataset should be annotated in a simple format so that it can be used easily. In addition, the dataset can be used to generate testing sets by transforming the result parts of causal relations in to why-questions. For example, the causal relation "Tom is not allowed to ride a bicycle because Tom is young" has the result part "Tom is not allowed to ride a bicycle". Thus, a why-question "why Tom is not allowed to ride a bicycle?" can be built by transforming the result part. In order to make more complex why-questions, synonyms or similar semantic phrases can be used to expand the original result parts.

The process of building VAAD dataset has four steps that are documents collecting, argument annotating, patterns extracting and argument annotated fragments collecting.

3.1   Documents Collecting

During the process of collecting documents containing arguments, the observations show that there are many news posts or comments without any arguments in them. These news posts or comments are often about new products, instructions, sports news. In order to collect documents containing arguments, Google[1] is used to search for document containing phrases which are more likely to appear in an argument, such as "tại sao" ("why"), "công dụng của" ("the use of"), "hạn chế của" ("the disadvantages of"). Then, the links in google search results are extracted and used to download the origin web pages. After that, the scripts, banners, etc. of the web pages are eliminated and the texts of main content of the web pages are extracted. These texts form a dataset for annotating in the next step.

3.2   Argument Annotating

According to the simplicity of the RST representation, the dataset is annotated follow these rules:

- All spans which are not in any argument are unchanged.
- Spans, which are in a certain argument, are place in a pair of symbols "[" and "]"
- A span which is an argument is annotated as follow: causal part and result part are place in a pair of symbols "{" and "}" in which they follow a notation of their role in the argument; the cue phrase which informs the type of causal relation is unchanged. Figure 1 illustrates an annotated argument fragment.

---

[1] https://www.google.com.

> [{CIRCUMSTANCE Theo nghiên cứu công bố trên tạp chí khoa học PNAS hồi tháng 5 của CSIRO (Tổ chức Nghiên cứu Khoa học và Công nghiệp Liên bang Australia), hải sâm là nguồn dược liệu và thực phẩm có giá trị cao tại thị trường châu Á}. *Do đó*, {OUTCOME nó đang bị đánh bắt quá mức}]
>
> (source: VnExpress.net)

Fig. 1. A structure of an argument annotated fragment. The bold words are the roles of two parts in a causal relation (CIRCUMSTANCE - OUTCOME). The bold, italic words, "Do đó" (therefore) is a cue phrase indicates the circumstance - result relation.

– An argument can be a part of another argument as shown in Fig. 2.

> [{CIRCUMSTANCE Bóng đè là một hiện tượng tâm sinh lý điển hình của hệ thống tính năng cơ thể. [{CIRCUMSTANCE Nó được ví như hệ thống "Role" trong kỹ nghệ, nhằm bảo vệ cơ thể bằng cách vô hiệu hóa những mệnh lệnh "tái sinh" từ hệ điều khiển đến hệ thống vận động trong lúc cơ thể đang được duy trì ở trạng thái "nghi" -} *do vậy* {OUTCOME sự "đè nén" ở đây không có thực thể mà chỉ là hiệu ứng do "cái bóng" gây ra mà thôi}]. [{CIRCUMSTANCE Mệnh lệnh "tái sinh" chỉ là "mệnh lệnh ảo" được não bộ tái hiện lại, hoặc "sáng tác ra" trong giai đoạn ta đang ngủ}, *vì vậy* {OUTCOME mệnh lệnh loại này chỉ được "chiếu thử" lên màn hình của não bộ mà không được thực thi bởi các cơ quan chức năng của cơ thể}]}.
> *Chính vì vậy,* {OUTCOME trong suốt giai đoạn mộng mị của giấc ngủ, hoặc trong lúc bị "bóng đè", cơ thể vẫn được duy trì trạng thái "nằm yên" bởi các cơ bắp bỗng nhiên bị "mất điện" nhằm ngăn cản các hành động có thể diễn ra theo kịch bản phiêu lưu quái dị và lãng mạn của não bộ vẽ vời ra}].
>
> (source: VnExpress.net)

Fig. 2. An argument can be a part of another argument. In this figure, the first paragraph is the causal part and the second paragraph is the result part of an argument. There are two arguments in the first paragraph.

By using these rules, the arguments in document are easy to extract. In addition, if there is any further language analysis needed, it can be applied easily to discover more precise patterns. In this format, the causal relations in RST is divided into four types according to [4]: rationale - effect, purpose - outcome, circumstance - outcome and means - outcome.

3.3 Patterns Extracting

After identifying arguments by annotating the causal relations. The patterns containing cue phrases and some specific marks such as periods, commas, new-lines are also identified. A causal relation can be an inner-sentence, an inter-sentence or an inter-paragraph relation.

In an inner-sentence relation, as in Fig. 3 all parts of the relation are bounded in two periods and they do not contain any period. In an inter-sentence relation, as in Fig. 1 above, there is only one period; and in an inter-paragraph relation, as in Fig. 2 above, there are one more new-line symbols.

> [*Để* {RATIONALE tồn tại trên thế giới này}, {EFFECT mọi người cần phải gặp gỡ, giao tiếp với nhau và thói quen này cần bắt đầu từ khi còn nhỏ}]
>
> (source: VnExpress.net)

Fig. 3. The inner-sentence relation in which all parts of the relation are bounded in two periods and there is no period in all parts of the relation.

In this step, the cue phrases are used as core feature to identify the argument because the cue phrase have stably meaning of discourse function as shown in [7, 9]. Therefore, the patterns are manually identified and used to extract arguments having the same patterns in websites to enrich the dataset.

3.4 Argument Annotated Fragments Collecting

By using the patterns discovered in step 3, a crawler is used to fetch the news posts on websites to extract the argument annotated fragment. By using the crawler, the process of building VAAD is reduced greatly in cost of manually collecting and annotating. However, this method has a disadvantage of not collecting arguments of new patterns. The extracted arguments of collected news posts are automatically annotated with the proposed format according to the patterns which are used to extract them.

4   Experiment

In order to evaluate the method of building VAAD, 34 articles are collected according to step 1 and annotated as describing in step 2. Then, the 49 argument fragment patterns, as shown in Table 1 are manually identified. Then, these patterns are represented in regular expressions to collect argument fragments.

After identifying argument fragment patterns, a set of 608 articles downloaded from internet using crawler are process with the patterns to generate 2609 fragments. The cue phrases associated with these fragments are presented in Table 2 to show which cue phrases are frequently used. In order to evaluate the precision of the argument identification method, 250 fragments are randomly selected in 2609 fragments. These 250 fragments are then manually check if they are argument fragments. After checking, there are 195 fragments are argument fragments which yield the precision of 0.78.

Table 1. The list of manually identified cue phrases.

Phrase	Relation type
… . Vì vậy,	inter-sentence
… . Bởi vậy, …	inter-sentence
… . Vì thế …	inter-sentence
… . Điều này làm cho …	inter-sentence
… Do đó, …	inter-paragraph
… do …	inner-sentence
Nhờ …, …	inter-sentence
… .Thế nên	inter-sentence
… . Kết quả …	inter-sentence
… .Vì vậy …	inter-sentence
… . Do vậy, …	inter-sentence
Để …, …	inner-sentence
…, chính vì vậy …	inner-sentence
… . Do vậy …	inter-sentence
… do vậy …	inner-sentence
… . Vì lẽ đó, …	inter-sentence
… là nguyên nhân chính dẫn tới …	inner-sentence
Do … mà …	inner-sentence
… . Điều này khiến …	inter-paragraph
… là do …	inner-sentence
… cho nên …	inner-sentence
…, do vậy …	inner-sentence
… Chính vì vậy, …	inter-paragraph
… Vậy, …	inter-paragraph
… dẫn đến …	inner-sentence
… vì …	inner-sentence
… , vì vậy …	inner-sentence
… . Điều này dẫn đến …	inter-sentence
… . Đây là lý do …	inter-sentence
… , đây là lý do tại sao …	inner-sentence
Bởi vì … nên …	inner-sentence
… là nhờ …	inner-sentence
Nguyên nhân … do …	inner-sentence
Với … , …	inner-sentence
Nhờ … mà …	inner-sentence
… để …	inner-sentence
… với mục đích …	inner-sentence
… nên …	inner-sentence
… gây …	inner-sentence
… Như vậy, …	inter-paragraph
… ảnh hưởng tới …	inner-sentence
Vì … nên …	inner-sentence
Bởi … , …	inner-sentence
… . Và đó là lý do …	inter-sentence
để … thì …	inner-sentence
… cho thấy …	inner-sentence
… khiến …	inner-sentence
… bằng cách …	inner-sentence
… bởi …	inner-sentence

Table 2. The list of cue phrases used to extract 2609 fragments and their number of use.

Phrase	Number of use
... để ...	923
... do ...	328
... nên ...	277
... vì ...	240
... khiến ...	158
... gây ...	163
... bởi ...	114
... cho thấy ...	91
... . Vì thế, ...	69
... nhằm ...	55
... biến thành ...	47
... bằng cách ...	30
... . Kết quả ...	21
... dẫn đến ...	21
... ảnh hưởng đến ...	21
... . Do đó ...	14
... . Vì vậy, ...	13
Để ... , ...	6
... , vì thế ...	3
... . Nhờ đó, ...	3
... là nhờ ...	3
... làm cho ...	3
... với mục đích ...	3
... . Do vậy, ...	1
... cho nên ...	1
... nguyên nhân chính ...	1

The reasons of the wrong identifying argument fragments are the ambiguity of the cue phrase and the misidentifying inter-paragraph relation. The ambiguity of cue phrase such as, "để" (in order to) and "để" (to put), can be overcome by POS tag process before identifying patterns and extracting argument fragments. The misidentifying inter-paragraph relation is more difficult to overcome. It requires a completely RST structure of the document to identify which paragraphs form a span in RST. However, the number of inter-paragraph argument fragments collected are not very large. Therefore this method can be used to build VAAD for developing a why-QA method.

The experiment result shows that the proposed method can be applied in practice with the higher precision by applying POS tagging task.

5   Conclusions and Future Works

In this paper, the research on building VAAD for developing why-QA method is presented. This dataset is important to find out the characteristics of argument of text fragments to answer the why-questions in Vietnamese. In addition, the testing dataset for why-QA method can be generated from this dataset. The testing dataset is also important to evaluate the answering method. Because the arguments are some kinds of

RST relations, this paper proposes a method of automatically identifying argument fragments from news posts in the internet using cue phrases. The cue phrases are used in this method because their linguistic functions of discourse are stable. Therefore, the process of four steps which are collecting documents, argument annotating, patterns extracting and argument annotated fragments collecting is proposed to build the dataset.

According to the proposed process, an experiment has been conducted and it shows that the process can be apply to automatically build the practical VAAD for developing why-QA method after POS tagging the documents for extracting patterns and collecting argument fragments.

In future, Vietnamese RST parser should be developed to overcome the misidentifying inter-paragraph causal relation to enrich VAAD.

References

1. Hovy, E.H., Hermjakob, U., Ravichandran, D.: A question/answer typology with surface text patterns. In: 2nd International Conference on Human Language Technology Research, California, pp. 247–251 (2002)
2. Verberne, S., Boves, L., Oostdijk, N., Coppen, P.: Using syntactic information for improving why-question answering. In: 22nd International Conference on Computational Linguistics, Manchester, United Kingdom, pp. 953–960 (2008)
3. Verberne, S.: Developing an approach for why-question answering. In: 11th Conference of the European Chapter of the Association for Computational Linguistics: Student Research Workshop, Trento, Italy, pp. 39–46 (2006)
4. Delmonte, R., Pianta., E.: Answering why-questions in closed domains from a discourse model. In: Conference on Semantics in Text Processing, pp. 103–114. ACL, Stroudsburg (2008)
5. Oh, J., Torisawa, K., Hashimoto, C., Sano, M., Saeger, S. D.: Why-question answering using intra- and inter-sentential causal relations. In: 51st Annual Meeting of the Association for Computational Linguistics, pp. 1733–1743. ACL Anthology, Sofia (2013)
6. Higashinaka, R., Isozaki, H.: Corpus-based question answering for why-questions. In: 3rd International Joint Conference of Natural Language Processing, Hyderabad, India, pp. 418–425 (2008)
7. Mann, W.C., Thompson, S.A.: Rhetorical structure theory: towards a functional theory of text organization. Text 3(8), 243–281 (1988)
8. Power, R., Scott, D., Bouayad-Agha, N.: Document Structure. Comput. Linguist. 29(2), 211–260 (2003)
9. Marcu, D.: The rhetorical parsing of natural language texts. In: 35th Annual Meeting of the Association for Computational Linguistics and 8th Conference of the European Chapter of the Association for Computational Linguistics, pp. 96–103. ACL, Stroudsburg (1997)
10. Hwee, T.N., Leong, H.T., Lai, J.P.K.: A machine learning approach to answering questions for reading comprehension tests. In: The 2000 Joint SIGDAT Conference on Empirical Methods in Natural Language Processing and Very Large Corpora, pp. 124–132. ACL, Stroudsburg (2000)
11. Riloff, E., Thelen, M.: A rule-based question answering system for reading comprehension tests. In: The 2000 ANLP/NAACL Workshop on Reading Comprehension Tests as Evaluation for Computer-Based Language Understanding Systems, pp. 13–19. ACL, Stroudsburg (2000)

12. Saint-Dizier, P.: Processing Natural Language Arguments with the <TextCoop> Platform. Argument Comput. 3(1), 49–82 (2012). Taylor and Francis
13. Zheng, Z.: AnswerBus question answering system. In: The 2nd International Conference on Human Language Technology Research, pp. 399–404. Morgan Kaufmann Publishers Inc., San Francisco (2002)
14. Clarke, C., Cormack, G., Kemkes, G., Laszlo, M., Lynam, T., Terra, E., Tilker, P.: Statistical selection of exact answers (multitext experiments for TREC 2002). In: TREC, pp. 823–831. NIST (2002)
15. Brill, E., Dumais, S., Banko, M.: An analysis of the AskMSR question-answering system. In: The ACL 2002 Conference on Empirical Methods in Natural Language Processing, pp. 257–264. ACL, Stroudsburg (2002)
16. Buchholz, S., Daelemans, W.: Shapaqa: shallow parsing for question answering on the world wide web. In: Euroconference Recent Advances in Natural Language Processing, Tzigov Chark, Bulgaria, pp. 47–51 (2001)
17. Katz, B., Felshin, S., Yuret, D., Ibrahim, A., Lin, J.J., Marton, G., McFarland, A.J., Temelkuran, B.: Omnibase: uniform access to heterogeneous data for question answering. In: Andersson, B., Bergholtz, M., Johannesson, P. (eds.) NLDB 2002. LNCS, vol. 2553, pp. 230–234. Springer, Heidelberg (2002)
18. Kamp, H.: Discourse representation theory. In: Gabbay, D., Guenthner, F. (eds.) Handbook of Philosophical Logic, vol. 15, pp. 125–394. Springer, Netherlands (2011)

FRFE: Fast Recursive Feature Elimination
for Credit Scoring

Van-Sang Ha[1(✉)] and Ha-Nam Nguyen[2]

[1] Department of Economic Information System, Academy of Finance, Hanoi, Vietnam
sanghv@hvtc.edu.vn
[2] Department of Information Technology, VNU-University of Engineering and Technology,
Hanoi, Vietnam
namnh@vnu.edu.vn

Abstract. Credit scoring is one of the most important issues in financial decision-making. The use of data mining techniques to build models for credit scoring has been a hot topic in recent years. Classification problems often have a large number of features, but not all of them are useful for classification. Irrelevant and redundant features in credit data may even reduce the classification accuracy. Feature selection is a process of selecting a subset of relevant features, which can decrease the dimensionality, reduce the running time, and improve the accuracy of classifiers. Random forest (RF) is a powerful classification tool which is currently an active research area and successfully solves classification problems in many domains. In this study, we constructed a fast credit scoring model based on parallel Random forests and Recursive Feature Elimination (FRFE) . Two public UCI data sets, Australia and German credit have been used to test our method. The experimental results of the real world data showed that the proposed method results in a higher prediction rate than a baseline method for some certain datasets and also shows comparable and sometimes better performance than the feature selection methods widely used in credit scoring.

Keywords: Credit risk · Credit scoring · Feature selection · Random forests · RFE · Machine learning

1 Introduction

The main purpose of credit risk analysis is to classify customers into two sets, good and bad ones [1]. Over the last decades, there have been lots of classification models and algorithms applied to analyze credit risk, for example decision tree [2], nearest neighbor K-NN, support vector machine (SVM) and neural network [3–7]. One important goal in credit risk prediction is to build the best classification model for a specific dataset.

Financial data in general and credit data in particular usually contain irrelevant and redundant features. The redundancy and the deficiency in data can reduce the classification accuracy and lead to incorrect decision [8, 9]. In that case, a feature selection strategy is deeply needed in order to filter the redundant features. Indeed, feature selection is a process of selecting a subset of relevant features. The subset is sufficient to

© ICST Institute for Computer Sciences, Social Informatics and Telecommunications Engineering 2016
P.C. Vinh et al. (Eds.): ICTCC 2016, LNICST 168, pp. 133–142, 2016.
DOI: 10.1007/978-3-319-46909-6_13

describe the problem with high precision. Feature selection thus allows decreasing the dimensionality of the problem and shortening the running time.

Credit scoring is a technique using statistical analysis data and activities to evaluate the credit risk against customers. Credit scoring is shown in a figure determined by the bank based on the statistical analysis of credit experts, credit teams or credit bureaus. In Vietnam, some commercial banks start to perform credit scoring against customers but it is not widely applied during the testing phase and still needs to improve gradually. For completeness, all information presented in this paper comes from credit scoring experience in Australia, Germany and other countries.

Many methods have been investigated in the last decade to pursue even small improvement in credit scoring accuracy. Artificial Neural Networks (ANNs) [10–13] and Support Vector Machine (SVM) [14–19] are two commonly soft computing methods used in credit scoring modelling. In order to achieve higher classification performance, SVM recursive feature elimination (SVM-RFE) filter relevant features and remove relatively insignificant feature variables. SVM-RFE uses numerical attribute but credit data sets has a lot of categorical attributes. How to deal with an SVM-RFE with categorical attributes? The conversion of categorical attributes into numerical attributes will lack information and reduce accuracy. Random forest is a popular classification method which deal with this problem. Recently, other methods like evolutionary algorithms [20], stochastic optimization technique and support vector machine [21] have shown promising results in terms of prediction accuracy.

This study proposed a new method for feature selection based on recursive feature elimination and integrated with a parallel Random Forest classifier in credit scoring tasks. The proposed method reduces the set of features via feature ranking criterion. This criterion re-evaluates the importance of features according to the Gini index and the correlation of training and validation accuracy which are obtained from RF algorithm. By that way, we take both feature contribution and correlation of training error into account. We applied the proposed algorithm to classify credit datasets. Integration with H2O parallel random forest, the FRFE showed better classification accuracy and faster than RF.

The rest of the paper is organized as follows: Sect. 2 presents the background of credit scoring, random forests and feature selection. Section 3 is the most important section that describes the details of the proposed model. Experimental results are discussed in Sect. 4 while concluding remarks and future works are presented in Sect. 5.

2   Feature Selection

Feature selection is the most basic step in data pre-processing as it reduces the dimensionality of the data. Feature selection can be a part of the criticism which needs to focus on only related features, such as the PCA method or an algorithm modeling. However, the feature selection is usually a separate step in the whole process of data mining.

There are two different categories of feature selection methods, i.e. filter approach and wrapper approach. The filter approach considers the feature selection process as a precursor stage of learning algorithms. The filter model uses evaluation functions to evaluate the classification performances of subsets of features. There are many evaluation functions such as feature importance, Gini, information gain, the ratio of information gain, etc. A disadvantage of this approach is that there is no relationship between the feature selection process and the performance of learning algorithms.

The wrapper approach uses a machine learning algorithm to measure the good-ness of the set of selected features. The measurement relies on the performance of the learning algorithm such as its accuracy, recall and precision values. The wrapper model uses a learning accuracy for evaluation. In the methods using the wrapper model, all samples should be divided into two sets, i.e. training set and testing set. The algorithm runs on the training set, and then applies the learning result on the testing set to measure the prediction accuracy. The disadvantage of this approach is highly computational cost. Some researchers proposed methods that can speed up the evaluating process to decrease this cost. Common wrapper strategies are Sequential Forward Selection (SFS) and Sequential Backward Elimination (SBE). The optimal feature set is found by searching on the feature space. In this space, each state represents a feature subset, and the size of the searching space for n features is $O(2^n)$, so it is impractical to search the whole space exhaustively, unless n is small.

3   H2O Parallel Random Forests

H2O is a platform for distributed in memory predictive analytics and machine learning. H2O uses pure Java which easy deployment with a single jar, automatic cloud discovery. H2O does in-memory analytics on clusters with distributed parallelized state-of-the-art Machine Learning algorithms. Figure 1 show H2O architecture:

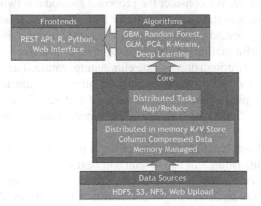

Fig. 1. H2O architecture

Random Forest is an ensemble classifier consisting of a set of CART classifiers using bagging mechanism. Each node of a tree only selects a small subset of features for a split, which enables the algorithm to create classifiers for highly dimensional data very quickly. One has to specify the number of randomly selected features *(mtry)* at each split. The default value is *sqrt(p)* for the classification where p is the number of features. The Gini index is used as the splitting criterion.

Random Forest is an ensemble classifier consisting of a set of CART classifiers using bagging mechanism. Each node of a tree only selects a small subset of features for a split, which enables the algorithm to create classifiers for highly dimensional data very quickly. One has to specify the number of randomly selected features *(mtry)* at each split. The default value is *sqrt(p)* for the classification where p is the number of features. The largest possible tree is grown and not pruned. The big enough number of trees *(ntree)* is chosen to ensure that every input feature is predicted at least several times. The root node of each tree in the forest keeps a set of bootstrapped samples from the original data as the training set to build a tree. The rest of the samples, called out-of-bag (OOB) samples are used to estimate the performance of classification. The out-of-bag (OOB) estimation is based on the classification of the set of OOB samples which is roughly one third of the original samples. H2O's Random Forest algorithm is parallel processing which produces a dynamic confusion matrix. As each tree is built, OOBE (out of bag error estimate) is recalculated. The expected behavior is that the error rate increases before it decreases, as it is a natural outcome of Random Forest's learning process. When there are only a few trees built on random subsets, the error rate is expected to be relatively high. As more trees are added, resulting in more trees "voting" for the correct classification of the OOB data, the error rate should decrease.

4   The Proposed Method

Our proposed method uses H2O parallel random forest (PRF) to estimate performance and reduce running time. We consider the proposed method has two phases. In the first phase, the training set was trained and tested by PRF in order to select the best features. The most important procedure in phase one is to estimate feature ranking value for each feature. A recursive elimination approach was applied to evaluated contribution of each feature to the classifier through one-by-one eliminating feature. The irrelevant feature(s) are eliminated and only the important features are survived by means of feature ranking value. Output of the phase one is a set of selected features. To deal with over-fitting problem, we apply n-fold cross validation technique to minimize the generalization error.

In the second phase, result of learning phase is used as a filter of test dataset. The detail of proposed algorithm will be presented in next section.

In wrapper approaches, they only focus on accuracies of the features when computing the ranking criteria, but not much on the correlation of the features. A feature with good ranking criteria may not turn out a good result. Also, the combination of several features with good ranking criteria may not give out a good result. On the other hand, Recursive

Feature Elimination takes a lot of time to run. To remedy this problem, we propose a procedure named Fast Feature Elimination based on parallel RF (FRFE).

1. Train data by Random Forest with the cross validation
2. Calculate the ranking criterion for all features F_i^{rank} where i = 1..n (n is the number of features).
3. Remove a feature by using *FastFeatureElimination* function (may be more efficient if we remove several features at a time)
4. Back to step 1 until reach the desired criteria.

In step 1, from the jth cross validation we get set of (F_j, A_j^{learn}, $A_j^{validation}$, AUC_j^{learn}, $Gini_j^{Learn}$) that are the feature importance. The learning accuracy, the validation accuracy, the area under curve (AUC). Those values will be used to compute the ranking criterion in step 2.

In step 2, we use the results from step 1 to build the ranking criterion which will be used in step 3. The ranking criterion of feature i^{th} is computed as follow:

$$F_i^{rank} = \sum_{j=1}^{n} F_{i,j} \times \left(\frac{\left(A_j^{learn} + A_j^{validation} \right)}{\left| A_i^{learn} - A_j^{validation} \right| + \varepsilon} + AUC_j^{learn} \right) \quad (1)$$

where $j = 1, .., n$ is the number of cross validation folders;

$F_{i,j}$ is the feature importance in terms of the node impurity which can be computed by Gini impurity

A_j^{learn} the learning accuracy

$A_j^{validation}$ the validation accuracy of feature j^{th} obtained from H2O Random Forest module, respectively.

ε is the real number with very small value.

AUC_j^{learn}: the area under curve (AUC)

The first factor $\left(F_{i,j} \right)$ is presented the Gini decrease for each feature over all trees in the forest when we train data by RF. Obviously, the higher decrease of $F_{i,j}$ is obtained, and the better rank of feature we have. We use the second factor to deal with the over fitting issue as well as the desire of high accuracy. The numerator of the factor presents for our desire to have a high accuracy. The larger value we get, the better the rank of the feature is. We want to have a high accuracy in learning and also want not too fit the training data which so called over fitting problem. To solve this issue, we apply the n-folder cross validation technique. We can see that the less difference between the learning accuracy and the validation accuracy, the more stability of accuracy. In the other words, the purpose of the denominator is to reduce over fitting. In the case of the learning accuracy is equal to the validation accuracy, the difference is equal to 0, we use ε with very small value to avoid the fraction to be ∞. We added AUC measure because the AUC is a commonly used evaluation metric for binary classification problems like predicting a Good (Buy) or Bad (Sell) decision (binary decision). The interpretation is that given a random positive observation and negative observation, the AUC gives the proportion of the time you guess which is correct. It is more affected by sample in-balance than accuracy. A perfect model will score an AUC of 1, while random guessing will score an AUC of around 0.5. AUC is in fact often predicted over accuracy for binary classification for a number of different reasons.

In step 3: we execute the feature elimination strategy based on backward approach. The proposed feature elimination strategy depends on both ranking criterion and the validation accuracy. The ranking criterion makes the order of features be eliminated and the validation accuracy is used to decide whether the chosen subset of features is permanently eliminated. The new subset is validated by H2O Random Forest module. The obtained validation accuracy plays a role of decision making. It is used to evaluate whether the selected subset is accepted as a new candidate of features. If the obtained validation accuracy is lower than the previous selected subset accuracy, it tries to eliminate other features based on their rank values. This iteration is stopped whenever the validation accuracy of the new subset is higher than the previous selected subset accuracy. If there is either no feature to create new subset or no better validation accuracy, the current subset of features is considered as the final result of our learning algorithm. Otherwise the procedure goes back to step 1. The set of features, which is a result of learning phase, is used as a filter to reduce the dimension of the test dataset before performing predicting those samples in classification phase.

5   Experiment and Results

Our proposed algorithm was coded using R language (http://www.r-project.org), using H2O Random Forest package. This package is optimized for doing "in memory" processing of distributed, parallel machine learning algorithms on clusters. A "cluster" is a software construct that can be fired up on your lap-top, on a server, or across the multiple nodes of a cluster of real machines, including computers that form a Hadoop cluster. We tested the proposed algorithm with several datasets including two UCI public datasets, German and Australian credit approval, to validate our approach. The learning and validation accuracies were determined by means of 5-fold cross validation. In this paper, we used RF with the original dataset as the base-line method. The proposed method and the base-line method were executed on the same training and testing datasets to compare their efficiency.

5.1   Australian Credit

The Australian credit dataset is composed of 690 applicants, with 383 credit worthy and 307 default examples. Each instance contains eight numerical features, six categorical features, and one discriminant feature, with sensitive information being transferred to symbolic data for confidentiality reasons. The averages of classification results are depicted in Fig. 2.

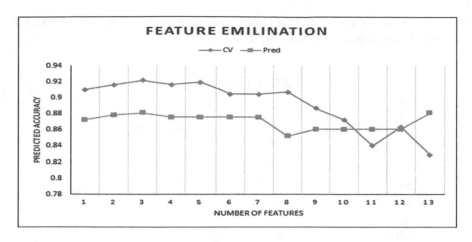

Fig. 2. Accuracy in case of Australian dataset

Table 1 shows the performances of different classifiers over the Australian credit datasets. Baseline is the classifier without feature selection. Classifiers used in [22] include: Linear SVM, CART, k-NN, Naïve Bayes, MLP. Filter methods include: t-test, Linear Discriminant analysis (LDA), Logistic regression (LR). The wrapper methods include: Genetic algorithms (GA) and Particle swarm optimization (PSO).

Table 1. Compare performances of different classifiers over the Australian credit dataset

Classifier	Filter methods			Wrapper methods		Baseline
	t-test	LDA	LR	GA	PSO	
Linear SVM	85.52	85.52	85.52	85.52	85.52	85.52
CART	85.25	85.46	85.11	84.85	84.82	85.20
k-NN	86.06	85.31	84.81	84.69	84.64	84.58
Naïve Bayes	68.52	67.09	66.74	86.09	85.86	68.55
MLP	85.60	86.00	85.89	85.57	85.49	84.15
Random forests						87.25
Our method	**89.16** (± 3.09)					

The prediction the performances of different classifiers over the Australian credit dataset. The table shows the classification accuracy of our method is much higher than these studies' one. Relying on parallel processing, time to run 20 trails with 5-fold cross validate taken by our method is only 2974 s (~50 min).

5.2 German Credit Dataset

The German credit approval dataset consists of 1000 loan applications, with 700 accepted and 300 rejected. Each applicant is described by 20 attributes. Our final results were averaged over these 20 independent trials. In our experiments, we use the default value for the mtry parameter and the ntree parameter was tried with value of 100. The averages of classification results are depicted in Fig. 3.

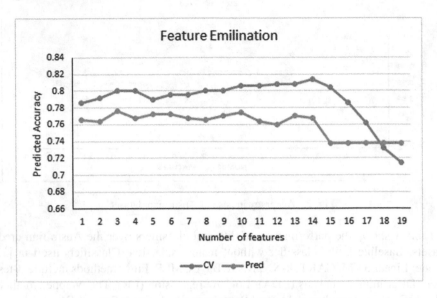

Fig. 3. Accuracy in case of German credit dataset

Table 2 shows the performances of different classifiers over the German credit datasets. Baseline is the classifier without feature selection. Classifiers used in [22] include: Linear SVM, CART, k-NN, Naïve Bayes, MLP. Filter methods include: t-test, Linear Discriminant analysis (LDA), Logistic regression (LR). The wrapper methods include: Genetic algorithms (GA) and Particle swarm optimization (PSO).

Table 2. Performances of different classifiers over the German credit dataset

Classifier	Filter methods			Wrapper methods		Baseline
	t-test	LDA	LR	GA	PSO	
Linear SVM	76.74	75.72	75.10	85.52	85.52	85.52
CART	74.28	73.52	73.66	84.85	84.82	85.20
k-NN	71.82	71.86	72.62	84.69	84.64	84.58
Naïve Bayes	72.40	70.88	71.44	86.09	85.86	68.55
MLP	73.28	73.44	73.42	85.57	85.49	84.15
Random forests						76.60
Our method	**78.95** (± 2.62)					

Moreover, relying on a parallel processing strategy, time to run 20 trails with 5-fold cross validate taken by our method is only 4311 s (~72 min) while other methods must run several hours. This result highlights the efficiency in terms of running time of our method when filtering the redundant features.

6   Conclusion

In this paper, we focused on studying feature selection and Random Forest method. Features selection involves in determining the highest classifier accuracy of a subset or seeking the acceptable accuracy of the smallest subset of features. We have introduced a new feature selection approach based on feature scoring. The accuracy of classifier using the selected features is better than other methods. Fewer features allow a credit department to concentrate on collecting relevant and essential variables. The parallel processing procedure leads to a significant decrement in runtime. As a result, the workload of credit evaluation personnel can be reduced, as they do not have to take into account a large number of features during the evaluation procedure, which will be somewhat less computationally intensive. The experimental results show that our method is effective in credit risk analysis. It makes the evaluation more quickly and increases the accuracy of the classification.

References

1. Altman, E.I., Saunders, A.: Credit risk measurement: developments over the last 20 years. J. Bank. Finance **21**(11–12), 1721–1742 (1997)
2. Davoodabadi, Z., Moeini, A.: Building customers' credit scoring models with combination of feature selection and decision tree algorithms **4**(2), 97–103 (2015)
3. Khashman, A.: A neural network model for credit risk evaluation. Int. J. Neural Syst. **19**(4), 285–294 (2009)
4. Bellotti, T., Crook, J.: Support vector machines for credit scoring and discovery of significant features. Expert Syst. Appl. **36**(2), 3302–3308 (2009)
5. Wen, F., Yang, X.: Skewness of return distribution and coefficient of risk premium. J. Syst. Sci. Complexity **22**(3), 360–371 (2009)
6. Zhou, X., Jiang, W., Shi, Y., Tian, Y.: Credit risk evaluation with kernel-based affine subspace nearest points learning method. Expert Syst. Appl. **38**(4), 4272–4279 (2011)
7. Kim, G., Wu, C., Lim, S., Kim, J.: Modified matrix splitting method for the support vector machine and its application to the credit classification of companies in Korea. Expert Syst. Appl. **39**(10), 8824–8834 (2012)
8. Liu, H., Motoda, H.: Feature Selection for Knowledge Discovery and Data Mining. Kluwer Academic Publishers, Dordrecht (1998)
9. Guyon, I., Elisseeff, A.: An introduction to variable and feature selection. J. Mach. Learn. Res. **3**, 1157–1182 (2003)
10. Oreski, S., Oreski, D., Oreski, G.: Hybrid system with genetic algorithm and artificial neural networks and its application to retail credit risk assessment. Expert Syst. Appl. **39**(16), 12605–12617 (2012)
11. Saberi, M., Mirtalaie, M.S., Hussain, F.K., Azadeh, A., Hussain, O.K., Ashjari, B.: A granular computing-based approach to credit scoring modeling. Neurocomputing **122**, 100–115 (2013)
12. Lee, S., Choi, W.S.: A multi-industry bankruptcy prediction model using back-propagation neural network and multivariate discriminant analysis. Expert Syst. Appl. **40**(8), 2941–2946 (2013)
13. Ghatge, A.R., Halkarnikar, P.P.: Ensemble neural network strategy for predicting credit default evaluation **2**(7), 223–225 (2013)

14. Chaudhuri, A., De, K.: Fuzzy support vector machine for bankruptcy prediction. Appl. Soft Comput. J. **11**(2), 2472–2486 (2011)
15. Ghodselahi, A.: A hybrid support vector machine ensemble model for credit scoring. Int. J. Comput. Appl. **17**(5), 1–5 (2011)
16. Huang, L., Chen, C., Wang, J.: Credit scoring with a data mining approach based on support vector machines. Comput. J. Expert Syst. Appl. **33**(4), 847–856 (2007)
17. Eason, G., Li, S.T., Shiue, W., Huang, H.: The evaluation of consumer loans using support vector machines. Comput. J. Expert Syst. Appl. **30**(4), 772–782 (2006)
18. Martens, D., Baesens, B., Gestel, T., Vanthienen, J.: Comprehensible credit scoring models using rule extraction from support vector machines. Eur. Comput. J. Oper. Res. **183**(3), 1466–1476 (2007)
19. Wang, Y., Wang, S., Lai, K.: A new fuzzy support vector machine to evaluate credit risk. Comput. J. IEEE Trans. Fuzzy Syst. **13**(6), 25–29 (2005)
20. Oreski, S., Oreski, G.: Genetic algorithm-based heuristic for feature selection in credit risk assessment. Expert Syst. Appl. **41**(4), 2052–2064 (2014)
21. Ling, Y., Cao, Q.Y., Zhang, H.: Application of the PSO-SVM model for credit scoring. In: Proceedings of the 2011 7th International Conference on Computational Intelligent and Security, CIS 2011, pp. 47–51 (2011)
22. Liang, D., Tsai, C.-F., Wua, H.-T.: The effect of feature selection on financial distress prediction. Knowl. Based Syst. **73**, 289–297 (2015)

Joint Load Balancing and Coverage Optimizing Based on Tilt Adjusting in LTE Networks

Phan NhuQuan[1,2], Jiang Huilin[1], Bui ThiOanh[1], Li Pei[1], Pan Zhiwen[1(✉)], and Liu Nan[1]

[1] National Mobile Communications Research Laboratory, Southeast University, Nanjing 210096, Jiangsu, China
oanhbui918@gmail.com,
{nhuquan2410,huilin.jiang,lipei,pzw,nanliu}@seu.edu.cn
[2] Faculty of Mechatronics-Electronics, Lac Hong University, Bien Hoa City 810000, Vietnam

Abstract. The coverage optimization and Load Balancing (LB) for LTE networks based on adjusting Antenna Tilt Angle (ATA) of the cell are investigated. The network coverage is presented by the Coverage Factor (CF), which is defined as the ratio of the served user number to the total user number. The level of LB is evaluated by the Load Balancing Index (LBI). Both of the CF and the LBI are optimized by adjusting the tilt angle based on the Modified Particle Swarm Optimization (MPSO) algorithm. Simulation results show that the CF of our algorithm can obtain 98 %. The LBI, the network bandwidth efficiency and the system throughput are appreciably improved.

Keywords: Antenna Tilt Angle · Coverage Optimization · Modified Particle Swarm Optimization · Load Balancing

1 Introduction

Load Balancing (LB) and coverage optimization are two essential techniques in LTE networks to boost the user experience and improve the system performance [1–3]. Under traditional antenna configuration scheme without LB and coverage optimization, each cell is assigned a fixed antenna tilt and each user selects the cell with the highest received power as its serving cell [3]. On one hand, this may lead to unbalanced traffic load among the cells and hence congestion to the cells with large amount of users while the Physical Resource Blocks (PRB) in the cells with few users are not efficiently used; on the other hand, this may cause low coverage ratio due to the fixed antenna tilt. Furthermore, the LB optimization always force users to access the cells with large amounts of spare PRB, which may further harm the received signal quality of the users and degrades the coverage ratio of the network. Therefore, to efficiently use the network resource and guarantee the basic service of users, it is indispensable to jointly consider the LB and coverage optimization in the LTE networks.

© ICST Institute for Computer Sciences, Social Informatics and Telecommunications Engineering 2016
P.C. Vinh et al. (Eds.): ICTCC 2016, LNICST 168, pp. 143–152, 2016.
DOI: 10.1007/978-3-319-46909-6_14

LB has been extensively considered in literatures. In [4], LB problems through down-link power modification are formulated as game models. Using game theory, the LB problem is also studied in [5], where each cell independently makes decision on the volume of load to maximize its individual utility in an uncoordinated way. In [6], the traffic load was balanced by changing handover (HO) parameters considering the capacity available in the neighboring cells of the heavy load cell. In the aforementioned literatures, coverage problem caused by the LB was not taken into consideration, and only few people focus on jointly solving LB and coverage problem.

As stated in [3,7], the antenna tilt of cell plays an important role in reducing or expanding the coverage ratio of the cell, and also has a potential impact on LB. [1] proposed a joint down-link and up-link tilt-based coverage optimization scheme based on the sparse system knowledge to increase the cell edge user throughput while simultaneously decreasing the number of uncovered users. The authors of [8] optimized antenna tilt settings to improve the LB in terms of the quality of service and the user throughput. All the above works focused either on LB or on maximizing coverage ratio. How to jointly optimize the LB and coverage ratio through adjusting Antenna Tilt Angle (ATA) is still an open issue.

In our previous works [9,10], we concurrently adjusted ATA to optimize the coverage of the cell considering the network load. However, in area with very high user density, there may be many users with broken service in heavy load cell due to the lack of the resource, while the residual resources in the light load cell are under-used. Particularly, the boundary users may occupy many PRBs in the serving cell, leaving little resource to the new coming users thus results in a higher Call Blocking Rate (CBR). However, if only consider load conditions as the previous works stated without consideration of LB, the users with poorer channel conditions may suffer poor handover and occupy excessive resources in the target cell. Hence, the network resource is inefficiently used, a unbalanced load happens between cells, and Coverage Factor (CF) will be poor [10].

Different from our works in [9,10], in this paper, we jointly optimize LB and coverage. The CF must be guaranteed to be more than 90 % according to former study [10]. The main problems are how to adjust the ATA to jointly balance cell load and enlarge the cell coverage and how to avoid handover caused by boundary users with poorer channel conditions. To overcome these problems, we propose an effective ATA adjusting scheme by using the Modified Particle Swarm Optimization (MPSO) algorithm.

The paper is organized as follows: The system model and problem formulation is detailed in Sect. 2. The MPSO-based ATA adjusting algorithm is described in Sect. 3. Section 4 shows the simulation results and analysis, and conclusions are drawn in the final Section.

2   System Model and Problem Formulation

2.1   System Model

Consider a system consisting of N cells, M antennas and K users, in which cell is partitioned into three sectors each with one antenna. Assume the user selects the cell providing the strongest signal as its serving cell, received signals from the neighbor cells are considered as interferences.

2.2   Link Model

The antennas radiation pattern and path-loss are in accordance with the antenna model proposed by [11]. And the shadow fading is logarithmically distributed.

The received signal power of user j from antenna k of cell i is

$$p_{j,i,k} = P_i L_{j,i} s_j G_{j,i,k} (x_j, y_j, \varphi_{j,i}, \psi), \forall i \in N, j \in K, k \in M \tag{1}$$

where P_i is the transmit power of cell i, $L_{j,i}$ is the path-loss at user j from cell i, (x_j, y_j) are the geographical position coordinates of user j. ψ is the ATA k of cell i, s_j is position related shadow fading of user j, $G_{j,i,k}$ is the antenna gain at user j from antenna k of cell i in dBi, and $\varphi_{j,i}$ is the azimuth angle between user j and cell i.

The received signal to interference plus noise ratio of the user j served by antenna k of cell i is

$$\gamma_{j,i,k} = \frac{p_{j,i,k}}{\sum_{n_c} p_{j,n_c,k} + n_0}, \forall i \in N, j \in K, k \in M, n_c \in N_{\bar{i}} \tag{2}$$

where n_c represents all neighboring interfering cells of cell i, n_0 is the power of additive white Gaussian noise.

The user j will select cell i antenna k with the strongest received signal p as its serving cell. Then, the connection indication is as follows

$$u_{j,i,k} = \begin{cases} 1, & if\ (i,k) = \underset{(l,m)}{\arg\max}\, p_{j,l,m} | p_{j,l,m} > p_{thr} \\ 0, & otherwise\ (j \in K, i, l \in N, k, m \in M) \end{cases} \tag{3}$$

where p_{thr} is the threshold used to judge which cell and antenna are serving the user. $u_{j,i,k}$ equals 1 if the inequality condition can be satisfied i.e. user j connects to antenna k of cell i, otherwise equals 0.

The bandwidth efficiency of user j from antenna k of cell i is

$$e_{j,i,k} = \log_2 [1 + \gamma_{j,i,k}] \tag{4}$$

The amount of PRBs occupied by user j of cell i at the antenna k is

$$o_{j,i,k} = \frac{r_j}{e_{j,i,k} B_{PRB}} \tag{5}$$

where r_j is requirement data rate (expressed in bps) of user j, B_{PRB} is the bandwidth of each PRB.

The load caused by user j to cell i at antenna k is defined as

$$\rho_{j,i,k} = \frac{o_{j,i,k}}{N_{PRB}}, \forall i \in N, j \in K, k \in M \tag{6}$$

where N_{PRB} is the total number of PRBs of cell i.

Then, the load of cell i is as follows

$$\eta_i = \sum_{j \in K} u_{j,i,k} \rho_{j,i,k}, \forall i \in N, j \in K, k \in M \tag{7}$$

Assume the serving cell i has enough resource for its existing served users, then $\eta_i \leq 1$. The number of users being served by antenna k of cell i is then determined by

$$n_{i,k}^{\text{cov}} = \sum_{j=1}^{K} u_{j,i,k}, \forall i \in N, j \in K, k \in M \tag{8}$$

The CF is defined as the ratio of the total number of covered users to the sum of the number of users in the network.

$$C = \frac{n^{\text{cov}}}{K} \tag{9}$$

where, $n^{\text{cov}} = \sum_{i \in N, k \in M} n_{i,k}^{\text{cov}}$ is the total number of covered users in network.

The level of LB is evaluated through LBI Γ according to Jains fairness index [12] as follows

$$\Gamma = \frac{\left[\sum_{i \in N} \eta_i \right]^2}{|N| \left[\sum_{i \in N} \eta_i^2 \right]} \tag{10}$$

Γ ranges among $[1/N, 1]$. $\Gamma = 1$ denotes that all cells have equal load at time t. For LB, we aim to maximize Γ.

2.3 Problem Formulation

A multiple objectives function is constructed to maximize the LBI and guarantee the CF. Denote $\boldsymbol{\psi} = \{\psi_1, \psi_2, ..., \psi_M\}$ as the ATA set of the cells and ψ_k ($\forall k \in [1, M]$) is the ATA of antenna k. Then, the optimization problem can be formulated as

$$\max_{\boldsymbol{\psi}} \; f(\boldsymbol{\psi}) = \alpha C(\boldsymbol{\psi}) + \Gamma(\boldsymbol{\psi}),$$
$$s.t \begin{cases} \psi_{\min} < \boldsymbol{\psi} \leq \psi_{\max} \\ \eta_i(\boldsymbol{\psi}) \leq 1 \\ C(\boldsymbol{\psi}) \geq 0.9 \end{cases} \tag{11}$$

The goal is to jointly maximize the CF and the LBI through finding the optimal ATA set $\boldsymbol{\psi}$. The first constraint means the minimum and maximum values of ATA. Second constraint means load should be small enough for the new coming users. And the final constraint states that the CF must be guaranteed, which is defined according to results of [10]. The coefficient α is used to jointly maximize the CF and LBI.

3 Algorithm

The optimization problem is a non-convex one, which is complex to solve by computational efficient algorithms. Fortunately, taking the manifest non-linear and multimodal features of the solution into account, and considering the fast convergence of the MPSO algorithm, the optimization problem (11) can be solved by means of MPSO [13]. Therefore, an MPSO-based ATA adjusting algorithm is proposed.

In the MPSO based algorithm, a particle swarm known as a group of potential solution sets of ATA is available. Each particle characterizes a candidate solution to the joint optimization problem and corresponds to a fitness value calculated by the fitness function determined by the objective function of the optimization problem. All particles are evolved according to the evolution velocities known as the ATA adjusting scale calculated by the local experience of each particle and the global experience of the whole swarm. To be specific, in the MPSO based ATA adjustment algorithm, the ATA of the cells are adjusted according to the objective function value. First, a lot of ATA sets are initialized randomly, each of which corresponds to a fitness value according to the objective function. Then, all sets of ATA are updated in each iteration according to the past experience of the best utility of each ATA set and the global best utility of all ATA sets. Finally, the global best ATA set can be obtained by iteratively updating these initial ATA sets when achieving better fitness value.

Assume the particle swarm consists of p particles, i.e., p sets of ATA. Each particle $n \in \{1, 2, ..., p\}$ known as the n-th potential solution set of ATA is notated by $\boldsymbol{\psi}^n = \{\psi_1^n, \psi_2^n, ..., \psi_M^n\}$, where $\psi_k^n \in [\psi_{\min}, \psi_{\max}]$ $(\forall k \in [1, M])$ is the tilt angle of the antenna k in set n. The MPSO-based ATA adjusting algorithm consists of the following main steps:

Step 1. Initialization

Set the maximum number of the iteration times as $t_{\max}$ and the current iteration time t as $t = 0$. Initialize p ATA sets, i.e., $\boldsymbol{\psi}^1(t), \boldsymbol{\psi}^2(t), ..., and \boldsymbol{\psi}^p(t)$, randomly, and initialize p sets of ATA adjustment scale $\{\boldsymbol{v}^1(t), \boldsymbol{v}^2(t), ..., \boldsymbol{v}^p(t)\}$, where $\boldsymbol{v}^n = \{v_1^n, v_2^n, ..., v_M^n\}$ is the ATA adjustment scale set (known as evolution velocities) for ATA set $\boldsymbol{\psi}^n$. And $\alpha \in \{0.1, 0.2, ..., 1\}$. To avoid the newly generated ATA being far away from the feasible searching space, the adjustment scale v_k^n $(\forall k \in [1, M])$ for each ATA in the n-th solution is restricted within $[-\psi_{\max}, \psi_{\max}]$.

Then go to the iteration procedure of Step 2 to update the ATA and ATA adjustment scale.

Step 2. Iteration procedure of the algorithm

In this step, for any ATA set $\boldsymbol{\psi}^n(t)$ belonging to the member of ATA sets, the fitness value $f(\boldsymbol{\psi}^n)$ of each set $\boldsymbol{\psi}^n(t)$ is calculated according to the fitness function (11). Base on the constraint of cell load and the constraint of coverage, the best local ATA set experienced by the n-th potential solution at time t is

$$\boldsymbol{\psi}_s^n(t) = \operatorname*{argmax}_{\psi^n(\tau)} f^n(\boldsymbol{\psi}^n(\tau)),$$

$$\forall \tau \in \{0, 1, ..., t\}, \eta_i(\boldsymbol{\psi}_k^n) \leq 1, C(\boldsymbol{\psi}_k^n) \geq 0.9 \tag{12}$$

which is the best ATA set corresponding to the so far obtained maximum value of the joint optimization problem (11) of CF C and LBI Γ for potential solution ψ^n before time t. The global best ATA set is

$$\boldsymbol{\psi}_g(t) = \operatorname*{arg\,max}_{\psi_s^n(t)} f(\boldsymbol{\psi}_s^n(t)),$$

$$\forall n \in [1, p], \eta_i(\boldsymbol{\psi}_k^n) \leq 1, C(\boldsymbol{\psi}_k^n) \geq 0.9 \tag{13}$$

which corresponds to the best ATA set obtained so far for all sets of ATA with the constraint of cell load and constraint of CF. Then update the ATA adjustment scale for a typical set $\boldsymbol{v}^n$ and the ATA set $\boldsymbol{\psi}^n$ according to

$$\boldsymbol{v}^n(t+1) = \Omega(t)\,\boldsymbol{v}^n(t) + c_1\xi\,[\boldsymbol{\psi}_s^n(t) - \boldsymbol{\psi}^n(t)]$$
$$+ c_2\chi\,[\boldsymbol{\psi}_g(t) - \boldsymbol{\psi}^n(t)]\,, \tag{14}$$

$$\boldsymbol{\psi}^n(t+1) = \boldsymbol{\psi}^n(t) + \boldsymbol{v}^n(t+1) \tag{15}$$

where $\Omega \in [\Omega_{\min}, \Omega_{\max}]$ is the inertia weight that can control the impact of the last velocity on the current velocity, and is set as

$$\Omega = \Omega_{\max} - \frac{t(\Omega_{\max} - \Omega_{\min})}{t_{\max}}. \tag{16}$$

According to the experimental studies, $\Omega_{\min} = 0.4$ and $\Omega_{\max} = 1$. The acceleration coefficients c_1 and c_2 together with the parameters ξ and χ will judge the sense of the variation of the velocity, with the empirical studies, c_1 and c_2 are taken 1.49, and ξ and χ are arbitrary within $[0, 1]$ [14].

This update procedure is repeated in each iteration cycle. In case the serving cell does not satisfy the CF, i.e., the remainder PRB of serving cell is not enough or the CF is less than 0.9, consider the adjacent cell offload through repeating the calculation of the ATA set $\boldsymbol{\psi}_s^n(t)$ until the load and CF constraints can be satisfied.

Step 3. Output optimization results

When the maximum number of iterations is satisfied, stop the algorithm and set the ATA of the cells according to the global best $\boldsymbol{\psi}_g(t)$. Then the value of fitness function $f(\boldsymbol{\psi}_g)$ can be calculated according to the objective function in (11). Finally, record the global best ATA set $\boldsymbol{\psi} = \boldsymbol{\psi}^n(t+1)$ and the corresponding maximum value $f(\boldsymbol{\psi})$ of the objective function.

4   Simulation Results and Analysis

Figure 1 presents the system with 7 cells (the green triangles located in the heart of the hexagons represent the base stations) under cell layout in three sectors, and the users (red dots) are generated according to Poisson process, with arrival rate λ. To differentiate load of cells we chose cell 1 as the heavy load one with arrival rate $0.8user/second$, stepped by $0.3user/second$, and $0.4user/second$ for other ones. All users have the same requirement data rate (100 kbps). The azimuth angle is kept fixed, but the ATA can be adjusted. The system simulation parameters are in accordance with 3 GPP standard [11]. The transmit power of cell is 46 dBm, the system bandwidth is 10 MHz, the minimum and maximum of antenna elevation angle are 0 and 16 degree, respectively, and the received signal threshold is -107 dBm.

Figure 2 shows that, the algorithm needs few iteration times to obtain the global optimum. The computational complexity of the solution is polynomial. The MPSO algorithm for Joint Coverage Factor Optimization and Load Balancing Index (JCFLB) is slightly delayed compared to LB in its convergence, because in JCFLB both CF and LB are considered.

The effect of α on the CBR is shown in Fig. 3. The CBR decreases as the value of α increases until 0.9. A larger α means that we put more weight on CF, thus more users in cell 1 are served. The CBR of $\alpha = 1$ is larger than that of $\alpha = 0.9$, which means that handover users for LB alone with no consideration of CF will switch improper users to other cells, and may consume too many resources in target cells thus resulting in a higher CBR.

The effect of α on LBI is shown in Fig. 4. One can observe that the LBI increases continuously with α. Comparing Fig. 4 with Fig. 3 when $\alpha = 1$, we can find that a larger LBI does not bring a lower CBR. According to the above results we can see that when $\alpha = 0.9$, the CBR is lowest and the LBI achieves about 1. Therefore, we select $\alpha = 0.9$ for the below simulations.

The LBI vs. λ of cell 1 is illustrated in Fig. 5. One can observe that the LBI of LB decreases continuously with the increase of λ. It is because that the extent of load unbalance depends on λ when users keeping in different cells follows the same distribution. A bigger λ of cell 1 brings a less balanced load distribution of the network. One can observe the LBI of JCFLB is the biggest. In our proposed

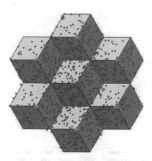

Fig. 1. System model (Color figure online)

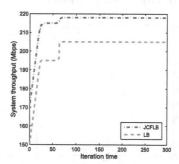

Fig. 2. Convergence of algorithm

algorithm, the LBI is close to 1 at all times, which indicates that JCFLB can achieve a significantly better LBI compared to that of LB.

The average network loads of LB and JCFLB for different λ are illustrated in Fig. 6. A bigger λ means more users appear, thus in both cases, average network load increases with λ of cell 1. Since handover users for LB unavoidably need more resource occupation in target cells, the average network load of JCFLB are

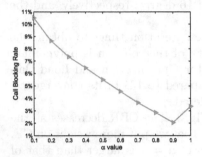

Fig. 3. Effect of α on Call Blocking Rate

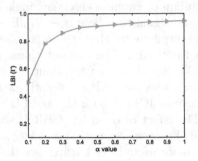

Fig. 4. Effect of α on LBI Γ

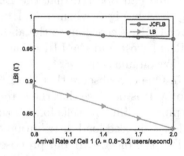

Fig. 5. Load Balancing Index

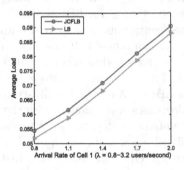

Fig. 6. Average Load of the system

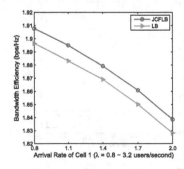

Fig. 7. Bandwidth Efficiency

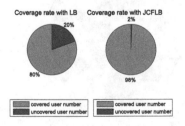

Fig. 8. Coverage Factor

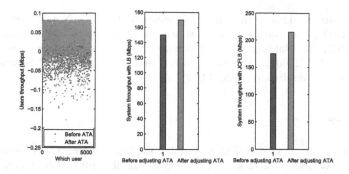

Fig. 9. System throughput

larger than that of just LB. However, JCFLB needs less resource in cell 1 than LB with all λ, which is the benefit when using JCFLB.

The network Bandwidth Efficiency (BE) of JCFLB and LB is shown in Fig. 7. One can observe that for all λ, JCFLB has larger BE than that of LB. The reason is that for a handover user, the channel condition in its neighboring cells may be worse than that in its original cell, which means the handover for LB will decrease BE. Moreover, we can see the BE of JCFLB and LB all decrease continuously as λ of cell 1 increases. It is reasonable that a bigger λ brings more users and a larger opportunity of switching users for LB, which may result in lower BE.

The coverage ability of the cell represented by the CF is optimized and obtains 98 % by using JCFLB (Fig. 8). It is reasonable that, when we optimize LB only, a large amount of improper users with poor channel condition are forced to connect to the neighboring light load cell with abundant residual resource while the signal quality cannot be guaranteed which deteriorates the CF of LB only. This brings the higher CF of the proposed JCFLB.

The users throughput and system throughput is illustrated in Fig. 9. One can observe that the JCFLB scheme shows significantly better performance than the LB only.

5   Conclusions

In this paper, we jointly consider the CF and LBI optimization in LTE networks. We formulate the problem as a multi-objective optimization problem, and an MPSO algorithm based adjusting ATAs scheme is proposed. Simulation results show that our algorithm can efficiently increase the network coverage. This significantly improves the load balancing, and appreciably increases the network bandwidth efficiency. Also, the system throughput is considerably improved. In this work, we only consider the down-link transmission of the LTE cellular systems. But in the practical system, the down-link and up-link interference scenarios are fundamentally different. Both the up-link and down-link will be considered in the future works.

Acknowledgment. This work is partially supported by the National 863 Program (2014AA01A702), the National Basic Research Program of China (973 Program 2012CB316004), the National Natural Science Foundation of China under Grants (61571123) and (61221002), Qing Lan Project, and the Fundamental Research Funds for the Central Universities (CXLX13 093).

References

1. Berger, S., et al.: Joint downlink and uplink tilt-based self-organization of coverage and capacity under sparse system knowledge. IEEE Trans. Veh. Technol. (2015). Accepted
2. Wang, H., et al.: A unified algorithm for mobility load balancing in 3GPP LTE multi-cell networks. Sci. China Inf. Sci. **56**(2), 1–11 (2013)
3. Partov, B., Leith, D.J., Razavi, R.: Utility fair optimization of antenna tilt angles in LTE networks. IEEE/ACM Trans. Netw. **23**(1), 175–185 (2015)
4. Awada, A., et al.: A game-theoretic approach to load balancing in cellular radio networks. In: 2010 IEEE 21st International Symposium on Personal Indoor and Mobile Radio Communications (PIMRC), pp. 1184–1189 (2010)
5. Hao, H., et al.: Game theory based load balancing in self-optimizing wireless networks. In: 2nd International Conference on Computer and Automation Engineering (ICCAE), pp. 415–418 (2010)
6. Kwan, R., et al.: Balancing, on mobility load for LTE systems. In: IEEE 72nd Vehicular Technology Conference Fall (VTC 2010-Fall), pp. 1–5 (2010)
7. Bratu, V., Beckman, C.: Base station antenna tilt for load balancing. In: 7th European Conference on Antennas and Propagation (EuCAP), pp. 2039–2043 (2013)
8. Fehske, A.J., et al.: Concurrent load-aware adjustment of user association and antenna tilts in self-organizing radio networks. IEEE Trans. Veh. Technol. **62**(5), 1974–1988 (2013)
9. NhuQuan, P., Huilin, J., ThiOanh, B., et al.: A modified particle swarm optimization based antenna tilt angle adjusting scheme for LTE coverage optimization. J. SE Univ. **31**(4), 443–449 (2015)
10. NhuQuan, P., ThiOanh, B., Huilin, J.: Coverage optimization of LTE networks based on ATA adjusting considering network load. J. China Commun. (2015). Accepted
11. 3GPP TR 36.814 V9.0.0, Further advancements for E-UTRA physical layer aspects, release 9 (2010)
12. Sediq, A.B., et al.: Optimal tradeoff between sum-rate efficiency and Jain's fairness index in resource allocation. IEEE Trans. Wirel. Commun. **12**(7), 3496–3509 (2013)
13. Qinghai, B.: Analysis of particle swarm optimization algorithm. Comput. Inf. Sci. **3**(1), 180–184 (2010)
14. Jiang, H., et al.: A power adjustment based eICIC algorithm for hyper-dense HetNets considering the alteration of user association. Sci. China Inf. Sci. **58**(8), 1–15 (2015)

Resource-Bounded Context-Aware Applications: A Survey and Early Experiment

Ijaz Uddin[1], Hafiz Mahfooz Ul Haque[1], Abdur Rakib[1(✉)],
and Mohamad Rafi Segi Rahmat[2]

[1] School of Computer Science, The University of Nottingham,
Malaysia Campus, Semenyih, Malaysia
{khyx4iui,khyx2hma,abdur.rakib}@nottingham.edu.my
[2] School of Applied Mathematics, The University of Nottingham,
Malaysia Campus, Semenyih, Malaysia
mohd.rafi@nottingham.edu.my

Abstract. The recent advancement of mobile computing technology and smartphones have changed the way we live, communicate, interact, and understand the world. Smartphones have various salient features that make them promising system platforms for the development of context-aware applications, e.g., embedded sensors in smartphones make them more convenient to be used for making context-rich information available to applications. Although the state of the art development of smartphones has endued developers to build advanced context-aware applications, many challenges still remain. Those are mostly due to the limited resources available in the mobile devices including computational and communication resources. This paper surveys the recent advances in context-aware applications in mobile platforms, and proposes a decentralized context-aware computing model that makes use of the smartphone platform, a P2P communication model, and declarative rule-based programming.

Keywords: Context-aware · Resource-bounds · Rule-based reasoning · Distributed reasoning · Android SDK

1 Introduction

The rapid growth of the cell phones across the world creates a platform for new computing systems. Within a decade the basic idea of cell phones has changed from a mobile phone towards a smartphone. Smartphones are capable to assist us in our daily routine tasks as well as providing basic communication features and connections to the wide services of the internet [3]. The exponential growth of smartphone products, softwares and communication ease have a tremendous effect on human lives. People use smart technology to connect and share experiences with each other including social networking, VoIP and other freely available messaging and call services [23].

© ICST Institute for Computer Sciences, Social Informatics and Telecommunications Engineering 2016
P.C. Vinh et al. (Eds.): ICTCC 2016, LNICST 168, pp. 153–164, 2016.
DOI: 10.1007/978-3-319-46909-6_15

In recent years, smartphones are equipped with wide range of sensors. For example, the global positioning system (GPS), shake sensors, accelerometers, proximity sensors are now basic sensors to be found on such devices [13]. These kind of sensing devices generate enough information about the users, such as location, time, movement, and so on. That is, such devices and technologies could be used to sense the surrounding environment of a user, acquire user's contexts and act accordingly. While a suitable communication mechanism would help to enrich the user interaction with the application and between these devices [16]. In principle, context-aware computing systems which include multiple interacting devices and human users can often be usefully modelled as multi-agent systems. Non-human agents in such a system may be running a very simple program, however they are increasingly designed to exhibit flexible, adaptable and intelligent behaviour. A common methodology for implementing the latter type of agents is implementing them as rule-based reasoners. In the literature, ontology-based context-modeling and rule-based reasoning have already been used in the field of context-aware systems [6,8]. In previous work [18,20], we have shown that ontological approach is a good way for modeling context-aware systems, and it allows us to model context-aware systems as rule-based agents. In [18], we developed a logical model for resource-bounded context-aware multi-agent systems which handles inconsistent context information using non-monotonic reasoning, but we have not explored the practical implementation yet. Rule-based systems and traditional rule engines have found significant application in practice, though mostly for desktop environment where the resources are abundantly available compared to smartphone devices. The main issue with those engines is that they cannot be easily used on smartphones or resource bounded devices due to platform differences and different hardware profiles. Some rule engines, which are discussed in Sect. 4, have already been tested for porting into mobile environment but the results were not satisfactory or the porting were only partially successful. In view of the above, there is a need to develop a decentralized context-aware computing model that makes use of the smartphone platform, a suitable communication model and declarative rule-based programming as a preferred development language. By developing a pure smartphone compatible context-aware framework, any kind of domain specific context-aware applications can be developed, e.g., elder care system, hospital critical situation, traffic control and office security, among others.

The remainder of the paper is organized as follows. In Sect. 2, we briefly introduce context-aware computing and its limitations and challenges in resource-constrained settings. Section 3 presents a brief survey on general theoretical context aware resource bounded frameworks, while Sect. 4 focuses on discussing Android based theoretical and ported context aware frameworks. Section 5 presents the proposed solution which includes a framework design for a specific platform, a communication model along with a proposed Android based application for context-aware programming. Section 6 concludes and discusses some suggestions for future work.

2   Context-Aware Computing: Limitations and Challenges

In a survey [14], it has been revealed that many definitions of *context* in different views exist. According to Dey et al. [2]: *"Context is any information that can be used to characterize the situation of an entity. An entity is a person, place, or object that is considered relevant to the interaction between a user and an application, including the user and applications themselves"*. In the same paper context-aware is defined as, *"A system is context-aware if it uses context to provide relevant information and/or services to the user, where relevancy depends on the user's task"*. Context can be further specified by its entities [24]. For example, a person's context entities can be his identity, location, mood and his surrounding, among others. The context-aware computing emerged in early 1990s when small mobile devices were introduced. In 1992, Olivetti Labs active badges used the infrared badger assigned to staff members for tracing their locations in office and according to the locations calls were forwarded [27]. Further developments in the context-aware systems lead to the development of various frameworks to support such systems including for example Georgia Tech's Context Toolkit [21]. In recent years, more research has been carried out and advanced context-aware systems exist [4], and the contributions to research and development over the years promise a bright future of such systems. Although various context-aware frameworks have been developed over the years, however, their functions remain primitive. This is because these systems are more complex due to the mechanism for sensing and reasoning about contextual information and their changes over time, and they often run on tiny resource-bounded devices in highly dynamic environments. Many challenges might arise when these context-aware devices perform computation to infer implicit contexts from a set of given explicit contexts and reasoning rules, and perhaps exchange information via messages. We list some constraints those often arise while designing and developing context-aware systems.

- **Space constraint:** The memory space available for storing contexts is often limited on most of the mobile devices. These devices usually are not privileged to store all the contexts acquired by itself or received via interaction with other agents.
- **Communication constraint:** Context-aware devices often acquire contextual information from other smart devices via messages. These devices communicate among themselves in a highly dynamic environment, they exchange information via message which causes quick reduction of the battery energy level. And most of the smart devices are not specifically designed to support this feature due to battery power constraints.
- **Time constraint:** Mobile devices often have limited computational power and simultaneous execution of multiple programs make this process more slower.

Due to the above constraints, execution of some applications on smart mobile devices may be impossible or may not be able to produce expected behavior, execution of some applications may need more energy or space than available in a mobile device.

3 Context-Aware Resource-Bounded Frameworks

Recent developments in the field of context-aware systems have led to a renewed interest in probing different approaches in developing different kinds of context models and reasoning techniques, which heightened the significance of the applications used by different resource-bounded mobile devices. In the literature [5,6,8,17], several approaches have been proposed for context modeling and reasoning techniques considering specific architectures and home health monitoring as an exemplar system. In [5], a ontology-based context management (GCoM) model is presented to facilitate context modeling and reasoning considering (user defined and ontological) rules and their semantics. This context modeling approach shows how a context can be acquired, manipulated, stored and expressed. This model is designed for dynamicity and re-usability in different domains where resource limitation is a crucial issue.

The authors in [8] present an ontology based programming framework for rapid prototyping of context-aware application development. The design goal of the authors is to support a wide user's category and cooperation and collaboration in the applications development. The framework further emphasizes that being a collaborative environment, users have to agree on shared conceptualization of the domain. The authors also targeted three categories of users based on their technical abilities into High level, Middle level, and Low level users who can use the framework in different environment. The main components of the framework are context providers, the context manager, programming toolkits and the resource sharing server. The framework although has various options to cater users from diverse technical skills, however the use of resource sharing server suggests limitation on distributed approach, and also the Android limitations demands a more compact and Android compatible framework.

In [17], an ontology-based framework has been presented to show how context-aware systems can be modeled as resource-bounded rule-based systems using OWL 2 RL and Semantic Web Rule Language (SWRL). Emphasize is given in the distributed problem-solving for the systems of communicating context-aware rule-based agents and specify bounds on time and number of messages exchanged to derive a goal. However, memory bound was not considered. Memory requirement is an important factor for reasoning because context-aware systems often run on resource limited devices. In [20], a logical framework $\mathcal{L}_{\mathcal{OCRS}}$ is presented for modeling and verifying context-aware multi-agent systems where agents reason using ontology-driven first order horn clause rules. In this model, authors have considered space requirement for reasoning in addition to time and communication resources. This work is based on monotonic reasoning where beliefs of an agent cannot be revised based on some contradictory evidence.

To some extent we believe that inconsistency may occur in the agent's memory and context-aware agents take decisions based on the available information that may become unreliable at certain circumstances. To overcome this issue, another framework [18] has been proposed for resource-bounded context-aware multi-agent systems which handles inconsistent context information using non-monotonic reasoning. The resulting logic $\mathcal{L}_{DROCS}$ allows a system designer to describe a set of rule-based non-monotonic context-aware agents with bounds on space and communication resources. In [19], it has been shown how to state various qualitative and quantitative properties of resource-bounded context-aware systems and formally verify resource requirements of such systems using model checking techniques.

Although the works discussed above make novel attempts to improve modeling resource-bounded context-aware systems, however the practical implementation has not yet been studied in depth.

4   Context-Aware Rule-Based Frameworks for Mobile Devices

There are quite a few frameworks that are specifically designed for the context-aware resource-bounded devices. The authors of [11] argue that there does not exist any comprehensive design and development tool which covers all the aspects of context aware applications in mobile platform including e.g., methodology, language, inference engine and communication protocols. They further state that such development environment is essential and will benefit both the researchers and developers. In an attempt to address some of these issues researchers tried to port the existing desktop based framework into mobile platform, e.g., in [22] authors proposed to port the JADE framework to Android, however still it is an ongoing project. Another attempt to port JADE in Android system by extending the JADE agent classes also shares the same problem of an earlier attempt [26] that it is not purely distributed and services are provided by a server which acts as a back end while the mobile devices act as the front end of the platform. From the development point of view, a general purpose programming language such as Python, is widely used among the complicated system development languages. The reason to mention Python is that there is a tool available which can convert a Python code into Android or its equivalent of iOS code. Although it works well at the basic code level, things get complex when a user wants access to program the internal hardware or sensors of the Android device. In order to make it works, there is a three step turn around required which will make it possible to use the sensors of the devices and it is out of the scope to be discussed here which also makes it least desirable as when new sensors are available their support may not be readily available. Some researchers tried to develop android based frameworks as discussed in [28] which provides a mechanism based on expression for Android. An expression is a Boolean, in which axioms are the context condition on the context entities. Although the work is based on the Android framework, the framework doesn't have its own language. Furthermore,

instead of reasoning, various scenarios are monitored using the evaluators (==
, >=, >, <, <==, regular expression, distance). The authors intend to provide
distributed environment compatibility in their future work.

Based on the literature, there does not exist any platform specific framework
where it is completely Android compatible. In all of the above mentioned frameworks, one has to use the traditional desktop computers for agent programming
and then agents are made Android compatible. One such (Prolog based) project
is also an ongoing research work called HeaRT [25], which is also in its early development stage and needs effort and time to see the product quality. Although the
rule text representation is written in Prolog code, the author intends to change
it and makes its own parser and semantic analyzer for writing rules in its own
language.

5   Proposed Context-Aware Application Framework

To the best of our knowledge, various theoretical rule-based context-aware
resource-bounded frameworks are available and some of them are discussed
above, however so far they have not been implemented, tested or deployed.
Nevertheless, there are some frameworks available that are ported from desktop to the Android framework where usability cannot be guaranteed, as they
have problems associated with the frameworks' differences. They may be able
to facilitate the currently available device sensors and architecture but in the
future if the Android architecture design changes or new sensors are added then
a user has to wait for the support to be available for the ported frameworks.

Based on the literature studied, we propose that there should be an independent framework for resource-bounded devices, which may not depend on the
traditional desktop computers from any aspects. A user may be able to develop
an agent on a device and run it on the device itself. The next sections further
elaborate our idea and the proposed implementation framework, communication
model and the application.

5.1   Intended Implementation Platform

In order to make a purely resource-bounded context-aware framework imple-
mentable, a specific platform from the leading platforms may be targeted. The
state of the art available platforms are Android, iOS, Windows mobile, Black
Berry and Symbian, among others. The frameworks used for the rule-based systems, to name some, are JADE, JARE JESS [15] and many more use platform
independent Java for their frameworks and implementation. These also add the
power of the Java programming into their rule-based platform. The downside of
using Oracle Java is that it has some compatibility issues with the smart devices
platforms such as Android or iOS which have their own development tools. The
main language for Android development is using Google implementation of Java
using the Android Software Development Kit (SDK) and the Android Studio.
There are differences between Java programming for desktop systems and Java

programming for the Android systems. As for the Java, the syntax of the language remains the same. The basic difference lies between their low level machine code generations. The desktop systems use JVM to translate Java code into machine understandable code or byte code while in Android system the applications are executed using the Dalvik Virtual Machine (DVM). DVM is a compact VM and is used in resource-bounded devices including cell phones, smart TVs and tablets, and is used to run programs on resource-bounded devices [9]. The Java language that can be used for Android does not support all the classes of Java as it has been optimized for the use with the resource bounded devices, so the obvious choice left is to use the Google Android SDK to program any application or software for the Android framework. Besides the focus of this study is for the resource bounded devices and the Android itself is made up resource bounded device and its programming is mainly done using the Google Android SDK, which can be used over Eclipse IDE or directly from the Google provided Android studio which is Officially supported by Google. According to a survey from Business Insider, the Google Android has the major user base as of 2015 report [1]. We chose the Google Android SDK to implement resource-bounded context-aware applications, however this choice does not restrict the research objective to Android only, and in the future we aim to develop a context-aware implementation framework that can be used to run application programs on multiple platforms seamlessly.

5.2   Proposed Communication Protocol: P2P

Since majority of the smart devices are wireless, there is also a need for efficient communication between devices whenever they interact with one another. Keeping in view the distributed scenario, one of the suitable protocols according to our proposed solution is Peer-to-Peer (P2P) protocol [12]. The P2P communication is a famous protocol widely available on the internet specially in the file sharing software like BitTorrent, Amule and Skype, among others. Skype uses it for their communication purpose with a slight changes. The P2P protocol is designed on the bases to provide a communication model without using any centralized server or computer, hence it is a natural fit for a distributed communication model where no central command is desired.

5.2.1   Open Peer

Open Peer is an open P2P signalling protocol. It is available for the Android as well as iOS platform. It lets the user find their peers by using various methods which include but not limited to social network websites, phone numbers, email ID and other ID authorization. It allows to communicate between two domains which are not on the same platform after providing strong identity validation. The communication mechanism is very secure and privacy is maintained. The open peer is designed to be stable on domains with high load of data. This protocol can use the signalling protocol in both encrypted and unencrypted formats. A message can be sent by any means of HTTPS/MLS/TLS/Message/RUDP/UDP or SCP protocols. Each request type must have its own ID and method of invocation and the same is for reply to include the sender ID. Another protocol that can be used for the same reason is Wifi-Peer to Peer, which provides almost all the functionalities that a standard protocol provides.

5.3   An Android-Based Context-Aware Application Example

The proposed solution is being developed for a complex context-aware application using the Google Android SDK, where smart devices sense the surrounding environments to acquire low level contexts and infer high level contexts based on the rules which are derived from a smart environment ontology domain [18,19]. In this system design, a number of agents (devices) have been considered which behave according to the use of the current contexts. The system is being implemented and run on smart devices and act as a dedicated system based on customized features. The communication among devices in based on messages passing and they exchange only facts (contexts). The application relies on rule-based systems where rules are distributed in a customized way and they don't change during execution. Each device has capability to produce implicit contextual information (derived facts) from given (or sensed) contexts. The core components of the application are elaborated in the following sections.

5.3.1   Internal Development Mechanism

The proposed model is based on the previous work [19], agents are programmed using defeasible rules and they use defeasible reasoning technique to infer implicit contextual information from given (or sensed) explicit contexts. The execution of rules accuracy also depends on the designer of rules, as rules have priority and the priorities are set by the domain expert. The proposed model is distributed, and every device acts as a module (see Fig. 1). We modularize the rule base for two reasons: (i) to reduce the amount of rules to be searched, and (ii) to make the rules specific to the role of a user e.g., patient or a doctor.

In order to load the initial facts the agents has pre-loaded facts in its static memory which cannot be changed. As these facts are the pre requisites for an agent to start its activity. As the agents are believed to have its inference so it will generate new facts from its inference and will store them accordingly. For that reason the dynamic memory

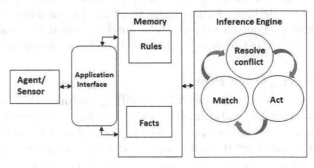

Fig. 1. System overview (single agent's perspective)

is used which can be changed as required by the agent itself. But keeping the resources minimum, the dynamic memory is also limited and some facts can be stored. To overcome the problem of storing newly derived facts the logical model uses a mechanism to overwrite existing facts in two condition: (i) only if the memory is full to store new facts, and (ii) when a contradictory context arrives in the memory [19]. In the first case if there is no contradictory context residing in the memory, it will randomly overwrite any memory slot to store the newly derived context. While in the second case even if the memory is not full, it will check first for any contradictory context, if there exists a contradictory context it will be replaced with the new context.

It is pertinent to mention that in resource bounded devices where memory space is at a premium, the well known pattern matching RETE algorithm [7] may not be a good choice while implementing rule engines [10]. In our prototype implementation, the rules of an agent are logically divided into two categories, the rules that are fired frequently are stored separately from those which are fired rarely. The rarely fired rules are gathered by using a counter with every rule, if a rule counter increases frequently it will be stored in the frequently fired rules category. And the rules with very low counter rate can be stored in the simple rule set. Threshold cannot be determined as the frequency may vary from role to role and device to device. Instead, the difference is based on the counters associated with the rules. The reason for this division is to restrict the rule engine to traverse the rules which are more likely to fire, saving time in computation, and memory space.

5.4   The User Interface

The prototype of Android based experimental results are shown in Fig. 2. These user interfaces reflect the system behavior based on the set of horn-clause rules

Fig. 2. Proposed application interfaces

distributed to the agents. As all the above mechanisms are running in the background, a good interface is as important as the code efficiency. We have developed an Android prototype that upon start ask for the role of either a doctor or a patient. Upon choosing one it will install the rules associated with the role selected and proceed accordingly. The step by step snapshots are provided in Fig. 2. The end product would be flexible enough to implement intelligent behaviour and at the same time this would work efficiently with limited processing power and on memory bounded devices. Hence, the proposed system is first verified using formal verification techniques before its implementation.

6   Conclusions

In this paper, we surveyed context-aware resource-bounded frameworks from both theoretical and practical points of view. The survey shows that purely Android platform based context-aware resource-bounded frameworks are not available yet. We propose a concrete Android platform based solution for context-aware resource-bounded systems, which makes use of the smartphone platform, a P2P communication model and rule-based programming language. In the future work, we will study the social impacts of state-of-the-art prototypes, which will be tailored to the specific needs of exploration of state-of-the art technologies to improve human lives; and particularly be suitable for development of systems for smart spaces.

References

1. Android is the world's largest mobile platform but it has to overcome these massive hurdles to keep the lead - business insider, October 2015. http://www. businessinsider.my/how-android-is-biggest-mobile-platform-ecosystem-google/? r=US&IR=T#uuUfWCcZ8WDUhJTg.97
2. Abowd, G.D., Dey, A.K., Brown, P.J., Davies, N., Smith, M., Steggles, P.: Towards a better understanding of context and context-awareness. In: Gellersen, H.-W. (ed.) HUC 1999. LNCS, vol. 1707, pp. 304–307. Springer, Heidelberg (1999). doi:10. 1007/3-540-48157-5_29
3. Ballagas, R., Borchers, J., Rohs, M., Sheridan, J.G.: The smart phone: a ubiquitous input device. IEEE Pervasive Comput. 5(1), 70–77 (2006)
4. Bardram, J.E., Nørskov, N.: A context-aware patient safety system for the operating room. In: Proceedings of the 10th International Conference on Ubiquitous Computing, pp. 272–281 (2008)
5. Ejigu, D., Scuturici, M., Brunie, L.: An ontology-based approach to context modeling and reasoning in pervasive computing. In: Fifth Annual IEEE International Conference on Pervasive Computing and Communications Workshops, PerCom Workshops 2007, pp. 14–19. IEEE (2007)
6. Esposito, A., Tarricone, L., Zappatore, M., Catarinucci, L., Colella, R., DiBari, A.: A framework for context-aware home-health monitoring. In: Sandnes, F.E., Zhang, Y., Rong, C., Yang, L.T., Ma, J. (eds.) UIC 2008. LNCS, vol. 5061, pp. 119–130. Springer, Heidelberg (2008). doi:10.1007/978-3-540-69293-5_11

7. Forgy, C.L.: Rete: a fast algorithm for the many pattern/many object pattern match problem. Artif. Intell. **19**(1), 17–37 (1982)
8. Guo, B., Zhang, D., Imai, M.: Toward a cooperative programming framework for context-aware applications. Pers. Ubiquit. Comput. **15**(3), 221–233 (2011)
9. Jackson, W.: Android Apps for Absolute Beginners, 3rd edn. Apress, Berkeley (2014). ISBN13: 978-1-484200-20-9
10. Kim, M., Lee, K., Kim, Y., Kim, T., Lee, Y., Cho, S., Lee, C.G.: Rete-adh: an improvement to rete for composite context-aware service. Int. J. Distrib. Sens. Netw. **2014**, 1–11 (2014)
11. Nalepa, G.J., Bobek, S.: Rule-based solution for context-aware reasoning on mobile devices. Comput. Sci. Inf. Syst. **11**(1), 171–193 (2014)
12. Park, H., Izhak-Ratzin, R., van der Schaar, M.: Peer-to-peer networks - protocols, cooperation and competition. In: Streaming Media Architectures, Techniques, and Applications: Recent Advances. IGI Global (2010)
13. Pei, C., Guo, H., Yang, X., Wang, Y., Zhang, X., Ye, H.: Sensors in smart phone. In: Li, D., Liu, Y., Chen, Y. (eds.) CCTA 2010, Part II. IFIP AICT, vol. 345, pp. 491–495. Springer, Heidelberg (2011). doi:10.1007/978-3-642-18336-2_59
14. Perera, C., Zaslavsky, A.B., Christen, P., Georgakopoulos, D.: Context aware computing for the internet of things: a survey. IEEE Commun. Surv. Tutorials **16**(1), 414–454 (2014)
15. Petcu, D., Petcu, M.: Distributed jess on a condor pool. In: Proceedings of the 9th WSEAS International Conference on Computers, pp. 1–5 (2005)
16. Raento, M., Oulasvirta, A., Petit, R., Toivonen, H.: Contextphone: a prototyping platform for context-aware mobile applications. IEEE Pervasive Comput. **4**(2), 51–59 (2005)
17. Rakib, A., Faruqui, R.U.: A formal approach to modelling and verifying resource-bounded context-aware agents. In: Vinh, P.C., Hung, N.M., Tung, N.T., Suzuki, J. (eds.) ICCASA 2012. LNICST, vol. 109, pp. 86–96. Springer, Heidelberg (2013). doi:10.1007/978-3-642-36642-0_9
18. Rakib, A., Haque, H.M.U.: A logic for context-aware non-monotonic reasoning agents. In: Gelbukh, A., Espinoza, F.C., Galicia-Haro, S.N. (eds.) MICAI 2014, Part I. LNCS (LNAI), vol. 8856, pp. 453–471. Springer, Heidelberg (2014). doi:10.1007/978-3-319-13647-9_41
19. Rakib, A., Haque, H.M.U.: Modeling and verifying context-aware non-monotonic reasoning agents. In: Proceedings of the 13th ACM-IEEE International Conference on Formal Methods and Models for System Design, pp. 453–471. IEEE (2015)
20. Rakib, A., Ul Haque, H.M., Faruqui, R.U.: A temporal description logic for resource-bounded rule-based context-aware agents. In: Vinh, P.C., Alagar, V., Vassev, E., Khare, A. (eds.) ICCASA 2013. LNICST, vol. 128, pp. 3–14. Springer, Heidelberg (2014). doi:10.1007/978-3-319-05939-6_1
21. Salber, D., Dey, A.K., Abowd, G.D.: The context toolkit: Aiding the development of context-enabled applications. In: Proceedings of the SIGCHI Conference on Human Factors in Computing Systems, pp. 434–441. ACM, New York (1999)
22. Sartori, F., Manenti, L., Grazioli, L.: A conceptual and computational model for knowledge-based agents in android. In: WOA@ AI*IA 2013, pp. 41–46 (2013)
23. Schrittwieser, S., Frühwirt, P., Kieseberg, P., Leithner, M., Mulazzani, M., Huber, M., Weippl, E.R.: Guess who's texting you? evaluating the security of smartphone messaging applications. In: 19th Annual Network and Distributed System Security Symposium (2012)

24. Sehic, S., Nastic, S., Vögler, M., Li, F., Dustdar, S.: Entity-adaptation: a programming model for development of context-aware applications. In: Proceedings of the 29th Annual ACM Symposium on Applied Computing, pp. 436–443. ACM (2014)

25. Slazynski, M., Bobek, S., Nalepa, G.J.: Migration of rule inference engine to mobile platform. Challenges and case study. In: Proceedings of 10th Workshop on Knowledge Engineering and Software Engineering (KESE 2010) co-located with 21st European Conference on Artificial Intelligence (ECAI 2014), Prague, Czech Republic (2014)

26. Ughetti, M., Trucco, T., Gotta, D.: Development of agent-based, peer-to-peer mobile applications on android with jade. In: The Second International Conference on Mobile Ubiquitous Computing, Systems, Services and Technologies, UBICOMM 2008, pp. 287–294. IEEE (2008)

27. Want, R., Hopper, A., Falcão, V., Gibbons, J.: The active badge location system. ACM Trans. Inf. Syst. **10**(1), 91–102 (1992)

28. van Wissen, B., Palmer, N., Kemp, R., Kielmann, T., Bal, H.: ContextDroid: an expression-based context framework for android. In: Proceedings of the International Workshop on Sensing for App Phones (PhoneSense) 2010, pp. 1–5 (2010)

Optimizing the Light Trap Position for Brown Planthopper (BPH) Surveillance Network

Huong Hoang Luong[1($\boxtimes$)], Tuyen Phong Truong[2], Ky Minh Nguyen[3],
Bao Hoai Lam[4], and Hiep Xuan Huynh[5]

[1] CUSC-CTU, Cantho, Vietnam
`lhhuong@ctu.edu.vn`
[2] Universite de Bretagne Occidentale, Brest, France
`tptuyen@ctu.edu.vn`
[3] Can Tho University of Technology, Cantho, Vietnam
`nmky@ctuet.edu.vn`
[4] CICT-CTU, Cantho, Vietnam
`lhbao@cit.ctu.edu.vn`
[5] DREAM-CTU/IRD, CICT-CTU, Cantho, Vietnam
`hxhiep@ctu.edu.vn`

Abstract. To forecast the population of brown planthopper (BPH), a major insect pest of rice in Mekong Delta in Viet Nam, a light trap network is used in the experiments where the BPH trapped density is considered as monitoring called BPH light trap surveillance network (BSNET). There are two problems in order to deploy the BSNET: the number of the light traps and their positions. In this paper, we propose a new approach to optimize the BSNET by determining the number of light traps needed and the position for every light trap node in the surveillance region based on **HoneyComb** architecture. The experiment results are performed on the Brown Planthoppers surveillance network for Mekong Delta in Viet Nam.

Keywords: Light trap · BPH · Surveillance Network · Optimization · Optimal-design · HoneyComb

1 Introduction

The light trap surveillance network [1] in Mekong Delta region is one kind of representative sampling applying for the geographical region. The light trap surveillance network that can capture multiple kinds of insects, especially BPH, and which data (the density of insects per trap) is collected and analyzed daily. The light trap surveillance network is deployed in the experiments where the BPH trapped density is considered as monitoring called BPH light trap surveillance network (BSNET). BSNET is a spatial sampling network applying for the geographical region.

Automatic light trap [2] consists of autonomous sensors to monitor environment conditions such as temperature, sound, and so on. The automatic light trap

© ICST Institute for Computer Sciences, Social Informatics and Telecommunications Engineering 2016
P.C. Vinh et al. (Eds.): ICTCC 2016, LNICST 168, pp. 165–178, 2016.
DOI: 10.1007/978-3-319-46909-6_16

can pass their data to the others. The BSNET is considered as a automatic light trap surveillance network. To deploy the BSNET, there are two factors need to consider including where the light trap is localized and the number of the light trap needed.

In this paper, we propose a new approach to optimize the light trap position for BPH surveillance network. The approach in use is the honeyComb architecture [3] to determine the light trap position with minimum the number of light traps needed.

This paper contains 7 sections. Some related works are introduced in the next section. Automatic Brown PlantHopper surveillance network is presented in the Sect. 3. Section 4 will describe how to optimize the light trap position for Brown PlantHopper surveillance network (OBSNET) and the OBSNET implementation is presented in Sect. 5. Section 6 will introduce some experimental results by applying the new approach. The last section summarizes the contribution and suggests some researches in the future.

2 Related Works

The surveillance network is applied in many domain of environment and ecological research such as in the agricultural management [4], in the fishery surveillance, and in the forest management [1,5]. Light traps are used to monitor the kinds of insect in the agricultural such as BPHs.

Optimal design is a kind of the experiment design that affects respect to some statistical criteria [1,6,7]. Many optimal designs proposed are A-optimal design, D-optimal design, and E-optimal design [7].

Optimization for wireless sensor network or particular light trap network is an important research. In fact, there are many related researches such as layout optimization [8], optimization for energy [9], optimization for coverage - connectivity - topology... [10], schemes optimization [11], optimizing for environment surveillance network [12], and etc. [13–15].

In optimal design, optimization for location wireless sensor network or light trap network that ensures the network is coverage or connectivity and so on, which is a popular research. Many researches for that are presented in [10,12,16–18]

The Unit Disk Graph (UDG) technique was introduced by Clark [19] and has been used widely in ad-hoc communication. In this model, a sensor device is a node where and edge between two nodes is established if the distance between them is at most the disk radius r. There aren't many investigations of UDG in manage an ecosystem. Some researches based on UDG for estimating the BPH density and modeling the surveillance network were introduced in [20,21].

The HoneyComb architecture [3] is applied in wireless and mobile communication. Many research such as optimization the location for base transceiver station, virtual infrastructure for data dissemination in multi-sink mobile wireless sensor network and so on are proposed in [22,23]

3   Automatic Brown PlantHopper Surveillance Network

3.1   Automatic BPH Light Trap

The light trap [24] is one kind of passive trap helping to catch only the mature insects, and it operates only at night. A light trap uses light as an attraction source [25]. Light traps depend on the positive phototactic response of the insects, physiological as well as abiotic environmental factors which can influence the behavior [26]. Many kinds of insect will be caught and counted every day to observe the current density of them. BPH monitoring process is done manually.

To automate the process of monitoring BPHs, a network of automatic BPH light traps need building. An automatic BPH light trap includes some functions such as detecting the BPHs and counting the number of BPHs in the trap. Also, the automatic BPH light trap can transmit data to other(s).

An automatic BPHs light trap [2] was equipped with light source, tray, a camera, communication devices, some sensors and a power. The camera is programmed to capture the images from tray. Also, it can recognize the BPHs and count the number of BPHs in the image. The sensors includes temperature, light, humidity, wind speed and wind direction. The communication devices which use radio are used to transmit or receive data.

3.2   Automatic BPH Light Trap Surveillance Network

A automatic BPH light trap surveillance network is a graph $G=(V, E)$. This graph built from a set of vertices $V = \{v_1, v_2, ..., v_n\}$ and the set of edges $E = \{e_1, e_2, ..., e_m\}$. The vertice v_i with $i \in \{1..n\}$ is an automatic light trap. The edge e_k with $k \in \{1..m\}$, $i \in \{1..n\}$, $j \in \{1..m\}$ is an edge between two vertices v_i and v_j. The weights of the edges are defined by W=$\{w_1, w_2, ..., w_m\}$ where the value of w_k is given by distance function $f_d(v_i, v_j)$.

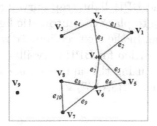

Fig. 1. A light trap network is presented as a graph (Color figure online)

Figure 1 illustrates the logical graph of a light trap network where the black dots mean the vertices in V and the red lines mean the edges in E. The graph contains 9 vertices $V = \{v_1, v_2, v_3, v_4, v_5, v_6, v_7, v_8, v_9\}$ and 10 edges $E = \{e_1 = e(v_1, v_2), e_2 = e(v_1, v_4), ..., e_9 = e(v_6, v_7), e_{10} = e(v_7, v_8)\}$.

Each node of light trap network has a communication range that is indicated by a circle with radius r. Conditions to define existence of an edge are introduced as following:

Definition 1 (Established edge). An edge is established if and only if the distance between a pair of vertices is less or equal to the minimum value of their radius - $f_d(v_i, v_j) \leq min(r_i, r_j)$.

Definition 2 (Unestablished edge). An edge is not established if distance between a pair of vertices is greater than the minimum value of their radius - $f_d(v_i, v_j) > min(r_i, r_j)$.

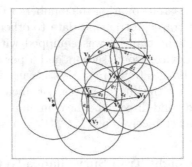

Fig. 2. The communication range of light traps that is used to establish the edges between the light traps

In the Fig. 2, the graph contains 1 subgraph and an isolated node. The sub graph consists of 8 nodes since distances among these nodes are less than the radius r while the vertex v_9 is an isolated node because all distance values between it to others are insufficient to the Definition 1.

To deploy the automatic BPH light trap surveillance network, we need to consider the positions where to place the automatic light traps so that the number of light traps is minimum. In the next section, we will present a new approach to optimize the light trap position for BPH surveillance network (The light trap network which is created by using this approach is called *Optimized BPH Surveillance Network*, contracted *OBSNET*).

4   OBSNET

4.1   Optimization for Surveillance Network

The BSNET will be deployed in regular pattern. The pattern can be a hexagon grid or triangular lattice [27]. In [28], this paper specifies for each pattern a condition that ensures the coverage of the region and guarantees network connectivity [27,29–34]. If R $\geq$ r and $0 \leq \frac{R}{r} \leq \frac{1}{2}3^{\frac{3}{4}}$, the hexagonal grid is the best deployment, it ensured the region is full coverage, the network is connected and it requires the minimum number of light trap nodes. Otherwise, if $R \geq \sqrt{3}r$, the triangle lattice is the optimal deployment pattern to ensure full region coverage and network connectivity.

For simplicity, triangular lattice is used to build surveillance network. The construction of this method is initiated by placing a light trap in the center of surveillance region. The others will be set based on the first light trap. For example, the first light trap is located at (x,y) in Euclidean space, the neighbor light traps are located at $(x, y \pm \sqrt{3}r)$, and $(x \pm 1.5r, y \pm \frac{\sqrt{3}r}{2})$. Through the recursive this construction, we not only determine the position for all the light traps in the surveillance region with the minimum number of the light traps but also ensure the surveillance region that is full coverage about the communication.

There are two cases in the deployment of OBSNET. In the first case, the deployment region will be divided into smaller units based on some conditions such as river, road, province, district and so on. After that, the biggest unit will be considered and hexagon cell at this unit will be created. Also, a hexagon grid will be created based on the first hexagon cell. The light traps will be located at the center of the hexagon cell. The pseudo-code for this case is presented in Algorithm 1.

Algorithm 1. OBSNET with the first case

---

begin
    Divide deployment region into smaller unit;
    Get the biggest unit;
    Let w is the width of the biggest unit;
    Let c is center coordinates of the biggest unit;
    list<hexagon> ⟵ hexagonGridBuilder(c,w);
    list<lighttrap> ⟵ lighttrapBuilder(list<hexagon>);
    network<lighttrap> ⟵ honeyCombNetworkBuilder(list<lighttrap>);
    return network<lighttrap>;
end

In the second case, a hexagon grid will be created by using the same method of the first case. If there are more than an unautomated light traps in a hexagon cell, build the unautomated light trap which is nearest from center of the hexagon cell to become the automatic light trap. After that, if the BSNET is not connected or not covered the deployment region about the communication, a light trap will be added at the center of the blank hexagon cell. Then, the connectivity will be checked again. If the BSNET is still not connected, move the light trap in the hexagon cell which is not connected with the honeycomb network to the center of that hexagon cell or intersection of communication range between two automatic light traps (choose the nearest point). The pseudo-code for the second case is presented in Algorithm 2.

Algorithm 2. Create a honeyComb network on deployment region with existing light traps

---

begin

> Divide deployment region into smaller unit;
> Get the biggest unit;
> Let w is the width of the biggest unit;
> Let c is center coordinates of the biggest unit;
> list<hexagon> ⟵ hexagonGridBuilder(c,w);
> **foreach** *cell in the list<hexagon>* **do**
>> **if** *There are more than unautomated light trap in a hexagon cell* **then**
>>> Build the nearest unautomated light trap from center to automatic light trap;
>>
>> **end**
>
> **end**
> Build the automatic light trap network;
> **repeat**
>> **if** *automatic light trap network is not connectivity* **then**
>>> Find all isolated light trap;
>>> **repeat**
>>>> **foreach** *every isolated light trap* **do**
>>>>> Move it to center of hexagon cell or intersection of communication range between two automatic light trap;
>>>>
>>>> **end**
>>>
>>> **until** *automatic network is connectivity*;
>>
>> **end**
>> **if** *automatic light trap network is not coverage* **then**
>>> **foreach** *cell in hexagon list* **do**
>>>> **if** *no light trap in a cell* **then**
>>>>> Create a light trap at the center of the cell;
>>>>
>>>> **end**
>>>
>>> **end**
>>
>> **end**
>> Build the automatic light trap network;
>
> **until** *automatic light trap network is connectivity and coverage*;
> return the automatic light trap network;

end

4.2   OBSNET Implementation

There are many factors that effect the implementation of the OBSNET. In this scope, we present the basic factors that effect the implementation of the OBSNET. Each factor has attributes and behaviors to interact each other.

Main factors are province, district, commune, light trap, and hexagon cell. When a map data is loaded, the commune factor will be created automatically and has certain attributes such as code, name, and area (Fig. 3). Each district

```
1  species commune{
2      string ID_commune;
3      string name_commune;
4      string ID_district;
5      rgb color <- #white;
6      float area <- 0.0;
7  }
```

```
1  species hexagon{
2      float size <- 0.0;
3      point center;
4      float range <- 0.0;
5      list<hexagon> neighbors;
6      rgb color <- #red;
7  }
```

Fig. 3. A definition of commune   **Fig. 4.** A definition of hexagon grid

factor knows which commune factor it includes. A hexagon grid includes attributes such as coordinate of center, radius and its neighbors as in Fig. 4.

5   Experiment

5.1   Case Study: Mekong Delta Region

Mekong Delta has 13 provinces. Every province is divided into smaller regions called districts. A district is also divided into smaller regions called communes. The Mekong Delta region can be considered as a surveillance region where need deploying the automatic light traps to monitor the BPHs. The region is divided as a grid of hexagonal cells. A cell is the smallest unit in this region and it is considered as a commune in Mekong Delta. Every cell has 6 neighbors. Each cell has the same width and height in the implementation. In other words, each cell has the same radius. The radius is considered from biggest commune in the surveillance network. The automatic light traps are located in the center of the cell. The HoneyComb network for Can Tho province is presented in the Fig. 5.

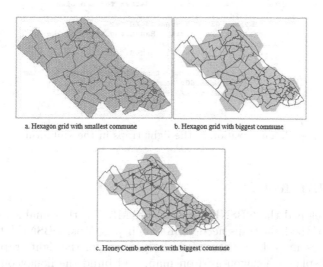

a. Hexagon grid with smallest commune   b. Hexagon grid with biggest commune

c. HoneyComb network with biggest commune

Fig. 5. OBSNET in a province of Mekong Delta region

5.2 Data Used

The data of experiment is a GIS map data of the *Hau Giang* province at administrative levels including province, district, and commune. The data is stored as a table includings id, name (province, district, commune), shape length, shape area and so on (Fig. 6).

id_province	name_province	id_district	name_district	id_commune	name_commune	type	shape_leng	shape_area
38254	Hau Giang	103164	Chau Thanh	34429	Nga Sau	Townlet	0.142665	0.00088672
38254	Hau Giang	103164	Chau Thanh	34428	Dong Thanh	Commune	0.172407	0.00093227
38254	Hau Giang	103164	Chau Thanh	34427	Dong Phuoc A	Commune	0.200755	0.00139623
38254	Hau Giang	103164	Chau Thanh	34426	Dong Phuoc	Commune	0.209359	0.00180681
38254	Hau Giang	103164	Chau Thanh	34432	Phu Huu	Commune	0.165654	0.00142994
38254	Hau Giang	103164	Chau Thanh	34433	Mot Ngan	Townlet	0.130744	0.00067739

Fig. 6. Data of Hau Giang province

The position of the light traps are stored in the plain text with xml format (*.gpx) that are used as input data. Figure 7 presents the structure of the data with three types of information including date, coordinate of the light trap (longitude, latitude), and name. This file is created by using NetGen platform (a platform is developed by Brest university - France) [35]. Also, an abstract network of the light traps for BPH surveillance region at *Hau Giang* province was generated from NetGen [35].

```
1    <?xml version="1.0"?>
2    <gpx version="1.0" creator="NetGen for Hau Giang">
3      <metadata>
4        <name>Hau Giang's sensors</name>
5        <desc>Sensors in city: Hau Giang, Vietnam</desc>
6      </metadata>
7      <wpt lat="9.957438" lon="105.743126">
8        <sym>sound</sym>
9        <cmt>title1</cmt><time>2013-031916:02:42</time>
10       <name>Node:60</name>
11       <desc>Noise:</desc>
12     </wpt>
```

Fig. 7. The position of the light traps in the xml format

5.3 OBSNET Tool

We have developed the OBSNET tool in GAML [36] that enables to optimize the number of the light traps needed and their positions. OBSNET tool enables to show the gis map data, determine the position of the light trap on a map, create and display a hexagon grid on map, and build the honeycomb network. Besides, OBSNET tool is also used to determine the communication range for automatic light trap based on honeyComb network.

5.4   Experiment 1: Optimizing the Light Trap Position for BPH Surveillance Network on the Surveilance Region Without Existing Unautomated Light Trap

The requirement for this experiment must create a honeyComb network for Hau Giang province. First, the experiment will display the gis map data of Hau Giang province as communes. Then, it will determine the biggest commune on the map and construct the hexagon grid based on that commune. The result shown as Fig. 8.

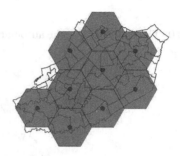

Fig. 8. Hexagon grid for Hau Giang province

Fig. 9. Light trap position in hexagon grid for Hau Giang province (Color figure online)

In Fig. 8, we obtain a hexagon grid with 9 hexagons. Each hexagon has a radius with 8.842 (m). Therefore, the minimum communication range is proposed 8.842*$\sqrt{3}$= 15.315 (m). After building the hexagon grid, place a automatic light trap at the center of hexagon (blue circle). The result shown as Fig. 9. The communication range of the automatic light trap is shown as yellow circle (Fig. 10)

5.5   Experiment 2: Optimizing the Light Trap Position for BPH Surveillance Network with Existing Unautomated Light Trap

In this experiment, we will build the hexagon grid on the surveillance region that have some existing unautomated light traps. First, we need to consider to build some unautomated light traps to become automatic light traps. Second, we will build the honeyComb network. If the network is not connected (there are some isolated automatic light traps), these automatic light traps will be considered moving to a new location. The hexagon grid on the surveillance region with existing unautomated light trap is shown as in Fig. 11. There are two cases about the unautomated light trap position. They are the unautomated light trap is located inside or outside the hexagon grid.

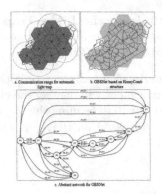

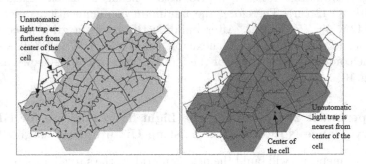

Fig. 10. The OBSNET for the automatic light traps in Hau Giang (Color figure online)

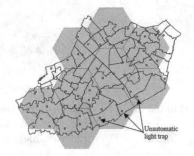

Fig. 11. The hexagon grid on Hau Giang with existing non-auto light traps

Fig. 12. Get unautomated light trap is nearest from center of the hexagon cell

Then, skip all the unautomated light traps outside the hexagon grid. After that, we will traverse every hexagon cell in hexagon grid, and get the unautomated light trap nearest from the center of the cell and skip all the others. The result is shown as in Fig. 12

The nearest unautomated light traps from center of the hexagon cell will become an automatic light trap with communication range that is calculated in

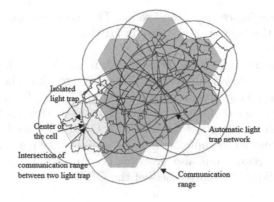

Fig. 13. Skip the unautomated light trap

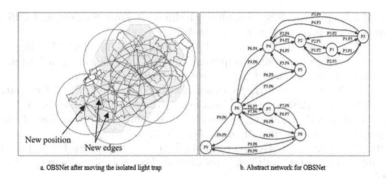

a. OBSNet after moving the isolated light trap   b. Abstract network for OBSNet

Fig. 14. OBSNet is built after moving the isolated automatic light trap to new position

the experiment 1. Now, we will build the honeyComb network for the automatic light traps (Fig. 13).

In the Fig. 13, there is an isolated automatic light trap, so the network is not connected. Therefore, we must move the isolated to new position that helps the network connect. There are two new positions including the center of the cell and the intersection between two communication of two automatic light traps in neighbor cells. In this experiment, we will choose the nearest position that helps network connect. It is the intersection between two communication ranges.

The Fig. 14 shows the network after moving the isolated light trap to new position (intersection between two communication ranges of two automatic light traps).

6 Conclusion

The research on the optimization the light trap position for surveillance network is one of the important trends in the environment and ecological research. This trend solves some questions such as where light traps are placed, how to fully cover the surveillance region and so on. Therefore, we propose a new approach to optimize the light trap position for BPH surveillance network based on honeyComb structure.

Building the hexagon grid and honeyComb network helps to determine the number of light traps needed and their positions. The result of the network model is deployed in Hau Giang province, a province in Mekong Delta. Based on the experiment results, we can deploy the OBSNET in the Mekong Delta region.

The experiment results show the effects of OBSNET based on honeyComb structure. Using this method not only helps to optimize the light trap position for BPH surveillance network but also saves the cost in actual deployment. Actual data is used to validate the correctness of the OBSNET.

References

1. Köhl, M., Magnussen, S.S.: Sampling Methods, Remote Sensing and GIS Multi-resource Forest Inventory. Springer, Heidelberg (2006)
2. Nguyen, K.M., Lam, B.H., Truong, T.P., Pham, H.M.T., Ho, C.V., Bernard, P., Huynh, H.X.: Automatic light-trap using sensors. In: Proceeding in National Conference on Information and Communication Technology (2015)
3. Wang, B.: Coverage problems in sensor networks: a survey. ACM Comput. Surv. **43**(4), 32:1–32:53 (2011). http://doi.acm.org/10.1145/1978802.1978811
4. Kozak, R.W.M.: PS sampling versus stratified sampling comparison of efficiency in agricultural surveys. Stat. Transit. **7**(1), 5–12 (2005)
5. Talvitie, M., Leino, O., Holopainen, M.: Inventory of sparse forest populations using adaptive cluster sampling. Finnish Soc. For. Sci. Silva Fennica, 0037–5330 (2006)
6. Warrick, A.W., Myers, D.E.: Optimization of sampling locations for variogram calculations. Water Resour. Res. **23**(3), 496–500 (1987). http://dx.doi.org/10.1029/WR023i003p00496
7. Brus, D.J., Heuvelink, G.B.: Optimization of sample patterns for universal kriging of environmental variables. Geoderma **138**(12), 86–95 (2007)
8. Jourdan, D., de Weck, O.: Layout optimization for a wireless sensor network using a multi-objective genetic algorithm. In: 2004 IEEE 59th Vehicular Technology Conference, VTC 2004-Spring, vol. 5, pp. 2466–2470 (2004)
9. Lee, J.-H., Moon, I.: Modeling and optimization of energy efficient routing in wireless sensor networks. Appl. Math. Model. **38**(78), 2280–2289 (2014)
10. Gogu, A., Nace, D., Dilo, A., Mertnia, N.: Optimization problems in wireless sensor networks. In: 2011 International Conference on Complex, Intelligent and Software Intensive Systems (CISIS), pp. 302–309, June 2011
11. Niewiadomska-Szynkiewicz, E., Marks, M.: Optimization schemes for wireless sensor network localization. Int. J. Appl. Math. Comput. Sci. **19**(2), 291–302 (2009)
12. Xuan, V.T., Huynh, X.-H., Le Ngoc, M., Drogoul, A.: Optimizing an environmental surveillance network with Gaussian process entropy - an optimization approach by agent-based simulation. In: 7th International KES Conference on Agents and Multi-agent Systems - Technologies and Applications, Vietnam, May 2013
13. Aioffi, W., Mateus, G., Quintao, F.: Optimization issues and algorithms for wireless sensor networks with mobile sink. In: Proceedings of INOC (2007)
14. Iqbal, M., Naeem, M., Anpalagan, A., Ahmed, A., Azam, M.: Wireless sensor network optimization: multi-objective paradigm. Sensors **15**(7), 17572 (2015)

15. Madan, R., Cui, S., Lall, S., Goldsmith, A.: Modeling and optimization of transmission schemes in energy-constrained wireless sensor networks. IEEE/ACM Trans. Network. **15**(6), 1359–1372 (2007)
16. Gopakumar, A., Jacob, L.: Localization in wireless sensor networks using particle swarm optimization. In: IET International Conference on Wireless, Mobile and Multimedia Networks, 2008, pp. 227–230, January 2008
17. Ghari, P.M., Shahbazian, R., Ghorashi, S.A.: Localization in Wireless Sensor Networks Using Quadratic Optimization, ArXiv e-prints, August 2014
18. Monica, Stefania, Ferrari, Gianluigi: Particle swarm optimization for auto-localization of nodes in wireless sensor networks. In: Tomassini, Marco, Antonioni, Alberto, Daolio, Fabio, Buesser, Pierre (eds.) ICANNGA 2013. LNCS, vol. 7824, pp. 456–465. Springer, Heidelberg (2013). doi:10.1007/978-3-642-37213-1_47
19. Cressie, N.A.C.: Statistics for Spatial Data. Wiley-Interscience, New York (1993)
20. Truong, V.X., Huynh, H.X., Le, M.N., Drogoul, A.: Estimating the density of brown plant hoppers from a light-traps network based on unit disk graph. In: Zhong, N., Callaghan, V., Ghorbani, A.A., Hu, B. (eds.) AMT 2011. LNCS, vol. 6890, pp. 276–287. Springer, Heidelberg (2011). doi:10.1007/978-3-642-23620-4_30. http://dl.acm.org/citation.cfm?id=2033896.2033931
21. Truong, V.X., Huynh, H.X., Le, M.N., Drogoul, A.: Modeling a surveillance network based on unit disk graph technique – application for monitoring the invasion of insects in Mekong Delta region. In: Rahwan, I., Wobcke, W., Sen, S., Sugawara, T. (eds.) PRIMA 2012. LNCS (LNAI), vol. 7455, pp. 228–242. Springer, Heidelberg (2012). doi:10.1007/978-3-642-32729-2_16
22. Erman, A.T., Dilo, A., Havinga, P.J.M.: A virtual infrastructure based on honeycomb tessellation for data dissemination in multi-sink mobile wireless sensor networks. EURASIP J. Wirel. Commun. Network. **2012**, 17 (2012)
23. Palanivelu, T.G., Nakkeeran, R.: Wireless - Mobile communication
24. Vaithilingam, D.C.: Role of insect light trap in organic agriculture, Romvijay Biootech Private Limited (2013)
25. Linker, D.B.O.H.M., Barbercheck, M.E.: Insect management on organic farms (2009)
26. Brown planthopper: Threat to rice, International Rice Research Institute (1979)
27. Khoufi, I., Minet, P., Laouiti, A., Mahfoudh, S., Survey of Deployment Algorithms in Wireless Sensor Networks: Coverage and Connectivity Issues and Challenges. Int. J. Auton. Adapt. Commun. Syst. (IJAACS), p. 24 (2014)
28. Baltzis, K.B.: Hexagonal vs Circular Cell Shape: A Comparative Analysis and Evaluation of the two Popular Modeling Approximations. INTECH Open Access Publisher, Rijeka (2011)
29. Sun, Y., Yu, Z., Ge, J., Lin, B., Yun, Z.: On deploying wireless sensors to achieve both coverage, connectivity. In: Proceedings of the 5th International Conference on Wireless Communications, Networking, Mobile Computing, WiCOM 2009, Piscataway, NJ, USA, pp. 3369–3372. IEEE Press (2009). http://dl.acm.org/citation.cfm?id=1737966.1738288
30. Ghosh, A., Das, S.K.: Coverage and connectivity issues in wireless sensor networks: a survey. Pervasive Mob. Comput. **4**(3), 303–334 (2008)
31. Zhu, C., Zheng, C., Shu, L., Han, G.: Review: a survey on coverage and connectivity issues in wireless sensor networks. J. Netw. Comput. Appl. **35**(2), 619–632 (2012). http://dx.doi.org/10.1016/j.jnca.2011.11.016
32. Zhang, H., Hou, J.C.: Maintaining sensing coverage and connectivity in large sensor networks. Ad Hoc Sens. Wirel. Netw. **1**(1–2), 89–124 (2005)

33. Bai, X., Kumar, S., Xuan, D., Yun, Z., Lai, T.H.: Deploying wireless sensors to achieve both coverage, connectivity. In: Proceedings of the 7th ACM International Symposium on Mobile Ad Hoc Networking, Computing, MobiHoc 2006, pp. 131–142. ACM, New York (2006). http://doi.acm.org/10.1145/1132905.1132921

34. Wang, Y.-C., Hu, C.-C., Tseng, Y.-C.: Efficient deployment algorithms for ensuring coverage and connectivity of wireless sensor networks, In: Imre, S., Crowcroft, J. (eds.) WICON, pp. 114–121. IEEE Computer Society, Washington (2005)

35. Netgen website, A generator of concurrent systems. http://wsn.univ-brest.fr/NetGenNews

36. Gama website, Modeling, simulation platform. https://github.com/gama-platforms

Some Efficient Segmentation-Based Techniques to Improve Time Series Discord Discovery

Huynh Thi Thu Thuy[✉], Duong Tuan Anh, and Vo Thi Ngoc Chau

Faculty of Computer Science and Engineering, Ho Chi Minh City University of Technology,
Ho Chi Minh City, Vietnam
huynhthithuthuy@tdt.edu.vn, {dtanh,chauvtn}@cse.hcmut.edu.vn

Abstract. Time series discord has proved to be a useful concept for time series anomaly detection. To search for discords, various algorithms have been developed. HOT SAX has been considered as a well-known and effective algorithm in time series discord discovery. However this algorithm still has some weaknesses. First, users of HOT SAX are required to choose suitable values for the discord length, word-length and/or alphabet-size, which are unknown. Second, HOT SAX still suffers from high computation cost. In this paper, we propose some novel techniques to improve HOT SAX algorithm. These techniques consist of (i) using some time series segmentation methods to estimate the two important parameters: discord length and word length and (ii) speeding up the discord discovery process by a new way of shifting the sliding window. Extensive experiments have demonstrated that the proposed approach can not only facilitate users in setting the parameters, but also improve the discord discovery in terms of accuracy and computational efficiency.

Keywords: Time series · Discord discovery · HOT SAX · Segmentation

1   Introduction

The problem of detecting unusual (abnormal, novel, deviant, anomalous, *discord*) subsequences in a time series has recently attracted much attention. Time series anomaly detection brings out the abnormal patterns embedded in a time series. Areas that explore such time series anomalies are, for example, fault diagnostics, intrusion detection, fraud detection, auditing and data cleansing. Anomaly detection is a challenging topic, mainly because we need to obtain the lengths of anomaly patterns before detecting them.

Some popular algorithms for time series anomaly detection include window-based methods such as brute-force and HOT SAX by Keogh et al. (2005) [6] and WAT by Bu et al. (2007) [1]; a method based on segmentation and Finite State Automata by Salvador and Chan (2005) [15]; a method based on neural-network by Oliveira et al. (2004) [13]; a method based on time series segmentation and anomaly scores by Leng et al. (2008) [9]; a method based on PAA bit representation and clustering by Li et al. (2013) [10]; and a method which applies cluster-based outlier detection by Kha and Anh (2015) [8]. Among these above-mentioned algorithms for time series discord discovery, HOT SAX has been considered as the most popular algorithm. HOT SAX is an unsupervised

© ICST Institute for Computer Sciences, Social Informatics and Telecommunications Engineering 2016
P.C. Vinh et al. (Eds.): ICTCC 2016, LNICST 168, pp. 179–188, 2016.
DOI: 10.1007/978-3-319-46909-6_17

method of anomaly detection and has been applied in several real applications. However, this algorithm still has some weaknesses. First, users of HOT SAX are required to choose suitable values for the discord length, word-length and/or alphabet-size, which are not intuitive. Second, HOT SAX still suffers from high computation cost and cannot satisfy the requirement of real applications with large datasets.

Time series segmentation can be considered as a preprocessing step and core task for variety of data mining tasks [12]. Segmentation focuses on dividing the time series into appropriate, internally homogeneous segments so that the structure of time series, through pattern discovery in the behavior of the observed variable, could be revealed. Segmentation is not a trivial problem. Common segmentation methods include Piecewise Linear Approximation (PLA) by Keogh et al. (2002) [5], major extreme points by Fink and Pratt (2002) [14], and Perceptually Important Points (PIP) proposed by Fu et al. (2006) [3]. Segmentation has been used in some time series data mining tasks, which can be listed as follows. Salvador and Chan (2005) [15] applied segmentation and Finite State Automata to detect anomaly in time series. Gruber et al. (2006) [4] applied major extreme points in identifying candidate patterns for time series motif discovery. Leng et al. (2008) [9] used segmentation and anomaly scores for anomaly detection in time series with dynamic time warping distance. Dani et al. (2015) used segmentation and local means and standard deviations for time series anomaly detection [2]. Through these previous works, it is obvious that there is a strong relationship between time series segments brought out by a segmentation method and the meaningful patterns for motif/ anomaly discovery in time series. Motivated by this direction, in this work we attempt to apply some segmentation techniques in improving HOT SAX, especially in estimating two important parameters n and w.

In this work, we propose some novel techniques to improve HOT SAX algorithm. These techniques consist of (i) using two time series segmentation methods (PLA and major-extreme points) to estimate the two important parameters in HOT SAX: discord length n and word length w; and (ii) speeding up the discord discovery process by shifting the sliding window one PAA frame at a time. Extensive experiments on several datasets have demonstrated that the proposed approach can not only facilitate users in setting the parameters but also improve discord discovery in terms of accuracy and computational efficiency.

2   Background and Related Works

In this section, we introduce some background on time series discords, HOT SAX algorithm and some basic ideas on time series segmentation.

2.1   Time Series Discords

According to Keogh et al., 2005 [6] a time series discord is a subsequence that is very different from its closest matching subsequence. However, in general, the best matches of a given subsequence tend to be very close to the subsequence under consideration.

Such matches are called *trivial matches* and are not useful. When finding discords, we should exclude trivial matches and keep only *non-self matches* as defined as follows.

Definition 1 (*Non-self match*): Given a time series T containing a subsequence C of length n beginning at position p and a matching subsequence M beginning at the position q, we say that M is a non-self match to C if $|p - q| \geq n$.

Definition 2 (*Time series discord*): Given a time series T, the subsequense D in T is called the most significant discord in T if the distance to its nearest non-self match is largest.

The naïve method for finding discords (called Brute Force Discord Discovery algorithm - BFDD) is also given in [6]. The algorithm is implemented by a two layer nested loop. The outer loop considers each possible candidate subsequence and the inner loop is a linear scan to find the nearest non-self match of the candidate. The subsequence that has the largest distance to its nearest non-self match is the discord. This method is simple, easy to implement, and can produce the exact solution. The main problem is that it has $O(m^2)$ time complexity where m is the length of the time series.

2.2 HOT SAX Algorithm

The BFDD algorithm is mainly designed for raw time series. By applying time series dimensionality reduction techniques, discord can be detected also based on approximate representation. HOT SAX algorithm, proposed by Keogh et al. [6], is the heuristic method which applies Symbolic Aggregate Approximation (SAX) representation [13] into a discord discovery algorithm. To symbolize a time series by SAX representation, first, HOT SAX has to reduce its dimensionality by applying Piecewise Aggregate Approximation (PAA) transform [11].

Having converted a time series into the PAA representation, HOT SAX applies a further transformation to obtain a discrete SAX representation. Notice that SAX representation requires that the data should meet Gaussian distribution. To find discords of length n in a time series T, HOT SAX first shifts a sliding window of length n across time series T, extracting subsequences, encoding them into charactering strings (called *SAX words*) and placing them in a table where the index refers back to the original subsequence. Once having this ordered list of SAX words, HOT SAX can store them in a tree structure (called *augmented trie*) where the leaf nodes keep a linked list of all word occurrences that map there. HOT SAX relies on three important parameters: the length of discords n, the cardinality of the SAX alphabet a, and the SAX word size w.

To realize early exit of the for loops, HOT SAX applies the two following heuristics. (a) In the outer loop, the subsequence with larger distance to its nearest neighbor has a priority to be selected for comparison. This kind of subsequences corresponds to the entries in the leaf nodes of the augmented trie which have the small word count. (b) In the inner loop, the subsequence with smaller distance to the current candidate has a priority to be compared. This kind of subsequences corresponds to the entries in the same leaf node with the current candidate.

2.3 Time Series Segmentation

In this work, we try to apply some segmentation techniques in improving HOT SAX algorithm, especially in estimating two important parameters: discord length n and word length w. Among many popular time series segmentation methods, we select to use the two most well-known methods: PLA and a method which based on major extreme points.

Identifying Major Extreme Points. Pratt and Fink [14] proposed a method for compressing time series which is based on the concept of major extreme points. But in this work, we apply the concepts of major extreme points for time series segmentation rather than for time series compression.

Major extreme points in a time series contain important features of the time series. The definition of major extreme points is given as follows.

Definition 3. *Major extreme points:* A point t_k of a time series $T = t_1,..., t_m$ is a *major minimum* if there are indices i and j, where $i < k < j$, such that t_k is the minimum among $t_i,..., t_j$ and $t_i/t_k \geq R$, and $t_j/t_k \geq R$.

Intuitively, t_k is a minimum value of some segment $t_i,..., t_j$ and the endpoint values of this segment are much larger than t_k. Similarly, a point t_k is an *major maximum* if there are indices i and j, where $i < k < j$, such that t_k is the maximum among $t_i,..., t_j$ and $t_k/t_i \geq R$, and $t_k/t_j \geq R$.

Figure 1 illustrates the definition of major minima and maxima.

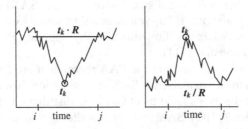

Fig. 1. Illustration of major extreme points, (left) minimum and (right) maximum

Notice that in the above definition, the parameter R is called *compression rate* which is greater than one and an increase of R leads to selection of fewer major extreme points.

Given a time series T, starting at the beginning of the time series, all major minima and maxima of the time series are computed by using the algorithm given by Pratt and Fink [14]. The algorithm takes linear time and constant memory.

PLA Segmentation using the Sliding Window Algorithm. The approximation of a time series T, of length m, with K straight lines that tightly fit the original data points is the essence of Piecewise Linear Approximation (PLA). The algorithms which input a time series and returns a piecewise linear representation are called *PLA segmentation algorithms*. The PLA segmentation problem can be formulated as follows. Given a time series, scan and divide the entire time series into a number of segments such that the maximum error for any segment does not exceed some user-specified threshold, *max_error*.

According to Keogh et al. [5], most time series PLA segmentation algorithms can be classified into three categories: Sliding Window, Top-Down and Bottom-Up. In this work, we select to use Sliding Window algorithm for PLA segmentation due to its procedural simplicity and its online nature.

3   Improving the HOT SAX Algorithm

In this work, we attempt to improve the HOT SAX algorithm through the following three techniques:

- Estimating the suitable size of PAA frame based on PLA segmentation.
- Estimating the suitable value for discord length *n* and SAX word length *w* based on identifying major extreme points.
- Applying a new way of shifting the sliding window.

So, our improved HOT SAX is a two-pass approach. In the first pass, we estimate the size of PAA frame, the discord length *n* and the word length *w*. Then, we apply HOT SAX with a new way of shifting sliding window and subsequence distance computation.

3.1   An Efficient Way to Estimate the Size of PAA Frame

The use of PAA representation in HOT SAX is mainly for dimensionality reduction. But in [6], Keogh et al. have not mentioned how much dimensionality reduction we should do for a given time series in order to guarantee the accuracy of discord discovery. It is obvious that too much dimensionality reduction may cause the loss of information in the original time series and this can be harmful to the accuracy of discord detection. Therefore, the size of PAA frame, which indicates how much dimensionality reduction we want, should be considered as an important parameter in HOT SAX and we should have a principled method to estimate it.

In this work, we propose a technique for estimating the size of PAA frame which is based on PLA segmentation. We select PLA segmentation for estimating the size of PAA frame due to the following reason. Because of the linear representation bias, PLA segmentation algorithms are much more effective at producing fine grain partitioning, rather than a smaller set of segments that represent characteristic patterns in a time series.

Among three algorithms for PLA segmentation: Top-Down, Bottom-Up and Sliding Window, Sliding Window algorithm is selected. After applying Sliding Window algo-rithm to divide the time series into linear segments, we can set the PAA frame for dimensionality reduction equal to the average length of all PLA segments obtained.

Notice that the complexity of the Sliding Window algorithm for PLA segmentation is just linear [5] and the estimation of the parameter *max_error* in the Sliding Window algorithm is intuitive. If the time series is very complex, we would favor a fine grain partitioning, which corresponds to a small PAA frame, then a small *max_error* is a good choice. Otherwise, relatively smooth and slowly changing datasets favor a larger value of *max_error*.

3.2   An Efficient Way to Estimate Discord Length and SAX Word Length

Identifying major extreme points [14] is a good method for segmentation that can extract characteristic patterns in a time series. Applying this method, we assume that any candidate patterns for discord discovery must start from a major extreme point and ends at the next major extreme point. With this assumption, we can estimate the discord length for a given time series by the following scheme. After identifying all the major extreme points in the time series, we extract subsequence segments one by one from each pair of adjacent major extreme points in the time series. We keep track of the lengths of all extracted subsequence segments. Next, we set the discord length equal to the average length of all the extracted subsequence segments.

For the algorithm that identifies all the major extreme points in the time series, we have to determine the compression rate R. According to [14], Pratt and Fink only suggested that R should be greater than 1. In this work, to find the right value for R, we have to try some values for R in the range from 1 to 10 and identify the value which seems to bring out an appropriate segmentation for a particular time series. Thank to the ease of visualization of segmented time series, we can estimate the right value for R with not much effort.

Furthermore, from the discord length n and the size of the PAA frame, we can easily determine the SAX word length w for HOT SAX algorithm by the following formula.

$$w = n/(\text{size of PAA frame})$$

3.3   A New Way to Shift the Sliding Window

The original HOT SAX creates a SAX representation of the entire time series by sliding a window of length n across the time series T one data point at a time. Hence, the original HOT SAX is computational expensive. A question can be raised "Is it necessary to shift the sliding window only one data point at a time?". To our knowledge, several previous works did not apply the same way of shifting sliding window as in HOT SAX. Chuah and Fu (2006) [2] proposed an adaptive window-based discord discovery (AWDD) approach for anomaly detection in ECG time series. AWDD shifts the sliding window across the ECG time series from a peak to its adjacent peak at a time. Tanaka et al. (2005) [16] proposed EMD, a time series motif discovery algorithm which also applies PAA and SAX transformation. EMD shifts the sliding window, called the *analysis window*, across the time series one PAA frame at a time. Following the spirit from EMD algorithm, in this work, we select to shift the sliding window one PAA frame at a time in order to speed-up the discord discovery process.

3.4   Other Issue: How to Compute Subsequence Distance in Improved HOT SAX

In HOT SAX, the conversion of subsequences to SAX words in this algorithm implies the use of the MINDIST distance between two SAX words, which is given in [11]. Besides this way to compute the distance between two SAX words, we can refer back to the two corresponding subsequences of these two SAX words in the original time series and compute the Euclidean distance between them. The latter way of computing subsequence distance can bring out a better accuracy of discord discovery than the former one.

4   Experimental Evaluation

We implemented all three algorithms, Brute Force, HOT SAX and Improved HOT SAX. The experiments aim to compare Improved HOT SAX with original HOT SAX in terms of time efficiency and discord detection accuracy. The Bruce Fore is used as the baseline algorithm.

Our experiments were conducted over the datasets from the UCR Time Series Data Mining archive for discord discovery [7]. There are 11 datasets used in these experiments. The datasets are from different areas (finance, medicine, manufacturing, science). After applying PLA segmentation to estimate the size of PAA frame and identifying major extreme points to estimate the discord length n for each dataset, we obtained the two important parameters for each dataset as shown in Table 1. We set the threshold *max_error* in the range from 0.3 to 0.000002.

Table 1.   Discord length and size of PAA frame for each dataset

Dataset	Length	*max_error*	R	Discord length (n)	Size of PAA frame
218c3EEG	8500	0.00007	1.499998	62	2
stock_20_0	5000	0.006	1.500001	138	3
memory	6000	0.000003	1.500000	357	3
ECG	6000	0.0025	1.499990	183	3
Power_demand_italy	6000	0.015	1.499997	267	3
ERP	5545	0.08	1.500014	164	2
chromosome	6000	0.0009	1.499996	99	3
eeg	6000	0.3	1.499996	63	3
koski_ecg	10000	0.00001	1.499999	633	3
power	5000	0.0015	1.499994	234	2
stock	6000	0.00002	1.499992	1410	3

4.1   Accuracy

Table 2 shows the experimental results about the discords found on each of 11 time series datasets by the three algorithms: Brute Force, HOT SAX and Improved HOT SAX. Over 11 datasets, we found out that the discord detected by Improved HOT SAX or HOT SAX is exactly the same as the discord detected by Brute Force. However, for each dataset there is some difference between the start location of the discord found by the HOT SAX or Improved HOT SAX to that of the same discord found by Brute Force.

From Table 2, we found out that the location difference between Brute Force and Improved HOT SAX is always much smaller than the location difference between Brute Force and HOT SAX. This phenomenon indicates that our Improved HOT SAX can detect time series discords better than the original HOT SAX.

Table 2. Locations of discords detected by Brute-Force, HOT SAX and Improved HOT SAX

Dataset	n	Position of discord			Location differences	
		BFDD	HOT SAX	Improved HOTSAX	HOT SAX vs. BFDD	Improved HOT SAX vs. BFDD
218c3EEG	62	6052	6145	6057	93	5
stock_20_0	138	97	4862	97	4765	0
memory	357	5217	3012	5197	2205	20
ECG	183	4015	4083	4015	68	0
Power_demand_italy	267	5323	2504	5323	2819	0
ERP_data	164	2551	2671	2551	120	0
chromosome	99	428	1973	430	1545	2
Eeg	63	3082	3019	3079	63	3
koski_ecg	633	8583	8393	8584	190	1
power	234	4615	41	4615	4574	0
Stock	1410	1	4544	1	4543	0

4.2 Efficiency

Following the tradition established in [1, 6], the efficiency of the three algorithms is measured by the number of calls to the distance function. Table 3 shows the numbers of distance function calls by Bruce Force, HOT SAX and Improved HOT SAX.

Table 3. Numbers of distance function calls by Bruce Force, HOT SAX and Improved HOT SAX

Dataset	The number of distance function calls		
	BFDD	HOTSAX	Improved HOTSAX
218c3EEG	70182506	6504476	481691
stock_20_0	22330350	2135119	383117
memory	27957656	3025101	328580
ECG	31758860	1785801	278003
Power_demand_italy	29893556	9165021	846848
ERP	27232742	1857263	511564
chromosome	33680612	205302	28455
Eeg	34521500	2689901	138630
koski_ecg	76308960	13903056	1219958
power	20552622	2506976	864376
Stock	10121942	2373381	203773

Experimental results in Table 3 show that HOT SAX brings out about 1 order of magnitude of a speedup to Brute Force while Improved HOT SAX has about 2 orders of magnitude of a speedup to Brute Force. Additionally, for sanity check, we measured the execution times of the three algorithms over 11 datasets. The experimental results in Table 4 reveal that in average, HOT SAX can work faster than Brute-Force about 4 times and Improved HOT SAX runs faster than HOT SAX about 2.5 times.

Table 4. Execution times (in seconds) of Brute-Force, HOT SAX and Improved HOT SAX

Dataset	Runtime (sec)		
	BFDD	HOTSAX	Improved HOTSAX
218c3EEG	66.023	22.153	7.266
stock_20_0	45.785	11.115	5.923
memory	143.013	16.611	7.131
ECG	84.032	15.566	6.394
Power_demand_italy	115.062	29.671	8.145
ERP	67.370	24.336	10.80
chromosome	50.372	15.011	7.119
eeg	34.104	11.263	3.473
koski_ecg	678.439	104.546	22.212
power	70.261	17.256	10.214
stock	203.061	41.343	12.42

We also conducted an experiment to compare the performance of HOT SAX in two ways of computing subsequence distances: MINDIST on SAX words and Euclidean Distance between two subsequences in original time series. The results of this experiment shows that the location difference between the discord detected by Brute Force and the discord detected by HOT SAX using MINDIST is always greater than the location difference between the discord detected by Brute Force and the discord detected by HOT SAX using Euclidean distance. These results indicate that HOT SAX with Euclidean distance on subsequences performs better than HOT SAX with MINDIST on SAX words.

5   Conclusions

In this paper, we proposed some new techniques to improve HOT SAX algorithm in time series discord discovery. This work has two major contributions. Firstly, we mitigate the difficulty of setting two important parameters, discord length n and word length w of HOT SAX by replacing them with the two other easy parameters, max_error and R in the two time series segmentation methods: major extreme points and PLA segmentation. Secondly, we speed-up HOT SAX by shifting the sliding window with one PAA frame at a time rather than one data point at a time.

In the future, we plan to devise some other method for outer and inner heuristics in HOT SAX for more effectiveness and efficiency.

References

1. Bu, Y., Leung, T.W., Fu, A., Keogh, E., Pei, J., Meshkin, S.: WAT: Finding top-K discords in time series database. In: Proceedings of the 2007 SIAM International Conference on Data Mining (SDM 2007), Minneapolis, MN, USA, 26–28 April 2007
2. Dani, M.C., Jollois, F.X., Nadif, M., Freixo, C.: Adaptive threshold for anomaly detection using time series segmentation. In: Arik, S., Huang, T., Lai, W.K., Liu, Q. (eds.) ICONIP 2015, Part III. LNCS, vol. 9491, pp. 82–89. Springer, Switzerland (2015)
3. Fu, T.C., Chung, F.L., Ng, C.M.: Financial time series segmentation based on specialized binary tree representation. In: Proceedings of 2006 International Conference on Data Mining, pp. 3–9 (2006)
4. Gruber, C., Coduro, M., Sick, B.: Signature verification with dynamic RBF network and time series motifs. In: Proceedings of 10th International Workshop on Frontiers in Hand Writing Recognition (2006)
5. Keogh, E., Selina, C., David, H., Michel, P.: An online algorithm for segmenting time series. In: Proceedings of the IEEE International Conference on Data Mining, pp. 289–296 (2001)
6. Keogh, E., Lin, J., Fu, A.: HOT SAX: efficiently finding the most unusual time series subsequence. In: Proceedings of 5th ICDM, Houston, Texas, pp. 226–233 (2005)
7. Keogh, E.: www.cs.ucr.edu/~eamonn/discords/. (Accessed on 24 Jan 2015)
8. Kha, N.H., Anh, D.T.: From cluster-based outlier detection to time series discord discovery. In: Li, X.L., Cao, T., Lim, E.-P., Zhou, Z.-H., Ho, T.-B., Cheung, D. (eds.) PAKDD 2015. LNCS (LNAI), vol. 9441, pp. 16–28. Springer, Switzerland (2015)
9. Leng, M., Chen, X., Li, L.: Variable length methods for detecting anomaly patterns in time series. In: International Symposium on. Computational Intelligence and Design (ISCID 2008), vol. 2 (2008)
10. Li, G., Braysy, O., Jiang, L., Wu, Z., Wang, Y.: Finding time series discord based on bit representation clustering. Knowl.-Based Syst. **52**, 243–254 (2013)
11. Lin, J., Keogh, E., Lonardi, S., Chiu, B.: Symbolic representation of time series, with implications for streaming algorithms. In: Proceedings of the 8th ACM SIGMOD Workshop on Research Issues in Data Mining and Knowledge Discovery, San Diego, CA, 13 June 2003
12. Lovric, M., Milanovic, M., Stamenkovic, M.: Algorithmic methods for segmentation of time series: an overview. JCEBI **1**(1), 31–53 (2014)
13. Oliveira, A.L.I., Neto, F.B.L., Meira, S.R.L.: A method based on RBF-DAA neural network for improving Novelty detection in time series. In: Proceedings of 17th International FLAIRS Conference. AAAI Press, Miami Beach (2004)
14. Pratt, K.B., Fink, E.: Search for patterns in compressed time series. Int. J. Image Graph. **2**(1), 89–106 (2002)
15. Salvador, S., Chan, P.: Learning states and rules for time series anomaly detection. Appl. Intell. **23**(3), 241–255 (2005)
16. Tanaka, Y., Iwamoto, K., Uehara, K.: Discovery of time series motif from multi-dimensional data based on MDL principle. Mach. Learn. **58**, 269–300 (2005)

Improving SPRING Method in Similarity Search Over Time-Series Streams by Data Normalization

Bui Cong Giao[(✉)] and Duong Tuan Anh

Faculty of Computer Science and Engineering,
Ho Chi Minh City University of Technology, Ho Chi Minh City, Vietnam
giao.bc@cb.sgu.edu.vn, dtanh@cse.hcmut.edu.vn

Abstract. Similarity search in streaming time series is a crucial sub-routine of a number of real-time applications dealing with time-series streams. In finding subsequences of time-series streams that match with patterns under Dynamic Time Warping (DTW), data normalization plays a very important role and should not be ignored. SPRING proposed by Sakurai et al. conducts the similarity search by mitigating the time and space complexity of DTW. Unfortunately, SPRING produces inaccurate results since no data normalization is taken into account before the DTW calculation. In this paper, we improve the SPRING method to deal with similarity search for prespecified patterns in streaming time series under DTW by applying incremental min-max normalization before the DTW calculation. For every pattern, our proposed method uses a monitoring window anchored at the entry of one streaming time series to keep track of min-max coefficients, and then the DTW distance between the normalized subsequence and the normalized pattern is incrementally computed. The experimental results reveal that our proposed method obtains *best-so-far* values better than those of another state-of-the-art method and the wall-clock time of the proposed method is acceptable.

Keywords: Similarity search · Streaming time series · Data normalization · Dynamic Time Warping

1 Introduction

A streaming time-series is a sequence of real values, where new values are continuously appended at a steady high-speed rate as time progresses, so time-series streams are potentially unbounded in size. There have been more and more applications of data mining on streaming time series recently. The typical examples are traffic monitoring using GPS, sensor network monitoring, and online stock analysis. In these applications, pattern discovery by similarity search is a core function to identify immediately which new-coming time-series subsequences of streaming time series match with prespecified patterns.

For the past, the Euclidean metric was widely used to compute the distance between two time-series sequences. However, the distance measure is unsuitable

© ICST Institute for Computer Sciences, Social Informatics and Telecommunications Engineering 2016
P.C. Vinh et al. (Eds.): ICTCC 2016, LNICST 168, pp. 189–202, 2016.
DOI: 10.1007/978-3-319-46909-6_18

when the two time-series sequences have the same shape but they are variable in the time axis and in the circumstance, Dynamic Time Warping (DTW) [1] shows its superiority in accuracy over the Euclidean metric. DTW has been noted in several domains, including bioinformatics, robotics, and finance, especially in multimedia such as speech recognition [2]. For instance, in a query-by-humming system [3], the computer searches a list of melodies that are most similar to a tune or a sung query echoed from a user, yet users almost tend to sing slower or faster than the digital song stored in a music database. Consequently, the system can hardly find the intended song from the out-of-phase query if the similarity search is conducted with the Euclidean metric. The DTW metric enables the system to retrieve the desirable song since it is able to find two similar time-series sequences although they are out of phase with each other. Nevertheless, using DTW is not enough for accurate retrievals of the song, since most users do not sing queries in the same pitch levels as the song. Normalization of both time-series subsequences of digital songs and the queries is needed to eliminate any existing offsets prior to any distance calculations.

There have been very few methods proposed for similarity search in streaming time-series under DTW. In 2007, Sakurai et al. [4] proposed SPRING, an outstanding method that can quickly find *best-so-far* subsequences for patterns over time-series streams under DTW. The authors claimed that SPRING can offer significantly improvements in speed (up to 650,000 times) over the naïve implementation of similarity search under DTW. However, the obtained results of SPRING are inaccurate in our experiments because the authors did not normalize the data before the DTW distance between any pair of time-series sequences is calculated. In 2012, Rakthanmanon et al. [5] introduced UCR-DTW, a method that can find *best-so-far* subsequences in static time series for patterns under DTW. UCR-DTW applies incremental z-score normalization and performs the task quickly and accurately. Recently, we have improved UCR-DTW to SUCR-DTW [6] so that the similarity search can be done in streaming time-series context. SUCR-DTW also performs the task as quickly and precisely as UCR-DTW does in static context. However, UCR-DTW and SUCR-DTW can find only the subsequences which have the same length as patterns. This characteristic of the two methods limits the benefit of DTW: the distance measure can be done on two sequences of different lengths.

The above shortcomings of some previous methods motivate us to develop a new method which can find accurately new-coming subsequences of streaming time series that are most similar to patterns under DTW. The proposed method is an improvement of SPRING method by applying incremental min-max normalization before the DTW calculation. Furthermore, our method can work in a very important scenario of streaming context where incoming data are from many concurrent high-speed time-series streams, and patterns for query are prespecified time-series sequences.

The rest of paper is organized as follows. Section 2 presents the background including an overview of DTW, data normalization, and the problem definition. Section 3 reviews related work. Section 4 describes the proposed method.

Section 5 discusses experimental evaluation, and Sect. 6 gives conclusions and future work.

2 Background

2.1 Dynamic Time Warping

Dynamic Time Warping (DTW) is a robust distance measure for time series. DTW allows time-series sequences stretched along the time axis to minimize the distance between them. DTW is calculated by dynamic programming depicted as follows. Consider two time-series sequences $C = c_1, c_2, \ldots, c_m$ and $Q = q_1, q_2, \ldots, q_n$. The DTW distance between C and Q is defined as:

$$DTW(C,Q) = f(m,n)$$

$$f(m,n) = d(c_i, q_j) + \min \begin{cases} f(i, j-1) \\ f(i-1, j) \\ f(i-1, j-1) \end{cases} \tag{1}$$

$$f(0,0) = 0, f(i,0) = f(0,j) = \infty$$
$$(1 \leq i \leq m, 1 \leq j \leq n)$$

in which $d(c_i, q_j) = (c_i - q_j)^2$ is the Euclidean metric between two numerical values, c_i and q_j. Notice that any choice (e.g. $d(c_i, q_j) = |c_i - q_j|$) would be fine. Our proposed method is absolutely independent of such choices.

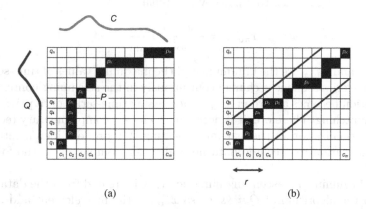

Fig. 1. (a) To align C and Q, a warping path P, shown with solid squares, is constructed. (b) The Sakoe-ChiBa band with a warping scope r is used as a global constraint to limit the scope of P.

To align C and Q using DTW, an n-by-m matrix, which is also referred to as an accumulated cost matrix, is constructed. The (i^{th}, j^{th}) cell of the matrix contains the value of $f(c_i, q_j)$. A warping path P is a sequence of continuous cells in the matrix, which defines a mapping of C and Q such that $f(m, n)$ is minimum. An example of P is illustrated as in Fig. 1(a).

Since DTW uses a dynamic programming algorithm whose the time and space complexity are $\mathcal{O}(mn)$, the distance measure is almost very slow, especially for long time-series sequences. To accelerate the DTW calculation, we can limit the number of cells evaluated in the accumulated cost matrix. Figure 1(b) depicts a Sakoe-Chiba band [2] that prevents pathological warping paths, where a data point in one time series matches to too many data points of another as in Fig. 1(a). The Sakoe-Chiba band makes a warping window constrained by two lines parallel to the diagonal of the matrix.

2.2   Data Normalization

In temporal data mining, data normalization is essential to achieve a meaningful calculation of the distance between two time series because the normalized data have similar offset and distribution, regardless of any distance measure used, especially for the DTW measure. There are two popular ways to normalize time-series data: min-max and z-score. The normalized data would be computed from the coefficients of the two data normalization types. Min-max coefficients (minimum and maximum values) of evolving subsequences in streaming time series are changed now and then, whereas z-score coefficients (mean and standard deviation) of the subsequences are almost changed whenever there is a new-coming data. For the reason, we use min-max normalization in our proposed method so that its time complexity is lower. Min-max normalization maps a value x of time series $X = x_1, x_2, \ldots, x_n$ to x_{norm} by computing

$$x_{norm} = \frac{x - x_{min}}{x_{max} - x_{min}} \tag{2}$$

where x_{min} and x_{max} are the minimum and the maximum values of time-series X.

As time-series sequences change continuously in the streaming context, data normalization becomes a burden for pre-processing time-series data prior to subsequence matching. Therefore, it is necessary to have a complementary technique for data normalization in the streaming setting. We propose incremental min-max normalization to preclude data normalization completely in the following paragraph.

In the beginning, an ascending numeric array is created from the data points of X with the algorithm of *Quicksort*, so x_{min} is the first element and x_{max} is the last one of the ordering array. After that, when there is a new-coming data point, the oldest data point of X is deleted out of the array, and then the new data point is inserted into the array. The course of the deletion and insertion must retain the ascending order of the array, so the algorithm of *Binary search* is used to find the element which needs deleting and the suitable position in the array to insert the new data point. As a result, the time complexity of the incremental min-max normalization is $\mathcal{O}(log(n))$.

2.3   *Best-so-far* Search in Streaming Time Series

The problem is defined as follows. A time-series stream S is a discrete, semi-infinite time-series sequence of real numbers $x_0, x_1, \ldots, x_n \ldots$ where x_n is the most recent value. In other words, X is a univariate time series, which is evolving with an increase of n after each time tick. Let $S[x_s : x_e]$ be the subsequence starting from time tick s, and ending at time tick e; and $NS[nx_s : nx_e]$ be the normalized subsequence of $S[x_s : x_e]$. Let $P[p_0 : p_{m-1}]$ be a time-series pattern of length m, and $NP[np_0 : np_{m-1}]$ be the normalized sequence of P. We want to find such a NS that is most similar to NP. This means that $DTW(NS, NP)$ is smallest until the most recent time tick n (see Fig. 3(a)). The smallest value is the *best-so-far* value, which is denoted as $P.bsf$, and S is also the *best-so-far* subsequence of P till time tick n.

3   Related Work

The section describes SPRING and SUCR-DTW which are closely related to our proposed method.

3.1   SPRING

The method detects high-similarity subsequences over time-series streams. Since SPRING works on un-normalized data, we only consider S and P. The method uses a subsequence time warping matrix (STWM) whose cells record the starting position of each candidate subsequence. Let denote the starting position as s for the (i, j) cell. In addition, the cell contains the value $f(i, j)$, which is the best distance to match the prefix of length $j - s + 1$ from a certain $S[x_s : x_h](h \geq j)$ with the prefix of length i from $P[p_0 : p_{m-1}]$. In other words, the values s and $f(i, j)$ in the STWM mean that the subsequence from s through j obtains $f(i, j)$, which is the minimum distance for the i- and j- prefix of P and S, respectively.

$p_3 = 4$	0 – 27	1 – 15	1 – 10	1 – 18	1 – 38	1 – 28	1 – 52	
$p_2 = 9$	0 – 26	1 – 6	1 – 10	1 – 2	1 – 3	1 – 3	1 – 7	
$p_1 = 6$	0 – 10	1 – 2	1 – 1	3 – 4	3 – 16	5 – 10	5 – 26	
$p_0 = 8$	0 – 9	1 – 1	2 – 4	3 – 0	4 – 4	5 – 1	6 – 9	
	$x_0 = 5$	$x_1 = 7$	$x_2 = 6$	$x_3 = 8$	$x_4 = 10$	$x_5 = 9$	$x_6 = 11$	$x_7 = \ldots$

Fig. 2. The subsequence time warping matrix shows *best-so-far* values until time tick 6.

We consider an illustration of SPRING. Assume that $P = 8, 6, 9, 4$ and $S = 5, 7, 6, 8, 10, 9, 11, \ldots$. The evolution of the STWM from time tick 0 to 6 is depicted as in Fig. 2. In the beginning, at time tick 0, the candidate subsequence $S[x_0 : x_0]$ has the distance $f(0, 3) = 27$. At time tick 1, the *best-so-far* value is 15 with the subsequence $S[x_1 : x_1]$. Next, we found the *best-so-far* value is 10 with the subsequence $S[x_1 : x_2]$ at time tick 2. Until the most recent time tick 6, the *best-so-far* value is still 10 with the subsequence $S[x_1 : x_2]$. From the example, we note that SPRING is of low computational time. If the length of P is m, SPRING requires the time complexity of $\mathcal{O}(m)$ per time tick. Besides, every column is computed from its preceding column.

Recently, Gong et al. [7] have introduced NSPRING, an extension of SPRING supporting z-score normalization. The authors normalize data of the current column in the STWM with the current z-score coefficients, and then compute this normalized data with the normalized data of the preceding column, which were derived from the z-score coefficients of the preceding time tick. Since z-score coefficients are frequently changed during the course of streaming time series, data of the preceding time tick need normalizing again with the current z-score coefficients. For the reason, in our opinion, NPRING is inaccurate.

3.2   SUCR-DTW

The method uses the Sakoe-Chiba band and many lower bounding functions to speedup DTW. The lower bounding functions prune off unpromising time-series subsequences in a cascading fashion. These functions are arranged in the ascending tightness of the lower bounding property such that front lower bounding functions with low time complexities rule out most unpromising subsequences. As a result, the number of post-checking times using the classical DTW so as to determine if a candidate subsequence is a true hit is very tiny. For a detailed explanation, SUCR-DTW [6] employs improved LB_{-Kim} [8] with the computation complexity $\mathcal{O}(1)$, LB_{-Keogh} [9] with $\mathcal{O}(m)$, and finally reversed LB_{-Keogh} [5] with $\mathcal{O}(m)$. The experiments in [6] indicated that the pruning powers of improved LB_{-Kim}, LB_{-Keogh}, and reversed LB_{-Keogh} are roughly 55 %, 35 %, and 9 %, respectively. Therefore, the calculation of the classical DTW is about 1 % in the post-checking phase.

Since SUCR-DTW integrates data normalization in similarity search under DTW, the finding results are relatively accurate. As mentioned in Sect. 1, the major limit of SUCR-DTW is that the method retrieves only time-series subsequences that have the same length as patterns.

4   Proposed Methods

The proposed method is an improvement of SPRING by combining with incremental min-max normalization. Let denote the proposed method as ISPRING (Improved SPRING). In comparison with SPRING, ISPRING consists of two novel ideas.

Firstly, each pattern has a monitoring window anchored at the entry of one time-series stream to keep track of min-max coefficients in the window. Thanks to these coefficients, the normalized new-coming subsequence of the time-series stream is derived. The time warping distance between the normalized subsequence and the normalized pattern is incrementally computed. Let l be the size of the monitoring window. If the min-max coefficients in the monitoring window are changed, the time warping distances need completely calculating from the starting time tick of the monitoring window $n - l + 1$, to the most recent time tick n, in order that the course ensures that finding results are still accurate. Figure 3(a) shows that while a streaming time series is evolving; the monitoring window must check minimum and maximum values of the corresponding subsequence.

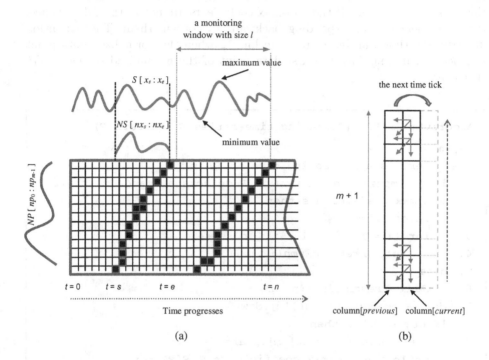

(a)   (b)

Fig. 3. (a) A window monitors the min-max coefficients. (b) The time warping distances are incrementally computed in a bottom-up fashion with the two columns.

Secondly, ISPRING uses two columns with size of $m + 1$ to maintain time warping distances computed incrementally. Hence, the memory space of ISPRING reduces significantly instead of using the subsequence time warping matrix (STWM) in SPRING. The space complexity is reduced from $\mathcal{O}(mn)$ of SPRING to $\mathcal{O}(m)$ of ISPRING. At the beginning of the similarity search, the two columns are initiated by Procedure *Reset_columns*. The two columns are exchanged the role with each other in every time tick. If a column is current at time tick i, then it will become previous at $i + 1$. Similar to SPRING, each cell of the column contains two kinds of information. The first is the starting time tick from which the time warping distance is calculated. The second is the time warping distance. While streaming time-series is evolving, the information of cells in the current column is computed in a bottom up fashion. Figure 3(b) illustrates the calculation of the time warping distances in cells complies with the formula (1), so the time warping distance in the mth cell of the current column will be the minimum distance from the starting time tick to the most recent time tick n. Next, this time warping distance is compared with the current *best-so-far* value of the pattern.

ISPRING is briefly described in Algorithm *ISPRING*. Notice that line 10 checks whether the subsequence $S[x_s : x_n]$ contains the min-max coefficients of the monitoring window. If the min-max coefficients are not in the subsequence, the subsequence needs expanding backward to contain them. The expansion increases the time warping distance in line 12 when the normalized data point nx_s needs matching with the first data point of the normalized sequence NP, that is np_0.

Algorithm *ISPRING*(Streaming time-series S, Pattern P)

begin

When there is a new-coming data of S: x_n

1. **if** the monitoring window of P detects a change in their
    min-max coefficients **then**

2.   *Reset_columns*

3.   **for** ($i = n - l + 1$; $i \leq n$; i++)

4.   *Set_current_column*(i, nx_i)

5. **else**

6.   *Set_current_column*(n, nx_n)

7. $dtw \leftarrow$ column[*current*][m].dtw

8. **if** $dtw < P.bsf$ **then**

9. $s \leftarrow$ column[*current*][m].start

10.   **while** the min-max coefficients $\notin S[x_s : x_n]$

11. s--

12. dtw += $d(nx_s, np_0)$

13.   **if** $dtw \geq P.bsf$ **then**

14.   **break**

15.   **end while**

16.   **if** $dtw < P.bsf$ **then**

17. $P.bsf \leftarrow dtw$

18.   Record $S[x_s : x_n]$ as the *best-so-far* subsequence of
            P

end

The two procedures *Reset_columns* and *Set_current_column* are presented in detail to clarify the subtle techniques in manipulating the two columns.

```
Procedure Reset_columns
begin
1.  for (i = 0 ; i ≤ m ; i++)
2.      column[1][i].dtw ← ∞
3.  current ← 1
4.  previous ← 0
end
```

```
Procedure Set_current_column(i, nx)
begin
1.  if current = 1 then
2.      current ← 0
3.      previous ← 1
4.  else
5.      current ← 1
6.      previous ← 0
7.  column[current][0].dtw ← 0
8.  column[current][0].start ← i
9.  for (i = 0 ; i ≤ m ; i++)
10.     temp ← column[current][i - 1]
11.     if temp.dtw > column[previous][i - 1].dtw  then
12.         temp ← column[previous][i - 1]
13.     if temp.dtw > column[previous][i].dtw  then
14.         temp ← column[previous][i]
15.     column[current][i].dtw ← temp.dtw + d(nx, np_{i-1})
16.     column[current][i].start ← temp.start
end
```

5   Experimental Evaluation

ISPRING and SUCR-DTW have been compared in terms of accuracy and wall-clock time. SUCR-DTW has been modified to implement *best-so-far* search and incremental min-max normalization instead of doing range search and incremental z-score normalization as in our previous work [6]. We use 5 % constraint on the warping path in SUCR-DTW. For example, if the length of a query is 200, then the warping scope r in Sakoe-Chiba band is 10. ISPRING is implemented with monitoring windows whose lengths are same as those of patterns.

The experiments have been conducted on an Intel Dual Core i3 M350 2.27 GHz, 4 GB RAM PC. Because of the characteristic of the search methods and the strength of today's CPU, we employ multi-threading in the implementation of ISPRING and SUCR-DTW. This means each threading process handles one time-series stream to perform the similarity search. For the sake of fairness, all threading processes are the same priority. Microsoft C# is powerful for multithreaded programming, so we use the programming language to implement the two methods. Another point we cannot ignore is that since many threading processes can compete to update the *best-so-far* value of one pattern at a time; the system must lock the shared resources and check the *best-so-far* value again before the update can be done.

Seven text files are used to simulate time-series streams. The sources of the text files are given in column 4 of Table 1. A pattern set is created from the text files. The number of patterns of the set is 20 and the lengths of all patterns are 256. Notice that ISPRING can work with many patterns concurrently, and every pattern that needs to find the *best-so-far* subsequence over time-series streams has its own monitoring window on each time-series stream. We used patterns of same length for the sake of clarity but no loss of generality. The number of patterns is created from a time-series file is proportional to the number of data points in the file. Every pattern is extracted from random positions in the time-series files. Next, all data points of a pattern are added by a numerical constant, and then the data points are virtually increased or decreased by a relatively small numeric value (e.g. 0.3 or −0.3). After that, 33 % of the data points are changed in which they get the value of the preceding data point or successive one, or the mean of neighboring ones.

Table 1. Text files are used to simulate time-series streams.

No	Time-series file	Length	Source
1	D2	50,000	[10]
2	ItalyPowerDemand_TEST	25,725	[11]
3	Lightcurve	27,204	[10]
4	MedicalImages_TEST	76,000	[11]
5	SonyAIBORobotSurface_TEST	42,671	[11]
6	SonyAIBORobotSurfaceII_TEST	62,898	[11]
7	TwoLeadECG_TEST	94,537	[11]

Since in reality, time-series streams are potentially unbounded in size, we design circular buffers whose sizes are 1,024, to store data points of time-series streams. This size of a circular buffer makes sure that ISPRING does not cause false dismissals for patterns whose lengths are 256.

The experimental results of the two methods are depicted in Table 2. We consider an illustration of the *best-so-far* search in case of pattern 3. By SUCR-DTW, while the seven time-series streams are arriving continuously,

Table 2. Statistic of the experimental results

Pattern	SUCR-DTW				ISPRING			
	#TS	#Position	Length	*bsf* value	#TS	#Position	Length	*bsf* value
1	3	5,420	256	1.9439	3	12,445	168	1.8089
2	3	5,435	256	1.9794	3	12,479	150	1.8518
3	5	24,164	256	2.0358	3	4,464	179	1.8659
4	2	19,606	256	1.2783	2	19,608	258	1.2779
5	3	21,199	256	2.2661	3	23,374	227	2.2059
6	4	75,955	256	0.8458	4	23,652	153	0.6341
7	4	52,014	256	0.4502	4	52,015	266	0.4144
8	4	1,812	256	1.1243	5	51,891	42	1.0536
9	4	29,699	256	0.5394	4	13,998	235	0.5012
10	5	60,364	256	0.9283	5	60,363	253	0.9270
11	5	37,530	256	0.9967	5	37,524	249	0.9937
12	5	32,947	256	1.48737	5	2,132	217	1.4151
13	6	22,872	256	1.0436	6	22,871	255	1.0426
14	6	17,702	256	0.9500	6	17,702	256	0.9500
15	7	33,139	256	0.9978	6	33,139	263	0.9938
16	7	86,976	256	1.1809	3	3,450	153	1.1597
17	7	69,489	256	0.9239	7	69,483	250	0.9207
18	7	40,087	256	1.0497	7	71,328	287	1.0264
19	7	76,957	256	0.9125	7	76,975	275	0.9110
20	7	24,316	256	0.9857	7	38,114	279	0.9757

the *best-so-far* (*bsf*) value of the pattern is discovered in streaming time-series 5 at time point 24,164 with a time-series subsequence of length 256. This means the starting time point of the subsequence is $24,164 - 256 - 1 = 23,907$. Similarly, ISPRING discovers the *best-so-far* value of pattern 3 in streaming time-series 3 at time point 4,464 with a time-series subsequence of length 179. The subsequence begins at time point $4,464 - 179 - 1 = 4,284$. As regards the pattern, the *best-so-far* value obtained by SUCR-DTW is 2.0358, whereas ISPRING returns 1.8659. Of twenty cases, there is one case (pattern 14) in which ISPRING has the same results as SUCR-DTW. Therefore, in the testbed, there are 5 % cases in which ISPRING and SUCR-DTW obtain the same results. In remaining 95 % cases, ISPRING gives better *best-so-far* values. However, as regards SUCR-DTW, the wall-clock time is 3:42.884 min and the average CPU time to process a new-coming data point is 5,880 ticks; whereas in respect of ISPRING, theses values are 4:42.68 min and 7,217 ticks, respectively. The evidence shows that the recalculation of the time warping distances in ISPRING is costly whenever the min-max coefficients of the monitoring window are changed. Another note is that there are seven cases (35 %) in which the *best-so-far* subsequences obtained by ISPRING are longer than those done by SUCR-DTW, and remaining twelve cases (60 %) in which the *best-so-far* subsequences obtained by ISPRING are shorter than those done by SUCR-DTW. Hence, we note that ISPRING tends to find *best-so-far* subsequences shorter than the patterns.

We also experimented on the two methods with various testbeds and the obtained results indicated that ISPRING is better than SUCR-DTW in finding *best-so-far* results. Space limits preclude the presentation of the statistic of these testbeds.

Notice that sometimes ISPRING finds *best-so-far* subsequences, whose lengths are very short in comparison with the lengths of the patterns. For instance, in the above testbed, pattern 8 has the *best-so-far* subsequence whose length is 40, compared with 256 of the pattern. This implies that there is a relatively small section of the subsequence mapped onto a relatively large section of pattern 8. As a result, the matching between the subsequence and the pattern creates an unavoidable pathological warping path in the accumulated cost matrix. Figure 4 depicts an illustration of matching between two time-series sequences S and P whose lengths are very uneven, so a pathological warping path is built to match these two sequences. It is obviously that the undesirable matching of the two time-series sequences is a shortcoming of ISPRING.

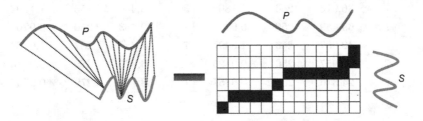

Fig. 4. The pathological matching between P and S

To determine which length of the monitoring window for every pattern is optimal, we vary the length by the formula:

$$\text{The length of the pattern} \times (1 + \Delta)$$
$$\Delta \text{ is changed to} - 5\%, -4\%, ..., 4\%, \text{ and } 5\% \text{ in turns.} \tag{3}$$

We used again the dataset in Table 1 and the same pattern set for the test. Table 3 shows that with each Δ, the number of patterns has the *best-so-far* values better and worse when these values are compared to those with Δ of 0 %. Figure 5 presents the wall-clock times of ISPRING when the method is experimented with Δ from -5% to 5%. With Δ of -5%, there is one case in which ISPRING finds a better *best-so-far* subsequence compared with the corresponding *best-so-far* subsequence with Δ of 0 %. However, the wall-clock time with Δ of -5% is larger than that with Δ of 0 %, since if the length of the monitoring window is

Table 3. The number of cases in which *best-so-far* values are better and worse than Δ of 0 %

Δ (%)	−5	−4	−3	−2	−1	1	2	3	4	5
# better	1	0	0	0	0	0	0	0	1	1
# worse	0	1	1	1	1	1	1	1	1	1

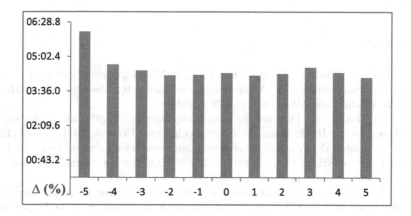

Fig. 5. The wall-clock times of ISPRING with various Δs

shorter, the min-max coefficients are changed more often. For the reason, the time warping distances are frequently recalculated. With other remaining values of Δ, their results are generally not better than the result of Δ of 0 % in terms of the *best-so-far* quality as well as the wall-clock-time, so the monitoring window should have the same length as the pattern.

6 Conclusions and Future Work

The paper has introduced a new method for finding new-coming subsequences in streaming time-series that are most similar to prespecified patterns under DTW. The proposed method, ISPRING, is an improvement of SPRING by applying incremental min-max normalization before the DTW calculation, so that obtained results are accurate. As regards each query pattern, a monitoring window is anchored at the entry of one streaming time series and then the min-max coefficients of the corresponding subsequence are extracted to infer the normalized subsequence. The experiments show that ISPRING can find *best-so-far* subsequences more accurate than those of SUCR-DTW, a state-of-the-art method of similarity search over time-series streams under DTW. The size of the monitoring window should be equal to the length of the pattern. Moreover, ISPRING can discover *best-so-far* subsequences whose lengths are different with those of patterns. Since whenever the min-max coefficients in the monitoring window are changed, the time warping distances need incrementally recalculating. Consequently, the wall-clock time of ISPRING is relatively longer than that of SUCR-DTW.

In future work, we plan to improve ISPRING to find *best-so-far* subsequences whose lengths are reasonable to those of patterns. This means that the found *best-so-far* subsequences should not be too short in comparison to the lengths of patterns.

References

1. Berndt, D., Clifford, J.: Using Dynamic Time Warping to find patterns in time series. In: Proceedings of AAAI Workshop on Knowledge Discovery in Databases, Seattle, Washington, USA, pp. 359–370 (1994)
2. Sakoe, H., Chiba, S.: Dynamic programming algorithm optimization for spoken word recognition. IEEE Trans. Acoust. Speech Signal Process. **26**(1), 43–49 (1978)
3. Zhu, Y., Shasha, D.: Warping indexes with envelope transforms for query by humming. In: Proceedings of the 2003 ACM SIGMOD International Conference on Management of Data, pp. 181–192 (2003)
4. Sakurai, Y., Faloutsos, C., Yamamuro, M.: Stream monitoring under the time warping distance. In: The IEEE 23rd International Conference on Data Engineering, Istanbul, Turkey, pp. 1046–1055 (2007)
5. Rakthanmanon, T., Campana, B., Mueen, A., Batista, G., Westover, B., Zhu, Q., Zakaria, J., Keogh, E.: Searching and mining trillions of time series subsequences under Dynamic Time Warping. In: Proceedings of the 18th ACM SIGKDD Conference on Knowledge Discovery and Data Mining (KDD 2012), Beijing, China, pp. 262–270 (2012)
6. Giao, B. C., Anh, D.T.: Similarity search in multiple high speed time series streams under Dynamic Time Warping. In: Proceedings of the 2015 2nd National Foundation for Science and Technology Development Conference on Information and Computer Science (NICS), Ho Chi Minh City, Vietnam, pp. 82–87 (2015)
7. Gong, X., Fong, S., Chan, J., Mohammed, S.: NSPRING: the SPRING extension for subsequence matching of time series supporting normalization. J. Supercomput. 8, 1–25 (2015). doi:10.1007/s11227-015-1525-6
8. Kim, S.-W., Park, S.: An index-based approach for similarity search supporting time warping in large sequence databases. In: Proceedings of the 17th IEEE International Conference on Data Engineering, Heidelberg, Germany, pp. 607–614 (2001)
9. Keogh, E., Ratanamahatana, C.: Exact indexing of Dynamic Time Warping. Knowl. Inf. Syst. **7**(3), 358–386 (2004)
10. Weigend, A.: In Time series prediction: Forecasting the future and understanding the past. http://www-psych.stanford.edu/~andreas/Time-Series/SantaFe.html. Accessed December 2013
11. Keogh, E.: The UCR time series classification/clustering page. http://www.cs.ucr.edu/~eamonn/time_series_data/. Accessed August 2013

Hybrid Mean-Variance Mapping Optimization for Economic Dispatch with Multiple Fuels Considering Valve-Point Effects

Khoa H. Truong[1(✉)], Pandian Vasant[1], M.S. Balbir Singh[1], and Dieu N. Vo[2]

[1] Department of Fundamental and Applied Sciences, Universiti Teknologi Petronas,
Tronoh, Malaysia
trhkhoa89@gmail.com, pvasant@gmail.com, balbir@petronas.com.my
[2] Department of Power Systems, HCMC University of Technology, Ho Chi Minh City, Vietnam
vndieu@gmail.com

Abstract. Many thermal generating units of an electric power system are supplied with multi-fuel sources such as coal, natural gas and oil. These fuels represent irreplaceable natural resources and conservation is used as a way to increase energy efficiency. Economic dispatch (ED) is one of the significance optimization problems in power system operation for fuel cost savings. This paper proposes a new approach which is hybrid variant of mean-variance mapping optimization (MVMO-SH) for solving this problem. The MVMO-SH is the improvement of original mean-variance mapping optimization algorithm (MVMO). This method adopts a swarm scheme of MVMO and incorporates local search and multi-parent crossover strategies to enhance its global search ability and improve solution quality for optimization problems. The proposed MVMO-SH is tested on 10-unit and large-scale systems with multiple fuels and valve-point effects. The obtained results are compared to those from other optimization methods available in the literature. The comparisons show that the proposed method provides higher quality solutions than the others. Therefore, the MVMO-SH is a promising method for solving the complex ED problems in electric power system.

Keywords: Economic dispatch · Multiple fuels · Valve-point effects · Mean-variance mapping optimization · MVMO · MVMO-SH

Nomenclature

N	total number of generating units
F	total operation cost
$a_{ik}, b_{ik}, c_{ik},$	fuel cost coefficients of generator i
B_{ij}, B_{0i}, B_{00}	total system load demand
P_D	total system load demand
P_i	power output of generator i
$P_{i,max}$	maximum power output of generator i
$P_{i,min}$	minimum power output of generator i

© ICST Institute for Computer Sciences, Social Informatics and Telecommunications Engineering 2016
P.C. Vinh et al. (Eds.): ICTCC 2016, LNICST 168, pp. 203–216, 2016.
DOI: 10.1007/978-3-319-46909-6_19

P_L	total transmission loss
K	the penalty factor for the slack unit
P_s	power output of slack unit
n_var	number of variable (generators)
n_par	number of particles
$mode$	variable selection strategy for offspring creation
$iter_{max}$	the maximum number of iterations
Np	number of particles
$archive\ zize$	n-best individuals to be stored in the table
Δd_0^{ini}	initial smoothing factor increment
Δd_0^{final}	final smoothing factor increment
g_{p_ini}	max percentage of good particles
g_{p_ini}	min percentage of good particles
m_{ini}	initial number of variables selected for mutation
m_{final}	final number of variables selected for mutation

1 Introduction

Economic dispatch (ED) is determination of optimized real power output from a number of electricity generators needed to meet load requirements at lowest possible cost while satisfying all unit and system constraints. Traditionally, the cost fuel function of each generating unit is presented as the quadratic function approximations [1, 2]. However, in practical power system operation conditions, thermal generating units can be supplied with multiple fuel sources like coal, natural gas and oil. This requires their fuel cost functions to be segmented as piecewise quadratic cost functions where each function reflects the effects of different fuel types. The ED problem has piecewise quadratic cost functions which is a non-convex optimization problem with multiple local optima. This problem is more complicated when the effect of valve point loadings is considered [3]. Therefore, the classical solution methods are difficult to deal with this problem. One approach for solving the problem with such units having multiple fuel options is linearization of the segments and solving them by traditional methods [4]. A better approach is to retain the assumption of piecewise quadratic cost functions and proceed to solve them. A hierarchical approach based on the numerical method (HNUM) has been proposed in [5] as one way to deal with the problem. However, the exponential growing time complexity of the numerical methods is a major problem for large-scale systems, especially for non-convex constraints. More advanced optimization methods based on artificial intelligence concepts have been effectively implemented to the ED problem with MF and VPE such as Enhanced Lagrangian Artificial Neural Network (ELANN) [6], genetic algorithm with multiplier updating (IGA_MU) [7], evolutionary algorithm (EA) [8], new PSO with local random search (NPSO-LRS) [9], an improved quantum-behaved particle swarm optimization (SQPSO) [10], Self-organizing hierarchical particle swarm optimizer (SOH-PSO) [11], and Pseudo-Gradient Based Particle Swarm Optimization Method (PGPSO) [12]. However, the search ability of these methods often provides near global optimal solution for non-convex optimization problems. The non-convex ED problem is always a challenge for solution methods. Therefore, there is always a need for developing new techniques for solving this problem.

Recently, Mean-variance mapping optimization (MVMO) is developed and introduced by István Erlich [13]. This algorithm possesses conceptual similarities to other known heuristic algorithms in three evolutionary operators including selection, mutation and crossover. However, the special feature of MVMO is the mapping function applied for the mutation based on the mean and variance of n-best population saved in an archive. The original of MVMO utilizes single particle to start the search process. In order to enhance its global searching ability, the search space of MVMO is extended by initializing a set of particles, which formed a swarm variant of MVMO (MVMOS) [14, 15]. The subsequent improvement is hybrid variant of MVMO, referred to as MVMO-SH [16]. It adopts a swarm scheme of MVMO and incorporates local search components. Therefore each particle has its own memory which is represented by the corresponding archive and mapping function. All particles are arranged according to their local best fitness and classified into two groups including good and bad particles. For each good particle, the parent assignment is done by considering the first ranked solution in its particular knowledge archive whereas a multi-parent crossover is used to reorient each bad particle towards different sub-regions of the search space. An interior-point method (IPM) is included for local improvement option. In this paper, the MVMO-SH is proposed as a new method for solving the non-convex ED problem with multiple fuels and valve-point effects. The non-convex and large-scale ED problem is always a challenge for solution methods in terms of optimal solution and computational time. The proposed MVMO-SH is tested on 10-unit and large-scale systems with multiple fuels and valve-point effects. The obtained results have shown that the MVMO-SH method is more effective than many other methods in the literature in terms of optimal solution, especially for large-scale systems. Therefore, the MVMO-SH is a favorable method for solving the non-convex ED problem.

2   Problem Formulation

The main objective of the ED problem with MF and VPE is to minimize total cost of thermal power plants with many different fuels while satisfying equality and inequality constraints. The power system consists of N thermal generating units. Each unit has a fuel cost function, shown as F_i, to generates a power out P_i. The total fuel cost of the system, F_T, is sum of fuel cost of each unit. The optimization problem of the ED is to minimize the total fuel cost F_T, which be written as:

$$\text{Minimize } F_T = \sum_{i=1}^{N} F_i(P_i) \quad i = 1, 2, 3, \dots, N \tag{1}$$

where the fuel cost function of each generating unit is represented by [12]:

$$F_i(P_i) = \begin{cases} a_{i1} + b_{i1}P_i + c_{i1}P_i^2 + \left|e_{i1}\cdot\sin(f_{i1}\cdot(P_{i1}^{\min} - P_{i1}))\right|, & \text{for fuel 1, } P_i^{\min} \leq P_i \leq P_{i1} \\ a_{i2} + b_{i2}P_i + c_{i2}P_i^2 + \left|e_{i2}\cdot\sin(f_{i2}\cdot(P_{i2}^{\min} - P_{i2}))\right|, & \text{for fuel 2, } P_{i1} \leq P_i \leq P_{i2} \\ \vdots \\ a_{ik} + b_{ik}P_i + c_{ik}P_i^2 + \left|e_{ik}\cdot\sin(f_{ik}\cdot(P_{ik}^{\min} - P_{ik}))\right|, & \text{for fuel } k, P_{ik-1} \leq P_i \leq P_i^{\max} \end{cases} \tag{2}$$

The constraints of the ED problem must be satisfied during the optimization process are presented as follows:

1. *Real power balance equation:* The total active power output of generating units must be equal to total active load demand plus power loss:

$$\sum_{i=1}^{N} P_i = P_D + P_L \tag{3}$$

The power loss P_L is calculated by [1]:

$$P_L = \sum_{i=1}^{N}\sum_{j=1}^{N} P_i B_{ij} P_j + \sum_{i=1}^{N} B_{0i} P_i + B_{00} \tag{4}$$

2. *Generator capacity limits:* The active power output of generating units must be within the allowed limits:

$$P_{i,\min} \leq P_i \leq P_{i,\max} \tag{5}$$

3 Hybrid Variant of Mean-Variance Mapping Optimization

3.1 Review of Mean - Variance Mapping Optimization (MVMO)

The key feature of MVMO is a special mapping function which applied for mutating the offspring based on mean-variance of the solutions stored in the archive.

The mean $\overline{x}_i$ and variance v_i are calculated as follows [13]:

$$\overline{x}_i = \frac{1}{n}\sum_{j=1}^{n} x_i(j) \tag{6}$$

$$v_i = \frac{1}{n}\sum_{j=1}^{n} (x_i(j) - \overline{x}_i)^2 \tag{7}$$

where $j = 1, 2, \ldots, n$ (n is population size).

The transformation of x_i^* to x_i via mapping function is depicted as Fig. 1.

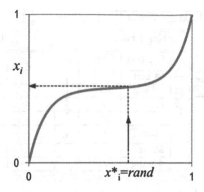

Fig. 1. Variable mapping

The transformation mapping function, h, is calculated by the mean $\bar{x}$ and shape variables s_{i1} and s_{i2} as follows [13]:

$$h(\bar{x}_i, s_{i1}, s_{i2}, x) = \bar{x}_i.(1 - e^{-x.s_{i1}}) + (1 - \bar{x}_i).e^{-(1-x).s_{i2}} \tag{8}$$

where

$$s_i = -\ln(v_i).f_s \tag{9}$$

The scaling factor f_s is a MVMO parameter which allows for controlling the search process during iteration. s_i is the shape variable.

All variables are initialized within the limit range [0,1]. The output of mapping function is always inside [0,1]. However, the function evaluation is carried out always in the original scales.

3.2 Hybrid Mean-Variance Mapping Optimization (MVMO-SH)

The hybrid variant Mean-variance mapping optimization (MOMO-SH) is a subsequent improvement of the original MVMO. It adopts a swarm scheme of MVMO and incorporates local search and multi-parent crossover strategies to increase the innate power of global searching ability of MVMO. The flowchart of MVMO-SH is depicted in [16].

The variables of optimization problem are recalculated from [0,1] to their original boundaries before fitness evaluation or local search is carried out. An interior-point method (IPM) based strategy is included for local improvement option. The IMP is performed with a probability γ parameter for any child of the population.

The solution archive stores the n-best achieved offspring of each particle in a descending order of fitness. For each particle, its archive is only updated once the new better solution is produced after every step of fitness evaluation or local search. The archive is illustrated in Fig. 2.

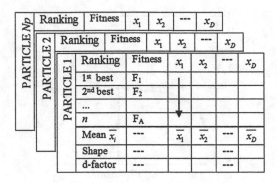

Fig. 2. Structure of the solution archive.

At least two fitness functions are independently evaluated by each particle in the early stage of the search process, and those solutions are saved in archive. All particles are ranked based on their local best fitness. Among of them, a set of good particles is determined as in (10), and the remainder is classified as a set of bad particles (Np-Gp) [16].

$$Gp = round(Np.g_p) \tag{10}$$

where

$$g_p = g_{p\_ini} + \frac{i}{i_{final}}(g_{p\_final} - g_{p\_ini}) \tag{11}$$

For each good particle, the first ranked solution in its particular knowledge archive is chosen as the parent for the next offspring. For each bad particle, a multi-parent strategy is used to produce the parent as (12). The detail of parent selection is described in [16].

$$x_k^{parent} = x_{RG}^{best} + \beta(x_{GB}^{best} - x_{LG}^{best}) \tag{12}$$

The x_{RG}^{best} is randomly selected between the x_{GB}^{best} and x_{LG}^{best}, where represent the first and the last global best in the group of good particles, respectively. The factor is a random number which is calculated as in (13). This number is recalculated if any element of the vector x_k^{parent} is outside the [0, 1] bound [16].

$$\beta = 2\left(rand + 0.5\left(\frac{i}{i_{final}}\right)^2 - 0.5\right) \tag{13}$$

In the selection variables of MVMO-SH, the number m of dimensions to be selected for mutation operation is progressively decreased as follows [16]:

$$m = round(m_{final} + irand(m^* - m_{final})) \tag{14}$$

$$m^* = round(m_{ini} - \left(\frac{i}{i_{final}}\right)^2 (m_{ini} - m_{final})) \tag{15}$$

4   Implementation of MVMO-SH to ED

4.1   Handling of Constraints

The constraints of the ED problem with MF and VPE include the real power balance constraint (3) and the generator capacity limits constraint (5). To satisfy all these constraints, the slack variable method is used for handling real power balance constraint (3) and the penalty function is used for handling the generator capacity limits constraint (5).

Neglecting the power transmission losses, the real power balance constraint (3) is rewritten by:

$$\sum_{i=1}^{N} P_i = P_D \tag{16}$$

Slack variable method is used for handling equality constraints in optimization problems where the value of variables is calculated from the others based on the equality constraints. This method is used for calculation of the power output for a slack unit from the power outputs of the remaining units in the system based on the real power balance constraint (3). By using the slack variable method [17], the slack unit can be randomly selected among the available units in the systems to calculate its power output as follows:

$$P_s = P_D - \sum_{\substack{i=1 \\ i \neq s}}^{N} P_i \tag{17}$$

In this study, the first unit is selected as slack unit for all test system. The power output of the slack unit is then included in the fitness function (18) with high penalty factor for a violation. The fitness function for the proposed MVMO-SH will include the objective function (2) and penalty terms for the slack unit if inequality (5) is violated. The fitness function is as follows:

$$F_T = \sum_{i=1}^{N} F_i(P_i) + K \times \left[\left(\max(0, P_s - P_{s,\max})\right)^2 + \left(\max(0, P_{s,\min} - P_s)\right)^2 \right] \tag{18}$$

4.2   Implementation of MVMO-SH to ED

The steps of procedure of MVMO-SH for the ED problem are described as follows:

Step 1:   Setting the parameters for MVMO-SH including $iter_{max}$, Np, n_par, $mode$, d_i, Δd_0^{ini}, Δd_0^{final}, $archive$ $zize$, $f_{s\_ini}^*$, $f_{s\_final}^*$, $n\_randomly$, $n\_randomly\_min$, $Indep.runs$

Set $i = 0$, i denotes the function evaluation

Step 2:   Normalize initial variables to the range [0,1]

```
for i=1:n_par
    for j=1:n_var
    xx(i,j)= p_min(j) + rand*(p_max(j)-p_min(j));
    end
    x_norm(i,:)=(xx(i,:)-p_min)./(p_max(j)-p_min(j));
end

x_normalized=x_norm;
```

Step 3:   Set $k = 1$, k denotes particle counters

Step 4:   If rand $< \gamma$ parameter, start local search. Otherwise, calculate power output for the slack generator by using (17) to evaluate fitness function in (18)

Step 5:   Fill/update individual archive

Step 6:   Classify Np particles into two groups including a set of GP good particles and a set of $(Np-Gp)$ bad particles according to (10)

Step 7:   If the particles are bad, the parent is produced by using a multi-parent strategy (12). Otherwise, the parent selection is single parent crossover based on local best

Step 8:   Create offspring generation through three evolutionary operators: selection, mutation and crossover

Step 9:   If $k < Np$, increase $k = k + 1$ and go to step 4. Otherwise, go to step 10

Step 10:   Check termination criteria. If stopping criteria is satisfied, stop. Otherwise, go to step 3. The algorithm of the proposed MVMO techniques is terminated when the maximum number of iterations $iter_{max}$ is reached

5   Numerical Results

The proposed MVMO-SH has been tested on 10-unit and large-scale system including 20, 40, 60, 80 and 160 units with multiple fules and valve-point effects. The convergence of metaheuristic methods may not obtain exactly same solution because these methods initialize variables randomly at each run. Hence, their performances could not be judged by the results of a single run. Many trials should be carried out to reach an impartial conclusion about the performance of the algorithm. Therefore, the implementations of the proposed method are carried out 50 independent trials in this study. The mean cost, max cost, average cost and standard deviation obtained by the proposed method are used to evaluate the robustness characteristic of the proposed method for ED problem. The algorithm of MVMO-SH is run on a Core i5 CPU 3.2 GHz PC with 4 GB of RAM. The implementation of the proposed MVMO-SH is coded in the Matlab R2013a platform.

By experiments, the typical parameters for MVMO-SH are selected as follows:

- $iter_{max}$: The maximum number of iterations is set to 20000, 40000, 60000, 80000 and 100000 for 10-unit, 20-unit, 40-unit, 80-unit and 160-unit, respectively

- *n_var*: number of generators (D), D = 10.
- *n_par*: number of particles is set to 50 in all cases.
- γ: The probability parameter is set to $\gamma = 1/100/D$.
- *archive size*: Size of solution archive is set to 4 in all cases.
- $g_{p\_ini} = 0.7$, $g_{p\_ini} = 0.2$
- *mode*: There are four variable selection strategy for offspring creation. After all simulations, strategy 4 (*mode* = 4) is suporior to the other strategy.
- $m_{final} = round\ (n\_var/2)$, $m_{ini} = 1$
- Δd_0^{ini}, Δd_0^{final}: The range of Δd_0 in (14) is [0.01 – 0.4]. By experiments, Δd_0^{ini} and Δd_0^{final} is set to 0.4 and 0.05, respectively.
- $f_{s\_ini}^*$, $f_{s\_final}^*$: $f_{s\_ini}^*$ is set to 1 and $f_{s\_final}^*$ is set to 10.
- *Indep_run* is set to 3.

5.1   10-Unit System

The data of 10-unit test with VPE and MF is given in [7]. This system supplies to the power load demand of 2700 MW with transmission power loss neglected.

The result obtained by the proposed MVMO-SH including power outputs, minimum total cost, average total cost, maximum total cost, standard deviation for this system are shown in Table 1. As seen in Table 1, the difference between the maximum and minimum costs obtained the proposed MVMO-SH is very small and the standard deviation is very low (0.0306). It clearly shows that the performance the proposed MVMO-SH is robust.

Table 1. Results obtained for 10-unit system with MF and VPE for load demands 2700 MW by MVMO-SH

Unit	Fuel F_i	P_i (MW)
1	2	218.1050
2	1	210.9169
3	1	280.6571
4	3	239.9551
5	1	279.9208
6	3	239.3922
7	1	287.7207
8	3	239.0145
9	3	428.4452
10	1	275.8725
Total power (MW)		2700.000
Min total cost ($/h)		623.8301
Average total cost ($/h)		623.8997
Max total cost ($/h)		623.9619
Standard deviation ($/h)		0.0306

The best total cost and computational time obtained by MVMO-SH are compared to other methods including CGA_MU, IGA_MU [7], DE, RGA, PSO [8], PSO-LRS, NPSO, NPSO-LRS [9], SQPSO [10], PSO-TVIW, PSO-TVAC, SOH-PSO [11], and PGPSO [12], which are shown in Table 2. The comparison of best fuel cost is also depicted in Fig. 3. The best total cost obtained by MVMO-SH for this system is less than the other methods as observed from Table 2 and Fig. 3.

Table 2. Comparison of best total cost for 10-unit system with MF and VPE

Method	Best cost ($/h)
CGA_MU [7]	624.7193
IGA_MU [7]	624.5178
DE [8]	624.5146
RGA [8]	624.5081
PSO [8]	624.5074
PSO-LRS [9]	624.2297
NPSO [9]	624.1624
NPSO-LRS [9]	624.1273
SQPSO [10]	623.8476
PSO-TVIW [11]	623.8444
PGPSO [12]	623.8431
PSO-TVAC [11]	623.8399
SOH-PSO [11]	623.8362
MVMO-SH	623.8301

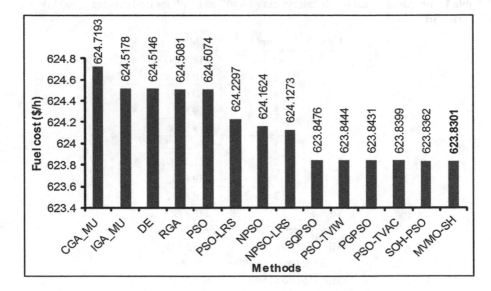

Fig. 3. Comparison of best fuel cost for 10-unit test system with VPE and MF

5.2 Large-Scale Systems

The large-scale systems are created by duplicating the basic 10-unit system with the load demand of 2700 MW adjusted to the system size proportionally. Table 3 shows the results obtained by the MVMO-SH for these systems including minimum total costs, average total costs, maximum total costs, standard deviations, and computational times. As seen from Table 3, the difference between the maximum and minimum costs obtained the MVMO-SH is small.

Table 3. Results for systems with VPE and MF

No. of units	20	40	80	160
Min total cost ($/h)	1247.7143	2495.6100	4991.8861	9992.6725
Average total cost ($/h)	1247.8435	2496.1662	4996.3716	10002.6651
Max total cost ($/h)	1248.0171	2497.7533	5006.5585	10016.9936
Standard deviation ($/h)	0.0863	0.5193	4.0995	6.1357
Average CPU time (s)	9.728	20.474	42.651	101.120

Table 4 shows the comparison of the average total costs and CPU times between the proposed MVMO-SH and the CGA_MU, IGA_MU [5] and PGPSO [10]. The comparison of best fuel cost is also depicted in Fig. 4 for this case. As seen from Table 4 and Fig. 4, in all cases, the MVMO-SH obtains the average total costs less than CGA_MU, IGA_MU and PGPSO, especially for the large-scale systems.

Table 4. Comparison of average total cost and CPU times for systems with VPE & MF

Method	No. of units	Total cost ($)	CPU time (s)
CGA_MU [7]	20	1249.3893	80.48
	40	2500.9220	157.39
	80	5008.1426	309.41
	160	10143.7263	621.30
IGA_MU [7]	20	1249.1179	21.64
	40	2499.8243	43.71
	80	5003.8832	85.67
	160	10042.4742	174.62
PGPSO [12]	20	1248.9623	4.078
	40	2499.6127	18.645
	80	5003.0250	43.191
	160	10032.4883	91.570
MVMO-SH	20	1247.8435	9.728
	40	2496.1662	20.474
	80	4996.3716	42.651
	160	10002.6651	101.120

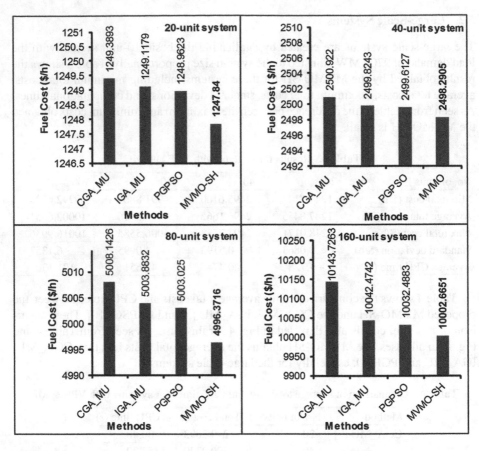

Fig. 4. Comparison of average fuel cost for large-scale test systems with both VPE and MF

6 Discussion

The proposed MVMO-SH has been implemented to the non-convex ED problem which takes into account multiple fuels and valve-point effects. From the numerical results, the power outputs obtained by MVMO-SH are between the minimum and maximum generator capacity limits and the total power output of generating units equals to the power load demand. It is indicated that the equality and inequality constraints always satisfy. In addition, the comparisons from Tables 2 and 4 show that the MVMO-SH can obtain better total fuel costs than most of other reported methods, especially for large-scale systems. Consequently, the MVMO methods can obtain very good solution quality for ED problems. However, the computation time is relatively high for large-scale systems. In this study, the proposed algorithm is run 50 independent trials. The mean cost, max cost, average cost and standard deviation obtained by the proposed method to evaluate the robustness characteristic of the proposed method for ED problems. The standard deviation is small. It shows that the performance the proposed MVMO-SH is robust. The disadvantage of MVMO-SH is computational time. The computation time of the MVMO-SH is relatively high for large-scale systems. Similar to the original MVMO, the number of iterations in MVMO-SH is equivalent to the number of offspring fitness evaluations which is usually time consuming in practical applications. In the future, the proposed method will be further improved for efficient dealing with complex and large-scale optimization problems in power systems.

7   Conclusion

The proposed MVMO-SH has been successfully applied to the ED problem with multiple fuels considering valve-point effects. The proposed method is based on the conventional MVMO enhanced with the embedded local search and multi-parent cross-over to improve its global search ability and solution quality for optimization problems. The method has been tested on 10-unit system and large-scale systems to demonstrate its effectiveness and efficiency. The numerical results showed that the proposed MVMO-SH has better performance than other optimization techniques exist in the literature in terms of global solution and robustness. Therefore, the proposed MVMO-SH could be favorable for solving other non-convex ED problems.

Acknowledgement.   The researchers would like to sincerely thank Universiti Teknologi PETRONAS for providing the research laboratory facilities under Graduate Assistance Scheme. This work is supported by the Centre of Graduate Studies with the help of the Department of Fundamental & Applied Sciences, Universiti Teknologi PETRONAS.

References

1. Wollenberg, B., Wood, A.: Power Generation, Operation and Control, pp. 264–327. John Wiley & Sons Inc, New York (1996)
2. Khoa, T.H., Vasant, P.M., Singh, M.S.B., Dieu, V.N.: Swarm based mean-variance mapping optimization (MVMOS) for solving economic dispatch. AIP Conf. Proc. **1621**(1), 76–85 (2014). doi:10.1063/1.4898448
3. Khoa, T.H., Vasant, P.M., Balbir Singh, M.S., Dieu, V.N.: Solving economic dispatch problem with valve-point effects using swarm-based mean–variance mapping optimization (MVMOS). cogent. Engineering **2**(1), 1076983 (2015). doi:10.1080/23311916.2015.1076983
4. Eberhart, R.C., Shi, Y.: Comparison between genetic algorithms and particle swarm optimization. In: Porto, V.W., Waagen, D. (eds.) EP 1998. LNCS, vol. 1447. Springer, Heidelberg (1998)
5. Ratnaweera, A., Halgamuge, S., Watson, H.C.: Self-organizing hierarchical particle swarm optimizer with time-varying acceleration coefficients. IEEE Trans. Evol. Comput. **8**(3), 240–255 (2004)
6. Lee, S.-C., Kim, Y.-H.: An enhanced Lagrangian neural network for the ELD problems with piecewise quadratic cost functions and nonlinear constraints. Electr. Power Syst. Res. **60**(3), 167–177 (2002)
7. Chiang, C.-L.: Improved genetic algorithm for power economic dispatch of units with valve-point effects and multiple fuels. IEEE Trans. Power Syst. **20**(4), 1690–1699 (2005)

8. Manoharan, P., Kannan, P., Baskar, S., Iruthayarajan, M.: Penalty parameter-less constraint handling scheme based evolutionary algorithm solutions to economic dispatch. IET Gener. Transm. Distrib. **2**(4), 478–490 (2008)
9. Selvakumar, A.I., Thanushkodi, K.: A new particle swarm optimization solution to nonconvex economic dispatch problems. IEEE Trans. Power Syst. **22**(1), 42–51 (2007)
10. Niu, Q., Zhou, Z., Zhang, H.-Y., Deng, J.: An improved quantum-behaved particle swarm optimization method for economic dispatch problems with multiple fuel options and valve-points effects. Energies **5**(12), 3655–3673 (2012). doi:10.3390/en5093655
11. Luong, L.D., Vasant, P., Dieu, V.N., Khoa, T.H., Khanh, D.V.: Self-organizing hierarchical particle swarm optimization for large-scale economic dispatch with multiple fuels considering valve-point effects. presented at the 7th Global Conference on Power Control and Optimization (PCO 2013), Prague, Czech Republic (2013)
12. Dieu, V.N., Schegner, P., Ongsakul, W.: Pseudo-gradient based particle swarm optimization method for nonconvex economic dispatch. In: Zelinka, I., Vasant, P., Barsoum, N. (eds.) Power, Control and Optimization, vol. 239, pp. 1–27. Springer, Cham (2013)
13. Erlich, I., Venayagamoorthy, G.K., Worawat, N.: A mean-variance optimization algorithm. In: IEEE Congress Evolutionary Computation 2010, pp. 1–6 (2010)
14. Rueda, J., Erlich, I.: Evaluation of the mean-variance mapping optimization for solving multimodal problems. In: IEEE Symposium Swarm Intelligence (SIS) 2013, pp. 7–14. IEEE (2013)
15. Khoa, T.H., Vasant, P.M., Singh, B.S.M., Dieu, V.N.: Swarm-based mean-variance mapping optimization (MVMOS) for solving non-convex economic dispatch problems. In: Handbook of Research on Swarm Intelligence in Engineering, p. 211 (2015)
16. Rueda, J.L., Erlich, I.: Hybrid mean-variance mapping optimization for solving the IEEE-CEC 2013 competition problems. In: IEEE Congress Evolutionary Computation (CEC) 2013, pp. 1664–1671. IEEE (2013)
17. Kuo, C.-C.: A novel coding scheme for practical economic dispatch by modified particle swarm approach. IEEE Trans. Power Syst. **23**(4), 1825–1835 (2008)

Heuristic Solutions for the Lifetime Problem of Wireless Sensor Networks

Nguyen Thanh Tung[1(✉)] and Phan Cong Vinh[2]

[1] International School, Vietnam National University, Hanoi, Vietnam
tungnt@isvnu.vn
[2] Nguyen Tat Thanh University, Ho Chi Minh City, Vietnam
pcvinh@ntt.edu.vn

Abstract. In [5, 7, 8] an analytical model of the lifetime problem of wireless sensor networks is developed. The solution given by the model is not practical for WSNs. Each time, there is a change in a sensor network, the solution needs to be recalculated. Also, it is difficult to build ILP solvers inside the small sensors. Furthermore, when the number of sensor nodes and CHs increases, it quickly becomes infeasible to calculate an optimum solution. As the analytical model is not able to be used to solve complicated networks, heuristic solutions are then examined that can compute the solutions for large sensor networks. Finally, the simulation results of the heuristic solutions are presented and discussed.

Keywords: Base station location · Wireless sensor network · Routing · Non-linear programming

1 Introduction

It is important to design heuristic algorithms [6, 9, 10] to approximate the performance of the optimum solution. Heuristic algorithms are summarized below:

Heuristic solutions for the lifetime problem

LEACH:
In every round, select a sensor node as a CH randomly from all sensor nodes in sensor networks.

```
Given:
N : The number of sensor nodes indexed from 1 to N
s : The current CH solution
For every round of data transmission
```
$$s = Random[1...N]$$
```
Result: s is the CH solution for the round obtained from
the LEACH algorithm. (End of code)
```

© ICST Institute for Computer Sciences, Social Informatics and Telecommunications Engineering 2016
P.C. Vinh et al. (Eds.): ICTCC 2016, LNICST 168, pp. 217–223, 2016.
DOI: 10.1007/978-3-319-46909-6_20

EEEAC (Avera):

In every round, select a sensor node to be a CH randomly from sensor nodes that have the energy level above the average energy of all nodes.

Given:
N : The number of sensor nodes indexed from 1 to N
s : The current CH solution
k : The number of sensor nodes that have energy above the average energy of all sensors
For every round of data transmission
$$s = Random[1...k]$$
Result: s is the CH solution for the round obtained from the Avera algorithm. (End of code)

LEACH_C:

In every round, select a sensor node, which has energy above the average energy of all nodes as a CH in order to minimize the total energy usage required to send traffic in that round to base station.

Given:
N : The number of sensor nodes indexed from 1 to N
s : The current solution
k : The number of sensor nodes that have energy above the average energy of all sensors
$f(s)$: The total energy consumption of all sensor nodes with solution s
s_0 : Best solution so far

Initialization: $s_0 \leftarrow \infty$

For (s from 1 to k)
$$\delta = f(s) - f(s_0)$$
    If $\delta < 0$ **then** $s_0 = s$

Result: s_0 is the CH solution obtained from the LEACH_C algorithm. (End of code)

2   A New Heuristic Solution

RE:

In every round of data transmission to the base station, select a sensor node as a CH in order to maximize the minimum remaining energy of all sensor nodes.

Given:
N : The number of sensor nodes indexed from 1 to N
s : A current solution
$f(s)$: The minimum residual energy of all nodes with solution s
s_0 : Best solution so far

Initialization: $s_0 \leftarrow 0$

For (s from 1 to N)

$$\delta = f(s) - f(s_0)$$

If $\delta > 0$ **then** $s_0 = s$

Result: s_0 is the CH solution obtained from the RE algorithm. (End of code)

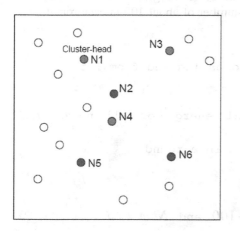 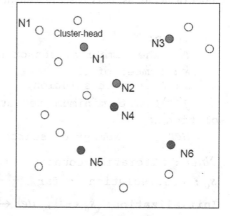

a)   Full search   b) Simple search

🔘 : Cluster-head for round i

⚫ : Cluster-head for round $i+k$

Search Method	Full search			Simple search		
Round i	N1	N3	N4	N1	N2	N3
Round $i+k$	N2	N5	N6	N4	N5	N6

Fig. 1. The order of cluster-head selection is not important (a) From a full search method, (b) From a simple search a method

3 Approximate Algorithm for RE

The authors in [1–4] mentioned that it is NP-hard to approximate Clustering Problem within a factor <2. Fortunately, the aim of the research is to extend the lifetime of sensor networks. To achieve this, CHs are reallocated in different rounds. We do not consider the cluster solution in each particular round, but the lifetime of the system (the total number of rounds) until the first sensor runs out of energy. As the CHs are reallocated from round to round, obtaining a poor solution of CHs in one round will not affect the whole performance in other rounds. In other words, a missed best solution of CHs can be revisited in other rounds. Therefore, a simple heuristic search scheme with a few hundred iterations could be enough to perform approximately as the full search. Figure 1 illustrates that a full search achieves different clustering solutions with a simple search in round i and round $i + k$. However, the simple search will achieve approximate lifetime performance of the full search, as the combination solution for the two rounds is the same (Node 1 to Node 6 are CHs).

The implementation of RE with a simple search is given below, in which the number of iterations, *iters* is set to a small number of about 100 in each round.

Given:
N : The number of sensor nodes indexed from 1 to N
k : Number of CHs
s : A current solution
$f(s)$: The minimum residual energy of all nodes with solution s
iter   : Number of searches in a round

Niter : Iteration counter
s_0 : Best solution so far

Initialization: $s_0 \leftarrow 0$, *iter* $\leftarrow 100$ and *Niter* $\leftarrow 0$

While (*Niter* < *iter*)
```
        Num_cluster=0;
        While (Num_cluster<k)
```

```
            new_node= Random[1...N]
            Num_cluster++;
```
$$\delta = f(s) - f(s_0)$$
```
            If  δ > 0  then s0 = s
```
            Niter ++
End While
Result: s_0 is the solution for RE in a round with *iter* number of iterations. (End of code)

4 Simulation Results

In order to compare the performance of the simple method with the solution of a full search, 50 random 50-node sensor networks are generated. Each node begins with 250,000 units of energy. The energy provides a system lifetime about 100 to 150 rounds. The number of CHs is set to 3. A full-search method requires 50^3 numbers of searches in each round. In each topology, RE with 100 searches in each round and the full search are run and their performances are compared. The network parameters are given below:

Network size $(100m \times 100m)$

Base station $(50m, 175m)$

Number of sensor nodes   50 nodes
Position of sensor nodes: Uniform placed in the area

Energy model: $E_t = \alpha d^2$, where α is set to 1

The position of sensors on the network is defined in Fig. 2.

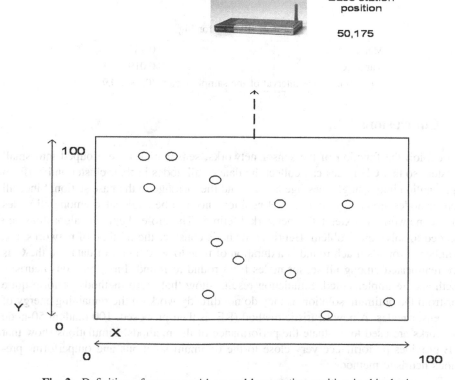

Fig. 2. Definition of sensor positions and base station position in this thesis

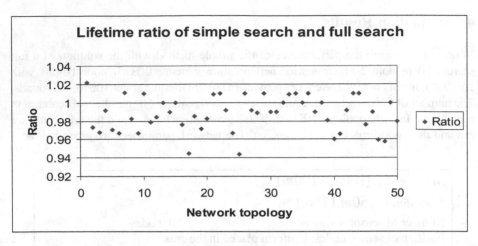

Fig. 3. Ratio of number of rounds between a simple search and a full search

Figure 3 plots the ratio of the lifetime (number of rounds) of RE method and the full search method on the same 100 network topologies. This can be seen from Fig. 4.10 that after from 100 to 150 rounds, the RE method provides almost the same lifetime as the full search method (Table 1).

Table 1. Results for Fig. 3

Mean	0.987
Variance	0.019
90 % confidence interval of the sample mean	(0.983, 0.991)

5 Conclusions

To exploit the function of the sensor networks, sensor nodes are grouped into small clusters so that CH nodes can collect the data of all nodes in their cluster and perform aggregation into a single message before send the message to the base station. Since all sensor nodes are energy-limited, CH positions need to be reallocated among all nodes in the network to extend the network lifetime. Therefore, heuristic algorithms are needed to solve the problem. Heuristic methods consider the lifetime of networks as a number of rounds. Each round is a duration of time to send a unit of data and the CHs are reallocated among all sensor nodes from round to round. First, previous heuristic methods are implemented. Simulation results show that these methods perform quite far from the optimum solution as they do not directly work on the remaining energy of all sensor nodes. A new heuristic method (RE) is then proposed. 100 random 50-node networks are used to evaluate the performance of the methods. Simulations show that RE provides performance very close to the optimum solutions and outperforms previous heuristic methods.

References

1. Nash, S.G., Sofer, A.: Linear and Nonlinear Programming. McGraw-Hill, New York (1996)
2. Kanungo, T., et al.: A local search approximation algorithm for k-means clustering. In: Proceedings of the Eighteenth Annual Symposium on Computational Geometry (2002)
3. Arora, S., Raghavan, P., Rao, S.: Approximation schemes for Euclidean k-median and related problems. In: Proceedings of the Thirtieth Annual ACM Symposium on Theory of Computing, Dallas, TX, pp. 106–113, May 1998
4. Kolliopoulos, S.G., Rao, S.: A nearly linear-time approximation scheme for the Euclidean k-median problem. In: Nešetřil, J. (ed.) ESA 1999. LNCS, vol. 1643, pp. 378–389. Springer, Heidelberg (1999)
5. Tung, N.T., Binh, H.T.T.: Base station location - aware optimization model of the lifetime of wireless sensor networks. In: Mobile Networks and Applications (MONET), May 2015. doi:10.1007/s11036-015-0614-3. (SCIE IF 2013 1.496)
6. Tung, N.T.: Energy-aware optimization model in chain-based routing. ACM/Springer Mobile Netw. Appl. (MONET) J. **19**(2), 249–257 (2014). (SCIE IF 2013 1.496)
7. Tung, N.T., Van Duc, N.: Optimizing the operating time of wireless sensor network. EURASIP J. Wirel. Commun. Netw. (2012). doi:10.1186/1687-1499-2012-348. (SCIE IF 2013 0.8), ISSN: 1687-1499
8. Tung, N.T., Ly, D.H., Binh, H.T.T.: Maximizing the lifetime of wireless sensor networks with the base station location. In: Vinh, P.C., Vassev, E., Hinchey, M. (eds.) ICTCC 2014. LNICST, vol. 144, pp. 108–116. Springer, Heidelberg (2015)
9. Tung, N.T., Vinh, P.C.: The energy-aware operational time of wireless ad-hoc sensor networks. ACM/Springer Mobile Netw. Appl. (MONET) J. **18**(3), 454–463 (2013). (SCIE IF 2013 1.496)
10. Tung, N.T., Minh, N.S.: Power-aware routing for underwater wireless sensor network. In: Vinh, P.C., Alagar, V., Vassev, E., Khare, A. (eds.) ICCASA 2013. LNICST, vol. 128, pp. 97–101. Springer, Heidelberg (2014)

Harnessing Collective Intelligence to Preserve and Learn Endangered Languages

Asfahaan Mirza$^{(\boxtimes)}$ and David Sundaram

Department of Information Systems and Operations Management,
University of Auckland, Auckland, New Zealand
asfahaan@mirzabros.com, d.sundaram@auckland.ac.nz

Abstract. The languages are disappearing at a frightening rate; half of 7105 plus languages spoken today may disappear by end of this century. When a language becomes extinct, communities lose their cultural identity, practices tied to a language and intellectual wealth. The rapid loss of languages motivates this study.

Current language revitalization approaches and systems are focused on creating language learning resources from already documented artifacts rather than a holistic approach towards language preservation, curation and learning. Harnessing and leveraging collective intelligence within communities through cooperation, coordination and cognition can help preserve endangered languages.

In this paper we first introduce collective intelligence, endangered languages, and language revitalization. Secondly we discuss and explore how to leverage collective intelligence to preserve, curate, discover, learn, share and eventually revitalize endangered languages. Thirdly we compare and synthesize existing language preservation and learning systems. Finally, this chapter proposes the design and implementation of "Save Lingo" and "Learn Lingo" mobile apps for preserving and revitalizing endangered languages. The systems are instantiated and validated in context of te reo Māori, which is the native language of the Māori population of New Zealand.

Keywords: Collective intelligence · Language revitalization · Endangered languages · Crowd sourced · Language learning · Mobile apps

1 Introduction

Language is a living and dynamic phenomenon that plays a significant role in our daily lives. It is essential for acquisition, accumulation, maintenance, and transmission of human knowledge regarding the natural environment and ways of interacting with it [1]. Language defines a culture, through which people communicate. Currently, languages are at greater risk of extinction than species of animals and plants [2]. Most linguists believe that at least half of the world's 7105 languages are endangered and they are not being learnt as first languages by children, and ultimately leading to the death of languages.

Firstly, to revitalizing a language, we need to document the language by capturing, curating and preserving various language artifacts such as words, phrases, songs,

© ICST Institute for Computer Sciences, Social Informatics and Telecommunications Engineering 2016
P.C. Vinh et al. (Eds.): ICTCC 2016, LNICST 168, pp. 224–236, 2016.
DOI: 10.1007/978-3-319-46909-6_21

idioms, stories and dialects for future use. Secondly, the preserved language can be disseminated and learnt by the wider community. The key success to any revitalization efforts is the contribution and collaboration by its native community. Hence, leveraging collective intelligence within the community will significantly help in preserving and learning the language. In the subsequent section we explore the fundamentals of collective intelligence, endangered languages and language revitalization efforts.

1.1 Collective Intelligence

Intelligence can be defined as the ability to see things, understand and reason at different capacities. It involves one being aware and conscious of individual actions and analysis of creative and critical thinking. In this context, collective intelligence can be described as the ability for different individuals to come together and form a group with the intention to share a common line of thought [3]. Lévy (1997) defines collective intelligence as a form of subjective mobilization, highly individual as well as ethical and cooperative.

Collective intelligence can either be beneficial or negative depending on the objectives set by the group. In this digitally enabled generation, the Internet is described as a useful tool that can be used to promote collective intelligence [5]. Currently, many individuals and groups are using the Internet to collectively provide content on various issues defining global trends as well as raising awareness on topics. Search engines and social media platforms are playing a significant role in facilitating these actions.

Collective intelligence dwells on three key principles that include cooperation, coordination and cognition [6]. Using these key principles, harnessing collective intelligence enables individuals and groups to solve practical problems. In this research we explore how to leverage concepts of collective intelligence to save endangered languages. Moreover, design and implement systems that can be used to mitigate the loss of languages and revitalize the affected languages [7].

1.2 Endangered Languages

Language is a primary means of interacting among people in various forms such as in person, writing, over the phone or the Internet. We all are so called 'social animals' therefore communication plays a very important role in our daily living, and language enables a person to express their feelings and opinions. Krauss (1992) estimates that 90 % of the world's 7105 languages would become endangered or extinct by the end of this century, if no language revitalization efforts are made [8]. Endangered languages are disappearing at a frightening rate; one language every two weeks [9]. The reasons for language endangerment are complex but generally it is linked to communities abandoning their minority native languages to a mainstream language that is more economically, politically and socially powerful.

Languages are one the richest part of human diversity. Currently there are 7105 living languages spoken by a world population of 6,716,664,407 [10]. The language distribution among the world population is heavily skewed. Approximately 79.5 % of the world population speaks only 75 languages. In contrary, 3894 smaller languages are spoken by only 0.13 % of the world population [1]. The rapid decline of languages highlights the need to revitalize endangered languages for the survival of culture, diversity and knowledge.

1.3 Language Revitalization

Language revitalization is to reverse the decline of a language from becoming extinct or endangered. Linguists have proposed various models for language revitalization [11, 12]. The language revitalization models include school-based programs (total and partial immersion), children's programs outside the school, adult language programs, documentation and materials development, home-based programs, and language reclamation.

Language preservation is one of the essential tasks when revitalizing a language. Language can be documented in multiple formats including, audio and video recordings, scanned images, or written notes. The documented data can then be archived and mobilized into various publications (print and digital). The preservation is highly dependent on the younger generation learning and using their indigenous language [13]. Most of the language revitalization models focus on language learning.

Language learning is an emerging research area known as "Language Acquisition" which overlaps in linguistics and psychology. We will focus on language learning techniques that assist in language revitalization efforts. Language learning is a key component to language revitalization, as teaching the future generation their indigenous language will help keep the language alive. Learning a language is dependent on the available resources for the language. Most of the language revitalization models consist of teaching and learning a language. Past research suggests that total immersion schools and classrooms have been very successful for language revitalization [12]. However, emerging technologies provide capabilities that were not available before which gives birth to new concepts towards language revitalization. In the next section we look at how we can leverage collective intelligence for language revitalization purposes.

1.4 Leveraging Collective Intelligence for Language Revitalization

One of the most important components of existence is language; it gives people a certain sense of belonging and originality. Language connects people of the same cultural values and makes them diversified to the general world. According to Evans and Levinson (2009), linguistic is the basis for cultural preference and belonging, the two authors note that the diversity offered by languages provide a crucial element in cognitive science [14]. Community driven projects are the best examples of how collective intelligence connects their interest. It is important for companies and other corporate bodies to develop programs that help connect language to daily work practice to help preserve the endangered language. Incorporating communities' practices and language preference in the day-to-day running of the corporations provide a sustainable step of language preservation [15].

Language provides deep insight of the culture associated with the language. Thus, gathering collective intelligence from various age groups and genders will help preserve, revitalize and pass the language to future generations. The language is rapidly evolving and like biology, only the fittest survive, similar to language, only the commonly used language will survive the change. The learning and usage of a language can be made possible by harnessing collective intelligence about a particular language and disseminating the knowledge among the community. Making the language available to wider society is made possible through the use of mobile devices and social media. This will enable the community to access their language anywhere anytime.

The diagram below illustrates the research dimensions (Fig. 1). Research in the past (inner circle) has focused predominantly on the design and implementation of traditional systems to capture and curate languages by experts in limited contexts focused on standard vocabulary and media. This research (red zone) tries to address these research problems by exploring a crowd sourced approach to harness collective intelligence using ubiquitous systems to capture, curate the linguistic diversity and richness anytime anywhere. Moreover, allow end users to discover and learn to use the endangered language.

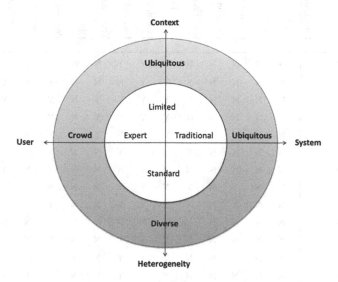

Fig. 1. Research Dimensions (Color figure online)

2 Existing Systems for Language Revitalization and Learning

Current language revitalization models and activities include school-based immersion programmes, children's programmes outside school, adult language programmes, documentation and materials development, home-based programs, and language reclamation [1, 11, 12, 16–18]. However, the focus of these efforts have been on language learning rather than a holistic approach towards language preservation, curation, and usage. Only few indigenous communities around the world have started adopting mobile apps to revitalize their language and cultural practices [19–22]. However, the apps are mostly learning-oriented using already documented information (e.g. Go Vocab, Hika Explorer, Te reo Māori dictionary, Duo Lingo, Ojibway and Saulteaux). Ma! Iwaidja, and Duo Lingo allow data capture but does not facilitate curation process. Moreover, there is limited research on models, frameworks, and/or architectures for the design and implementation of collective intelligence based language preservation and learning system. Hence, there is a gap in existing approaches and apps, because they do not facilitate a holistic approach to preserve, curate, and learn to use an endangered language (Table 1).

Table 1. Existing systems available for revitalizing endangered languages

Systems / Functionality	Capture Audio	Capture Video	Capture Images	Curation Process	User Feedback	Audio Playback	Learning	Dictionary	Translator	Dialect Support	Progress Tracking	Assessments	Gamification	Leader Board	Social Media
DIXEL Mobile	N	N	N	N	N	Y	Y	Y	N	N	N	Y	Y	N	N
Duolingo	Y	N	N	N	Y	Y	Y	N	N	N	Y	Y	Y	Y	Y
Go Vocab	N	N	N	N	Y	Y	Y	Y	Y	N	Y	Y	Y	Y	Y
Hika Explorer	N	N	N	N	N	Y	Y	N	Y	N	Y	Y	Y	N	N
iPhraseBook®	N	N	N	N	N	Y	Y	N	Y	N	Y	N	N	N	N
Language Perfect	N	N	N	N	Y	Y	Y	Y	N	Y	Y	Y	Y	Y	Y
MindSnacks	N	N	N	N	N	Y	Y	N	N	N	Y	Y	Y	Y	N
Ma Iwaidja	Y	N	Y	N	Y	Y	Y	Y	N	N	N	N	N	N	N
Memo Cards	N	N	N	N	N	Y	Y	Y	N	N	Y	Y	Y	Y	Y
myLanguage Pro	N	N	N	N	Y	Y	N	Y	Y	N	N	N	N	N	N
Ojibway	N	N	N	N	N	Y	Y	Y	N	N	N	N	N	N	Y
Saulteaux	Y	N	N	N	N	Y	Y	Y	N	N	N	Y	Y	N	N
Spanish 24/7	N	N	N	N	N	Y	Y	Y	N	N	Y	Y	Y	Y	N
Spanish!	N	N	N	N	N	Y	Y	Y	N	N	Y	Y	Y	N	N
Te Pūmanawa	Y	N	N	N	Y	Y	Y	N	Y	N	Y	Y	Y	N	N
Touch Trainer	N	N	N	N	N	Y	Y	Y	N	N	Y	Y	Y	N	N
Tusaalanga	Y	N	N	N	N	Y	Y	Y	N	Y	Y	N	N	N	N

3   Design and Implementation of a Collective Intelligence Based Language Preservation and Learning System

Majority of languages in the world are endangered and rapidly becoming extinct. The aim of this research is to design and implement a collective intelligence driven smart mobile apps to preserve and learn endangered languages. We adopted a design science research methodology to help develop concepts, models, processes, frameworks and architectures [23–26]. Subsequently, mobile apps will be designed and implemented leveraging key principles of collective intelligence including cooperation, coordination and cognition to support vital language revitalization processes: (1) **Capture/Preserve** - words, phrases, poems, idioms, and stories as text, audio, images, and video in multiple dialects; (2) **Curate** - filter and approve captured content, and (3) **Learn and use** – context-aware dynamic games and apps based on curated data to encourage the use of the endangered language in daily life. The apps and related concepts, models, processes, and frameworks will be initially designed for preserving and learning te reo Māori, which is the native language of New Zealand. These research artefacts will then be generalised to help save and learn other dying and endangered languages.

3.1   Concepts and Processes

This research employs a holistic crowd sourced approach to harness collective intelligence to revitalize endangered languages as illustrated in Fig. 2. This model is created by synthesising concepts from collective intelligence, knowledge management, and language revitalization literature [1, 4, 5, 11, 27, 28]. It has five stages and related processes namely: capture, curate, discover, learn and share. The *capture stage* allows contributors to create/capture words, phrases, idioms, stories and songs in multiple formats including text, image and video. The *curate stage* involves moderating and refining the captured data by language experts. The *discover stage* will facilitate the wider community to retrieve knowledge from the dynamic repository. The *learn* stage allows user to learn the language using interactive games. Lastly, the *share stage* enables the dissemination of knowledge through social media among the wider community to help promote the use of language.

Fig. 2. Concepts and Processes to harness collective intelligence to revitalize endangered languages

3.2   Framework

The generic design elements make up the Save Lingo framework are depicted in Fig. 3. The framework incorporates collective intelligence fundamentals to save endangered languages. The framework elements support the reuse of artifacts for multiple endangered languages. Ninety percent of the artifacts such as concepts, models, processes, framework, architecture and system are not associated with the language. Only user interface changes at a system level are required to tailor it to a particular language. The artifacts are key outputs of design science research [23, 24]. The first six layers of the framework are standard and well understood in research. However, applying the fundamentals for language revitalization and learning purposes is novel.

3.3   Implementation of Language Preservation System – Save Lingo

Many indigenous communities have started to adopt Ubiquitous Information Systems and Devices (UIS&D) to preserve, maintain and revitalize their language and cultural practices [19, 20]. UIS&D refer to systems and devices (tabs, pads, or boards) that are available abundantly without boundaries [29, 30]. There is a significant rise in adoption of UIS&D among everyone; both digital natives and digital immigrants. Ubiquitous devices provide many advantages: flexibility, low cost, mobility, user-friendliness, connectivity and multimedia capabilities. These advantages significantly help in implementing Save Lingo app – holistic crowd sourced language preservation system to harness collective intelligence. The prototypical implementation of Save Lingo adapted to revitalize te reo Māori, which is the native language of the Māori population of New Zealand.

Save Lingo app as shown in Fig. 4 extends upon fundamentals from social media, knowledge management, and collective intelligence to create a highly interactive platform that allows users to remotely contribute and collaborate towards capturing, curating, discovering and sharing the endangered language. These functionalities are described in book chapter [31].

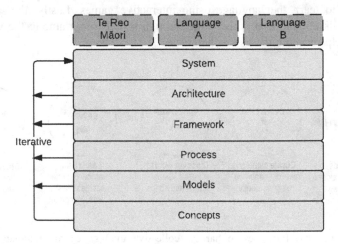

Fig. 3. Framework of generic design elements to preserve and learn endangered languages

Fig. 4. Save Lingo app - Holistic crowd sourced language preservation system [31]

3.4   Implementation of Language Learning Systems – Learn Lingo

Learning a language can be a difficult task regardless of age or gender. We aim to implement Learn Lingo apps that are user-friendly, dynamic and gamified to engage, retain and help users learn an endangered language. The underlying fundamentals and learning processes, modalities and mechanisms are synthesized from language acquisition and learning literature [11, 32–36] as presented in Table 2. Every individual progresses through various learning stages to learn a new language. Each stage is unique as the modalities and mechanisms applied for learning are different. There are many learning apps available including Flash card and Hangman for various languages.

Table 2. Learning processes, modalities and mechanisms synthesized from [11, 32–36]

Stage modality	Pre-production	Early production	Speech emergence	Intermediate fluency
Listening	(Audio-Lingualism) Listen word/phrase	Listen word/phrase.	Listen phrase, story, song, idiom.	Listen phrase, story, song, idiom.
Drawing	Draw & Colour the correct answer	Draw & Colour the correct answer	Draw & Colour the correct answer	Draw & Colour the correct answer
Observe & identifying	Chose the correct image. Match the words (drag and drop)	View and select correct answer Chose the correct image. Match the words (drag and drop)	Identify and select correct phrases, story, song, idiom. Match the correct pairs (drag and drop)	Identify and select correct phrases, story, song, idiom. Match the correct pairs (drag and drop)
Reading	Repeat what's on your screen	Repeat what's on your screen	Repeat what's on your screen	Read what's on the screen and complete the comprehension activities.
Role Play	Act out the activity via Video Capture	Act out/Retell the activity via Video Capture	Act out/Retell the activity via Video Capture	Act out, Retell, Create the scenario.
Speaking	*Not Applicable*	Repeat what is on your screen Respond/Record the correct answer.	Recall, Summarize, Retell, Describe, Define, Explain, Restate. Talk to Native Speaker	Record the complete phrase, song, story, idiom. Answer or debate the question or the speaker. Group Discussion
Writing	*Not Applicable*	Complete the word by filling the missing letters for what you see or hear.	Complete the phrase/story/song by filling the missing words for what you see or hear. Define, Describe, Summarize, Explain	Translate the phrase, story, song, idiom. Analyze and correct what is displayed on the screen.
Cognitive	*Not Applicable*	List, Categories, Group, and/or Compare using a combination of speaking, listening, reading and writing	List, Categories, Group, and/or Compare using a combination of speaking, listening, reading and writing	List, Categories, Group, and/or Compare using a combination of speaking, listening, reading and writing

Nevertheless, the novel contribution of Save Lingo and Learn Lingo is that we are using the collective intelligence/data of the community which was captured and curated via Save Lingo app is used as the content for Learn Lingo's Flash Card and Hangman apps.

Flash cards to support: Observe, Identify, Listening and Speaking

Flash cards are a relatively simple way of learning key words and phrases of a language. The flash cards app supports observe, identify, listening and speaking modalities to help users learn the language. The prototypical implementation of Flash cards app is shown below in Fig. 5. The app allows user to securely login and create various flash

Fig. 5. Learn Lingo – Flash card app workflow

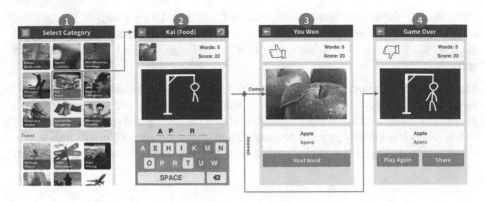

Fig. 6. Learn Lingo – Hangman app workflow

card sets. The set can be constructed using the data that was captured and curated using Save Lingo.

Hangman to support: Identify, Writing, and Reading
The Hangman app supports identify, writing and reading modalities to help users learn new words of the language. The prototypical implementation of Hangman app is displayed below in Fig. 6. The app allows user to securely login and simply select a category. The app will randomly select a curated word from the category selected by the user.

4   Conclusion

In conclusion, this research leverages from strengths of collective intelligence to address weakness in systems that attempt to preserve and/or teach languages. We first began by looking at the strengths of collective intelligence, practical problems of endangered languages and language revitalization efforts. Moreover, we explored how collective intelligence can be leveraged for language revitalization purposes. Consequently, we reviewed variety of language preservation and learning systems. Based on these finding and our previous work on Save Lingo [31], we proposed concepts, models, processes and framework to help preserve and learn endangered languages. Furthermore, we describe the implementation of Save Lingo and Learn Lingo – Flash card and Hangman, which are based on the proposed concepts, models, processes and framework in the context of an endangered language, te reo Maori. The system's functionality can easily be ported to facilitate cooperation, coordination and cognition within the community to revitalization other endangered languages. This crowd-sourced approach will harness collective intelligence to create a central repository for the distribution and revitalization of indigenous languages, knowledge, values and culture.

References

1. Romaine, S.: Preserving endangered languages. Lang. Linguist. Compass **1**, 115–132 (2007)
2. Sutherland, W.J.: Parallel extinction risk and global distribution of languages and species. Nature **423**, 276–279 (2003)
3. Kubátová, J.: Growth of collective intelligence by linking knowledge workers through social media. Lex Sci. Int. J. **1**, 135–145 (2012)
4. Lévy, P.: Collective Intelligence. Plenum/Harper Collins, New York (1997)
5. Malone, T.W., Laubacher, R., Dellarocas, C.: Harnessing crowds: Mapping the genome of collective intelligence (2009)
6. Engel, D., Woolley, A.W., Jing, L.X., Chabris, C.F., Malone, T.W.: Reading the mind in the eyes or reading between the lines? theory of mind predicts collective intelligence equally well online and face-to-face. PLoS ONE **9**, e115212 (2014)
7. Yun, J., Li, X., Wang, C.: Simulation of conducting early-warning to the endangered state of language. J. Multimedia **8**, 475–480 (2013)
8. Krauss, M.: The world's languages in crisis. Lang. (Baltim) **68**, 4–10 (1992)
9. Crystal, D.: Language Death. Cambridge University Press, Cambridge (2002)
10. Lewis, M.P., Simons, G.F., Fennig, C.D. (eds.): Ethnologue: Languages of the World. http://www.ethnologue.com
11. Hinton, L., Hale, K.L.: The Green Book of Language Revitalization in Practice. Academic Press, San Diego (2001)
12. Grenoble, L.A., Whaley, L.J.: Saving Languages: An Introduction to Language Revitalization. Cambridge University Press, Cambridge (2005)
13. Yang, M.-C., Rau, D.V.: An integrated framework for archiving, processing and developing learning materials for an endangered aboriginal language in Taiwan. ALR-2005, 14 October 2005
14. Evans, N., Levinson, S.C.: The myth of language universals: language diversity and its importance for cognitive science. Behav. Brain Sci. **32**, 429–448 (2009)
15. Lesser, E., Ranson, D., Shah, R., Pulver, B.: Collective intelligence: capitalizing on the crowd. IBM Inst. Bus. Value (2012)
16. UNESCO, Brenzinger, M., Yamamoto, A., Aikawa, N., Koundiouba, D., Minasyan, A., Dwyer, A., Grinevald, C., Krauss, M., Miyaoka, O., Sakiyama, O.: Language vitality and endangerment. UNESCO Intangible Cultural Unit - Safeguarding Endangered Languages (2003)
17. Tsunoda, T.: Language endangerment and language revitalization: an introduction. Walter de Gruyter, Berlin (2006)
18. Dwyer, A.M.: Tools and techniques for endangered-language assessment and revitalization (2011)
19. Holton, G.: The role of information technology in supporting minority and endangered languages. In: Austin, P., Sallabank, J. (eds.) The Cambridge Handbook of Endangered Languages, pp. 371–399. Cambridge University Press, Cambridge (2011)
20. Galla, C.: Indigenous language revitalization and technology from traditional to contemporary domains. Indig. Lang. Revital. Encourag. Guid. Lessons Learn. Flagstaff (Arizona, Estados Unidos) North. Arizona Univ. pp. 167–182 (2009)
21. Keegan, P., Te Taka Keegan, M.L.: Online māori resources and māori initiatives for teaching and learning: current activities, successes and future directions. Mai Rev. **1**, 1–13 (2011)
22. Nichols, D.M., Witten, I.H., Keegan, T.T., Bainbridge, D., Dewsnip, M.: Digital libraries and minority languages. New Rev. Hypermedia Multimedia **11**, 139–155 (2005)

23. Nunamaker Jr., J.F., Chen, M., Purdin, T.D.M.: Systems development in information systems research. J. Manag. Inf. Syst. **7**, 89–106 (1990)
24. Hevner, A.R., March, S.T., Park, J., Ram, S.: Design science in information systems research. MIS Q. **28**, 75–105 (2004)
25. Baskerville, R.: What design science is not. Eur. J. Inf. Syst. **17**, 441–443 (2008)
26. Nunamaker Jr., J.F., Chen, M.: Systems development in information systems research. In: 1990 Proceedings of the Twenty-Third Annual Hawaii International Conference on System Sciences, pp. 631–640. IEEE (1990)
27. Nonaka, I., Takeuchi, H., Umemoto, K.: A theory of organizational knowledge creation. Int. J. Technol. Manag. **11**, 833–845 (1996)
28. Alavi, M., Leidner, D.E.: Review: knowledge management and knowledge management systems: conceptual foundations and research issues. MIS Q. **25**, 107–136 (2001)
29. Sorensen, C., Yoo, Y., Lyytinen, K., DeGross, J.: Designing Ubiquitous Information Environments: Socio-Technical Issues and Challenges: IFIP TC8 WG 8.2 International Working Conference. Springer, Heidelberg (2005)
30. Weisser, M.: The computer for the twenty-first century. Sci. Am. **265**, 94–104 (1991)
31. Mirza, A., Sundaram, D.: Design and implementation of socially driven knowledge management systems for revitalizing endangered languages. In: Remko, H., Cranefield, J., Cranefield, J. (eds.) Social Knowledge Management in Action, in the Knowledge Management and Organizational Learning. Springer, Heidelberg (2016)
32. Viberg, O., Grönlund, Å.: Mobile assisted language learning: a literature review. In: mLearn, pp. 9–16 (2012)
34. Brown, H.D.: Principles of language learning and teaching (2000)
35. MacWhinney, B.: A unified model of language acquisition. In: Handbook of Bilingualism, p. 49 (2004)
36. Godwin-Jones, R.: Emerging technologies: mobile apps for language learning. Lang. Learn. Technol. **15**, 2–11 (2011)

An Abstract-Based Approach for Text Classification

Quoc Dinh Truong[1(✉)], Hiep Xuan Huynh[1],
and Cuong Ngoc Nguyen[2]

[1] College of Information and Communication Technology, Can Tho University,
Campus 2, 3/2 Street, Ninh Kieu District, Can Tho City, Vietnam
{tqdinh,hxhiep}@ctu.edu.vn
[2] Department of Computer and Mathematical, The People's Security University,
Km9 Nguyen Trai Street, Ha Dong District, Ha Noi, Vietnam
cuongnn@hvannd.edu.vn

Abstract. Text classification is a supervised learning task for assigning text document to one or more predefined classes/topics. These topics are determined by a set of training documents. In order to construct a classification model, a machine learning algorithm was used. Training data is often a set of full-text documents. The training model is used to predict a class for new coming document. In this paper, we propose a text classification approach based on automatic text summarization. The proposed approach is tested with 2000 Vietnamese text documents downloaded from vnexpress.net and vietnamnet.vn. The experimental results confirm the feasibility of proposed model.

Keywords: Text classification · Automatic text summarization · Machine learning

1 Introduction

Text classification is one of the basic problems of text mining. Text classification is the process of assigning text documents to predefined categories based on their content. Text classification has been used in a number of application fields such as information retrieval, text filtering, electronic library and automatic web news extraction. Text classification can be achieved manually or can be automated successfully using machine learning techniques: support vector machines – SVM [1], tolerance rough set model approach [2] and association rules approach [3]. Whatever approach used, the challenge is that full-text content of documents is always taken into account so classification process often deals with large number of features.

Traditionally, before deciding to read or buy a document (book, scientific article) we often read the abstract of this document to catch the main idea. This proves that abstract reflects the main content of document and it can be used for classifying text documents.

Nowadays, research in the field of automatic text summarization has achieved some initial successes. We can list some of the most significant works: automatic text summarization based on word-clusters and ranking algorithms [4], multi-document

P.C. Vinh et al. (Eds.): ICTCC 2016, LNICST 168, pp. 237–245, 2016.
DOI: 10.1007/978-3-319-46909-6_22

summarization by sentence extraction [5], inferring strategies for sentence ordering in multi-document news summarization [6]. These methods have been applied for solving the problem of Vietnamese text summarization.

Based on the success of research in the field of automatic text summarization and the assumption that topic of text document can be simply identified through its abstract, we propose an abstract-based approach for text classification. The objective of our research is to answer the question of whether abstract should be used for classifying text documents.

In the field of data mining, the problem of text classification is often solved by using machine learning techniques: support vector machine-SVM [1], decision tree [7], k-nearest neighbor [8] and neural network [9] in which the most used techniques are SVM and decision tree. So in the context of our research, we use SVM and decision tree as classifier for both classification models: our proposed model uses abstract of text documents as input samples and the baseline model uses full-text content of documents as input samples. To compare the performance of models, 2000 Vietnamese text documents are collected from two websites vnexpress.net and vietnamnet.vn. The abstracts of these text documents are generated by module which is programed according the model we proposed in [10]. Experimental results show that the proposed approach is effective and promising.

2   Proposed Model

The overall model architecture is depicted in Fig. 1. First a classification is trained and then this model is used for classifying input data in which abstract of full-text document is automatically generated.

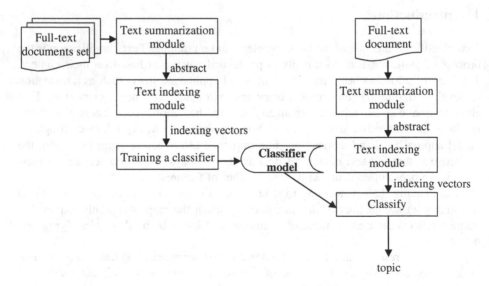

Fig. 1. Proposed model architecture

2.1   Text Document Representation

We use bag of words (BoW) model to represent text document. In order to do this, first the text document is segmented into word tokens using a tokenizer and then a term-weighting scheme was applied to compute the weights of word tokens. There exist some tools to separate Vietnamese words, by example vnTokenizer [11] which is used in this study. That tool was built based on the maximum matching method with the database used is the Vietnamese syllabary and Vietnamese dictionary with Java open source. Thus, it can be easily integrated into other systems. The following is an example of Vietnamese text segmentation:

- Original text: "Để có thể thực hiện rút trích tự động tóm tắt cũng như phân lớp văn bản với máy học vectơ hỗ trợ thì văn bản cần được biểu diễn dưới dạng thích hợp".
- Text after segmentation: "Để có_thể thực_hiện rút trích tự_động tóm_tắt cũng_như phân lớp văn_bản với máy học vectơ hỗ_trợ thì văn_bản cần được biểu_diễn dưới dạng thích_hợp".

To compute the weights of word tokens, we use TF-IDF term-weighting scheme, originated from information retrieval field, which is widely used in natural language processing field. The TF-IDF scheme combines two aspects of a word: the importance of a word within a document (TF: Term Frequency) and its discriminative power within the whole collection (IDF: Inverse Document Frequency). There are many variants of the TF-IDF scheme and the most used is:

- TF: number of occurrences of a word token in a given text document
- IDF: $\log(1 + \frac{N}{n})$, where N is number of documents in the collection and n is the number of documents which contain given word token.

2.2   Automatic Text Summarization

Our proposed model [10] for Vietnamese text summarization provides good result. The proposed model is based on the notion of similarity between sentences. The ranking scores of sentences are computed by using the advanced PageRank algorithm and then sentences with highest scores are extracted as abstract (summary).

The main steps for text summarization are the following:

- Split text document into sentences represented as vector in the space of indexing terms.
- Construct graph for representing document in which nodes are sentences and arcs represent the similarity between sentences.
- PageRank algorithm [12] has been modified to better suit the new context – undirected weighted graph. Sentence is selected to put into the summary based on its PageRank score.

Our proposed model belongs to the class of "extraction" approaches. The main advantages of this approaches are: since they are unsupervised approaches so no training set is needed; we can identify exactly how many sentences have been extracted.

First, after sentences are splitted by using separation characters such as '.', '?', '…' etc., we use bag of words model and TF-IDF weighting scheme to model sentences. In the next step, an undirected weighted graph will be constructed in which nodes represent sentences and each arc represents the similarity between two sentences. The arc's weight is computed by using the Jaccard coefficient [13]. We proved in [10] that by using Jaccard coefficient we can get a good result for the problem of automatic text summarization. In the last step, the PageRank algorithm that have been adjusted to suit the context of undirected weighted graph is used to compute the "importance" of nodes. The "importance" of nodes will be fixed after a number of iterations. The "importance" of nodes are updated every iteration by using following equation:

$$PR(A) = \frac{1-d}{N} + d(W_{AB}\frac{PR(B)}{L(B)} + W_{AC}\frac{PR(C)}{L(C)} + \dots)$$

Where

d is often chosen equal to 0.85

W_{ij} is the weight of arc connected two nodes i and j

$L(i)$ is $N-1$, N is the number of sentences.

Sentences are arranged in descending order according to their importance scores. A certain percentage of sentences with highest scores is selected as summary. In this work, 15 % of sentences or at least 2 sentences will be included in summary. The following example shows the result of summarization module:

Original text: Windows XP ngừng hỗ trợ vào ngày 8/4 năm sau. Nhiều nhân viên bán hàng bảo hiểm tại Nhật Bản sẽ được chuyển từ máy tính cũ lên tablet chạy Windows 8 để tương tác tốt hơn với khách hàng. Microsoft tại Nhật Bản hôm nay thông báo đang giúp một công ty bảo hiểm lớn của Nhật Bản là Meiji Yasuda nhằm nâng cấp hàng loạt máy tính chạy hệ điều hành sắp tròn 12 tuổi. Các thiết bị mới sẽ chạy Windows 8 do Fujitsu sản xuất cùng nhiều phần mềm và tiện ích cài đặt sẵn. "Trước đây, đội ngũ bán hàng sẽ chuẩn bị các đề xuất trên máy tính chạy Windows XP và sau đó in ra để chia sẻ với các khách hàng. Tuy nhiên, hệ thống thiết bị mới sẽ giúp chấm dứt các bước làm phiền toái này", thông báo của Microsoft có đoạn. Ngoài trang bị phần cứng mới, hãng phần mềm Mỹ cũng sẽ tổ chức khóa đào tạo và hướng dẫn sử dụng thao tác trên phần mềm mới. Các khách hàng cũng sẽ thuận tiện hơn trong việc sử dụng như đăng ký thông tin, tìm hiểu trực tiếp các gói bảo hiểm mà không phải ngập trong đống giấy tờ, văn bản như trước đây. Meiji Yasuda cũng sẽ là công ty bảo hiểm nhân thọ đầu tiên của Nhật thông qua việc sử dụng hoàn toàn hệ điều hành Windows 8 Pro. Microsoft dự kiến sẽ chấm dứt hỗ trợ hệ điều hành Windows XP từ ngày 8/4/2014. Tuy nhiên, đây vẫn là hệ điều hành có số lượng người dùng khổng lồ, kém không nhiều so với vị trí dẫn đầu thuộc về Windows 7. Hỗ trợ công ty bảo hiểm Nhật Bản là một trong những động thái "mạnh tay" của Microsoft giúp Windows XP sớm "nghỉ hưu" và nhường sự phát triển cho các hệ điều hành mới hơn.

Abstract (summary): Nhiều nhân viên bán hàng bảo hiểm tại Nhật Bản sẽ được chuyển từ máy tính cũ lên tablet chạy Windows 8 để tương tác tốt hơn với khách hàng. Microsoft tại Nhật Bản hôm nay thông báo đang giúp một công ty bảo hiểm lớn của

Nhật Bản là Meiji Yasuda nhằm nâng cấp hàng loạt máy tính chạy hệ điều hành sắp tròn 12 tuổi. "Trước đây, đội ngũ bán hàng sẽ chuẩn bị các đề xuất trên máy tính chạy Windows XP và sau đó in ra để chia sẻ với các khách hàng. Tuy nhiên, hệ thống thiết bị mới sẽ giúp chấm dứt các bước làm phiền toái này", thông báo của Microsoft có đoạn. Microsoft dự kiến sẽ chấm dứt hỗ trợ hệ điều hành Windows XP từ ngày 8/4/2014.

2.3   Text Classification

To do the classification, a classifier should be trained using training dataset in which the topic of each document is known in advance. The goal of our study was to verify the usability of the proposed model using abstract of text document instead of using the full text content so in this study, the abstracts of text documents are extracted automatically to perform the test. We use libSVM [14] and decision tree J48 which are integrated in WEKA [15] to verify the model.

For training a classifier using WEKA, training dataset should be in ARFF format. The sparse ARFF format is structured as follow:

```
@RELATION <relation-name>
@ATTRIBUTE <Attribute-name>        <datatype>
…
@ATTRIBUTE class      {class-label₁, class-label₂ …}
@DATA
{<index₁> <value₁> … <indexₙ> "class-label"}
```

3   Results and Discussion

The goal of our research was to verify the feasibility of the text classification model based on automatic text summarization so we will compare the results of using abstracts of text documents with the results of using full text documents. We use a PC with a CORE i3 CPU and 4 GB RAM to perform the test.

3.1   Experimental Dataset

For experiments, we use 2000 articles, under ten different topics, which are collected from online newspapers (vnexpress.net and vietnamnet.vn). The distribution of ten topics is shown on Table 1.

After collecting 2000 articles, text summarization method (described in Sect. 2.2) is applied on this set of articles to produce 2000 abstracts/summaries. The execution time is about 1 s per article (see Table 2).

Table 1. Distribution of 10 topics

Topic	Number of articles
IT	200
Business	200
Law	200
Education	200
Health	200
Sports	200
Science	200
Travel	200
Society	200
Culinary	200

Table 2. Execution time for creating the summaries

Topic	Dataset size (MB)	Execution time (second)
IT	5.91	201
Business	6.84	280
Law	6.01	229
Education	6.59	273
Health	6.21	230
Sports	6.28	229
Science	6.94	229
Travel	6.46	186
Society	6.89	202
Culinary	6.28	242

3.2   Exeperimental Results

We use two most frequently used machine learning methods for the case of text classification: support vector machine (libSVM) and decision tree (J48) for verifying the feasibility of the proposed model. In both case, we use 10-fold cross validation to test the model.

3.2.1   Using libSVM

We show the classification result in the case of using full text documents in Table 3.

In the case of using summaries dataset, classification result is shown in Table 4.

With this experiment, we can conclude that by using libSVM the classification result on the summaries dataset is better than the one on the full text dataset for all metrics. Especially, we can improve more than 7 % of the TP Rate on average.

3.2.2   Using J48

We show the classification result in the case of using full text documents in Table 5.

In the case of using summaries dataset, classification result is shown in Table 6.

Table 3. Classification result using libSVM on full text documents dataset

Topic	TP rate	FP rate	Precision	Recall	F-measure
IT	0.975	0.112	0.491	0.975	0.653
Business	0.735	0.004	0.948	0.735	0.828
Law	0.930	0.024	0.812	0.930	0.867
Education	0.795	0.007	0.924	0.795	0.855
Health	0.815	0.009	0.906	0.815	0.858
Sports	0.850	0.003	0.971	0.850	0.907
Science	0.910	0.002	0.978	0.910	0.943
Travel	0.700	0.011	0.881	0.700	0.780
Society	0.768	0.007	0.921	0.768	0.837
Culinary	0.855	0.005	0.950	0.855	0.900
Average	**0.833**	**0.019**	**0.878**	**0.833**	**0.843**

Table 4. Classification result using libSVM on summaries dataset

Topic	TP rate	FP rate	Precision	Recall	F-measure
IT	0.975	0.048	0.691	0.975	0.809
Business	0.799	0.002	0.975	0.799	0.878
Law	0.965	0.024	0.818	0.965	0.885
Education	0.859	0.004	0.961	0.859	0.907
Health	0.885	0.006	0.941	0.885	0.912
Sports	0.950	0.002	0.979	0.950	0.964
Science	0.960	0.006	0.946	0.960	0.953
Travel	0.805	0.009	0.904	0.805	0.852
Society	0.840	0.007	0.928	0.840	0.882
Culinary	0.945	0.003	0.969	0.945	0.957
Average	**0.898**	**0.011**	**0.911**	**0.898**	**0.900**

Table 5. Classification result using J48 on full text documents dataset

Topic	TP rate	FP rate	Precision	Recall	F-measure
IT	0.790	0.068	0.564	0.790	0.658
Business	0.665	0.037	0.668	0.665	0.667
Law	0.650	0.027	0.726	0.650	0.686
Education	0.865	0.017	0.848	0.865	0.856
Health	0.635	0.024	0.747	0.635	0.686
Sports	0.835	0.017	0.843	0.835	0.839
Science	0.709	0.020	0.797	0.709	0.750
Travel	0.620	0.030	0.697	0.620	0.656
Society	0.747	0.031	0.725	0.747	0.736
Culinary	0.840	0.022	0.808	0.840	0.824
Average	**0.736**	**0.029**	**0.742**	**0.736**	**0.736**

Table 6. Classification result using J48 on summaries dataset

Topic	TP rate	FP rate	Precision	Recall	F-measure
IT	0.845	0.023	0.805	0.845	0.824
Business	0.729	0.028	0.744	0.729	0.736
Law	0.835	0.021	0.819	0.835	0.827
Education	0.859	0.011	0.895	0.859	0.877
Health	0.775	0.032	0.731	0.775	0.752
Sports	0.920	0.007	0.934	0.920	0.927
Science	0.845	0.022	0.813	0.845	0.828
Travel	0.830	0.015	0.860	0.830	0.845
Society	0.755	0.021	0.799	0.755	0.776
Culinary	0.850	0.016	0.854	0.850	0.852
Average	**0.824**	**0.020**	**0.825**	**0.824**	**0.825**

Again, the obtained results indicate that the classification result on the summaries dataset is better than the one on the full text dataset for all metrics. We can improve more than 10 % of the TP Rate on average.

4 Conclusion

In this paper, we propose a text classification model based on automatic text summarization. This is a relatively new approach and there are not many studies in the literature. The initial results that we obtained are satisfactory. Indeed, the model we propose gives the better results than the traditional one on all evaluation metrics.

These positive results can be explained by several reasons: (1) abstract/summary of a text covers the main ideas of the whole text so it can be used to identify the topic; (2) by using the right words segmentation method (vnTokenizer library in this work) we do not lose too much semantic information; (3) the proposed text summarization method is effective. Indeed, as we mentioned in [10] our method can produce the summary of the text with the accuracy of 52 % (an acceptable accuracy for automatic text summarization).

Although the experimental results show the feasibility of the proposed model, we have also remaining issues: (1) the volume of experimental data is not large enough; (2) only Vietnamese texts are collected. In future, we will continue updating this work, e.g., increasing the volume of experimental dataset as well as improving the text summarization model accuracy.

References

1. Joachims, T.: Text categorization with support vector machines: learning with many relevant features. In: Proceedings of the 10th European Conference on Machine Learning, pp. 137–142 (1998)

2. Ho, T.B., Nguyen, N.B.: Nonhierarchical document clustering by a tolerance rough set model. Intl. J. Fuzzy Logic Intell. Syst. **17**(2), 199–212 (2012)
3. Zaïane, O.R., Antonie, M.-L.: Classifying text documents by associating terms with text categories. In: Proceedings of the 13th Australasian Database Conference, pp. 215–222, Melbourne, Victoria, Australia (2002)
4. Amini, M.R., Usunier, N., Gallinari, P.: Automatic text summarization based on word-clusters and ranking algorithms. In: Proceedings of the 27th European Conference on Advances in Information Retrieval Research, Santiago de Compostela, Spain (2005). doi:10.1007/978-3-540-31865-1_11
5. Goldstein, J., Mittal, V., Carbonell, J., Kantrowitz, M.: Multi-document summarization by sentence extraction. In: Proceedings of the 2000 NAACL-ANLP Workshop on Automatic Summarization, pp. 40–48, Seattle, Washington (2000). doi:10.3115/1117575.1117580
6. Barzilay, R., Elhadad, N., McKeown, K.: Inferring strategies for sentence ordering in multidocument news summarization. J. Artif. Intell. Res. **17**, 35–55 (2002)
7. Johnson, D., Oles, F., Zhang, T., Goetz, T.: A decision tree-based symbolic rule induction system for text categorization. IBM Syst. J. **41**(3), 428–437 (2002)
8. Han, E.H., Karypis, G., Kumar, V.: Text categorization using weighted-adjusted k-nearest neighbor classification. In: PAKDD Conference (2001)
9. Ruiz, M., Srinivasan, P.: Hierarchical neural networks for text categorization. In: ACM SIGIR Conference (1999)
10. Truong, Q-D., Nguyen, Q-D.: Automatic Vietnamese text summarization (in Vietnamese). In: Proceeding of The Fifteenth National Conference, pp. 233–238, Hanoi, Vietnam (2012)
11. Hông Phuong, L., Thi Minh Huyên, N., Roussanaly, A., Vinh, H.T.: A hybrid approach to word segmentation of Vietnamese texts. In: Martín-Vide, C., Otto, F., Fernau, H. (eds.) LATA 2008. LNCS, vol. 5196, pp. 240–249. Springer, Heidelberg (2008). doi:10.1007/978-3-540-88282-4_23
12. Page, L., Brin, S., Motwani, R., Winograd, T.: The PageRank citation ranking: bringing order to the web (1999)
13. Jaccard P.: Étude comparative de la distribution florale dans une portion des Alpes et des Jura, Bulletin de la Société Vaudoise des Sciences Naturelles **37**, 547–579
14. Chang, C.C., Lin, C.J.: LIBSVM: a library for support vector machines. ACM Trans. Intell. Syst. Technol. **2**, 27 (2011)
15. Hall, M., Frank, E., Holmes, G., Pfahringer, B., Reutemann, P., Witten, I.H.: The WEKA data mining software: an update. SIGKDD Explor. **11**(1), 10–18 (2009)

An Hierarchical Scheduled Algorithm for Data Dissemination in a Brown Planthopper Surveillance Network

Bao Hoai Lam[1]([✉]), Tuyen Phong Truong[1], Ky Minh Nguyen[2],
Hiep Xuan Huynh[3], and Bernard Pottier[1]

[1] Université de Bretagne Occidentale, LAB-STICC, UMR CNRS 6285, Brest, France
{bao-hoai.lam,tuyen-phong.truong,pottier}@univ-brest.fr
[2] Can Tho University of Technology, Can Tho, Vietnam
nmky@ctuet.edu.vn
[3] DREAM Team/UMI 209 UMMISCO-IRD, Can Tho University, Can Tho, Vietnam
hxhiep@ctu.edu.vn

Abstract. The paper proposes a new approach to model the hierarchical structure and implement a scheduled algorithm for disseminating data of a brown planthopper surveillance network based on Wireless Sensor Network (WSN) approach. In the hierarchical model, light trap sensor nodes in the same province compose a sub network at level 1 while sink nodes of these networks compose another sub network at level 0. Thanks to this structure, there are 2 types of data dissemination: local at sub networks at level 1 and cluster at sub network at level 0. These behaviors are monitored by a timer which calculates the next execution time for each node. The model and its algorithms are simulated using data collections of the brown planthopper surveillance network in Mekong Delta, especially in Cantho, Angiang, Dongthap - 3 typical rice provinces in the delta. Structure of the model is suitable for the hierarchical management policies of a light trap network in a large region and the role of WSN in collecting data is emerged via the simulation.

Keywords: BPHSUN · Brown planthopper surveillance network · BPH · WSN · Timer

1 Introduction

Light trap network is one of effective solutions for insect pest management in a large area. For example, Rothamsted light trap networks [1,2] have been established in Britain since the 1960s to monitor insect migrations and populations in order to provide warning systems. Another example is that a light trap network in Mekong Delta [7] with more than 340 light traps can provide hopper densities and thanks to data collection form the network, people may know what types of insects are there in their fields and if they are in a controllable level.

© ICST Institute for Computer Sciences, Social Informatics and Telecommunications Engineering 2016
P.C. Vinh et al. (Eds.): ICTCC 2016, LNICST 168, pp. 246–263, 2016.
DOI: 10.1007/978-3-319-46909-6_23

The idea of light trap network based on Wireless Sensor Network (WSN) approach [9] emerges as a suitable choice for insect, particularly Brown Planthopper (BPH) monitoring since they can help monitoring hopper behaviors automatically as well as providing meteorological factors. This kind of solution use sensors in each trap to sense surrounding conditions and a whole network becomes a massive coordinated sensing machine. These pieces of sensed data are collected and sent to a data center via a wireless network for post processing. This solution can be shortly called as BPH surveillance network.

Due to a large area of BPH surveillance network distribution, it is necessary to maintain an appropriate light trap network topology in order to collect data. This topology illustrates the topology of the observation WSN and influences on algorithms for collecting data from the WSN as well. Moreover, management policies of the surveillance network also rely on this topology such as: authorization of light traps, decision making.

This paper proposes a new hierarchical structure to model a BPH surveillance network topology as well as describes an appropriate scheduled algorithm for data dissemination in the network. In this work, the light trap sensor network is considered as a multi-level graph in which each light trap sensor node is modelled as a node and 2 sensor nodes located in their communication ranges, the maximum distance that radio signal from a node can be reached, can be considered as candidates to establish an edge. Based on the multi-level graph, an hierarchical structure with multi-level sub networks, along with a scheduled algorithm, is presented for data dissemination inside the BPH surveillance network in a large region.

The structure of this paper is as follows. Section 2 summarizes some previous work relating to insect surveillance network topology. Next section depicts the topology of a BPH surveillance network as an hierarchical graph model. Section 4 is about data behaviors of the BPH surveillance network including scheduled algorithms for sending and receiving collected data from sensor nodes. Next section illustrates some simulation results for data behaviors of the surveillance network with data collection in Cantho, Angiang and Dongthap. The last section is our conclusion and future plans.

2   Related Work

Light trap method is one of solutions to prevent high densities of spruce budworm in Canadian forests [3,4]. This method allows people to participate insect trapping by giving light traps to them and track their traps from June to end of August every year. Periodically, people only report estimated densities of insects via a website, an application or even with a paper and a pen. Finally, trap samples are collected and counted in a lab environment. Applications of data collections from these light traps are variant, for example, thanks to wing wear and body size measurements of adult spruce budworms captured at light traps in some previous years, some useful inference on seasonal patterns related to reproduction can be archived [5]. However, these light traps seem not to compose a network, instead, they create a combination of traps to collect data for post processing.

Rothamsted light trap networks [1,2] have been established in Britain since the early 1960 s to monitor pest insects. The initial ideas of these networks is to understand the population change when pest insects occur. By the time passing, these networks have also been used to monitor the responses of insects to climate and environmental change and as well as to measure and analyze biodiversity [18, 19]. Nevertheless, few information about topologies of these networks is found.

If a light trap network is based on wireless sensor network (WSN) approach (as proposed in [8,9]), its topology is identified by the observation WSN topology. Although these pieces of above work use mesh network to distribute data, there is no information about how data is transmitted via the network topology.

In addition, there are not many investigation of hierarchical structure in modeling insect surveillance network topology.

3   Multilevel Graph of the BPH Surveillance Network

3.1   Description

The BPH surveillance network in a large region depicts an hierarchical structure with 3 levels (Fig. 1). Level 2 illustrates light trap sensor nodes to collect data. These sensor nodes compose sub networks at level 1 and each sub network is represented by a sink node where data in the sub network is assembled. These sink nodes constitute another sub network at level 0 with a gateway where collected data from the whole network is aggregated for post processing.

3.2   Sub Network at Level 1

A sub network at level 1 (small circles in Fig. 1) can be considered as a graph $G_i = (V_i, E_i)$ where V_i is a collection of automatic light trap sensor nodes in the same province i and E_i is a collection of edges. An edge between 2 nodes in V_i is composed if the distance between them is at most the transmission range, the maximum distance that a single transmission of a node can be received by all nodes in its vicinity. All sensor nodes are assumed to have the same transmission range.

In the graph G_i, a special node is elected as a sink (leader) where data is assembled and stored. In this case, sensor nodes have abilities to sense surrounding conditions (environmental factors and hopper densities) and transmit sensed data to its neighbors. However, the sink node can only receive data from its neighbors in the same sub network at level 1.

3.3   Sub Network at Level 0

Sink nodes of all sub networks at level 1 can be considered as a graph $G = (V, E)$ where V is a collection of sink nodes, nodes concentrating data from sub networks

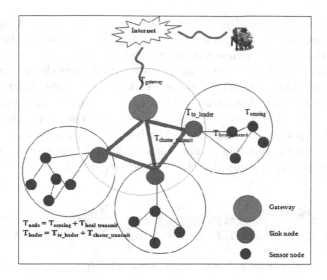

Fig. 1. Hierarchical structure of hopper observation WSN.

at level 1, and E is a set of edges. An edge is created between 2 nodes if the distance between them is at most the transmission range. Similar to sub networks at level 1, all sink nodes have the same transmission range.

In this sub network, each sink node can transmit aggregated data, data accumulated from collected data in the corresponding sub network at level 1, to its neighbors. There is no sensing activity in the sub network at level 0.

A special node is elected as a gateway. This node can be a sink or a new node to store the final data. The main task of the gateway is to receive the aggregated data from sinks and there could be an application to which connects for decision making.

3.4   BPHSUN

The composition of the sub network at level 0 and sub networks at level 1 depicts an hierarchical structure for the BPH surveillance network. Therefore, it can be called as **B**rown **P**lanthopper Hierarchical **SU**rveillance **N**etwork (BPHSUN).

4   Data Transmission in the BPHSUN

4.1   Data Packet

Data is packed as packets and transmitted through the hierarchical structure of the BPHSUN. In the BPHSUN, there are 2 types of packets:

- Local packet: data sensed at each sensor node is packed as a local packet.
- Cluster packet: a packet aggregated at each sink node.

The structure of a local packet is depicted as in Fig. 2. In this structure, ID is the unique ID of the packet and location ID represents the ID of the sensor node that senses environmental factors. The time that the sensor node senses data is described by a time stamp. Source ID depicts the sensor node that sends the packet while destination ID is the ID of next node that the packet is received. Normally, the destination ID is identified thanks to a routing table, a table that routes packets to a sink (or a gateway). These attributes compose a header of the packet. In addition to the header, the packet contains a data part which stores surrounding conditions such as light intensity, temperature, humidity, wind velocity, wind direction and hopper density.

HEADER						DATA					
ID	time Stamp	source ID	destID	location ID	data Size	density Hoppers	light Intensity	temperature	humidity	wind Velocity	wind Direction

Fig. 2. Local packet in the BPHSUN.

The structure of a cluster packet is almost similar to that of a local packet. However, the data part of the cluster packet contains min, mean, max values of environmental factors after a period of time.

A packet here depicts a structure to maintain a piece of spatial-temporal data. Indeed, time stamp illustrates the temporal aspect while location id describes the spatial one and the data part of the packet becomes data aspect. Figure 3 is an example of this piece of data. It can be translated as: at the time *01/02/2016 08:07:56 AM*, the sensor node *10* has *500 hoppers caught* at the temperature 29°C and *5.5* km/h wind velocity.

HEADER					DATA					
ID	01/02/2016 08:07:56 AM	...	...	10	...	500	...	29	...	5.5	...

Fig. 3. Example of a piece of spatial-temporal data.

Consequently, a local packet can be declared as the following C based pseudo code:

```
typedef struct{
        int ID;
        int sourceID , desID;
        int location;// local ID of sensor node that senses data
        int timeStamp; //time stamp of sensing
        int dataSize;
        float densityHoppers; // density of hoppers
        float lightIntensity; // light intensity
        float temperature , humidity; // temperature & humidity
        float velocityWind;       // wind velocity
        float directionWind;      // wind direction
}LocalPacket;
```

The declaration of a cluster packet is similar to that of a local packet. The difference is that the cluster packet may contain max, mean, min values of surrounding conditions as well as hopper densities.

4.2   Packet Dissemination

There are 2 procedures to disseminate data in the BPHSUN based on types of packets: local packet and cluster packet procedures.

Local packet dissemination. Local packet dissemination illustrates behaviors of a sensor node in each sub network at level 1. These behaviors compose of sensing surrounding conditions, packing into a local packet and sending the packet to a sink node (Fig. 4).

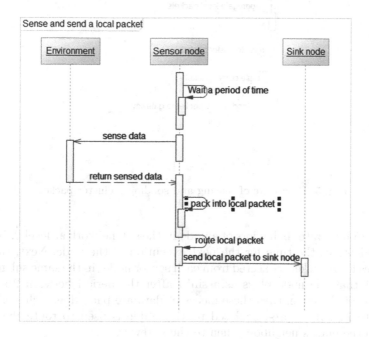

Fig. 4. Procedure of sensing and sending a local packet

Figure 4 depicts behaviors of a sensor node of each sub network at level 1. First, next execution time of a sensor node is identified by a timer. Next, the sensor node measures surrounding conditions and receives sensed data from environment, then these pieces of data are packed as a local packet (as in Fig. 2). A pre-calculated routing table is used to route the local packet to its sink node where sensed data is aggregated periodically.

Cluster packet dissemination. Cluster packet dissemination describes behaviors of a node in the sub network at level 0. These behaviors represent a procedure to aggregate packets collected at each sensor node at level 1, pack into a cluster packet and send to a gateway.

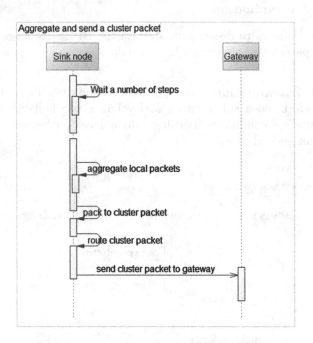

Fig. 5. Procedure of sensing and sending a cluster packet.

Figure 5 illustrates behaviors of a node in the sub network at level 0. Initially, a timer identifies the time for the next execution of the node. Next, the node aggregates local packets collected from each sensor node (in the same sub network at level 1 that the node plays as a sink) after the period between 2 adjacent executions of the node, then these pieces of data are packed as a cluster packet (similar to Fig. 2). A pre-calculated routing table is used to route the cluster packet to the node's neighbors, then to the gateway.

4.3   Timer

In the BPHSUN, timer is a mechanism calculating the time when nodes (sensor, sink and gateway) execute their tasks. This time can be figured out based on sensing times of sensor nodes and communication times to transmit packets to the gateway.

Assume that each sensor node contains n sensors, t_i is a duration of time to read sensor i. Therefore, $T_{read} = \{t_1, t_2, ..., t_n\}$ is a collections of times to read sensors in a sensor node.

Let $T_{sensing}(s)$ is the sensing time, a duration of time that a sensor node finish reading all its sensors. This time is calculated as:

$$\Rightarrow T_{sensing} = Max\{t_1, t_2, ..., t_n\} = Max\{T\} \tag{1}$$

To transmit data to the gateway, following factors are considered:

- f: the frequency used to transmit data (Hz).
- LocalDataSize, ClusterDataSize: sizes of a local packet and a cluster packet, respectively (bit).
- DataRate: the rate (speed) to transmit data ($Kbps$). This rate depends on the frequency used to transmit data.

The communication time $T_{local\_transmit}$ from one node to another node in a sub network at level 1 is shown as below:

$$T_{local\_transmit} = \frac{LocalDataSize}{DataRate} \tag{2}$$

Similarly, the communication time $T_{cluster\_transmit}$ in the sub network at level 0 is measured as:

$$T_{cluster\_transmit} = \frac{ClusterDataSize}{DataRate} \tag{3}$$

Therefore, the duration of time that a sensor finish executing its tasks (Fig. 1) is calculated as:

$$T_{node} = T_{sensing} + T_{local\_transmit} \tag{4}$$

Let T_{to_leader} be a duration of time that a leader (sink node) finish collecting data from all other nodes (Fig. 1), then T_{to_leader} is estimated as:

$$T_{node} \leq T_{to\_leader} \leq nT_{node} \tag{5}$$

where n is the number of sensor nodes in a sub network at level 1. Indeed, in the best case, all sensor nodes of a sub network at level 1 transmit its data directly to a sink node at the same time, then T_{to_leader} is approximately T_{node}. However, in the worst case, sensor nodes perform sequentially, then T_{to_leader} is around nT_{node}.

Assume that there are m sink nodes in the sub network at level 0. Let T_{leader} be a time that a sink node collects data from its sensor nodes at leaf level and sends these pieces of data to a neighbor of it in the sub network at level 0 (Fig. 1). Another assumption is that $T_{gateway}$ is a total of time that a packet reaches the gateway. Then:

$$T_{leader} = T_{to\_leader} + T_{cluster\_transmit} \tag{6}$$

$$T_{leader} \leq T_{gateway} \leq mT_{leader} \tag{7}$$

The interval time T between 2 next actions of a sensor node in the BPHSUN can be calculated as the maximum of $T_{gateway}$ after adding an error-time Δt. Therefore, T is estimated as:

$$T = mT_{leader} + \Delta t \tag{8}$$

$$\Rightarrow T = m(n(T_{sensing} + T_{local\_transmit}) + T_{cluster\_transmit}) + \Delta t \qquad (9)$$

The above interval time T is used for nodes of sub networks at level 1. However, sink nodes do not forward data sensed from sensor nodes to the gateway immediately, instead, they wait some working steps of sensor nodes in order to aggregate data. Thus, after a multiple of T time unit, nodes at level 0 aggregate data and transmit to the gateway.

4.4   Routing Table

Routing table [20] is a structure to store shortest paths from a node to other nodes in a WSN. In the BPHSUN, because automatic light trap sensor nodes located at fixed positions, routing table is prev-calculated and stored to disseminate data to sinks or the gateway.

Distance vector algorithm [20] is used to calculate routing tables for a WSN $G(V, E)$. The algorithm is shown as below:

ALGORITHM. Calculate a routing table for node v to other nodes in $G(V, E)$

INPUT: c(v, w): the direct cost from v to w $(w \in V)$.
OUTPUT: D(v, w): distance between v and w $(w \in V)$. Next(v, w): next node to reach to w from v. $(w \in V)$

```
createRoutingtable(){
    for each (w in V)
        D[v, w] = 0;
    D[v, v] = _INFINITY;
    // Find route from v to others
    for each (w in V){
        if (w == v) continue;
        /* Select the shortest distance from v to its neighbors
           after adding direct costs */
        minCost = D[v, w]; // old distance
        neighbor = -1;
        nextNode = Next(v, w);
        for each (j in v.getNeighbors()){
            neighbor = j;
            newCost = c[v,j] + D[j, w];
            if (newCost < minCost){
                minCost=newCost;
                nextNode=neighbor;
            }
        }
        // Update routing table
        D[v,w]=minCost;
        Next[v,w]=nextNode;
    }
}
```

The above algorithm is executed parallely for all nodes $v \in V$, then routing tables for all node $v \in V$ to other nodes are found after 1 execution step. This procedure of calculating routing tables for all nodes is looped until distances are unchanged.

Example. Let a WSN given by a graph $G(V, E)$ (Fig. 6). Assume that the direct cost from a node to its neighbors is 1.

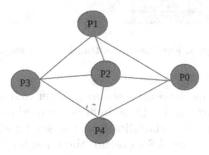

Fig. 6. Example of a graph to calculate routing tables.

The following result are routing tables of all nodes in the graph G after 2 execution steps. After 2 steps, routing tables of all nodes are unchanged, thus, they become final routing tables.

	P0		P1		P2		P3		P4	
	D	*Next*	*D*	*Next*	*D*	*Next*	*D*	*Next*	*D*	*Next*
P0	0	-1	1	0	1	0	2	1	1	0
P1	1	1	0	-1	1	1	1	1	1	1
P2	1	2	1	2	0	-1	1	2	1	2
P3	2	1	1	3	1	3	0	-1	1	3
P4	1	4	1	4	1	4	1	4	0	-1

Fig. 7. Routing tables after 2 steps.

4.5   Routing Local Packets

This procedure takes place in sub networks at level 1. It is a process of sending and receiving packets at each sensor node based on a routing table so that all packets are concentrated at the sink node.

Before sensed data is transmitted, it is packed as a local packet (as Fig. 2). The local packet consists of an ID, source ID, destination ID, location, time stamp and other measured values of environmental factors. The attribute location depicts the local ID of the sensor node that senses these surrounding conditions.

Example: Assume that P1, P2, P3, P4 are sensor nodes and P0 is the sink node of the graph in Fig. 6, according to routing tables in Fig. 7, collected data from P1, P2, P4 can send directly to P0 while P3 needs 2 hops to reach to P0 (P3 - P1 - P0). Figure 8 depicts a round how sensed data from sensor nodes reaches the sink node P0.

		HEADER				DATA				
1	...	P1	P0	P1	...	500	...	30	...	...	...
2	...	P2	P0	P2	...	550	...	29	...	...	...
3	...	P3	P1	P3	...	600	...	30	...	...	...
4	...	P4	P0	P4	...	650	...	29.5	...	...	...
5	...	P1	P0	P3	...	600	...	30	...	...	...

Fig. 8. Example of routing local packets.

To implement this mechanism, a sending buffer and a receiving buffer are maintained at each sensor node. These buffers are used in 2 following methods: sendLocalPackets() and receiveLocalPackets() to send and receive local packets at a node v. All nodes in the WSN execute these methods concurrently.

Sending packets. Sending packets takes place at sensor nodes of the WSN after they are granted execution times from the timer. First, environmental factors are sensed by sensors of a node and these pieces of sensed data are packed as a packet. Next, the packet is added to sending buffer of the node. The next step is to move all packets from the node's receiving buffer to its sending buffer in order to send to the gateway thanks to the routing table.

The algorithm is described as followed:

ALGORITHM. send local packets at a sensor node

INPUT: Node v, routing table t, receiving buffer $v.receiveBuff$
OUTPUT: sending buffer $v.sendBuf$

```
sendLocalPacket(){
  if (isExecutionTime()){
    if (!isLeader(v)){
      senseData();      //Sense data from environment
      createPacket(p);  //Create a packet
      l = Leader(v);    //Find leader of v

      //Next hop of v is destination ID of p
      p.destinationID = t.Next[v][l];

      v.sendBuff.Add(p);
      for each (packet p in v.receiveBuff)
        v.sendBuff.Add(p);
      v.receiveBuff.Clear();
    }
  }
}
```

Receiving local packets. When sensor nodes are granted execution times, they start receiving packets from their neighbors. Main idea of receiving packets at a node v is to locate in the sending buffer of each neighbor of v in order to find packets considering v as their destination IDs, then these packets are added to the receiving buffer of v.

ALGORITHM. receive local packets at a node

INPUT: Node v, routing table t
OUTPUT: receiving buffer $v.receiveBuf$

```
receiveLocalPacket (){
  if (isExecutionTime ()){
    l = Leader(v);  //Find leader of v
    for each (Neighbor j of v){
      for each (packet p in j.sendBuf){
        desID = p.destinationID;
        if (desID == v.ID){
          //Next hop of v is destination ID of p
          NextID =  t.Next[v][l];
          p.destinationID = NextID;
          v.receiveBuff.Add(p);
        }
      }
    }
  }
}
```

4.6   Routing Cluster Packets

Routing cluster packets relating to sending and receiving cluster packets at each sink nodes thanks to a routing table so that all cluster packets are concentrated at the gateway. To implement this procedure, each sink node has 2 more buffers: sending and receiving cluster buffers. 2 new buffers are used for transmitting packets in the sub network at level 0. Similar to routing local packets, this procedure is divided into 2 methods: sendClusterPackets() and receiveCluster-Packets(). Similar to routing local packets, nodes in the sub network at level 0 execute these above methods parallely.

Sending cluster packets. Sending cluster packets takes place at nodes of the sub network at level 0 when these nodes are granted execution times from the timer. First, each node aggregates data in packets from its sending local buffer grouping by each sensor node after a period of time identified by the timer. After grouping, each group of packets composes a cluster packet and the packet is added to the node's sending cluster buffer.

ALGORITHM. send cluster packets at a node

INPUT: Sink node v, routing table t, sending and receiving buffers of v: v.sendBuf, v.receiveBuf

OUTPUT: sending cluster buffer *v.sendClusterBuf*

```
sendClusterPacket(){
 if (isExecutionTime()){
   if (isLeader(v){
    //Aggregate packets in sending and receiving buffer of v
    //  results are in a temp buffer b
    aggregateData(v.sendBuf, v.receiveBuf, &b);
    for each (cluster packet p in b){
      p.sourceID = v.ID;
      //Next hop of v is destination ID of p
      p.destinationID = t.Next[v][gateway];
      v.sendClusterBuf.Add(p);
    }
   }
 }
}
```

ALGORITHM. receive cluster packets

INPUT: Sink node v, routing table t

OUTPUT: receiving cluster buffer *v.receiveClusterBuf*

```
receiveClusterPacket(){
 if (isExecutionTime()){
   if (isLeader(v) || isGateway(v)){
    for each (neighbor j of v){
      for each (packet p in j.sendClusterBuf){
        desID = p.destinationID;
        if (desID == v.ID){
         // //Next hop of v is destination ID of p
         NextID = t.Next[v][gateway];
         p.destinationID = NextID;
         v.receiveClusterBuf.Add(p);
        }
      }
    }
   }
 }
}
```

Receiving cluster packets. Similar to receiving local packets, the main idea of this algorithm is to locate in the cluster sending buffer of each neighbor of a node v in order to find cluster packets considering v as their destination IDs, then these packets are added to the receiving cluster buffer of v. The algorithm is shown as below:

5 Experiment

5.1 Data Used

The experiment uses the data collection of the light trap network in Mekong Delta by selecting some typical rice provinces to simulate. It uses 4 current light traps in Cantho, 3 in Angiang and 3 in DongThap as sensor nodes. Thus, the BPHSUN contains 3 sub networks at level 1 and 1 sub network at level 0 (Fig. 9). The sub network in Cantho contains sensor nodes P00, P01, P02, P03, P04 which P00 is a sink node. In Angiang, the sub network consists of 4 sensor nodes P05, P06, P07, P08 which P05 is a sink node. Similarly, P09, P10, P11, P12 compose a sub network of Dongthap which P09 is a sink node. At level 0, P00, P05, P09 and the gateway P13 compose another sub network at level 0.

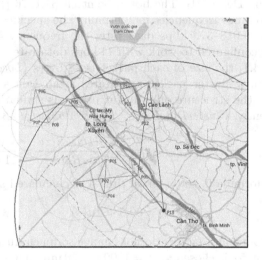

Fig. 9. The BPHSUN composed by light trap sensor nodes in Cantho, Angiang, Dongthap.

5.2 Tools Used

The map including Cantho, Angiang and Dongthap is processed by the tool PickCell in the framework NetGen [12]. Behaviors of the BPHSYN are implemented in CUDA to run the simulation on the NVIDIA card GeForce GTX 680 1.15 GHz with 1536 CUDA Cores (8 Multiprocessors x 192 CUDA Cores/MP).

5.3   Sensor Node Interval Time Calculation

According to Formula 9 the sensor node interval time of the BPHSUN depends on sensing times and communication times.

Actually, sensing time of a sensor is the response time of that sensor. This time relies on type of sensors as well as concrete surrounding conditions. A sensor node here is an automatic light trap [21] consists of following sensors shown in Fig. 10. This figure also depicts the response time of each sensor [14–16].

Sensor	Response time (s)
Wind sensor WindSonic M	0.25
Temperature and humidity sensor DT22	20
Light sensor BH1750FVI	Approximately human eye response

Fig. 10. Response times of sensors in a light trap sensor node

Therefore, the sensing time is $T_{sensing} = 20$ s.

LORA technology [17] is used to transmit data in the BPH surveillance network in Mekong Delta [21]. The board Semtech SX1276 [17] is used since it is suitable for allowance frequencies in Vietnam. The specification of this board shows that it has 0.018–37.5 kbps data rate, the frequency 433 MHz. Assume that the board is configured to work with 11 kbps data rate.

According to 4.1, the size of each packet is 48 bytes ($LocalDataSize = 48$). In this simulation, a cluster packet aggregates mean values of environmental factors, therefore, the structure of a cluster packet is similar to that of a local packet. Consequently, $ClusterDataSize = LocalDataSize = 48$ bytes.

$$\Rightarrow T_{cluster\_transmit} = T_{local\_transmit} = \frac{LocalDataSize}{DataRate} = \frac{48 * 8}{11 * 1000} = 0.035 \text{ s}$$

According to formula 9, the interval time T is calculated as:

$$\Rightarrow T = 60.5 + \Delta t(s)$$

Because environmental factors do not change so much during a short period of time, $\Delta t = 1739.5$ s is chosen $\Rightarrow T = 1800$ s $= 30$ min. Thus, the interval time between 2 adjacent actions of a sensor node is 30 min. If a light trap works 4 h every night, the sensor node senses environment and transmits data 9 times.

5.4   Scenario *Data Collection After 30 min*

In this scenario, assume that sink nodes aggregate data every 30 min, it means that these pieces of data are calculated after every 2 adjacent steps of a sensor node.

Figure 11 depicts a status of the BPHSUN when sensor nodes and sink nodes execute their tasks. The left of this figure is captured when the sensor nodes are

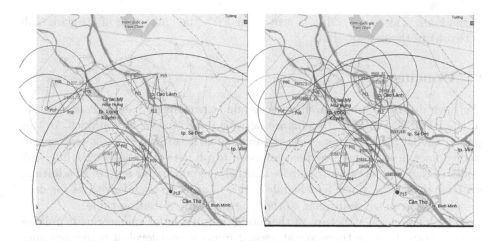

Fig. 11. Sensing and transmitting data in sensor nodes

in their first step to sense and transmit data. In the left, sensor nodes in 3 sub networks of Cantho, Angiang, Dongthap are working to measure environment as well as send data according to routing tables to sink nodes. The sub network at level 0 does not operate yet since it is not the time for its behaviors. On the other hands, the right of the figure illustrates data transmissions in the sub network at level 0. In this case, 3 sub network of Cantho, Angiang, Dongthap do not operate while aggregated data is transmitting through the sub network at level 0 to the gateway.

Figure 12 depicts aggregated data of the BPHSUN after the first 30 min. In the sub network at level 0, because all nodes are in their transmission ranges, aggregated data is transmitted directly to the gateway P13. These pieces of data are mean values of sense data at each sensor node locations after 30 min (2 steps). For example, the row 6 in this figure means that after the first 30 min, the mean value of hoppers collected at P07 (in Angiang sub network) is 9039.72

From	To	Location	Sub network	Mean of hopper density (individuals)
P00	P13	P01	Cantho	8176.4
P00	P13	P02	Cantho	20057.45
P00	P13	P03	Cantho	20302.36
P00	P13	P04	Cantho	19104.9
P05	P13	P06	Angiang	10615.5
P05	P13	P07	Angiang	9039.72
P05	P13	P08	Angiang	21219.6
P09	P13	P10	Dongthap	7341.44
P09	P13	P11	Dongthap	6159.4
P09	P13	P12	Dongthap	15557.32

Fig. 12. Aggregated data in BPHSUN after the first 30 min.

individuals. This mean value is sent from P05 (the sink node of Angiang sub network) to the gateway P13.

6   Conclusion

We have described an hierarchical scheduled algorithm for data dissemination in the BPHSUN, a BPH surveillance network based on WSN approach. In this paper, the BPHSUN forms as an hierarchical structure where light trap sensor nodes place in the same province compose a sub network at level 1 while sink nodes of these sub networks compose another sub network at level 0. In addition, we have depicted a timer to schedule nodes in order to use algorithms for data dissemination to transmit data to the gateway using a routing table.

The hierarchical structure of the model is suitable for management policies of light traps because there are at least 2 management level of traps: province level and region level. It can be considered that sub networks at level 1 is for provincial administrative administration and the sub network at level 0 is for regional management. This structure is simulated with the light trap network in Mekong Delta by using data collections in Cantho, Angiang, Dongthap. The simulation also shows the role of WSN not only in sensing data, but also in collecting data for decision making.

In practice, the distance of light traps is quite far (approximately 10–15 km), LORA technology [17] emerges as a suitable choice for transmitting data to a distant destination. In addition, it is necessary to maintain a database for sensed data as well as aggregated data for post processing. Ongoing investigations include meta data for light trap network to maintain data for post processing.

The paper assumes that data sensed from a sensor node is sent to its neighbors thanks to a routing table. To better routing data, it is necessary to implement some mechanisms such as SYN-ACK or checking/fixing errors during the data transmission.

Acknowledgments. The work of this paper was in the scope of the "OBSNET - Optimizing the Brown Planthopper surveillance network using automatic light traps in the Mekong Delta region" project of the Ministry of Education and Training, Vietnam. The first author was funded by the program 911 of Ministry of Education and Training, Vietnam.

References

1. Conrad, K.F., Fox, R., Woiwod, I.P.: Monitoring biodiversity: measuring long-term changes in insect abundance. In: Insect Conservation Biology, pp. 203–225. Cabi Publisher (2007). ISBN: 9781845932541
2. Crichton, M.I.: The interpretation of light trap catches of Trichoptera from the Rothamsted Insect Survey. In: Malicky, H. (ed.) Proceedings of the First International Symposium on Trichoptera, pp. 147–158. Springer, Netherlands (1976). ISBN: 978-90-6193-547-6

3. http://www.healthyforestpartnership.ca/
4. Rhainds, M., Heard, S.B.: Sampling procedures and adult sex ratios in spruce budworm. Entomol. Exp. Appl. **154**, 91–101 (2014)
5. Rhainds, M.: Wing wear and body size measurements of adult spruce budworms captured at light traps: inference on seasonal patterns related to reproduction. Appl. Entomol. Zool. **50**(4), 477–485 (2015). Springer, Japan. ISBN: 0003-6862
6. Phan, C.H., Huynh, H.X., Drogoul, A.: An agent-based approach to the simulation of Brown Plant Hopper (BPH) invasions in the Mekong Delta. In: 2010 IEEE RIVF International Conference on Computing & Communication Technologies, Research, Innovation, and Vision for the Future (RIVF), Hanoi, Vietnam, pp. 1–6. IEEE, Heidelberg (2010)
7. Truong, V.X., Huynh, H.X., Le, M.N., Drogoul, A.: Modeling a surveillance network based on unit disk graph technique – application for monitoring the invasion of insects in Mekong Delta region. In: Rahwan, I., Wobcke, W., Sen, S., Sugawara, T. (eds.) PRIMA 2012. LNCS (LNAI), vol. 7455, pp. 228–242. Springer, Heidelberg (2012). doi:10.1007/978-3-642-32729-2_16
8. Lam, H.B., Phan, T.T., Vuong, L.H., Huynh, H.X., Pottier, B.: Designing a brown planthoppers surveillance network based on wireless sensor network approach. In: ISCRAM (Information Systems for Crisis Response and Management) Vietnam 2013 Conference (2013)
9. Lam, B.H., Huynh, H.X., Traoré, M., Lucas, P.Y., Pottier, B.: Monitoring environmental factors in Mekong Delta of Vietnam using wireless sensor network approach. In: 8th International Conference on Simulation and Modelling in the Food and Bio-Industry, FoodSim 2014, pp. 71–78 (2014). ISBN: 978-90-77381-84-7
10. Heong, K.L., Hardy, B.: Planthoppers: new threats to the sustainability of intensive rice production systems in Asia. International Rice Research Institute, Asian Development Bank, Australian Government, Australian Centre for International Agricultural Research (2009). ISBN: 978-90-77381-84-7
11. Lynch, N.A.: Distributed Algorithms. Morgan Kaufmann Publishers Inc., San Francisco (1996). ISBN: 1558603484
12. Pottier, B., Lucas, P.-Y.: Dynamic networks NetGen: objectives, installation, use, and programming. Université de Bretagne Occidentale (2015). https://github.com/NetGenProject
13. NVDIA. https://developer.nvidia.com/cuda-zone
14. WindSonic M. http://gillinstruments.com/data/datasheets/windsonic-m.pdf?v=01.2014
15. DT22. http://www.dfrobot.com
16. BH1750FVI. http://www.electronic-circuits-diagrams.com
17. LORA technology. http://www.semtech.com/wireless-rf/rf-transceivers/sx1276/
18. Taylor, L.R.: Synoptic dynamics, migration and the Rothamsted Insect Survey. J. Anim. Ecol. **55**, 1–38 (1986)
19. Woiwod, I.P., Harrington, R.: Flying in the face of change: the Rothamsted Insect Survey. In: Leigh, R.A., Johnston, A.E. (eds.) Long-term Experiments in Agricultural and Ecological Sciences, pp. 321–342. CAB International, Wallingford (1994)
20. Vutukury, S., Garcia-Luna-Aceves, J.J.: MDVA: a distance-vector multipath routing protocol. In: Proceedings of the Twentieth Annual Joint Conference of the IEEE Computer and Communications Societies, INFOCOM 2001, vol. 1, pp. 557–564. IEEE (2001). doi:10.1109/INFCOM.2001.916780
21. Nguyen, K.M., Lam, B.H., Truong, T.P., Thi Pham, H.M., Van Ho, C., Pottier, B., Huynh, H.X.: Automatic hopper light trap. Cantho University Journal of Science, pp. 168–178. Cantho University (2015)

CFBM - A Framework for Data Driven Approach in Agent-Based Modeling and Simulation

Thai Minh Truong[1,2(✉)], Frédéric Amblard[2], Benoit Gaudou[2], and Christophe Sibertin Blanc[2]

[1] CIT, Can Tho University, Can Tho, Vietnam
tmthai@cit.ctu.edu.vn
[2] UMR 5505 CNRS-IRIT, Université Toulouse 1 Capitole, Toulouse, France
{frederic.amblard,benoit.gaudou,sibertin}
@ut-capitole.fr

Abstract. Recently, there has been a shift from modeling driven approach to data driven approach in Agent Based Modeling and Simulation (ABMS). This trend towards the use of data-driven approaches in simulation aims at using more and more data available from the observation systems into simulation models [1, 2]. In a data driven approach, the empirical data collected from the target system are used not only for the design of the simulation models but also in initialization, evaluation of the output of the simulation platform. That raises the question how to manage empirical data, simulation data and compare those data in such agent-based simulation platform.

In this paper, we first introduce a logical framework for data driven approach in agent-based modeling and simulation. The introduced framework is based on the combination of Business Intelligence solution and a multi-agent based platform called **CFBM (Combination Framework of Business intelligence and Multi-agent based platform)**. Secondly, we demonstrate the application of CFBM for data driven approach via the development of a Brown Plant Hopper Surveillance Models (BSMs), where CFBM is used not only to manage and integrate the whole empirical data collected from the target system and the data produced by the simulation model, but also to initialize and validate the models.

The successful development of the CFBM consists not only in remedying the limitation of agent-based modeling and simulation with regard to data management but also in dealing with the development of complex simulation systems with large amount of input and output data supporting a data driven approach.

Keywords: Agent-Based model · BI solution · Brown plant hopper · Data driven approach · Data warehouse · Multi-Agent based simulation

1 Introduction

Today, the agent-based simulation approach is increasingly used to develop simulation systems in quite different fields such as: (1) in natural resources management – e.g., an agent-based simulation system consisting of a set of management processes (i.e. water,

© ICST Institute for Computer Sciences, Social Informatics and Telecommunications Engineering 2016
P.C. Vinh et al. (Eds.): ICTCC 2016, LNICST 168, pp. 264–275, 2016.
DOI: 10.1007/978-3-319-46909-6_24

land, money, and labour forces) built to simulate catchment water management in the north of Thailand [3] or the agent-based modeling used to develop a water resource management and assessment system which combines spatiotemporal models of ecological indicators such as rainfall and temperature, water flow and plant growth [4]; (2) in biology - a model for the study of epidemiology or evacuation of injured persons [5–8]; and (3) in sociology - a multi-agent system to discover how social actors could behave within an organization [9] or an agent-based simulation model to explore rules for rural credit management [10].

In the building such systems, we are not only concerned with modeling driven approach – that is how to model and combine coupled models from different scientific fields - but also with data driven approach – that is how to use empirical data collected from the target system in modeling, simulation and analysis [1, 11–13]. Such systems mainly take the form of empirical data gathered from the target system and these data can be used in processes such as design, initialization, calibration and validation of models. That raises the question about which framework to deal with data driven approach that can help to manage empirical data, simulated data and compare those data in agent-based simulation systems as mentioned above.

In this paper, the first introduction is the general architecture for data driven approach which is called CFBM (the Combination Framework of Business Intelligence solution and Multi-agent platform). The CFBM in order to adapt "the logic of simulation" proposed in [13, 14] and it could serve the following purposes: model and execute multi-agents simulations, manage the input and output data of simulations, integrate data from different sources and enable to analyze high volume of data. We argue that BI (Business Intelligence) solutions are a good way to handle and analyze big datasets. Because a BI solution contains a data warehouse, integrated data tools (ETL, Extract-Transform-Load tools) and Online Analytical Processing tools (OLAP tools), it is well adapted to manage, integrate, analyze and present huge amounts of data [15, 16]. The second is a demonstration the application of CFBM into develop Brown plant hopper Surveillance network Models (BSMs) by using data driven approach.

2   Related Works

Technologies or tools from different fields used within integrated systems become a common trend today. In particular, for the development of decision support systems or prediction systems based on simulation approaches, data warehouse (DW), online analytical processing (OLAP) technologies and simulation often represent a good solution. Data warehouse and analysis tools as a BI solution can help users to manage a large amount of simulation data and make several data analyses that support the decision-making processes [17, 18]. The combination of simulation tools and DW is increasingly used and applied in different areas. In [19], Madeira et al. proposed a new approach dedicated to the analysis and comparison of large amounts of output data from different experiments or from similar experiments across different systems. Data warehouse and OLAP tools were recommended for collecting and analyzing simulation results of a system [20]. Although [19, 20] are only applications of OLAP technologies to a special problem, these works demonstrate that a multidimensional database is suitable to store several hundreds of thousands of simulation results. Simulation models, DW and analysis tools with OLAP technologies were also involved in decision support systems or forecast systems [21, 22]. Not only their researches solve specific problems but they also demonstrated a promising use of gathering and analyzing simulation results by using data warehouse and OLAP technologies. In [23], Mahboubi et al. also use data warehouse and OLAP technologies to store and analyze a huge amount of output data generated by the coupling of complex simulation models such as biological, meteorological and so on. In particular, they propose a multidimensional data schema of a data warehouse for storing and analyzing simulation results.

The state of the art demonstrates therefore the practical possibility and the usefulness of the combination of simulation, data warehouse and OLAP technologies. It also shows the potential of a general framework that has, as far as we are aware, not yet proposed in the literature.

3   A Framework for Data Driven Approach in Agent-Based Simulation

In this Section, we present a solution addressing the requirements concerning data (collected data from target system and simulated data) management, initialization (used collected data as input of simulation model) and analysis (e.g. validation the output of simulation) in data driven approach for agent-based simulation [24]. First, we introduce general architecture could serve the following purposes: to model and execute multi-agents simulations, manage input and output data of simulations, integrate data from different sources and enable to analyze high volume of data. The second, we introduce an implementation of the logical framework in the GAMA multi-agent based simulation platform

3.1   A Logical Framework to Manage and Analyze Data for Agent-Based Models

The Combination Framework of Business Intelligence solution and Multi-agent platform (CFBM) is designed based on our definition of an extended computer simulation system [25]. We have therefore designed CFBM with four major components: (1) model design tool; (2) model execution tool; (3) execution analysis tool; and (4) database management tool. CFBM is a logical framework to manage and analyze data in agent-based modeling and its architecture is summarized in Fig. 1.

Simulation System The simulation system plays the roles of model design tool and model execution tool, includes at the same time the model design (that we won't detail at this stage) and the model execution parts. It executes simulations and handles their input/output data. From a data management point of view, it plays the role of an OnLine Transaction Processing (OLTP) or of an operational source system. It is considered as an outside part of the data warehouse [26].

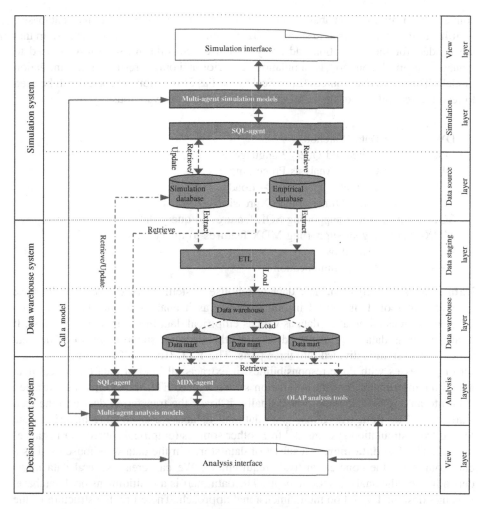

Fig. 1. CFBM architecture

Three layers with five components compose the simulation system. The **simulation interface** is a user environment that helps the modeler to design and implement his models, execute simulations and visualize some observations selected (through the design of the graphical interface) from the simulation. **Multi-agent simulation models** are used to simulate phenomena that the modeler aims at studying. The **SQL-agent** plays the role of the database management tool and can access a relational database. They can be considered as intermediary in between the simulation system and the data management part. It is a particular kind of agents that supports Structured Query Language (SQL) functions to retrieve simulation inputs from the database containing empirical data (Empirical database) as well as parameter values and scenarios (Simulation database). SQL-agent is able to store output simulation data. SQL-agent are also able to transform data (in particular the data type) from simulation model to relational database, and conversely. Empirical database and Simulation database are relational databases. **Empirical database** is used to store empirical data gathered from the target system that are needed for the simulation and analysis phases. **Simulation database** is used to manage the simulation models, simulation scenarios and output results of the simulation models. These two data sources (Empirical as well as Simulation databases) will be used to feed the second part of the framework, namely the Data warehouse system.

Note:
DW   : Data Warehouse
SQL   : Structured Query Language
OLAP   : OnLine Analysis Processing
ETL   : Extract – Transform – Load
MDX   : Multi Dimensional eXpressions
SQL-agent   : Agent supporting SQL features to query data.
MDX-agent   : Agent supporting MDX features to query data.
----►   : Data flow.
──────►   : Intercommunication

Data Warehouse System. The data warehouse system plays the role of database management tool. It is crucial in our approach as it enables to integrate data from different sources (simulation data as well as empirical data from the target systems). It is also used as data store to provide data to the decision support systems. The data warehouse system is divided into three parts. The **ETL** (Extract-Transform-Load) is a set of processes with three responsibilities: it extracts all kind of data (empirical data and simulation data) from the simulation system; then, ETL transforms the extracted data into an appropriate data format; finally, it loads the transferred data into the data warehouse. The **data warehouse** is a relational database used to store historical data loaded from simulation systems and from other sources (empirical sources for instance) by the ETL. The **data mart** is a subset of data stored in the data warehouse used as a data source for the concrete analysis requirement. We can create several data marts depending on the analysis requirements. The data mart is a multidimensional database, which is designed based on multidimensional approach. Therefore, the structure of the data mart is presented using star join, fact tables and dimension tables to present. Thanks to its multidimensional structure, data marts are particularly useful to help users to improve the performance of analytic processes.

Decision Support System. In CFBM, the decision support system component is a software environment supporting analysis, visualization of results and decision-making. It plays the role of execution analysis tool. In our design, we propose to use either existing OLAP analysis tools or a multi-agent platform equipped with analysis features or a combination of both. The decision support system of CFBM is composed of four parts. The **analysis interface** is a graphical user interface used to handle analysis models and visualize results. The **multi-agent analysis models** are a set of tools dedicated to the analysis of multi-agent simulations, they are created based on analysis requirements and handled via the analysis interface. The **MDX-agent** is a special kind of agents, which supports MultiDimensional eXpressions (MDX) functions to query data from a multi-dimensional database. The MDX-agent serves as a bridge in between multi-agent analysis models and data marts. It is used to retrieve data from the data marts into the data warehouse system. The **OLAP analysis tools** could be any analysis software that supports OLAP operators. The multi-agent analysis tools may need several kind of retrievals such as: (1) to retrieve detailed data from relational databases (simulation database or empirical database) for analyses for instance for comparison in-between models or in-between a model output and gathered empirical data; (2) to retrieve pre-aggregated data from multidimensional databases (data marts) for multi-scale analysis. Hence in the decision support system, we designed two kinds of database access agent: on the one hand SQL-agent uses structured query language to retrieve data from relational database and on the other hand MDX-agent uses multidimensional expressions to query data from multidimensional database. Therefore, the multi-agent analysis tools can also use SQL-agents (same SQL-agents as in the simulation system) or MDX agents to appropriately access data.

3.2 Implementation of CFBM with the GAMA Platform

The CFBM has been implemented in GAMA[1] within a three-tier architecture [25]: (1) the **Presentation tier** plays the role of the view layer of simulation system and decision support system in the CFBM architecture; (2) the **Logic tier** coordinates the application commands, as it plays the role of both simulation and analysis layers in the CFBM architecture; and (3) the **Data tier** plays two roles in the framework: data source layer and data warehouse layer. The main functions of this tier are to store and retrieve data from a database or a file system using JDBC and OLAP4 J[2].

Thanks to added database features of GAMA, we can create agents and define the environment of the simulation by using data selected from database, store simulation results into relational databases or query data from multidimensional database. Database features are implemented in the *irit.gaml.extensions.database* GAMA plug-in with the following features:

- Agents can execute SQL queries (create, insert, select, update, drop, delete) to various kinds of DBMS.
- Agents can execute MDX (Multidimensional Expressions) queries to select data from multidimensional objects such as cubes, and return multidimensional cell sets that contain the cube's data[3].

These features are implemented in two kinds of components: *skills* (SQLSKILL, MDXSKILL) and agent (AgentDB). They help us to gain flexibility in the management of simulation models and the analysis of simulation results. In this part, we do not demonstrate functions, which have been implemented in GAMA. More details are presented in website of GAMA[4].

---

[1] https://github.com/gama-platform/gama/wiki.

[2] http://www.olap4j.org/.

[3] http://msdn.microsoft.com/en-us/library/ms145514.aspx.

[4] https://github.com/gama-platform/gama/wiki/G__UsingDatabase.

4 Applying CFBM to Develop Brown Plant Hopper Surveillance Models

Thanks to added CFBM of GAMA, the features of CFBM in GAMA have been successfully applied in some projects such as Simulating the flooding progression by the influence of rainfall in Can Tho city [27], Optimization by simulation of an environmental surveillance network - application to the fight against rice pests in the Mekong Delta (Vietnam) [28] and To Calibrate & Validate an Agent-Based Simulation Model [29]. This Section demonstrates an application of CFBM to: (1) manage input and output data of pest surveillance models called Brown plant hopper Surveillance Models (BSMs). The BSMs was built to predict the invasion of Brown Plant Hoppers (BPHs) on the rice fields based on the data collected from the network light traps network in the Mekong Delta River in Vietnam. The models are part of the research project JEAI-DREAM project[5] and their methodology and implementations were presented in [28]; (2) initialization, using gathered data from target system as input data of BSMs; and validation the output of BSMs.

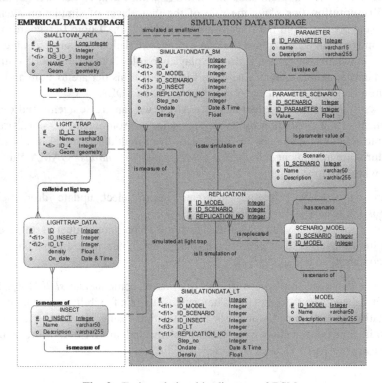

Fig. 2. Entity relationship diagram of BSMs

---

[5] http://www.vietnam.ird.fr/les-activites/renforcement-des-capacites/jeunes-equipes-aird/jeai-dream-umi-209-ummisco-2011-2013.

4.1 Data Management for the Models

In BSMs, an integrated model of an environment surveillance network on an insect ecosystem is built for an application at the regional scale. The input data (empirical data) of this model are divided into four main groups: Insect sampling data (daily sampling data of about 10 insect species at more than 300 light-traps in the Mekong Delta region of Vietnam), Administrative regions (province, district and small town scales), Land uses (seasonal crops of multiple tree species of the region), Natural phenomena (wind, temperature, humidity, etc.).

In experiments, we tested the BSMs with various scenarios and several replications for each scenario. We also classified the outputs of simulations into two groups: (1) number of insects in light traps and (2) mean density of insects for small towns. The Fig. 2 illustrates a part of the entity relationship diagram of input/out data of the BSMs.

In the case of a development of the model without using CFBM, for an example with only one insect species in the provinces of Mekong Delta, Vietnam [30, 31], the authors needed to manually filter the data by some tools and the selected data can be stored in some individual files. These files were used as the input of the model. With CFBM, these works are just replaced by some queries applied on database. This flexibility allows the modelers to easily change their temporal or spatial scale of their scenarios. In other words, CFBM supports to select and update the appropriate data at every micro scale of the model for every simulation step. Furthermore, the input and output data are also distributed and portable.

4.2 Initialization and Validation of BSMs

By applying CFBM, all kind of data of the BSMs are managed by a relational database management system, which makes it more easy to integrate and choose data for each scenario, calibration and validation without manipulating external tools [29]. For example, we can select data and define environment in Example 1 and agents for simulating the invasion of BPHs on the rice fields of three provinces (Dong Thap, Soc Trang and Bac Lieu) as the codes in Example 2; and if we want to add more provinces, then we only change the "WHERE" condition. Hence CFBM in GAMA not only helps modelers in the management of data but it also helps to build agent-based models in a more flexible way by parameterizing the inputs of the models.

Example 1: Specification of the boundary of simulation

```
    String PROVINCES<- ' (38254, 38257,38249)';//Dong Thap, Soc Trang, Bac
Lieu
    map<string,string> BOUNDS <-
        ['host'::'localhost','dbtype'::'postgres','database'::'SurveillanceNetDB'
        ,'port'::'5432','user'::'postgres','passwd'::'acb'
        ,'select'::'SELECT ST_AsBinary(geom) as geo from PROVINCE_AREA'
```

Example 2: Select appropriate data from database and create agents

```
//    Specify light trap
String NODE<-
    "SELECT
        id_lt , lt.name as lighttrap,
        regions_area.id_1 as id_1, province_are.id_2 as id_2,
        distric_area.id_3 as id_3, smalltown_area.id_4 as id_4,
        province_are.name as province, distric_area.name as district,
        smalltown_are.name as smalltown,  st_asbinary(lt.geom) as geo "
    FROM
        regions_area, province_are, distric_area, smalltown_area,
        light_trap as lt
    WHERE
            (province_are.id_1=regions_area.id_1) and
            (district_are.id_2=province_area.id_2) and
            (smalltown_are.id_3=district_area.id_3) and
            (lt.id_4 =smalltown.id_4) and
            province_area.id_2 in "'+ provinces;
...
//Create species
create species: db number: 1
{
    ...
    create species: node
        from: list(self select [params:: PARAMS, select:: NODE])
        with:[ id :: 'ID', name :: 'LightTrap', district_name :: 'District',
                province_name :: 'Province', id_0 :: 'ID_0', id_1 :: 'ID_1',
                id_2 :: 'ID_2',shape::'geo'];
    ...
}
```

Thanks to the combination of BI solution and multi-agent based simulation platform, CFBM can help us to integrate empirical and simulated data (cf. Sect. 3).
Because the simulation results and empirical data are already integrated in the data
warehouse, we can define the data marts in accordance to the change of aggregation
requirements without reproducing the results of the simulation models. Furthermore,
agent model analysis may become easier and modelers can conduct several analyses on
the integrated data such as comparing simulated data between models, calibrating and
validating models, or aggregating high volumes of data by using database features in
GAMA [29]. For example, we can validate the output of BSMs by calculating the
similarity coefficients such as the RMSE between the collected data and simulation data
(Example 3) or Jaccard index on ordered data set [29].

Example 3: Calculate RMSE by model, scenario and replication_no

```
string query_str <-
"SELECT  ml.model, ml.scenario, ml.replication_no,
sqrt(avg(square(lt.simulation_value - lt.collected_value)))as RMSE
FROM lighttrapdata_facts as lt, models_dim as ml
WHERE  lt.id_models=ml.id_models
GROUPBY ml.model, ml.scenario, ml.replication_no";
ask db
{
    list<list> rmse_list <- list<list> (self select(params: PARAMS,
            select: query_str));
}
```

There are some flexibility of data integration and aggregation via CFBM such as reducing the complex structure in programming and aggregating high volumes of data. By applying CFBM, modelers can split the complex simulation models aiming at simulating a phenomenon and analyzing the simulation outputs into two separate models (SIMULATION MODEL and ANALYSIS MODEL), one for simulating the phenomenon and another for analyzing the outputs of simulation [29].

5 Conclusion

The most important of CFBM is a logical framework dealing with data-adapted computer simulations, including four major tools: (1) a *model design tool*: a software environment that supports a modeling language and a user interface, and this is generic enough to model any kind of system; (2) a *model execution tool*: a software environment that can run models; (3) an *execution analysis tool*: a software environment that supports statistical analysis features for the analysis of the simulation output; and (4) a *database tool*: a software environment that supports appropriate database management features for all components in the system.

In addition, CFBM is the powerful integration of a data warehouse, OLAP analysis tools and a multi-agent based platform. CFBM is useful to develop complex simulation systems with large amount of input/output data such as a what-if simulation system, a prediction/forecast system or a decision support system.

In practice, we recognize that CFBM allows the handling of complex simulation system. In particular, we can build several models to simulate the same phenomenon, conduct a lot of simulations for each of them and compare these simulation results (e.g. to determine which one is better for which parameter value domain) [29]. In this case, it is very difficult for modelers to manage, analyze or compare the output data of simulations if they do not have an appropriate tool. With the embedding of SQL agents and MDX agents in the simulation system of CFBM, modelers can create a database to manage and store simulation models, scenarios and outputs of simulation models more easily. In our case study, we have fully handled the input/output simulation data of the models. Selecting and comparing the output data between different replications or between the simulation data and the empirical data can be done in an easier and more efficient way.

References

1. Edmonds, B., Moss, S.: From KISS to KIDS – *an 'anti-simplistic' modelling approach*. In: Davidsson, P., Logan, B., Takadama, K. (eds.) MABS 2004. LNCS (LNAI), vol. 3415, pp. 130–144. Springer, Heidelberg (2005)
2. Hassan, S.: Towards a Data-driven Approach for Agent-Based Modelling: Simulating Spanish (2009)
3. Becu, N., Perez, P., Walker, A., Barreteau, O., Page, C.L.: Agent based simulation of a small catchment water management in Northern Thailand. Ecol. Modell. **170**, 319–331 (2003)
4. Gaudou, B., Sibertin-Blanc, C., Therond, O., Amblard, F., Arcangeli, J.-P., Balestrat, M., Charron-Moirez, M.-H., Gondet, E., Hong, Y., Louail, T., Mayor, E., Panzoli, D., Sauvage, S., Sanchez-Perez, J.-M., Taillandier, P., Nguyen, V.B., Vavasseur, M., Mazzega, P.: The maelia multi-agent platform for integrated assessment of low-water management issues. In: Multi-Agent-Based Simulation XIV-International Workshop, MABS (2013)
5. Rao, D.M., Chernyakhovsky, A., Rao, V.: Modeling and analysis of global epidemiology of avian influenza. Environ. Model Softw. **24**, 124–134 (2009)
6. Stroud, P., Valle, S. Del, Sydoriak, S., Riese, J., Mniszewski, S.: Spatial dynamics of pandemic influenza in a massive artificial society. Artif. Soc. Soc. Simul. **10** (2007)
7. Amouroux, E., Desvaux, S., Drogoul, A.: Towards virtual epidemiology: an agent-based approach to the modeling of H5N1 propagation and persistence in North-Vietnam. In: Bui, T.D., Ho, T.V., Ha, Q.T. (eds.) PRIMA 2008. LNCS (LNAI), vol. 5357, pp. 26–33. Springer, Heidelberg (2008)
8. Dunham, J.: An agent-based spatially explicit epidemiological model in MASON. J. Artif. Soc. Soc. Simul. **9** (2005)
9. Sibertin-Blanc, C., Roggero, P., Adreit, F., Baldet, B., Chapron, P., El-Gemayel, J., Mailliard, M., Sandri, S.: SocLab: A Framework for the modeling, simulation and analysis of power in social organizations. J. Artif. Soc. Soc. Simul. **16** (2013)
10. Barnaud, C., Bousquet, F., Trebuil, G.: Multi-agent simulations to explore rules for rural credit in a highland farming community of Northern Thailand. Ecol. Econ. **66**, 615–627 (2008)
11. Hassan, S., Antunes, L., Pavón, J.: Mentat: a data-driven agent-based simulation of social values evolution. In: Di Tosto, G., Van Dyke Parunak, H. (eds.) MABS 2009. LNCS, vol. 5683, pp. 135–146. Springer, Heidelberg (2010)
12. Hassan, S., Pavon, J., Gilbert, N.: Injecting data into simulation: can agent-based modelling learn from microsimulation? In: The World Congress of Social Simulation 2008, Washington, D.C. (2008)
13. Hassan, S., Pavón, J., Antunes, L., Gilbert, N.: Injecting data into agent-based simulation. In: Takadama, K., Cioffi-Revilla, C., Deffuant, G. (eds.) Simulating Interacting Agents and Social Phenomena. Agent-Based Social Systems, vol. 7, pp. 177–191. Springer, Japan (2010)
14. Gilbert, N., Troitzsch, K.G.: Simulation for the Social Scientist. Open University Press, Buckingham (2005)

15. Mahboubi, H., Faure, T., Bimonte, S., Deffuant, G., Chanet, J.-P., Pinet, F.: A multidimensional model for data warehouses of simulation results. Int. J. Agric. Environ. Inf. Syst. **1**, 1–19 (2010)
16. Vasilakis, C., El-Darzi, E.: A data warehouse environment for storing and analyzing simulation output data. In: Simulation Conference (2004)
17. Inmon, W.H.: Building the Data Warehouse. Wiley Publishing Inc. (2005)
18. Kimball, R., Ross, M.: The Data Warehouse Toolkit: The Complete Guide to Dimensional Modeling. John Wiley & Sons Inc., New York (2002)
19. Madeira, H., Costa, J.P., Vieira, M.: The OLAP and data warehousing approaches for analysis and sharing of results from dependability evaluation experiments. In: International Conference on Dependable Systems and Networks, pp. 86–99 (2003)
20. Sosnowski, J., Zygulski, P., Gawkowski, P.: Developing data warehouse for simulation experiments. In: Kryszkiewicz, M., Peters, J.F., Rybiński, H., Skowron, A. (eds.) RSEISP 2007. LNCS (LNAI), vol. 4585, pp. 543–552. Springer, Heidelberg (2007)
21. Ehmke, J.F., Grosshans, D., Mattfeld, D.C., Smith, L.D.: Interactive analysis of discrete-event logistics systems with support of a data warehouse. Comput. Ind. **62**, 578–586 (2011)
22. Vasilakis, C., El-Darzi, E., Chountas, P.: A decision support system for measuring and modelling the multi-phase nature of patient flow in hospitals. In: Chountas, P., Petrounias, I., Kacprzyk, J. (eds.) Intelligent Techniques and Tools for Novel System Architectures. SCI, vol. 109, pp. 201–217. Springer, Heidelberg (2008)
23. Mahboubi, H., Faure, T., Bimonte, S., Deffuant, G., Chanet, J.P., Pinet, F.: A multidimensional model for data warehouses of simulation results. Int. J. Agric. Environ. Inf. Syst. **1**, 1–19 (2010)
24. Hassan, S., Antunes, L., Pavon, J., Gilbert, N.: Stepping on earth: a roadmap for data-driven agent-based modelling. In: The 5th Conference of the European Social Simulation Association (ESSA 2008), pp. 1–12 (2008)
25. Truong, T.M., Truong, V.X., Amblard, F., Sibertin-blanc, C., Drogoul, A., Le, M.N.: An Implementation of framework of business intelligence for agent-based simulation. In: The 4th International Symposium on Information and Communication Technology (SoICT 2013), pp. 35–44. ACM (2013)
26. Kimball, R., Ross, M.: Data Warehouse Toolkit: The Complete Guide to Dimentional Modeling. John Wiley & Sons Inc., New York (2002)
27. Ngo, T.D.: Simulating the flooding progression by the influence of rainfall in Can Tho city (2013)
28. Truong, V.X.: Optimization by simulation of an environmental surveillance network - application to the fight against rice pests in the mekong delta (vietnam) (2014)
29. Truong, T.M., Amblard, F., Benoit, G., Sibertin-blanc, C.: To calibrate & validate an agent-based simulation model an application of the combination framework of bi solution & multi-agent platform. In: The 6th International Conference on Agents and Artificial Intelligence (ICAART 2014), pp. 172–183 (2014)
30. Phan, C.H., Huynh, H.X., Drogoul, A.: An agent-based approach to the simulation of Brown Plant Hopper (BPH) invasions in the Mekong Delta. In: 2010 IEEE RIVF International Conference on Computing and Communication Technologies, Research, Innovation, and Vision for the Future (RIVF), pp. 1–6. IEEE (2010)
31. Truong, V.X., Drogoul, A., Huynh, H.X., Le, M.N.: Modeling the brown plant hoppers surveillance network using agent-based model - application for the Mekong Delta region. In: Proceedings of the Second Symposium on Information and Communication Technology, pp. 127–136. ACM (2011)

Graph Methods for Social Network Analysis

Quoc Dinh Truong[1(✉)], Quoc Bao Truong[2], and Taoufiq Dkaki[3]

[1] College of Information and Communication Technology,
Can Tho University, Campus 2, Can Tho University, 3/2 street,
Ninh Kieu district, Can Tho City, Vietnam
tqdinh@ctu.edu.vn
[2] College of Engineering Technology, Can Tho University, Campus 2,
Can Tho University, 3/2 street, Ninh Kieu district, Can Tho City, Vietnam
tqbao@ctu.edu.vn
[3] Institut de Recherche en Informatique de Toulouse, Université de Toulouse,
Toulouse, France
dkaki@irit.fr

Abstract. Social network is a structure in which nodes are a set of social actors that are connected together by different types of relationships. Because of the complexity of the actors and the relationships between actors, social networks are always represented by weighted, labeled and directed graph. Social network analysis (NSA) is a set of techniques for determining and measuring the magnitude of the pressure. Social network analysis is focused also on visualization techniques for exploring the networks structure. It has gained a significant following in many fields of applications. It has been used to examine how the problems have been solved, how organizations interact with others, to understand the role of an individual in an organization… In this paper, we focus on two methods: 1- graphs visualization; 2- network analysis based on graph vertices comparison.

Keywords: Social network · Graph · Graph drawing · Graph comparison

1 Introduction

In reality, social network is a common word but there are many definitions of it. Today, people think that social networks are Facebook, Twitter, Google+ or any website with the keyword "social network" in its description such as: www.ResearchGate.net (social networking site for scientists and researchers), Zing Me (Vietnamese social networking and entertainment)… In general, social network is known as a social structure in which actors (individuals or organizations), called nodes, are connected by a number of types of relationships such as: friendship, common interest, relationships of beliefs, knowledge or prestige [1]. The main characteristics of a social network are:

- There exist a collection of entities that participate in the network. Typically, these entities are people.
- There exist at least one type of relationships between entities. The relationship can be a type of "all-or-nothing" or has a degree.

© ICST Institute for Computer Sciences, Social Informatics and Telecommunications Engineering 2016
P.C. Vinh et al. (Eds.): ICTCC 2016, LNICST 168, pp. 276–286, 2016.
DOI: 10.1007/978-3-319-46909-6_25

- There exist an assumption of nonrandomness. It means that if A has relationships with both B and C, then there is a high probability that B and C are related.

Social network analysis is a field of study that attempt to understand relationships between entities in a network based on the assumption about the "importance" of relationship between entities. There are many definitions of social network analysis and the most used one is: "*Social network analysis has emerged as a set of methods for the analysis of social structures, methods which are specifically geared towards an investigation of the relational aspects of these structures. The use of these methods, therefore, depends on the availability of relational rather than attribute data [2]*". Social network analysis is focused also on visualization techniques for exploring the networks structure. Graph structure is often used to represent social networks and their size becomes increasingly large as the progression of the means for data gathering and storage steadily strengthens. This call for new methods in graph visualization and analysis for dealing with the problem of large graphs. In this paper, we present two methods: 1- method for clustered graphs drawing; 2- graph vertices comparison method for network analysis. The rest of paper is organized as follow. Section 2 introduces notion of clustered graph and presents a drawing method for this type of graphs. In Sect. 3, we present our proposed method for graph vertices comparison. Section 4 discuss the performance of our proposed methods through several application examples. In final section we derive conclusions and gives some suggestions.

2 Clustered Graph Drawing

2.1 Clustered Graph Structure

A graph is a couple (V, E), where V is an arbitrary set of vertices and E is a finite set of edges, that is, E consists of some couples (x, y) where x, y $\in$ V. A clustered graph is a triple (V, E, P) where V is a finite set of vertices, E $\subseteq$ V x V a finite set of edges and P is a partition over V. The Number of elements in P corresponds to the number of clusters in graph. The following figure illustrates structure of clustered graphs –the graph in the figure contains three clusters (Fig. 1).

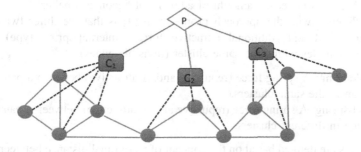

Fig. 1. Structure of a clustered graph associated to a cluster dendogram

2.2   Model

The objective of automatic graph drawing is the development of algorithms for creating nice and readable layout of graphs. In the two last decades, there are enormous works that have been undertaken in the field of graph drawing in order to generate intelligible graph layouts. In the case of basic graph structure, several representative approaches are described in [3–5].

When considering the case of clustered graph drawing, only a very few works can be cited. Among these works we can list some major works such as [6–8]. Ho [6] introduced a method for drawing clustered graph in space of three dimensions by using "divide and conquer" approach. He proposed to draw each cluster in a 2D plane and the 3D drawing of clustered graph is produced by combining these flat drawings. Chuang [7] considers the problem of clustered graph drawing as a problem of drawing graphs with nonuniform nodes represented as charged polygons/polyhedron exposed to both spring forces and magnetic forces induced by the potential fields generated by the other nodes in the graph. Eades [8] propose adding an extra vertex, called super node, to each cluster and using different types of spring force. In this work, the drawing zones of clusters are predefined by the users and can be modified by the proposed model.

We believe that clustered graph drawing rules differ to that of basic graph drawing. These heuristic rules that abstracts our approach for clustered graphs drawing. We present some visualization constraints for drawing clustered graph in priority order:

- The drawing zone of each cluster must be convex.
- The drawing zones associated to the clusters must not overlap.
- Edge crossings are reduced as much as possible within a cluster.

We distinguish also two problems of drawing clustered graph: self-generated cluster areas and predefined cluster areas. By considering the set of heuristic rules we list above, the two first rules are considered such as preconditions for the cluster areas in the case of predefined cluster areas. Our method is based on force directed placement method proposed in [4]. Like this method, our proposed method iterates two steps: computations of the forces among vertices on the one hand and the positioning adjustment of each vertex and the computation of its new coordinates following the temperature model on the other hand. The displacement of a vertex at every iteration is limited to the maximum displacement value decreasing over time. This means that, as the layout becomes better the amount of adjustment becomes smaller.

The difference with the approach proposed in [4] is that we differ two types of spring forces and add additional attractive forces (internal-spring type) between non-connected nodes within the same cluster (invisible edges).

- Internal-spring: A spring force (repulsive and/or attractive) between a pair of nodes which are in the same clusters.
- External-spring: A spring force (repulsive and/or attractive) between a pair of nodes which are in different clusters.

The forces are defined based on the concept of an optimal distance between vertices that are not connected. Generally, this distance can be computed as follow:

$$optDist = \sqrt{\frac{frame\_size}{number\ of\ vertices}} \qquad (1)$$

f_a, f_r are attractive and repulsive forces respectively which can be defined as follow:

$$f_a(d) = d^2/optDist \qquad (2)$$

$$f_r(d) = -optDist^2/d \qquad (3)$$

where d is the distance between the two vertices.

Since in our model, we distinguish two types of spring forces so two optimal distances are needed: one between vertices belonging to two different clusters –optDist- and the other relevant to vertices of a same cluster -optDistCluster. We believe that the optimal distance between vertices of a same cluster must be less than the global optimal distance because the size of a cluster occupied area must obviously be smaller than the size of the total drawing area (optDist = a *optDistCluster where a > 1).

Self-generated cluster areas. In this case, we propose adding invisible edges (additional attractive forces) between non-connected nodes within same cluster to keep them close together in the drawing. The forces generated by the invisible edges must then be lowered to prevent them from over affecting the internal layout of clusters. In other word, extra edges will be help to create separated cluster with relatively close nodes without over modifying the relative placement -of the cluster's nodes. To do that, the strength of additional attractive forces must be according to the proportion between the number of invisible edges and the number of real edges. The following figure shows our spring force model for this application case (Fig. 2).

Predefined cluster areas. In this case, our proposed model takes user predefined area of each cluster as parameter. So the process of adding "invisible" edges is not necessary. Two types of forces are defined in the same way as in the previous case. And

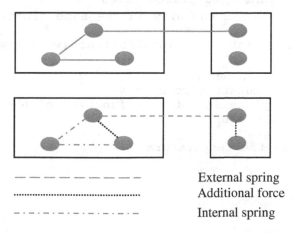

External spring
Additional force
Internal spring

Fig. 2. Spring forces model for self-generated cluster areas

then, to keep nodes inside their cluster area, we add repulsive forces between nodes and the border of visualization area of cluster (we call them as frontier forces). If f_f is the frontier force, d the distance between node and the border and δ predefined constant equal to the maximum possible displacement of node then it can be defined as following

$$f_f(d) = \begin{cases} \infty \ \textit{if} \ d \le \delta \\ \frac{optDistCluster}{d^3} \end{cases}$$ (4)

The following figure shows the spring force model in this case (Fig. 3).

Algorithm
Input: Clustered graph CG (V, E, P); Visualization area of each cluster (optional)
Output: Drawing of clustered graph CG

```
→ self-generated cluster area
random placement of nodes
→ predefined cluster area
placement of nodes according to their clusters areas
while temperature > 1 begin
    for v ∈ V do begin
        → predefined cluster area
            calculate frontier force on v
            for u ≠ v in V do begin
                calculate forces on v and u
            end
    end
    for (u, v) ∈ E do begin
        calculate force on u and v
    end
    → self-generated cluster area
    for (u, v) ∉ E and u, v in the same cluster do
    begin
        calculate additional attractive force on u, v
    end
    for v ∈ V do begin
        accumulate forces on v
        displacement of v in function of the
        temperature
    end
    decrease the temperature
end
```

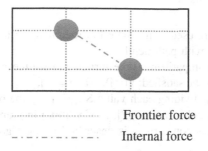

.... Frontier force

_ . _ . _ . _ . _ . _ . Internal force

Fig. 3. Spring forces model for predefined cluster areas

3 Graph Vertices Comparison

We proposed in [9] a method for graph vertices comparison. The starting point of our method is the one proposed in [10]. This method is applied on two graphs: one to be analyzed (the target graph) and the other serving as the model (the source graph). By using this method we can identify which vertices in the source graph are the most similar with the given vertex in the target graph (Fig. 4).

The main idea of our method is that the similarity between two vertices i and j respectively from target graph and source graph is computed by examining the similarity scores between their related vertices (vertices pointing to i or j and vertices pointed by i or j). In other word, the similarity score S_{ij} between vertex i of target graph and vertex j of source graph can be updated by following equation:

$$S_{ij} = \sum_{r:(r,i)\in E_B, t:(t,j)\in E_A} S_{rt} + \sum_{r:(i,r)\in E_B, t:(j,t)\in E_A} S_{rt} \tag{5}$$

However (5) does not take into account the notion of similarity inheritance. We modified (5) to comply with the similarity inheritance principle. In our work, we consider the similarity inheritance as a "flooding" similarity proposed in [11]. So the notion of graph closure is used to express the similarity inheritance. To do that, adjacency matrices of target and source graphs are formulated as follows:

$$A \leftarrow A + \sum_{n=2}^{\infty} f_A(n) \frac{A^n}{A^n} \qquad B \leftarrow B + \sum_{n=2}^{\infty} f_B(n) \frac{B^n}{B^n} \tag{6}$$

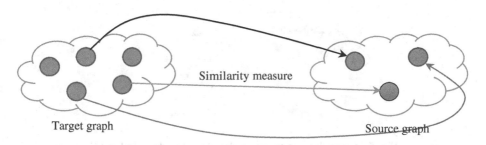

Similarity measure

Target graph

Source graph

Fig. 4. Graph vertices comparison

where $f_A(n)$ and $f_B(n)$ are used to translate the idea that the influence of 'generations' exponentially decreases with path depth.

In the case of self-comparison where target and source graphs are the same, the following condition must be satisfied: $\forall(i, j)$, $s(i, i) = s(j, j) \geq s(i, j)$. So we normalized similarity matrix S_{AB} by dividing each value $S_{AB}(i, j)$ by the product of self-similarity $S_{AA}(i, i)$ of vertex i in graph A and $S_{BB}(j, j)$ of vertex j in graph B. The final proposed method for graph vertices comparison is described in the algorithm below.

$$S_0 \leftarrow 1 \qquad k \leftarrow 0$$

$$A \leftarrow A + \sum_{n=2}^{\infty} f_2(n) g_2\left(\frac{A^n}{\|A^n\|}\right) \quad ; \quad B \leftarrow B + \sum_{n=2}^{\infty} f_1(n) g_1\left(\frac{B^n}{\|B^n\|}\right)$$

Repeat

$$\left| S_{AA_{k+1}} \leftarrow \frac{AS_{AA_k}A^T + A^T S_{AA_k}A}{\|AS_{AA_k}A^T + A^T S_{AA_k}A\|_F} \; S_{BB_{k+1}} \leftarrow \frac{BS_{BB_k}B^T + B^T S_{BB_k}B}{\|BS_{BB_k}B^T + B^T S_{BB_k}B\|_F} \; S_{AB_{k+1}} \leftarrow \frac{BS_{AB_k}A^T + B^T S_{AB_k}A}{\|BS_{AB_k}A^T + B^T S_{AB_k}A\|_F} \right.$$

$$\left| k \leftarrow k+1 \right.$$

Until convergence is achieved for k even

$$S_{AB} \leftarrow \bullet \frac{S_{AB} \bullet * S_{AB}}{diag(S_{AA}) \bullet * diag(S_{BB})^T}$$

Output $S_k(k \, is \, even)$ as similarity matrix

4   Results and Discussion

For verifying the performance of our proposed methods we use two social networks. This first network presents a collaboration network where vertices represent researchers that have been associated to eight clusters. First we perform a drawing of this network using the basic graph drawing method [4] (Fig. 5). As we can see, the resulting

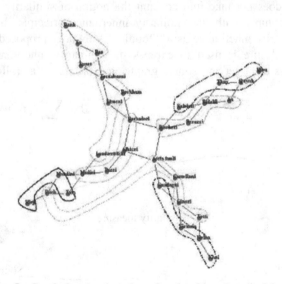

Fig. 5. Graph drawing based on the algorithm described in [4]

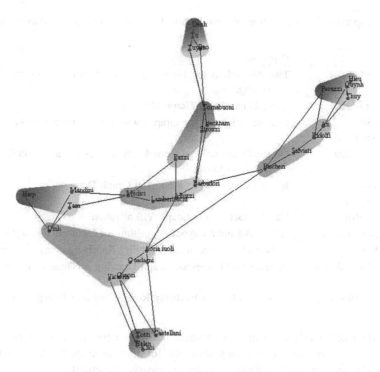

Fig. 6. Graph drawing based on our algorithm – the case of self-generated cluster area

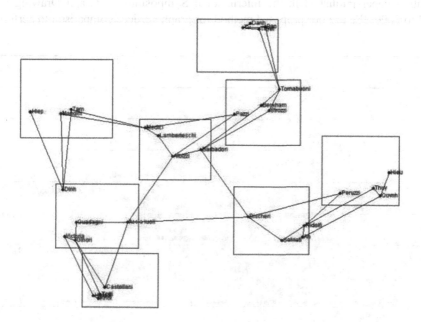

Fig. 7. Graph drawing based on our algorithm – the case of predefined cluster area

Table 1. Top authority papers from the international symposium on graph drawing (1994 to 2000)

Paper	Paper title
GD 96, 139 Eades, ...	Two Algorithms for Three Dimensional Orthogonal Graph Drawing.
GD 94, 1 Cohen, ...	Three-Dimensional Graph Drawing
GD 95, 254 Foessmeier, ...	Drawing High Degree Graphs with Low Bend Numbers
GD 94, 286 Garg, ...	On the Computational Complexity of Upward and Rectilinear Planarity Testing
GD 95, 419 Papakostas, ...	Issues in Interactive Orthogonal Graph Drawing
GD 95, 99 Bruss, ...	Fast Interactive 3-D Graph Visualization
GD 94, 388 Frick, ...	A Fast Adaptive Layout Algorithm for Undirected Graphs
GD 95, 8 Alt, ...	Universal 3-Dimensional Visibility Representations for Graphs
GD 97, 52 Papakostas, ...	Incremental Orthogonal Graph Drawing in Three Dimensions
GD 95, 234 Fekete, ...	New Results on a Visibility Representation of Graphs in 3D

drawing does not clearly show the cluster structure of the network. The two next figures (Figs. 6 and 7) present the resulting drawing for the same network by using our methods. As we can see the cluster structure is clearly presented.

The second example we present here is the citations network in the context of graph drawing [12]. The network consists of 311 vertices and 647 edges. Each vertex represents a paper published in the International Symposium on Graph Drawing from 1994 to 2000. We use our proposed method for graph vertices comparison to perform a

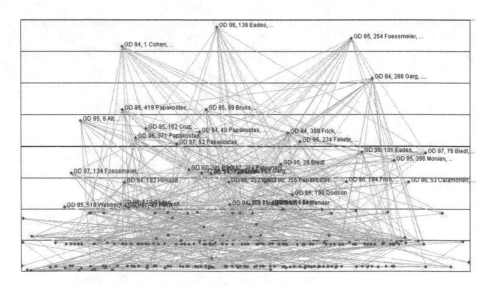

Fig. 8. Drawing of citation network

hub-authority analysis. In this example, we only care the authority of each vertex (Table 1). The authority scores are used to generate eight clusters. Each cluster is composed of papers that have similar authority scores. And then each cluster is associated to a prefixed rectangle area. Clusters on the top of the drawing correspond to papers that have best authority scores (Fig. 8).

5   Conclusion

In this paper we have proposed couple of methods for social network analysis: one for drawing clustered graph and another for graph vertices comparison. Our model for drawing clustered graph differs from previous works from two aspects: the forces in action and the nature of the clusters that can be handled. Indeed, the authors of these works define clusters as sets of vertices with many internal edges and few outside edges while clusters in our work are "freely" defined. We also presented and discussed a novel model for computing similarity scores between vertices of two graphs by extending methods previously submitted in [10, 11]. This method can be applied in the field of social network analysis in the way that we can identify the similar actors of two networks.

In the future work, we will extend the model for clustered-graph drawing to deal with geographic constraints when graphs vertices are clustered according to some of their geographic properties such as the authors' countries or locations in scientific citation networks.

References

1. Wasserman, S., Faust, K.: Social network analysis in the social and behavioral sciences. In: Social Network Analysis: Methods and Applications, pp. 1–27. Cambridge University Press (1994). ISBN 9780521387071
2. Scott, J.: Social Network Analysis. Sage, Newbury Park (1992)
3. Gajer, P., Kobourov, S.G.: GRIP: Graph dRawing with Intelligent Placement. In Marks, J. (ed.) Proceedings of the Graph Drawing, pp. 222–228. Colonial Wiliamsburg (2001)
4. Fruchterman, T.M.J., Reingold, E.M.: Graph drawing by force-directed placement. Softw. Pract. Exp. **21**(11), 1129–1164 (1991)
5. Kamada, T., Kawai, S.: An algorithm for drawing general undirected graphs. Inf. Process. Lett. **31**(1), 7–15 (1989)
6. Ho, J., Hong, S.-H., Gronemann, M., Jünger, M.: Drawing Clustered Graphs as Topographic Maps. In: Didimo, W., Patrignani, M. (eds.) GD 2012. LNCS, vol. 7704, pp. 426–438. Springer, Heidelberg (2013)
7. Chuang, J.-H., Lin, C.-C., Yen, H.-C.: Drawing graphs with nonuniform nodes using potential fields. In: Liotta, G. (ed.) GD 2003. LNCS, vol. 2912, pp. 460–465. Springer, Heidelberg (2004)
8. Eades, P., Huang, M.L.: Navigating clustered graphs using force-directed methods. J. Graph Algorithms Appl. **4**, 157–181 (2000)

9. Truong, Q.D., Dkaki, T., Mothe, J., Charrel, P-J.: GVC: a graph-based information retrieval model. In: Conférence francophone en Recherche d'Information et Applications (CORIA 2008), Trégastel (France), 12–14 Mar 2008, pp. 337–351. CNRS (2008)
10. Blondel, V.D., Gajardo, A., Heymans, M., Senellart, P., Van Dooren, P.: A measure of similarity between graph vertices: applications to synonym extraction and web searching. SIAM Rev. **46**(4), 647–666 (2004)
11. Melnik, S., Garcia-Molina, H., Rahm, E.: Similarity flooding: a versatile graph matching algorithm and its application to scheme matching. In: Proceedings of the 18th ICDE Conference (2002)
12. Biedl, T.C., Brandenburg, F.J.: Graph-Drawing Contest Report. In: Mutzel, P., Jünger, M., Leipert, S. (eds.) GD 2001. LNCS, vol. 2265, pp. 513–521. Springer, Heidelberg (2002)

Maintenance Process Control:
Cellular Automata Approach

Mustapha Ouardouz[1]([✉]), Abdessamed Bernoussi[2], Hamidou Kassogué[2],
and Mina Amharref[2]

[1] MMC Team, Faculty of Sciences and Techniques, BP. 416, Tangier, Morocco
ouardouz@gmail.com
[2] GAT Team, Faculty of Sciences and Techniques, BP. 416, Tangier, Morocco
a.samed.bernoussi@gmail.com, hamidoukass@gmail.com, amharrefm@yahoo.fr

Abstract. In this work we consider an industrial maintenance process
control problem using cellular automata approach. The problem consists
on finding an optimal control for the displacement of agents in a spatial
area to maintains the equipments running. The approach is based on a
feedback control. Some simulation are given to illustrate our approach.
The simulation software was developed under Java environment.

Keywords: Cellular Automata · Maintenance process · Feedback control

1 Introduction

From the 1980s with the development of computers, cellular automata (CA) theory has boomed in the world of science. They gradually emerged as an alternative for the microscopic realities, reflecting the macroscopic behavior of dynamic systems. They are now used as modeling tools in many sciences area.

Research in biology and chemistry were the first predisposed to exploit them. Today there are lots of applications in all areas involving the variables space and time. Indeed, by the cellular automata approach, they are taken discretely, as well as the physical quantities they describe.

Since their introduction in the 1940s as a model of self-replicative systems considered by Von Neumann and Ulam, many were the definitions around the CA, [2] (1998), [3] (2002) and [8] (2008).

Their simple conception, as well as their adaptation to strong computer architectures with respect to continuous models justify their heavy use as modeling tools in recent decades. Most recently Ouardouz et al. in [1] have proposed an CA model for the technicians allocation process in a maintenance problem in industry, to meet the needs of resources allocation under constraints of space, cost and time. The determination of the mathematical model for such phenomenon described by a distributed parameters system is the first step in the classic study

This work has been supported by the project PPR2-OGI-Env and the international
network TDS, Academy Hassan II of Sciences and Techniques.

© ICST Institute for Computer Sciences, Social Informatics and Telecommunications Engineering 2016
P.C. Vinh et al. (Eds.): ICTCC 2016, LNICST 168, pp. 287–296, 2016.
DOI: 10.1007/978-3-319-46909-6_26

of this kind of system (understanding the system, follow its evolution in the aim to control it). The cellular automata approach yet in this case present a huge advantage compared to its description relatively simple and for its adaptation to global realities of the problem studied.

Therefore, the need to define and characterize the concepts, long exposed in the systems theory is required for cellular automata approach. We quote for example the concepts of regional controllability, spreadability and observability [4–10]).

In this paper, we consider the controllability concept for cellular automata in order to approach the maintenance process problem. For that, we consider the model, proposed by Ouardouz et al. in [1] in the autonomous case, and we introduce a feedback control to optimize the assignments and agents displacements.

In the second section we present the problem statement and in the third section we recall some definition and the principle of cellular automata. In section four we present the methodology for the problem approach and some simulations results illustrating our approach.

2   Maintenance Process Control: Problem Statement

The maintenance problem is to assign available technicians to a set of down equipments taking into account there proximity, availability and competencies so as to maintain as long as possible all the equipments operational. The starting point is a set of operational machines falling down (not necessarily all of them) after a certain uptime.

This system is a system with spatiotemporal evolution described by the states of the machines and the interventions over time. It is a discrete system in time and space. Each machine and each agent occupies a geographic position at a given moment and the overall state of the system is a spatial configuration changing over time. That is why we opt for a cellular automaton approach.

It is proposed to develop a control based on the consideration of spatial and temporal factors in the allocation of resources allowing particularly, in the case of a manufacturing company to maintain all the machines operational.

We are interested in the control of the allocation of intervention tasks of preventive maintenance process for which allocation decisions and agent displacements are made by a simulation based on cellular automata.

The proposed control, must also apply in the case of unplanned interventions (random) due to corrective maintenance. Indeed, the application of control following the observation of the distribution of resources 'technicians' in the beggerhood of a down machine should allow to allocate maintenance tasks to the most appropriate agent, available and/or more close spatially and thus to ensure the reparation of the machine.

We consider the cellular automaton model as used in [1] but in this work we introduce the feedback control concept. We recall in the next section the definition and principle of cellular automata.

3   Cellular Automata: Generality

3.1   Cellular Automata Definition

A cellular automaton is given by a quadruplet

$$\mathcal{A} = (\mathcal{T}, \mathcal{V}, \mathcal{E}, f) \tag{1}$$

- $\mathcal{T}$ said cell space or lattice is a network which consists on a regular tiling of a domain Ω of $\mathbb{R}^n$, $n = 1, 2$ or 3. The elements of this paving denoted c are said cells and occupy the whole area.
- v said neighborhood, for a c cell is a set of cells affecting its evolution over time. Depending on the problem modeled, it can be given by

$$v(c) = \{c' \in \mathcal{T}; \ d(c, c') \le r\}, \quad \forall c \in \mathcal{T}. \tag{2}$$

d is a distance on $\mathcal{T} \times \mathcal{T}$ equivalent to the norm L_∞ defined by [5]

$$d(c, c') = \min\{\ell(c, c'); \ (c, c') \in J(c, c')\}, \quad \forall c, c' \in \mathcal{T} \tag{3}$$

where $\ell(c, c')$ a length between c and c' and $J(c, c')$ the set of all possible joins between c and c' from their center. $v(c)$ is said radius r and size $m = \operatorname{card} v(c)$.

- $\mathcal{E}$ designates all states, which is a finite set of values representing all states that may be taken by each cell. This is generally a cyclic ring, given by

$$\mathcal{E} = \{e_1, e_2, \ldots, e_k\} \quad \text{with} \ \operatorname{card} \mathcal{E} = \mathrm{k}. \tag{4}$$

We speak about a configuration of a CA in a given time t, the application

$$\begin{aligned} e_t : \mathcal{T} &\to \mathcal{E} \\ c &\mapsto e_t(c) \end{aligned} \tag{5}$$

which maps each cell c from $\mathcal{T}$ a value taken in $\mathcal{E}$ which will be the state of c at t.

- f is a transition function that defines the local dynamics of the system studied. It calculates the state $e_{t+1}(c)$ of a cell at $t+1$ depending on the state $e_t(v(c)) = \{e_t(c'), \ c' \in v(c)\}$ of the neighborhood at t. We consider then the form

$$\begin{aligned} f : \ \mathcal{E}^m &\to \mathcal{E} \\ e_t(v(c)) &\mapsto e_{t+1}(c) \end{aligned} . \tag{6}$$

3.2   Controllability for Cellular Automata

First let's see how we can introduce a control in a cellular automaton as outlined in [4]. As in the case of continuous systems, a precision on the control is to give its spatial support and its values. The spatial support of the CA will be a part of the lattice $\mathcal{T}$ noted $\mathcal{T}_u$, and the values of the control will be provided by the set of real values $U = \{u_1, u_2, \ldots u_q\}$. Some U values can of course be in the set of states $\mathcal{E}$. In what follows I is a discrete time interval.

Definition 1. *Let $\mathcal{A} = (\mathcal{T}, \mathcal{V}, \mathcal{E}, f)$ be a cellular automaton and let $\mathcal{T}_u \subset \mathcal{T}$. The control over $\mathcal{A}$ is a function*

$$u : \mathcal{T}_u \times I \to U \tag{7}$$

which to each cell c from $\mathcal{T}_u$ associates a value $u_t(c)$ in U at t. In this case $\mathcal{A}$ becomes a non-autonomous or a controlled cellular automaton denoted $\mathcal{A}_u((\mathcal{T}, \mathcal{V}, \mathcal{E}, f), u)$.

The support of the control u in some cases may be reduced to a single cell, in this case we speak of punctual control. In other cases, the support may vary in time and space. This is known as scanner control. In all cases, the support may be expressed by

$$\mathcal{T}_u = supp(u) = \bigcup_i \{c \in \mathcal{T}; u_t(c) = u_i \in U\}.$$

Similarly with continuous systems, we may adopt a formulation of the transition function in the case of a controlled CA as

$$f_u : \mathcal{E}^m \times U^m \to \mathcal{E}$$
$$(e_t(v(c)), u_t(v(c))) \mapsto e_{t+1} \tag{8}$$

where $u_t(v(c)) = \{u(c', t) \in U; c' \in v(c)\}$. Acts on the control cells only in $\mathcal{T}_u$. Another much more flexible formulation, which we will use for the following, is established that

$$f_u(e_t(v(c))) = f(e_t(v(c))) \oplus u(c, t)\chi_{\mathcal{T}_u}. \tag{9}$$

It is clear that here the control is applied to a cell c when it is in the action area $\mathcal{T}_u$ of control u. The sign $\oplus$ is interpreted as a mutual action of the control and the transition function.

Definition 2. *We say that a cellular automaton $\mathcal{A} = (\mathcal{T}, \mathcal{V}, \mathcal{E}, f, u)$ is controllable during a time interval $]0, T[$ if for each initial global configuration $e_0^{\mathcal{T}}$ and each desired global configuration $e_d^{\mathcal{T}}$ there exists a control u such that*

$$e_T^{\mathcal{T}} = e_d^{\mathcal{T}} \tag{10}$$

The CA $\mathcal{A}$ is said to be weakly controllable with a tolerance ε during a time interval $]0, T[$ if for each initial configuration $e_0^{\mathcal{T}}$ and each desired configuration $e_d^{\mathcal{T}}$ there exists a control u such that

$$\frac{card\{c \in \mathcal{T}; e_T(c) \neq e_d(c)\}}{card\mathcal{T}} \leq \varepsilon. \tag{11}$$

For more details about controllability of cellular automata we refer to [4,6,8,9] and the references therein.

4   Application to the Maintenance Process Control Problem

4.1   Presentation of the CA Model

Model principle. The CA Model $\mathcal{A} = (\mathcal{T}, \mathcal{V}, \mathcal{E}, f)$ for the studied case is constructed on a bi-dimensional lattice $\mathcal{T} \subset Z^2$ where the cells in $\mathcal{T}$ noted c_{ij} has as neighborhood the entire lattice $(v(c_{ij}) = \{c_{kl} \in \mathcal{T}; d(c_{ij}, c_{kl}) \leq cardT\} = \mathcal{T})$. The set of states is given by

$$\mathcal{E} = \{-3, -2, -1, 0, 1, 2\} \tag{12}$$

with

$$e_t(c_{ij}) = \begin{cases} -3 & \text{if the cell contains a down equipment} \\ -2 & \text{if the cell contains an equipment under reparation} \\ -1 & \text{if the cell contains an operationnal equipment} \\ 0 & \text{if the cell is empty} \\ 1 & \text{if the cell contains an available technician} \\ 2 & \text{if the cell contains an occupied technician} \end{cases}$$

We denote that $e_t(c_{ij}) < 0$ corresponding to a presence of an equipment in the cell, whereas a presence of a technician is indicated by $e_t(c_{ij}) > 0$. To each equipment we associate characteristic parameters determined from previous operating statistics

- $mtbf_{ij}$: the mean time between failures,
- $mttr_{ij}$: the mean time to repairs,
- zr_{ij}: an area of intervention which corresponds to a cell where the technician should stand up to repair the machine.

In this situation the equipment does not fail randomly, but after $MTBF$. The technicians likewise have the following properties

- zt_{ij}: a buffer zone where the technician returns at the end of the intervention.
- cc_{ij}: said target cell is the final destination of the technician.
- d_{ij}: is a couple $(d_1, d_2) \in \{-1, 0, 1\}^2$ with $|d_1| + |d_2| \leq 1$ reflecting a direction taken by the technician in the next moment. It is negotiated for the cell c_{ij} as a local destination $c_{i+d1, j+d2}$. $d = (0, 0) \equiv 0$ is a null direction, the technician is stationary. For cc_{ij} corresponding to the index cell c_{kl}, it is calculated as

$$d_{ij} = \begin{cases} (0, 0) & \text{if } k = i \text{ and } l = j \qquad (\cdot) \\ (1, 0) & \text{if } |k - i| \geq |l - j| \text{ and } k \geq i \ (\rightarrow) \\ (-1, 0) & \text{if } |k - i| \geq |l - j| \text{ and } k \leq i \ (\leftarrow) \\ (0, 1) & \text{if } |k - i| \leq |l - j| \text{ and } l \geq j \ (\uparrow) \\ (0, -1) & \text{if } |k - i| \leq |l - j| \text{ and } l \leq j \ (\downarrow) \end{cases} \tag{13}$$

- α_{ij}: a rotation angle of $\{\pm\frac{\pi}{2}, \pm\pi\}$ performed by the technician, in case of an obstacle relative to the local direction d_{ij}. The couple $[d_{ij}, \alpha_{ij}]$ indicates a direction d_{ij} followed by a rotation angle α_{ij}. For example $[(1, 0), -\frac{\pi}{2}] = (0, 1)$ and $[(1, 0), \frac{\pi}{2}] = (0, -1)$.

Autonomous system. The transition function f can be written firstly to define the dynamics of an autonomous system. Let $e_t(c_{ij})$ the cell state $c_{ij} \in T$ at t. The probable cell state at $t+1$ is fulfilled by

$$
e_{t+1}(c_{ij}) = f(e_t(v(c_{ij})))
$$
$$
= \begin{cases}
-3 & \text{if } e_t(c_{ij}) = -3 \text{ or if } e_t(c_{ij}) = -1 \text{ with } mtbf_{ij} = 0 \\
-2 & \text{if } e_t(c_{ij}) = -2 \text{ with } mttr_{ij} > 0 \\
-1 & \text{if } e_t(c_{ij}) = -1 \text{ or if } e_t(c_{ij}) = -2 \text{ with } mttr_{ij} = 0 \\
1 & \text{if } e_t(c_{ij}) = 2 \text{ and } e_t(cc_{ij}) = -2 \text{ with } mttr_{cc} = 0 \\
dep(c_{ij}) & \text{if } e_t(c_{ij}) = 1 \text{ or if } e_t(c_{ij}) = 2 \text{ with } d_{ij} \not\to cc_{ij}
\end{cases}
$$
$$(14)$$

Here $dep(c_{ij})$ is a function that is used to implement the process of moving a technician occupying the cell c_{ij}. In case of the intersection of several technicians, the priority to the right rule is performed. Displacement is thus made to avoid as much as possible blockage. The diagram in Fig. 1 describes the deplacement function where we used the following notations:

- d_{-1}: previous direction of the technician.
- c_o: obtained cell from the direction d_{ij}.
- c_{oo}: cell after c_o in the direction d_{ij}.
- c_α: obtained cell from a rotation $[d_{ij}, \alpha_{ij}]$.
- d_o, d_{oo}: direction of the technician if the cell c_o or c_{oo} contains a technician.

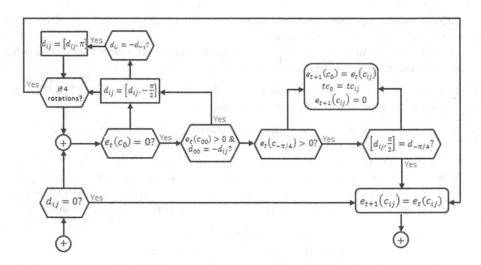

Fig. 1. Diagram of the technicians displacement function $dep(c_{ij})$.

Controlled system: Feedback control. We introduce here a feedback control on the autonomous system defined by the previous cellular automaton model. For T a given time horizon, the control will aim to keep all equipments operational. We therefore consider all down equipments

$$\omega = \{c_{ij} \in \mathcal{T}; e_t(c_{ij}) = -3\} \tag{15}$$

as a spatial distribution (or region) of the control. The support of the control, will, among other be

$$\mathcal{T}_u = \{c_{ij} \in \mathcal{T}; e_t(c_{ij}) = 1\} \tag{16}$$

the set of available technician. We choose as the control gains

$$U = \{1, 2\}. \tag{17}$$

For a desired configuration e_d of the system with

$$e_d(c_{ij}) = -1, \quad c_{ij} \in \omega, \tag{18}$$

the problem of the CA controllability we adopt is to find a control u that achieves this configuration at the time T. The one we found is a technicians assignment in $\mathcal{T}_u$ to down equipment in ω for repair, let then

$$\begin{aligned} u : \mathcal{T}_u \times I &\to U \\ (c, t) &\mapsto u(c, t) \end{aligned} \tag{19}$$

A technician is assigned to an equipment when he is nearest the equipment than any one other (principle of Voronoi diagram [11]). Both are updated and removed in the process of assignment and the operation is repeated until that there is no more technicians available or machines in failure. For the explicit expression of the control u, we construct Voronoi diagrams [1] associated to $\mathcal{T}_u$ and ω:

$$Vor(\mathcal{T}_u) = \bigcup_{c \in \mathcal{T}_u} R_c^T \text{ with } R_c^T = \{c' \in T; d(c, c') \leq d(c, c")\ \ c" \in \mathcal{T}_u\}, \tag{20}$$

$$Vor(\omega) = \bigcup_{c \in \omega} R_c^E \text{ with } R_c^E = \{c' \in T; d(c, c') \leq d(c, c")\ \ c" \in \omega\}. \tag{21}$$

Then the control u is expressed by

$$c \in \mathcal{T}_u, \ u(c, t) = \begin{cases} 2 \text{ if } \exists c' \in \omega / R_c^T \cap R_{c'}^E \neq \emptyset \\ 1 \text{ else} \end{cases}. \tag{22}$$

However, it is noted that $\mathcal{T}_u$ changes in time because a busy technician may become available upon control. It is the same with ω, a machine in good operating conditions could breakdown. And since the control is performed for a definite time horizon, then the control u can be seen in a loop farm with return on observation of the state of the system.

The transition function of the controlled CA

$$\mathcal{A}_u = ((\mathcal{T}, \mathcal{V}, \mathcal{E}, f), u) \tag{23}$$

shall be defined so that all updating operations are made between the instants $t, t + 1/2$ and $t + 1$.

– Between t and $t + 1/2$, observations are performed on the state of the cells to notify the equipment failed and available technicians (ω et $\mathcal{T}_u$) according to the function

$$y : \mathcal{E}^{\mathcal{T}} \to \mathcal{T} \times \mathcal{T}$$
$$e_t \mapsto (\mathcal{T}_u, \omega) \qquad (24)$$

– Between $t + 1/2$ and $t + 1$, we perform the control

$$u(c, t + 1/2), \quad c \in \mathcal{T}_u. \qquad (25)$$

– At $t + 1$, we update the state of each cell. And all technicians can move except those engaged before $t + 1/2$.

The transition function f_u of the controlled CA $\mathcal{A}_u$ is then written

$$e_{t+1}(c_{ij}) = f_u(e_t(v(c_{ij})) = f(e_t(v(c_{ij})) \oplus u(c_{ij}, t + 1/2)\chi_{\mathcal{T}_u}; \quad c_{ij} \in \mathcal{T} \qquad (26)$$

where f and u are explained respectively by the Eqs. 14 and 22 and $\oplus$ refers to the mutual action. The principle of closed loop control on our CA for maintenance problem is summarized in Fig. 2. Some examples of Computer simulations after implementation of the CA are provided in the next section.

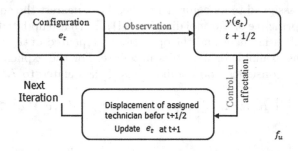

Fig. 2. Principle of feedback control for maintenance process

4.2　Simulation Results

The set of algorithms for cellular automaton built above was implemented in Java object oriented programming [12] using the architecture of Model View Controller design pattern in order to meet the simulation needs while ensuring flexibility and re-use of source code. A GUI is produced to facilitate the monitoring of maintenance process. To see some examples of simulations in accordance with the concepts of controls mentioned above, we adopt the following color connotation with respect to the state of the cells.

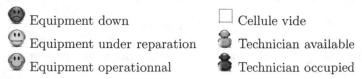

A boundary condition, fixed type is considered. We maintained empty, the cells involved in each iteration. The repair area of each equipment is assumed to be the cell above the container. Of course a free choice of the latter may be performed by the user from the user interface. We associate to each technician a buffer zone (a cell to which he returns after an intervention) it is the technicians initial position. The mean time to repair and the mean time between failure are considered constant for all the equipments, with respective values 3 and 15. In the simulation (Fig. 3), the inial configuration is given at $t = 0$.

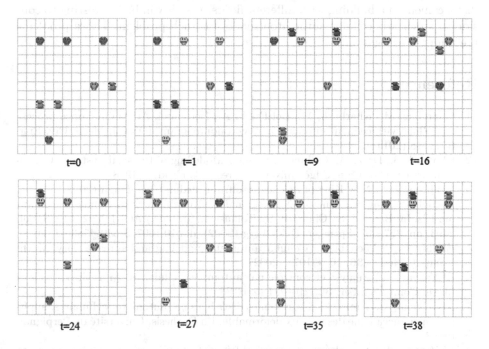

Fig. 3. Simulation results with a feedback control (Color figure online)

After the first assignment $t = 9$ a machine was repaired. An assignment is performed at $t = 10$. Between $t = 12$ and 14 four machines are operational. But at $t = 15$ an other machine fall down and the control is applied at $t = 16$. At $t = 24$ another failure is reported, and control is still established. This follows and during the time horizon, we set. The configuration at $t = 16$ returns at $t = 41$. A periodic succession of configurations, presenting three Operational equipment is then observed. And there are at least two equipments operational at each iteration, after $t = 8$. We remark in this case that the system is weakly controllable with respect to $\epsilon = 3/180$.

5   Conclusion and Perspectives

In this work we have considered the maintenance control problem with application in an industrial process using a cellular Automaton approach. The approach is based on the determination of a feedback control for the agent affectations through the observation of the state. The affectation is performed by Voronoi diagram based on the "nearest neighborhood" principle. In this work we have considered the case of 2D dimension cellular automata and it is will be very interesting to extend this results to the 3D dimension as for example the case of displacement in a building with different floors. Also it will be interesting to consider a stochastic cellular automaton model for such problem. Those problems are under investigation.

References

1. Ouardouz, M., Kharbach, M., Bel Fekih, A., Bernoussi, A.: Maintenance process modelling with cellular automata and Voronoi diagram. IOSR J. Mech. Civ. Eng. **3**, 11–18 (2014)
2. Chopard, B., Droz, M.: Cellular Automata Modelling of Physical Systems. Collection Alea-Sacley. Cambridge University Press, Cambridge (1998)
3. Wolfram, S.: A New King of Science. Wolfram Media, Champaign (2002)
4. Yacoubi, S., Jai, A., Ammor, N.: Regional controllability with cellular automata models. In: Bandini, S., Chopard, B., Tomassini, M. (eds.) ACRI 2002. LNCS, vol. 2493, pp. 357–367. Springer, Heidelberg (2002). doi:10.1007/3-540-45830-1_34
5. El Jai, A., El Yacoubi, S.: Cellular automata modeling and spreadability. Math. Comput. Model. **36**, 1059–1074 (2002)
6. El Yacoubi, S.: Analyse et controle par automates cellulaires. Ann. Univ. Craiova Math. Comp. Sci. Ser. **30**, 210–221 (2003)
7. Abdellaoui, M.: Approche des systèmes distribués par automates cellulaires, application en mécanique des milieux déformable. Ph.D. thesis, Université de Perpignan (2003)
8. El Yacoubi, S.: A mathematical method for control problems on cellular automata models. Int. J. Syst. Sci. **39**, 529–538 (2008)
9. Jellouli, O., Bernoussi, A., Amharref, M., Yacoubi, S.: Vulnerability and protector control: cellular automata approach. In: Wąs, J., Sirakoulis, G.C., Bandini, S. (eds.) ACRI 2014. LNCS, vol. 8751, pp. 218–227. Springer, Heidelberg (2014). doi:10.1007/978-3-319-11520-7_23
10. Anda Ondo, D.: Modélisation et analyse des systémes à paramètres distribués non linéaires par la méthde de Boltzman sur réseau: application aux écoulements à surface libre. Ph.D. thesis, Université de Grenoble (2013)
11. de Berg, M., van Kreveld, M., Overmars, M., Schwarzkopf, O.: Voronoi diagrams: the post office problem. In: de Berg, M., van Kreveld, M., Overmars, M., Schwarzkopf, O. (eds.) Computational Geometry: Algorithms and Applications, 2nd edn, pp. 147–163. Springer, Heidelberg (2000). doi:10.1007/978-3-662-04245-8_7. Chap. 7
12. Delannoy, C.: Programmer en Java. Editions Eyrolles, Paris (2008)

Modeling and Optimizing of Connections for Dynamic Sensor Fields Based on BT-Graph

Tuyen Phong Truong[1(✉)], Huong Hoang Luong[2], Hung Huu Huynh[3],
Hiep Xuan Huynh[2], and Bernard Pottier[1]

[1] Lab-STICC, UMR CNRS 6285, Université de Bretagne Occidentale, Brest, France
{phong-tuyen.truong,pottier}@univ-brest.fr
[2] Cantho University, Can Tho, Vietnam
{lhhuong,hxhiep}@ctu.edu.vn
[3] Danang University of Technology, Danang, Vietnam
hhhung@dut.udn.vn

Abstract. In this paper, we propose a new approach to model and optimize the dynamic sensor field for both internal network connections and LEO satellite connection based on BT-Graph. Due to the shift of LEO satellite's orbit at each revolution, a dynamic sensor field (DSF), which is able to redetermine its gateways, is suitable to improve successful data communications. It is convenient to present a DSF as a BT-Graph that aims to utilize optimization algorithms. The simulation experiments are performed on a forest fire surveillance network to validate our proposed approach.

Keywords: Associate analysis · Balltree structure · BT-Graph · Dynamic sensor field · Leo satellite

1 Introduction

Wireless Sensor Network (WSN) [1] is known as a network of sensors cooperatively operating in order to surveillance or collect the environmental parameters. Although the short transmission range can be compensated by applying a mesh topology, it would be economically infeasible to deploy in large geographic areas or behind obstacles (mountains, oceans, ...). To overcome these disadvantages, satellite-based wireless sensor networks have emerged as a promising technology with various applications.

Because the orbit of a LEO satellite shifts in westward direction around the polar axis at each revolution [10], the meeting points of a gateway on the Earth's surface and the LEO satellite will be changed over time. With a static sensor field, it can be occasionally unsuccessful in communication with the LEO satellite because the meeting time is not enough for data exchange [10]. To overcome this problem, a dynamic sensor field (DSF) [1], which has the ability to redetermine its gateway to adapt with the shifts of LEO satellite's paths, is suitable to improve the connection time.

© ICST Institute for Computer Sciences, Social Informatics and Telecommunications Engineering 2016
P.C. Vinh et al. (Eds.): ICTCC 2016, LNICST 168, pp. 297–310, 2016.
DOI: 10.1007/978-3-319-46909-6_27

In order to improve the connection time, it is necessary to choose proper gateways for the longest length of connection time. For this purpose, the connections between a LEO satellite and a dynamic sensor field should be presented by a graph-based model because it is convenient to determine number of neighbors in the satellite's communication range and then apply the optimization algorithms [3,5]. In addition, BT-Grap model [2] based on balltree structure is efficiently support not only for searching the range nearest neighbors (RNN) but also finding the shortest path to a given target node [6,13,15,20]. In this paper, we propose a new approach, namely dynamic sensor field optimization model based on BT-Graph (BT-DYNSEN), to model and optimize the DSF in communication with LEO satellite.

The rest of this paper is organized as follows. In Sect. 2, we overview related works. Section 3 presents the graph-based model for a DSF based on BT-Graph (BT-DYNSEN). How to optimize the DSF for satellite connection is presented in Sect. 4. Section 5 gives the simulation experiments on a forest fire surveillance network in Vietnam before a conclusion is drawn.

2   Related Work

The LEO satellite communication can be used in mobile satellite communications, surveillance the Earth surface, geological surveys, so on [1,11,14]. In the last decade, researches on communication services provided by LEO satellites have focused on several main directions such as optimizing the mechanics, interconnections, electric circuits, power supply. Another approach, many surveys show the research topics in design trajectory, handover traffic and constellation, as well as design protocols, radio frequencies, onboard transceivers and antenna designs [1,14]. However, the direct radio links between sensor fields and LEO satellites are not considered in literature. In recent years, it emerges as an attractive topic because of the current innovation solutions such as LoRa Semtech and solutions from vendors QB50 [9].

Additionally, graph-based model has emerged as well approach to present the structure and elaborate the performance of wireless sensor networks [3,4]. For example, random geometric graph [15] was used to determine the probability of the whole network being connected. Secure communications between large number of sensor nodes in WSNs can be elaborated on expander graph [19] and finding transmission path in network was performed based on Pascal graph [5,7]. Furthermore, hyper-graph [18] was utilized to support for reducing the transmission energy consumption and improving the fault-tolerant ability of the system. In the next section, we introduce BT-DYNSEN model for optimizing the DSF for the connection with LEO satellite.

3   BT-DYNSEN

3.1   BT-DYNSEN Model of DSF

BT-DYNSEN model of a dynamic sensor field (DSF) [1] based on BT-Graph [2] is a graph G(V,E). In this graph, set of vertices $V = \{v_i\}$, $i = 1..n$ corresponds to sensor nodes and set of edges, $E = \{e_j\}$, $j = 1..m$ are connections between the nodes with associated weight functions $W = \{w_j\}$, $j = 1..m$. The value of each w_j is given by Euclidean distance $d(v_i, v_j)$, $i \neq j$. Additionally, $R = \{r_i\}$, $i = 1..n$ are the radii of the communication ranges of nodes [2,6,8]. An edge is established if and only if the distance between two nodes is less or equal to the minimum value of their communication radii, $d(v_i, v_j) \leq \min(r_i, r_j)$, $i \neq j$. Note that the terms *node* and *vertex* are used interchangeably in this paper as a matter of convenience.

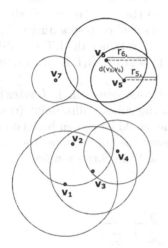

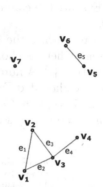

Fig. 1. A dynamic sensor field in which the communication ranges of sensor nodes are indicated by the radii of balls.

Fig. 2. A BT-Graph of the dynamic sensor field with 07 vertices $V = \{v_1, v_2, v_3, v_4, v_5, v_6, v_7\}$ and 5 edges $E = \{e_1 = e(v_1, v_2), e_2 = e(v_1, v_3), e_3 = e(v_2, v_3), e_4 = e(v_3, v_4), e_5 = e(v_5, v_6)\}$.

In Fig. 1, for an example, a pair of vertices (v_5, v_6) has communication ranges r_5 and r_6 respectively. Because the distance between v_5 and v_6 is less than r, $d(v_5, v_6) < r$, so there exists an edge e_5 connecting them as can be seen in Fig. 2. Similarly, the others edges of this graph namely $e_1 = e(v_1, v_2), e_2 = e(v_1, v_3), e_3 = e(v_2, v_3), e_4 = e(v_3, v_4)$ could be established. There are $2^n - 5$ edges between a pair of nodes of this graph that are not existed due to inadequacy of the condition. The vertex v_7 is isolated because all distance values between it and the other nodes are inadequate to the condition.

3.2   BT-DYNSEN Model of LEO Satellite Connection

The connections between a LEO satellite and a dynamic sensor field are also described in a BT-Graph. Let $V = \{v_i\}$, i=1..n, is a set of sensor node coordinates in a DSF. In this scenario, connection time is defined when any sensorset [1] of the

DSF under the satellite coverage. The LEO satellite communication range is considered as a circle whose center is sub-point on the ground (sub-satellite point), s. It is noted that sub-satellite point, s, is where on the ground the straight line connecting the center of the Earth and the satellite meets the Earths surface [10]. The associated BT-Graph consists of $n+1$ vertices $P = \{V, s\} = \{v_1, v_2, ..., v_n, s\}$. If a node is within the communication range of the satellite, there exists an edge with weight given by the Euclidean distance between them. Otherwise edge weight is set to infinity. Consequently, the number edges of the graph are $m + n$ by adding n new edges $C = \{c_1, c_2, ..., c_n\}$ with $c_i = c(s, v_i)$, $i = 1..n$. The weights of the n new edges are denoted by $Z = \{z_1, z_2, ..., z_n\}$. In this case the set of edges is $R = \{E, C\} = \{e_1, e_2, ..., e_m, c_1, c_2, ..., c_n\}$ and the set of corresponding weights is $Q = \{W, Z\} = \{\{w_k\}, \{z_i\}\}$ with $k = 1..m$, $i = 1..n$. Hence the BT-DYNSEN model for LEO satellite connections is presented by a graph G(P,R) with weight functions Q.

Furthermore, during the connection time only one sensor node (vertex) of a dynamic sensor field is chosen to connect with the sub-satellite point (center vertex) at one time [1]. A number of different nodes could be chosen based on the value of edge weights at different times. To manage the connections, the name of chosen node is kept in *Connection vector* [1] and the corresponding time is saved in *Time vector* [1] (as in Fig. 3).

Connection number	1	2	3	...
Connection vector	v_1	v_3	v_4	...
Time vector	t_1	t_2	t_3	...

Fig. 3. An example of satellite connection data with three rows: *Connection number*, *Connection vector* and *Time vector*.

Figure 3 shows that in *connection 1*, center vertex s connects with v_1 at time t_1. In a similar way, in *connection 2* at time t_2 and *connection 3* at time t_3, v_4 and v_2 are chosen to connect with s respectively.

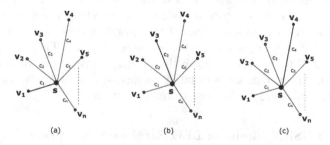

(a)   (b)   (c)

Fig. 4. The BT-Graph of a dynamic sensor field in three different connections (solid red lines) at times t_1, t_2 and t_3. (Color figure online)

For instance, Fig. 4 shows three graphs of the dynamic sensor field in three different connections with the center vertex s (a sub-satellite point) at different times t_1, t_2 and t_3. At time t_1 (see Fig. 4(a)), vertex v_1 is chosen and edge c_1 is established. Similarly, in Fig. 4(b) and Fig. 4(c) vertex v_3, v_4 are chosen for connections that leads to corresponding edges c_3, c_4 are established at time t_2 and t_3 respectively.

3.3   Compute the Connection Time

In this section, we describe the way to calculate connection time, t_{ij}, between a LEO satellite and a gateway of DSF, v_j [1, 10]. Similarly, the calculation could be applied for all other nodes. Note that every node of the sensor field is assumed as a gateway for the connection with the satellite in calculating the values of connection time.

First, it is necessary to define the angles and related distances between satellite, a gateway on the ground and the Earth's center. The parameters are indicated on Fig. 5. For angular radius of the spherical Earth, ρ_i, and the angular radius λ_{0_i} can be found from relations

$$\sin(\rho_i) = \cos(\lambda_{0_i}) = \frac{R_E}{R_E + H} \tag{1}$$

$$\rho_i + \lambda_{0_i} = 90 \ deg \tag{2}$$

where $R_E = 6378.14 \, \text{km}$ is the Earth's radius and H is the altitude of the satellite above the Earth's surface.

With the coordinates of a sub-satellite point, s_i $(Long_{s_i}, Lat_{s_i})$ along each satellite's ground track and a sensor node, nodes v_j of the DSF $(Long_{v_j}, Lat_{v_j})$, and defining $\Delta L_{ij} = |Long_{s_i} - Long_{v_j}|$, the azimuth, $\Phi_{E_{ij}}$, measured eastward from north, and angular distance, λ_{ij}, from the sub-satellite point to the sensor node (see Fig. 6) are given by

$$cos(\lambda_{ij}) = sin(Lat_{s_i})sin(Lat_{v_j}) + cos(Lat_{s_i})cos(Lat_{v_j})cos(\Delta L_{ij}) \tag{3}$$

$$cos(\Phi_{E_{ij}}) = ((sin(Lat_{v_i}) - cos(\lambda_{ij})//sin(Lat_{s_i}))/(sin(\lambda_{ij})cos(Lat_{s_i})) \tag{4}$$

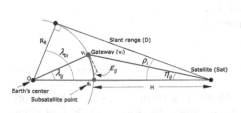

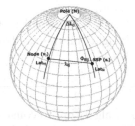

Fig. 5. Gateway of sensor field geometry [10].

Fig. 6. Relationship between sensor node of a DSF and sub-satellite point [10].

where $\Phi_{E_{ij}} < 180\ deg$ if v_i is east of s_i and $\Phi_{E_{ij}} > 180\ deg$ if v_i is west of s_i
Consider triangle Os_iv_j (in Fig. 5), the distance, d_{ij}, between s_i and v_j can be
found using the law of cosines:

$$d_{ij}^2 = R_E^2(1 - cos(\lambda_{ij})) \tag{5}$$

The *connection time*, t_{ij}, is given by

$$t_{ij} = (\frac{P}{180\ deg}) \arccos(\frac{\cos(\lambda_{ij_{max}})}{\cos(\lambda_{ij_{min}})}) \tag{6}$$

where P is the *orbit period* in minutes. From Eqs. (5) and (6), the communication duration, t_{ij}, strongly depends on how close the nodes v_j is to the
sub-satellite points s_i, the distances d_{ij}, along the ground track on any given
orbit pass [10].

4   Optimization Method

4.1   Verify the Connectivity of DSF

In this work, top down construction algorithm is chosen in order to build balltree
structure for verifying the network connectivity of the DSF. In this manner, the
time complexity can be found in $O(nlog^2n)$ [8].

Algorithm 1. verifyConnectivity(D)

---

   if D.hasAPoint() **then**
      create a leaf B is a point in D;
      return B;
   else
      let c is the dimension of greatest spread;
      let L, R are the set of points lying to 2 subsets;
      let r is a radius of ball;
      create B with two children:
         B.center ← c;
         B.radius ← r;
         B.leftChild ← balltreeConstruct(L);
         B.rightChild ← balltreeConstruct(R);
   return B;

Top down algorithm to construct the balltree is a recursive process from top
to down. The process at each step is to choose the split dimension it and then
split the set of values into two subsets. First, it is necessary to choose the point
in the ball which is farthest from its center, and then choose a second point (p_2)

that is farthest from (p_1). It is followed by assigning all points in the ball to closest one of two clusters corresponding to p_1 and p_2. Finally, the centroid of each cluster is calculated and the minimum cluster radius for enclosing all the points are determined. This process is stopped only when the leaf balls contain just two points. Note that D denotes current considered balltree structure and B denotes leaf node defined after each process.

4.2 Determine the Sensorsets Corresponding to Each Sub-satellite Point

Defining a sensorset [1] based on BT-DYNSEN is to find k nearest sensor nodes (neighbors) under the satellite's coverage area at each sub-satellite. It is a depth-first traversal algorithm for traversing tree or graph data structures, starting with the root node. The value of Q is updated during search process. At each considered node B, Q obtains k points which are nearest query q as following algorithm.

Algorithm 2. determineSensorset

```
input: balltreeNode, query
output: sensorset
begin
    centerNode ← balltreeNode.getCenter();
    radiusNode ← balltreeNode.getRadius();
    //calculate distance from query to centerNode
    d ← distance(centerNode.lat, centerNode.lon, query.lat, query.lon);
    if(balltreeNode.isALeaf) {
        if(d < query.range) {
            write name of balltreeNode to file;
        }
    }
    else {
        if(d < (query.range + radiusNode)) {
            left ← balltreeNode.leftChild;
            right ← balltreeNode.rightChild;
            rnn: left, query;
            rnn: right, query;
        }
    }
}
```

There are two different cases in $BT\text{-}DYNSEN$ algorithm as follows. If current considered node is a leaf node and the distance from query point q to B is less than r $(d < r)$, the obtained result is updated by adding B into Q. Otherwise, if B is not a leaf node and the distance from query point q to B is less than the total of r and the radius of B ($d < r + B.radius$), it is necessary to perform recursive algorithm for the two child nodes of a parent node B: left-child and right-child.

4.3   Select the Gateways of DSF

If a DSF V has n nodes, there are $2^n - 1$ connection items, $G = \{g_l\}$, l=1..($2^n - 1$). It is necessary to find out a set of proper nodes which play as gateways of DSF to provide the longest length of time for the connection. To do this, the *association analysis algorithm* [13] is applied. To do this, a DSF is represented in a binary format, where each row corresponds to a connection item and each column corresponds to a node. A node value is one if the node appears in a connection item and zero otherwise. Weight of a connection item determines how often a connection item is applicable to a set of connection items. The weight of a connection item, $g_i \in G$, can be defined as $w(g_i) = | \{g_l \mid g_i \subseteq g_l, g_l \in G\} |$, where the symbol $| \, . \, |$ denotes the number of elements in a set.

The algorithm for selecting the gateways of the DSF is briefly presented in following list.

Algorithm 3. selectGateway()

```
input: list of sensorsets
output: gateways of DSF
//C_k: candidate sensors (size k)
//L_k: set of selected gateways (size k)
begin
    L_1 ← {weight1 − sensorsets};
    for(k = 2; Lk.count > 0; k + +) {
        C_{k+1} ← generate candidate sensors L_k;
        foreach (transaction t in data) {
            Increment count of the candidate sensors in C_{k+1} that contained
            in t;
        }
        L_{k+1} ← candidate sensors in C_{k+1};
    }
    Write counted frequent of all sensors L_k to file;
end
```

For example, a DSF with 4 nodes, $V = \{v_1, v_2, v_3, v_4\}$ is shown in Fig. 7. There are 4 sensorsets $A_1 = \{v_1\}$, $A_2 = \{v_1, v_2, v_3\}$, $A_3 = \{v_2, v_3, v_4\}$ and $A_4 = \{v_3, v_4\}$. The weights of connection items are presented in Fig. 8. The connection with the highest weight corresponds to the least number of times required to change the gateways. It leads to the connection duration time of the connection is longest. Because the weight of connection item (v_1, v_3) is highest, this connection is chosen.

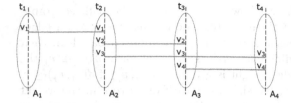

Connection items	Weights
(v_1, v_2, v_4)	1
(v_1, v_2, v_3)	1
(v_1, v_3)	3
(v_1, v_3, v_4)	1

Fig. 7. The connections between a 4-node DSF with a LEO satellite.

Fig. 8. The weights of connection items in a DSF with 4 nodes.

4.4 Find Shortest Path for Data Dissemination

The problem of finding shortest path from each sensor node of DSF to the gateway can be solved by a graph search method. The algorithm is presented as follows:

Algorithm 4. searchShortestPath()

```
Init matrix M;
S ← Start point;
T ← End point;
d is an array;
free is an array;
trace is as array;
d[S] ← 0;
    while (true){
        u ← -1;
        min ← INFINITE;
        for (i ← 1 to n-1) {
            if (free[i] AND (d[i] < min)) {
                min ← d[i];
                u ← i;
            }
        }
        if((u = -1) OR (u = T))
            Break;
        free[u] ← false;
        for (v ← 0 to n-1) {
            if(free[v] AND (d[v] > (d[u] + M[u, v]))) {
                d[v] ← d[u] = arr[u][v];
                trace[v] ← u;
        }
    }
}
```

The algorithm proceeds in three following steps. First, the balltree graph-based model, G, is constructed. At the next step, the weight matrix M for edges connect each pair of vertices (sensor nodes) in V is computed based on their coordinates. For v_i, v_j are two different vertices in V, in case of $v_i \equiv v_j$ the edge weight is 0. If $v_i \neq v_j$, the edge weight is given by $d(v_j, v_j)$ if $d(v_j, v_j) \leq r$, otherwise it is infinity, ∞. Finally, the shortest path from q to e in the weight matrix is figured out. Note that q is starting point (a sensor node) and e is the destination point (the gateway of DSF).

5   Experiment

5.1   Data Used

For experiments, an abstract structure of the long-range sensor field for fire forest surveillance was generated by using NetGen [16]. Figure 9(a) shows dynamic sensor field consists of 50 sensor nodes that is stretched from South Central Coastal to Southeast and extended up to Mekong River Delta in Vietnam.

From the constraints about the satellite's orbit altitude in [1], orbit 12974 of BEESAT-3 [17], a LEO satellite with orbit altitude is around 575 km, which was chosen in our experiments. The ground track data stored in a plain text (.txt file) was used as input data.

5.2   BT-DYNSEN Tool

We have developed the BT-DYNSEN tool in MATLAB, that enables to optimize the connection time between a dynamic sensor field with a LEO satellite. GPredict [12] is used to provide the information about BEESAT-3 satellite's path. Besides, NetGen tool [16] is utilized to generate the abstract network of a 50-node dynamic sensor field from geographic data provided by Google maps service. The obtained result are the nodes of the DSF which should be configured as gateways for the best connection duration time and the shortest paths for data dissemination from each node to these gateways.

5.3   Experiment 1: Verify Network Connectivity

The connectivity of the 50-node dynamic sensor network was verified by applying BT-DYNSEN as shown in Fig. 9(a). Figure 9(b) depicts the balltree structure of this DSF in which there are 49 balls with radii from 10.124 m to 321.165 m. BT-Graph model then was utilized to ensure the full connectivity of all network nodes, the radius 30.497 m was then chosen as shown in Fig. 9(c).

5.4   Experiment 2: Determine the Sensorsets

BT-DYNSEN tool was employed in determining sensorsets corresponding to sub-satellite points during visiting time. The map in Fig. 10 shows the sensorset was

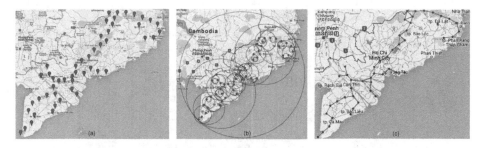

Fig. 9. Verify dynamic sensor network connectivity. (a) A 50-node dynamic sensor network, (b) Balltree structure of the DSF, (c) Connectivity of the DSF.

Fig. 10. Determine the sensorsets corresponding to each sub-satellite along the ground track of BEESAT-3 in orbit 12794. (Color figure online)

determined with sub-satellites of BEESAT-3 at (latitude: 14.00, longitude: 102.48) in orbit 12794. Sub-satellite and satellite coverage were indicated by solid red square and red circle respectively. The sensorset consists of 26 sensor nodes which were under the satellite's coverage area as indicated by a solid red circle. There are four sensorsets were created along the BEESAT-3's ground track in orbit 12794.

5.5   Experiment 3: Select the Gateways

With each sensorset, a subset of connections is established. The weights of each connection in subset are then computed. A set of connection items is created by combining these subsets. The best connection is chosen based on the weights of connection items. For instance, in Fig. 11 node v_{36} was chosen as the gateway of the 50-node DSF to connection with BEESAT-3 satellite in orbit 12794 because its weight is highest in sensor nodes.

Fig. 11. Select a set of nodes which play as gateways of the DSF according to the weights of connections.

5.6   Experiment 4: Optimize Data Dissemination

To ensure sensing data to be collected from all sensor nodes and then sent before the satellite leaving, it is necessary to find the shortest path from each sensor nodes to the gateway. The interconnection weights within the DSF are geographic distances between each pair of nodes that were carried out by applying BT-DYNSEN model. Figure 12, as an example, illustrates the chosen path (the bold blue line) for data dissemination from sensor node v_{50} to the gateway node v_{36}.

Fig. 12. The shortest path for data dissemination from node v_{50} to gateway node v_{36}. (Color figure online)

6   Conclusion

Based on BT-Graph, we have described a new approach in order to model and optimize the dynamic sensor field for LEO satellite connections. The distances between the sub-satellite points and each node of the sensor field is utilized as a key factor to find out the proper gateways for the longest connection time. The experimental results were obtained by applying several appreciate algorithms on BT-DYNSEN model to verify the connectivity of network, determine sensorsets at visiting time, choose set of gateway nodes and find shortest path for data dissemination in DSF. The simulation results show that our proposed graph-based model helps to increase the amount of time for data communications in long-range sensor field applications using satellite connections in order to monitor, control and collect environmental data.

Acknowledgment. The first author was funded by the program 911 of Ministry of Education and Training, Vietnam. This publication was made possible through support provided by the Lab-STICC, UMR CNRS 6285, France.

References

1. Truong, T.P., Van Tran, H., Huynh, H.X., Pottier, B.: Optimizing the connection time for LEO satellite based on dynamic sensor field. In: Vinh, P.C., Alagar, V. (eds.) Context-Aware Systems and Applications. Lecture Notes of the Institute for Computer Sciences, Social Informatics and Telecommunications Engineering, vol. 165, pp. 380–394. Springer, Heidelberg (2016)
2. Luong, H.H., Huynh, H.X.: Graph-based model for geographic coordinate search based on balltree structure. In: Proceeding of the 17th International Conference, Daklak, Vietnam, pp. 116–123 (2014)
3. Akoglu, L., Tong, H., Koutra, D.: Graph based anomaly detection and description: a survey. Data Min. Knowl. Discov. **29**(3), 626–688 (2015). IEEE Press
4. Khou, I., Minet, P., Laouiti, A., Mahfoudh, S.: Survey of deployment algorithms in wireless sensor networks: coverage and connectivity issues and challenges. Int. J. Auton. Adapt. Commun. Syst. (IJAACS), p. 24 (2014)
5. Chaparro, C., Eberle, W.: Detecting anomalies in mobile telecommunication networks using a graph based approach. In: FLAIRS Conference, pp. 410–415 (2015)
6. Abbasifard, M.R., Ghahremani, B., Naderi, H.: A survey on nearest neighbor search methods. Int. J. Comput. Appl. 39–52 (2014)
7. Panwar, D., Neogi, S.G.: Design of energy efficient routing algorithm for wireless sensor network (WSN) using Pascal graph. Comput. Sci. Inf. Technol. 175–189 (2013)
8. Omohundro, S.M.: Five Balltree Construction Algorithms. Technical report (1989)
9. Lucas, P.-Y., Van Truong, N.H., Truong, T.P., Pottier, B.: Wireless sensor networks and satellite simulation. In: Pillai, P., Hu, Y.F., Otung, I., Giambene, G. (eds.) Wireless and Satellite Systems. Lecture Notes of the Institute for Computer Sciences, Social Informatics and Telecommunications Engineering, vol. 154. Springer, Heidelberg (2015)
10. Larson, W.J., Wertz, J.R.: Space mission geometry. In: Space Mission Analysis and Design, Chap. 5, 3rd edn. pp. 95–230. Microcosm Press, Portland (2003)

11. Colitti, W., Steenhaut, K., Descouvemont, N., Dunkels, A.: Satellite based wireless sensor networks: global scale sensing with nano- and pico-satellites. In: Proceedings of the 6th ACM Conference on Embedded Network Sensor Systems (SenSys 2008), pp. 445–446 (2008)
12. Csete, A.: GPredict project. http://gpredict.oz9aec.net/
13. Tan, P.-N., Steinbach, M., Kumar, V.: Association analysis: basic concepts and algorithms. In: Introduction to Data Mining, Chap. 6, pp. 327–413. Addison-Wesley Longman Publishing Co., Inc., Boston, MA, USA (2005)
14. Celandroni, N., et al.: A survey of architectures and scenarios in satellite-based wireless sensor networks: system design aspects. Int. J. Satell. Commun. Network. **31**(1), 1–38 (2013). Wiley
15. Dong, J., Chen, Q., Niu, Z.: Random graph theory based connectivity analysis in wireless sensor networks with Rayleigh fading channels. In: Asia-Pacific Conference Communication, pp. 123–126 (2007)
16. Pottier, B., Lucas, P.-Y.: Dynamic networks NetGen. Technical report, Universit de Bretagne Occidentale, France (2015)
17. Berlin Experimental and Educational Satellite-2 and -3. https://directory.eoportal. org/web/eoportal/satellite-missions/b/beesat-2-3
18. Ting, Y., chunJian, K.: An energy-efficient and fault-tolerant convergecast protocol in wireless sensor networks. Int. J. Distrib. Sens. Netw. 8 pages (2012)
19. Camtepe, S., Yener, B., Yung, M.: Expander graph based key distrbution machinisms in wire sensor networks. In: IEEE International Conference of Communication, pp. 2262–2267 (2006)
20. Muja, M., Lowe, D.G.: Scalable nearest neighbor algorithms for high dimensional data. IEEE Trans. Pattern Anal. Mach. Intell. **36**(11), 2227–2240 (2014)

Toward an Agent-Based and Equation-Based Coupling Framework

Huynh Quang Nghi[1,6](✉), Tri Nguyen-Huu[2,3,4,5,6], Arnaud Grignard[3,4,6],
Hiep Xuan Huynh[1,6], and Alexis Drogoul[5,6]

[1] DREAM-CTU/IRD, CICT-CTU, Cantho, Vietnam
hqnghi88@gmail.com
[2] IRD, Centre Ile-de-France, 32 Avenue Henri Varagnat, 93140 Bondy, France
[3] Sorbonne University, Universit Pierre et Marie Curie Paris 6, Paris, France
[4] Faculté des Sciences de Semlalia, Université Cadi Ayyad, Marrakech, Morocco
[5] University of Science and Technology of Hanoi, Hanoi, Vietnam
[6] IXXI, ENS Lyon, 46 allée d'Italie, 69364 Lyon Cedex 07, France

Abstract. The ecology modeling generally opposes two class of models, equations based models and multi-agents based models. Mathematical models allow predicting the long-term dynamics of the studied systems. However, the variability between individuals is difficult to represent, what makes these more suitable models for large and homogeneous populations. Multi-agent models allow representing the attributes and behavior of each individual and therefore provide a greater level of detail. In return, these systems are more difficult to analyze. These approaches have often been compared, but rarely used simultaneously. We propose a hybrid approach to couple equations models and agent-based models, as well as its implementation on the modeling platform Gama [7]. We focus on the representation of a classical theoretical epidemiological model (SIR model) and we illustrate the construction of a class of models based on it.

Keywords: Equation-based model · Agent-based model · Coupling framework · Simulation platform · Epidemiology

1 Introduction

Mathematical modeling and agent-based modeling are two kind of modeling often used for describing dynamical systems [4]. Equation Based Models (EBM) are present in many domains, such as physical, chemical, biological, economical systems [4,5]. Agent-Based Models (ABM) appeared with the development of computer science, which allowed describing large complex systems [15]. In particular, both kind of modeling are used in epidemiology. The well known SIR model [2,9] is the first epidemiology model that has been developed in 1927. It is a compartment level that allows describing the dynamics of an epidemic at the population level according to very simple assumptions. SIR models and their derivative (spatial mathematical models using partial differential equations) were

© ICST Institute for Computer Sciences, Social Informatics and Telecommunications Engineering 2016
P.C. Vinh et al. (Eds.): ICTCC 2016, LNICST 168, pp. 311–324, 2016.
DOI: 10.1007/978-3-319-46909-6_28

extensively used for many diseases and real case studies. ABM models were later developed in order to introduce a description of processes at a finer level [10]. They describe the propagation of epidemics by representing the processes at the individual level.

Those two kinds of modeling paradigms are often used to represent the same systems, with different benefits and drawbacks. As a global approach, EBM models require very little resources and allow performing a complete mathematical analysis of the system (equilibria, stability, asymptotic behavior, etc.). However, heavy preliminary work is need in order to determine how the processes involved in the dynamics can be translated into mathematical equations. Furthermore, representing such processes at the global level leads to a loss of information corresponding to individual variability. Contrarily, ABM use a local approach and allow a detailed description of processes occurring at the individual level. Such description is more intuitive and better represents variability. On the other hand, ABM require a high amount of resource depending on the number of agents that are represented and a high amount of data depending on the level of details described, while EBM usually do not. Therefore, ABM are more difficult to analyze and have more risks of over fitting. The main objective of our work is to propose a coupling methodology of equation-based models and multi-agent-based models. With this method, modeler can take advantage of both approaches, switching from individual level to global level when needed. This work also offer a programmable environment for both formalisms.

This paper consists of six parts, the first being this introduction. The second part introduces related works about coupling the two modelling approaches. In the third part, we present a methodology for coupling the agent-based and the equation-based approaches. In the fourth part, we present an implementation of our method into the simulation platform GAMA. The fifth part is dedicated to experimental results, and the sixth part to discussion and ongoing work.

2   Related Work

In this part, we present the current state of the art of coupling two modeling approaches: Agent-Based Modeling and Equation-Based Modeling. Although these two approaches aim at a common objective, they are distinct by their modeling formalism. The necessity of coupling and comparing the two approaches has been raised in several research studies. They use a common methodology: exploration is always done by implementing an agent-base model beside an equation-based without the support of an agent-based modeling framework neither an equation-based framework.

In [17], the authors study the difference between agent-based modeling and equation-based modeling in a industrial supply network project in which network's domain supply are modeled with both agents and equations. They also summarize the resemblance and variety of two approaches with a suggestion to use one or another. Their study is part of the DASCh project (Dynamical Analysis of Supply Chains). DASCh includes three species of agents: Company agents, PPIC agents and Shipping agents. It also integrates a fixed set of ordinary differential equations (ODE).

Coupling and comparing agent-based and equation-based is also found in [14] where Rahmandad et al. examine in contrast the dynamic of well-know SEIR model which describe the common and important context of the spread of contagious disease. They compare and validate an ABM and EBM for epidemiological disease-spread models, as well as [16] who use an ABM and EBM of the 1918 Spanish flu. In their publication, they propose a model validation framework of choosing ABM or EBM.

Nguyen in [12] propose to use only one appropriate modeling formalism instead of two approaches, and infer an EBM from an ABM SIR model by exploring the deducible parameters like number of individual in population, rates of interactions base on dimension of environment, ... They have done a study with the measure based on disk graph theories [11] to link ABM with EBM dynamical systems applied to theoretical population ecology.

Another coupling approach is proposed in [1,13] or [3]. In the simulation of emergency evacuation of pedestrians in case of a tsunami in Nhatrang City, Vietnam, people move along the road networks as agents. The agent based model of individuals movements are replaced by equation models for the roads with higher traffic. This transformation give the model an addition of time and resource for such evacuation model which usually take into account huge populations (Fig. 1).

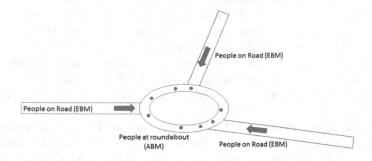

Fig. 1. Coupling approach example: people moving on the road are represented in the form of equation, and in form agents at the crossroads

All these approaches provide mechanisms that allow interaction between several models but they still have the following disadvantages:

- In general, these approaches are not generic and are difficult to be re-implemented in different domains and contexts.
- There are no consideration of the differences in spatial and temporal scales.
- Their are no framework that support coupling of heterogeneous models between equation-based modeling and agent-based modeling paradigm.

3 Coupling Between Equation-Based Model (EBM) and Agent-Based Model (ABM)

3.1 Equation-Based Model

The equation-based models [4] predict the long-term dynamics of the studied systems. They use mathematical formalism based on Ordinary Differential Equations or Partial Differential Equations. The modelling approach is generally driven by the principle of parsimony (or *Occam's razor*), which means that the model should be kept as simple as possible, with as few parameters as possible. Although, if a stochastic approach is possible, a deterministic approach is preferable when possible. In addition, processes are considered at a global scale (e.g. in ecology: at the population level instead of the individual level), assuming that the processes that govern the system at such a scale can be determined (often using mean field approximation). For example, the demographic dynamics of a population can be described at the global level using a parameter call *population growth rate*, which can be derivated from the mean of offsprings per individual per time unit. Due to such approximations, the variability between individuals is difficult to represent, making these models more suitable for large and homogeneous populations. Mathematics often provide useful analytical tools to find the properties of ODE models, such as equilibria and asymptotic dynamics. The evolution of the system can be determined from mathematical proofs, which are more robust than just simulations. For those reasons, such models can be easily analysed and are useful for making predictions. On the contrary, translating the studied processes into equations requires a good knowledge of similar physics or mathematical models. Processes also have to be sufficiently smooth in order to fit their mathematical description. As a summary, such models require a large amount of work upstreams, but they offer conceptually good possibilities of analysis downstreams (the technical issues that could be encountered in mathematical proofs is not discussed here).

EBMs have been wildly used for epidemiology modeling. A pragmatic reason is that mathematical analysis methods were the only available methods, as computers and EBM were not available to Kermack and McKendrick in 1927. However, there are many conceptual reasons why EBM are a reasonable choice for modeling epidemics. Firstly, epidemics arise in large populations, and the transmission and remission rates variability among individuals can be easily represented according to familiar distribution laws, making such processes easy to describe at the population level using mean field approximations. Secondly, the analysis of the equations provide useful prediction tools for epidemiology: one can determine conditions on the parameters for which the epidemics will arise or not. For example, the basic reproduction number R_0 can be computed with the parameters of the model, based generally on transmission and remission rates. Values greater than one mean that an epidemics outbreak will occur, such an event can be then predicted without simulations.

3.2   Agent-Based Model

Agent-based models [6] are used to represent the attributes and behavior at the individual level, and therefore to provide a greater level of detail. They can describe strong individual variability, not only for the attributes of the individuals of a same population, but also for their behavior. They are often associated to small time scales, which correspond to the individual processes time scales. In return, these systems may be more difficult to analyze and prediction almost rely on simulations (apart from some ABMs which are actually probabilistic mathematical models that can be analysed with mathematical tools). Because of the large number of parameters, it can be difficult to test the model sensitivity to one of them. A large amount of analysis, dependent on simulations and on the assumed prior distribution of parameters has to be performed in order to provide synthetic results. ABM use a specific language to describe in detail the aspects of agents: perception, action, belief, knowledge, goals, motivation, intention, reflexion, etc. Processes can be written as algorithms, offering more freedom to the modeler, as complex decision structures can be used (e.g. if the behaviour of individuals depends on some condition, an *if-then-else* construct can be used). The ABM approach also proposes a more intuitive way to build the model: processes can be represented as close to the perception of the modeler. As a summary, such approach proposes an easy and intuitive work upstreams, but requires a large amount of work downstream to provide relevant results. In addition, the large number of parameters combined with the often large size of population considered means that such a model may need a very important amount of resources to run simulations.

Interest of epidemiologists in ABMs relies on the ability to give a detailed description of the network of transmission, and such models have been developed alongside graph theory. Such models are useful to represent singular events (one infected individual entering a large susceptible population) and the stochasticity associated to such events. Such models are used to represent the worldwide propagation of infection due to air travel. Depending on the disease, a detailed behavior of the infection vector can be given.

3.3   Coupling EBM and ABM

These approaches have often been compared but rarely used simultaneously.

Coupling problems. In this part, we introduce the existing problems in many researches which have been done to couple the models of complex system in multi-discipline:

Different formalism of modeling: Coupling models often takes place when modelling is carried out with more and more models from many different domains, such that each one comes with a particular modeling formalism. Thus, modeler is led to the problem of diversifying the formalism of coupling models. In this research, ABM is based on agent formalism and the EBM is based on the algebraic equation paradigm.

Spatial - temporal scale: While coupling ABM and EBM models, modeler usually encounters with the need to change the spatial and temporal level of an object or of models components, to have benefit with diverse representation from one model to another. Each model has its own scales and needs to take into account entities at different spatial and temporal scales. For example, models in epidemiology may need to represent explicitly entities that belong to a hierarchy of containers, like molecules, cells and tissues. Their spatial scale has multiple levels of observations: ward, commune, district, city, region, etc., as well as multiple temporal levels of observation: days, weeks, months, quarters, years, couple of years...

Explicit description of the coupling: There are no ways to support the explicitly description of the coupling between ABM and EBM. The problem pose is to describe how the sub-model will interact each other. Most of all research proposed coupling research implicitly implement the integration of models. They have been done on the coupling between ABM and EBM, is based on the exchange value during or after simulations. In that case, the composing is fixed and could not be changed easily and dynamically with an explicit modeling language. It leaves aside the semantic problem to describe the dynamic of coupling and composition.

Propose methodology. In the act of our research domain which is present in [8] to propose a coupling framework that support the modeling and simulation of complex systems, we propose in that scope an approach to compose the two modeling types (ABM and EBM) in one modeling environment. This methodology will facilitate the comparison between the two types of models through the combination and simultaneous use (Fig. 2).

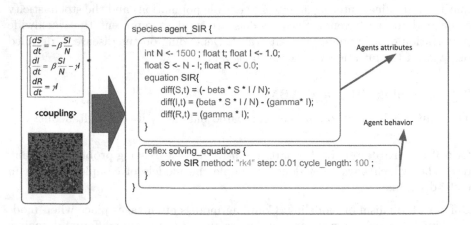

Fig. 2. Coupling between ABM and EBM: equations are integrated into agents

3.4 Model "Switch"

We illustrate our coupling methodology by implementing a hybrid model, called Switch, combining equations and agents on the modeling platform Gama. We build a class of SIR model based in both ABM and EBM (Fig. 3), in which people are represented by agents when the density is low, and by equations if the density is higher, a tilting mechanism for moving from an approach to another.

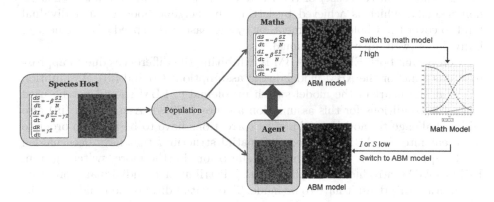

Fig. 3. Representation the dynamic of "Switch" model

Both models are based on the same assumptions. They involve two processes: contamination and recovery. The ABM model also adds spatial interactions and dispersal. The mathematical model is indeed a mean field approximation of the ABM and represents the dynamics at the global scale, while ABM shows the dynamics at local scale. The contamination and recovery processes happen frequently with a "uniform distribution" over time.

- Assumption (i) implies that processes can be represented at a continuous time;
- Assumption (ii) allows to replace probabilities of processes occurrences by expectancies; finally assumption (iii) allows to consider that all individual have the same number of neighbors.
- Assumption (iii) populations are considered to be at sufficiently high density; populations are considered as homogeneous for spatial distribution of individuals, as well as for the distribution of each type of individuals (S, I and R).

Considering that assumption (i) holds is rather natural, as processes occur along constant time steps. Epidemiological models usually assume that population densities are high, thus condition for assumption (ii) seems to be naturally fulfilled. However, in a large population, the density of infected (or even susceptible) individuals may be very low. Indeed, a usual condition for such kind of model is the introduction of a small group of infected inside a disease free population. Mathematical model are deterministic and ignore the variability due to stochasticity which alter the dynamics: if one infected individual is introduced in the population, if basic reproduction rate R0 > 1, and epidemic outbreak will be predicted by the mathematical model. However, in real cases or for ABM, there is a chance to avoid epidemic outbreak as contamination may not occur thanks to the stochasticity of infection process. Assumption (iii) may not be possible for spatially explicit ABM, as spatial distribution does not remain constant and spatial patterns could appear, like contamination waves. Assumption (iii) makes that the EBM, as mean-field approximation of ABM, is also the "limit" (in the mathematical sense) of the EBM when spatial process tends to spatial homogeneity, which is achieved by letting the neighborhood of an individual tend to cover the whole environment, or by increasing the speed of movement of individuals (well mixed populations).

Comparing both EBM and ABM is exhibiting the differences due to approximations done for the ABM model due to assumptions (ii) and (iii). Assumption (ii) is at the heart of the model switch problematic: EBM should not be used when the conditions for this assumption are not fulfilled. Assumption (iii) also add a challenge to model switching, as corrections have to be made in order to represent into the ABM the effects of spatial structures that have been hidden by the approximation made with this assumption. Furthermore, switching from EBM to ABM introduces an explicit spatial distribution of individuals, for which assumption (iii) doesn't have to be made. The spatial distribution, hidden in the EBM, may have to be generated.

The two models are based on SIR models assumptions. Individuals can be in three different states: susceptible individuals (S): the individual is disease-free and can be contaminated by contact with an infected individual (I). After some time, infected individuals recover from the disease (or die). They are assumed to be in a recovered state (R): they are immune to the disease and do not take part anymore in the infection dynamics. The models involve the following processes:

- infection: transmission of the disease from infected individuals. This depends on the contact rate between susceptible individuals and infected individuals;
- recovery: infected individuals heal and recover from infection;
- movements: individuals are assumed to move within the considered environment. There are two type of movement, one is random walking and other is not random, (Fig. 4).

Hypothesis found in both models:

- Recovery rate: the remission rate is very similar in the agent-based model and the equation-based model. In the ABM, parameter gamma is the probability to recover per time unit. In the EBM model, the parameter gamma is a mean-field approximation, which means that the number of recovered individuals given by the EBM model is exactly the expectancy of the number of recovered individuals given by the ABM model (provided that there is no infection occurring at the same time). Stochasticity of recovery rate appears at low I populations, otherwise both models fit.

– Contact rate: in the present models, contact are defined in a similar way for the mathematical model and the agent-based model. In the agent-based model, two individuals are considered to be "in contact" if they are in each other's vicinity for one time step. In mathematical model, space is not explicitly represented, but the average number of neighbours can be determined. Stochasticity of contact rate appear because of size of neighbourhood (strong variability in number of hosts neighbours) and speed of hosts (low speed means no mixing, neighbourhood proportion of R and I may greatly vary).

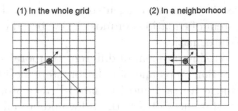

Fig. 4. Two type of deplacement of agent in an environment

We compare this model with existing models and present a method to determine the parameters for transitions between models. In particular, we establish a link between the parameters of the mathematical model, and the representation of contacts and travel agents in a spatial environment.

We are also interested in how to compensate for the loss of information on spatial structures when we move an agent model to a mathematical model. Currently, we save the attributes, especially the location and the status, of all agents and re-assign to agents when they need. We are also interested in how to compensate for the loss of information on spatial structures when we move an agent model to a mathematical model. Currently we have implemented two following method of creation new distribution after the switch from EBM to ABM.

4   An ODE-Integrated Environment

We tackle these problems of differences with our proposition of coupling by integrating these two approaches in a modeling and simulation platform, GAMA [7], in which the equation-based model is declared as an attribute of the agent. It has two famous examples of equation-based modeling which are the Lotka and Volterra [24] modeling of prey-predator dynamics or the Kermack and McKendrick [2] SIR model to represent epidemic dynamics.

We have introduced in GAMA the possibility to describe the dynamics of agents using a differential equation system and to integrate this system at each simulation step. With the enhancement of GAMA modeling language (GAML), modelers have possibility to write equations linking agents attributes and to

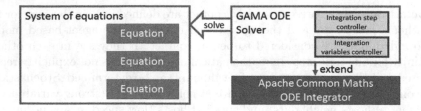

Fig. 5. An ODE solver structure inside a modeling and simulation platform

integrate equation-based system with agent-based system. The GAML syntax permit to write an system of equations of most EBM based on the implementation with Commons Mathematics Library.

To figure out the coupling problem of different temporal scale, we introduce the controller of integration steps and simulation steps beside the two current integration method Runge Kutta 4 and Dormand-Prince 8(5,3). This controller is maintain in the solve statement of GAML and would be call at each simulation step. In the Fig. 5, an equation-based model in form of algebrics is represented into GAML syntax that are called Equation. Set of equations make a System of equations. This type of entity will be integrated by our GAMA ODE (Ordinary Differential Equation) Solver package.

5   Experiments

5.1   Objective, Data and Tools Used

In this part, we do experiment to prove the capabilities of coupling framework that we have proposed to compose the ABM and EBM. The experiments will have three scenarios, each scenario The data used in the "Switch" model is bring in the real data of SIR model. The epidemiology's parameters are the spead of the flu and measles.

5.2   Represent Classical SIR Model in EBM and ABM Formalism

The first experiment show that we can easily modeling the classical SIR in form of equation-based and also agent-based. As in the Fig. 6, an differential equation can be declare with two expression. The first one on the left of "=" is the keyword diff followed by the name of integrated variable and the time variable t:

```
diff( <integrated variable>, t ) = <calculating expression>;
```

An EBM is then represented as a attributes of agent with a block of equations:

```
equation <name_identifier> {
    diff (...) = ...;
    diff (...) = ...;
    ...
}
```

equation SIR{

$$\begin{cases} \dfrac{dS}{dt} = -\beta \dfrac{SI}{N} \\[2mm] \dfrac{dI}{dt} = \beta \dfrac{SI}{N} - \gamma I \\[2mm] \dfrac{dR}{dt} = \gamma I \end{cases}$$

S diff(S,t) = (- beta * S * I / N);

I diff(I,t) = (beta * S * I / N) - (gamma * I);

R diff(R,t) = (gamma * I);

}

Fig. 6. Representation of an equation-based model in an simulation platform.

5.3 Adjust the Parameters to Calibrate EBM and ABM

The ABM simulation result is a stochastic result, instead of EBM'results are deterministic. Our proposition allow modeler to calibrate the SIR model in ABM fit with EBM. We launch the simulation with following parameter: N = 500; I = 1.0; S = N - I; R = 0.0; beta = 1/2.0; gamma = 1/3.0. After 100 simulations, the SIR model and agent model present significant differences from (Fig. 7): population initial (N), effect of size grid (grid size), effect of topologies (neighborhood size).

The transition beta from EBM to ABM is then adjust an amount alpha. We relaunch the simulation 100 times to explore the value of alpha. We found the best fixed alpha = 0,45 (Fig. 8). We have also found several criteria that would be effect the fitness between SIR EBM and ABM are: difference of synchronous/asynchronous (infect others vs is infected); random walk; effect of beta; dispersion; effect of movement speed.

$$\beta_m = \beta \frac{\text{neighborhood size}}{\text{grid size}} N \times a \quad , a \text{ adjustment parameter}$$

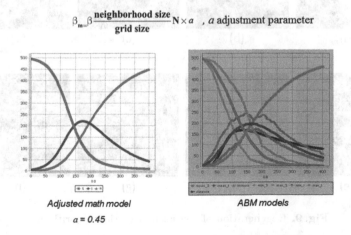

Adjusted math model
a = 0.45

ABM models

Fig. 7. Calibrate the beta parameter of SIR model of Switch model by adjusting an alpha parameter.

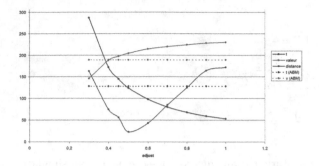

Fig. 8. Adjust the alpha parameter of SIR model to calibrate EBM with ABM result.

5.4 Regenerate Spatial Information from EBM to ABM

In this experiment (Fig. 9), we save the attributes, especially the location and the contamination status of all agents when we do a switch from ABM to EBM model. Then when re-assign to agents. The image represent the regeneration algorithm in order: (a) (e) step 0, (b) (f) before the switch, (c) (g) after the generation, (d) (h) step 100. The (a) (b) (c) (d) take the seed of random 0.123. The (e) (f) (g) (h) have the seed 3.14.

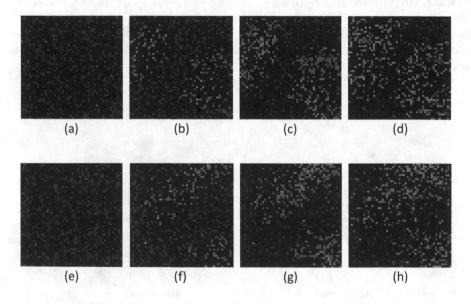

Fig. 9. Regeneration of spatial information algorithm.

6   Conclusion

This paper has proposed a hybrid approach combining modeling equations and agents, as well as its implementation on the modeling platform Gama. We are interested in the representation of this approach theoretical epidemiological models. We illustrate the construction of a class of models based on a SIR model in which people are represented by agents when their density is low, and equations with higher density, a tilt mechanism for moving from an approach to the other. We compare this model with existing models and present a method to determine the parameters during transitions between models. In particular, we seek to establish a link between the parameters of the mathematical model and representation of contacts and travel agents in a spatial environment. We are also interested in how to compensate the loss of information on spatial structures when moving an agent model to a mathematical model.

Acknowledgments. This publication has been made possible through support provided by the IRD-DSF.

References

1. Anh, N.T.N., Daniel, Z.J., Du, N.H., Drogoul, A., An, V.D.: A hybrid macro-micro pedestrians evacuation model to speed up simulation in road networks. In: Dechesne, F., Hattori, H., Mors, A., Such, J.M., Weyns, D., Dignum, F. (eds.) AMAS 2011 Workshops. LNCS (LNAI), vol. 7068, pp. 371–383. Springer, Heidelberg (2012). doi:10.1007/978-3-642-27216-5_28
2. Bacar, N.: McKendrick and Kermack on epidemic modelling (1926–1927). A Short History of Mathematical Population Dynamics, pp. 89–96. Springer, London (2011)
3. Brent Daniel, W., Hengartner, N.W., Rivera, M.K., Powell, D.R., McPherson, T.N.: An epidemiological model of spatial coupling for trips longer than the infectious period. Math. Biosci. **242**(1), 1–8 (2013)
4. Cavana, R.Y.: Modeling the Environment: An Introduction to System Dynamics Models of Environmental Systems. Andrew Ford Island Press, Washington (1999). viii + 401, pp. ISBN: 1-55963-601-7. Syst. Dyn. Rev. **19**(2), 171–173 (2003)
5. Ford, A.: Modeling the Environment, 2nd edn. Island Press, Washington (2010)
6. Gilbert, G.N.: Agent-Based Models. Number no. 07-153 in Quantitative Applications in the Social Sciences. Sage Publications, Los Angeles (2008)
7. Grignard, A., Taillandier, P., Gaudou, B., Vo, D.A., Huynh, N.Q., Drogoul, A.: GAMA 1.6: advancing the art of complex agent-based modeling and simulation. In: Boella, G., Elkind, E., Savarimuthu, B.T.R., Dignum, F., Purvis, M.K. (eds.) PRIMA 2013. LNCS (LNAI), vol. 8291, pp. 117–131. Springer, Heidelberg (2013). doi:10.1007/978-3-642-44927-7_9
8. Huynh, N.Q., Huynh, H.X., Drogoul, A., Cambier, C.: Co-modeling: an agent-based approach to support the coupling of heterogeneous models. In: Vinh, P.C., Vassev, E., Hinchey, M. (eds.) ICTCC 2014. LNICST, vol. 144, pp. 156–170. Springer, Heidelberg (2015). doi:10.1007/978-3-319-15392-6_16
9. Kermack, W.O., McKendrick, A.G.: A contribution to the mathematical theory of epidemics. Proc. R. Soc. Lond. A Math. Phys. Eng. Sci. **115**(772), 700–721 (1927)

10. Morvan, G.: Multi-level agent-based modeling - a literature survey, May 2012. arXiv:1205.0561
11. Nguyen, N.D., Phan, T.H.D., Nguyen, T.N.A., Drogoul, A., Zucker, J.-D.: Disk graph-based model: a graph theoretical approach for linking agent-based models and dynamical systems, pp. 1–4. IEEE, November 2010
12. Nguyen, N.D., Taillandier, P., Drogoul, A., Auger, P.: Inferring equation-based models from agent-based models: a case study in competition dynamics. In: Desai, N., Liu, A., Winikoff, M. (eds.) PRIMA 2010. LNCS (LNAI), vol. 7057, pp. 413–427. Springer, Heidelberg (2012). doi:10.1007/978-3-642-25920-3_30
13. Ngoc Ann, N.T., Daniel, Z.J., Hung, N.M., Alexis, D., Phuong, N.H.: Simulation of emergency evacuation of pedestrians along the road networks in Nhatrang City, pp. 1–6. IEEE, February 2012
14. Rahmandad, H., Sterman, J.: Heterogeneity and network structure in the dynamics of diffusion: comparing agent-based and differential equation models, vol. 54. Management science: journal of the Institute for Operations Research and the Management Sciences - Hanover, Md: INFORMS, ISSN: 0025-1909, ZDB-ID 2063451, vol. 54.2008, 5, pp. 998–1014. INFORMS, Hanover, Md (2008)
15. Railsback, S.F., Grimm, V.: Agent-Based and Individual-Based Modeling: A Practical Introduction. Princeton University Press, Princeton (2012)
16. Sukumar, S.R., Nutaro, J.J.: Agent-based vs. equation-based epidemiological models: a model selection case study, pp. 74–79. IEEE, December 2012
17. Van Dyke Parunak, H., Savit, R., Riolo, R.L.: Agent-based modeling vs. equation-based modeling: a case study and users' guide. In: Sichman, J.S., Conte, R., Gilbert, N. (eds.) MABS 1998. LNCS (LNAI), vol. 1534, pp. 10–25. Springer, Heidelberg (1998). doi:10.1007/10692956_2

Active Contour Based on Curvelet Domain in Medical Images

Vo Thi Hong Tuyet[✉]

Faculty of Information Technology, Ho Chi Minh City Open University,
Ho Chi Minh City, Vietnam
vothihongtuyet.dhbk@gmail.com

Abstract. Contours are important in computer vision. Among many algorithms proposed to describe the contours, snake is one of them. In snakes, the energy is minimized by the set of replacements. In natural images, Snake is easy for finding the traditional boundaries by the spline smoothness term. However, medical images are of a difficult problem. In this paper, we propose a method for active contour in medical images by combining the curvelet transform and B-spline. Our algorithm is to increase the ability for smoothing before reducing energy between boundaries which detects in curvelet domain. Compared with other recent methods, the proposed method is better.

Keywords: Active contour · Curvelet transform · Snake · B-spline · Smoothing

1 Introduction

Medical image processing is a concerning problem in the recent period. Some aspects are concerned such as: enhancing the quality – denoising and deblurring, object detection, contours, segmentation, etc. In case of contours, the boundary is detected by many methods to base on the object detection. After detecting, the active contour model continues to show the size and location of objects. In medicine, the contour detecting is very important because that is the basis for the doctor to make the diagnosis and treatment protocols. The faster and more accurate the treatment is, the better chance of living the patients have.

In the past, there are many algorithms which are proposed for object detection, such as: Sobel [3], Canny [2], Cuckoo Search [9], transform [7], etc. In these methods, the authors proposed the process for edge detection including: remove noise and make the input images smooth. They are very useful for other latter proposed methods which improve the quality of them. The curves are the idea of latter methods, and a prominent representative is B-spline [4–6]. B-spline is used to increase the smoothing steps. After the object detection step, the boundaries are described by Otsu method [14], active contour model [5, 6, 15], gradient vector flow [16], etc. Their results are not only in natural images but also in medical images as [17, 18, 20]. The combination between them is also very neccesary [5, 7, 18].

We can say that active contour model, Snake, is one of the popular methods used in recent years. The previous authors proposed the Snake processing based on the

© ICST Institute for Computer Sciences, Social Informatics and Telecommunications Engineering 2016
P.C. Vinh et al. (Eds.): ICTCC 2016, LNICST 168, pp. 325–333, 2016.
DOI: 10.1007/978-3-319-46909-6_29

transform, such as: wavelet transform [19, 20] or new generation of wavelet transform [18, 21]. In [20], the idea is to use self-affine mapping for weak boundaries in wavelet transform. That is the results of the improving quality from [19] also in wavelet domain.

In this paper, we propose a method to detect the objects and to show their contours in medical images. We use curvelet transform for remove noise and detect in objects. Then, we use B-spline for smoothing steps and also detect the objects in curvelet domain. When we have the object detection, we reconstruct and call it 1. We continue with period 2 which uses self-affine Snake to show the boundaries of output object detection in the previous step. The structure of this paper is as follows: the basis of curvelet transform, B-spline curves and active contour model are presented in Sect. 2. The proposed method is described clearly in Sect. 3. Our experiments and results are accentuated in Sect. 4, and Sect. 5 is the conclusions.

2 Curvelet and B-Spline Curves Model

2.1 Curvelet Transform

Curvelet is proposed by [12], this is the improvement from the ridgelet transform [11]. It is a popular method of representing edges and other singularities along curves. Curvelets decompose the input images into subbands with which each subband is a curve with width $\approx$ length^2. Then, each subband is analyzed by a local ridgelet transform [13]. The subbands in curvelet domain have the nonstandard form $[2^{2s}, 2^{2s+2}]$. The basic process of the digital realization for curvelet transform is given as follows [13]:

(i)   *Subband Decomposition.* The image f is decomposed into subbands:

$$f \mapsto (P_0 f, \Delta_1 f, \Delta_2 f, \ldots) \tag{1}$$

(ii) *Smooth Partitioning.* Each subband is smoothly windowed into "squares" of an appropriate scale (of sidelength $\sim 2^{-s}$):

$$\Delta_s f \mapsto (w_Q \Delta_s f)_{Q \in Q_s} \tag{2}$$

where w_Q is a collection of smooth window localized around dyadic squares:

$$Q = [k_1/2^s, (k_1 + 1)/2^s] \times [k_2/2^s, (k_2 + 1)/2^s] \tag{3}$$

(iii) *Renormalization.* Each resulting square is renormalized to unit scale

$$g_Q = (T_Q)^{-1}(w_Q \Delta_s f), \ Q \in Q_s \tag{4}$$

(iv) *Ridgelet Analysis.* Each square is analyzed via the discrete ridgelet transform.

2.2 B-Spline for Enhancing the Quality of Smoothing

In curves, a Bézier curve is a parametric curve and that is used popularly with model smooth curves in the previous, so is a B-spline. B-spline curve is similar to Bézier curve, but it gives more information. From the set of n + 1 control points, knot vector of m + 1 knots and a degree p. But it must satisfy: m = n + p + 1. The B-spline curve of degree p $(N_{i,\ u}(u))$ defined by these control points and knot vector U is [4]:

$$C(u) = \sum_{i=0}^{n} N_{i,p}(u)P \qquad (5)$$

where n + 1 control points $P_0, P_1, \ldots, P_n$ and a knot vector $U = \{u_0, u_1, \ldots, u_m\}$.

B-spline with the smoothing function $\beta_{2^{-1}}^{n+1}$ and $\beta_{2^{-1}}^{n+2}$ uses 2^{-1} level.

$$\psi^n(x) = \frac{d}{dx}\beta_{2^{-1}}^{n+1}(x) = 4(\beta^{n+1})^{(1)}(2x) \qquad (6)$$

$$\text{or} \quad \psi^n(x) = \frac{d^2}{dx^2}\beta_{2^{-1}}^{n+2}(x) = 8(\beta^{n+2})^{(2)}(2x) \qquad (7)$$

where n is the order of wavelet transform.

We define the desirable geometric characteristics of B-Spline curves and surfaces of degree p is defined as [4]:

$$N_{i,0}(u) = \begin{cases} 0 \ if \ u_i \le u \le u_{i+1} \\ 1, \ otherwise \end{cases} \qquad (8)$$

2.3 Active Contour Model

Active contour model with another name is snakes [5, 6, 15] which bases on an energy minimizing. In [15], the position of a snake parametrically by v(s) = (x(s), y(s)) and energy functional as:

$$E_{snake}^* = \int_0^1 E_{snake}(v(s))ds = \int_0^1 E_{int}(v(s)) + E_{image}(v(s)) + E_{con}(v(s))ds \qquad (9)$$

where E_{int} represents the internal energy of spline due to bending, E_{image} gives rise to the image forces, and E_{con} gives rise to the external constraint forces. Each element of (9) can be written:

$$E_{int} = (\alpha(s)|v_s(s)|^2 + \beta(s)|v_{ss}(s)|^2)/2 \qquad (10)$$

$$E_{con} = \frac{1}{2}(\alpha(s)|v_s(s)|^2) \qquad (11)$$

where $\alpha(s)$ and $\beta(s)$ are user-defined weights. The $\alpha(s)$ is a large weight for the continuity term penalizes. The distance between points in the contour is changed by $\alpha(s)$. And $\beta(s)$ is for the smoothing term of the contour. The energy of the images is the presentation of the features of the images. These features are calculated by [15]:

$$E_{image} = w_{line}E_{line} + w_{edge}E_{edge} + w_{term}E_{term} \tag{12}$$

where w_{line}, w_{edge}, w_{term} are weights of these salient features.

3   Describing Contours by the B-Spline and Active Contour Model in Curvelet Domain

Snake is one of the present contour methods by energy reducing. In recent methods, we have many ways to reduce the energy functions. In the previous methods, B-spline is used to combine with snake as [5] or single for edge detection [4]. In [19], the authors use self-affine snake as a new parametric for active contour in wavelet transform. They continued to improve in [20]. That is an example for using the parametric for active contour in transforms. In fact, the objects in medical images have many noises in them because of many reasons [10]. This is a difficult problem for object detection and then also for active contour. Curvelet transform is popular in denoising images [10, 13] because of the represented curves. In [18], the authors are proposed to segment in curvelet domain which includes two steps: the first step is the de-speckle noise from speckle images and the second step is the edge curves. In [21], curvelet continued to combine with snakes for segmentation. It means that curvelet is very useful for active contour or segmentation in medical images. Our idea is to use the transform in the proposed method because their aptitudes remove noise and detect objects in the detection process. We divide the proposed method into two periods which include: period 1 is the object detection in curvelet domain by combining between ridgelet in each subband of curvelet transform and B-spline for smoothing step; period 2 is to use self-affine Snake for active contour. This process is presented clear in Fig. 1.

In period 1, the proposed method begins with the decomposition into curvelet domain. The input of this period is the medical images, we use curvelet transform for denoising the image, curvelet's process is as follows:

(1) apply the à trous algorithm with scales and set $b_1 = b_{min}$
(2) for $j = 1, ..., j$ do
    a. partition the subband w_j with a block size b_j and apply the digital ridgelet transform to each block;
    b. if j modulo 2 = 1 then $b_{j+1} = 2b_j$;
    c. else $b_{j+1} = b_j$

The side length of the localizing windows is doubled at every other dyadic subband. In this step, we use threshold T for denoising:

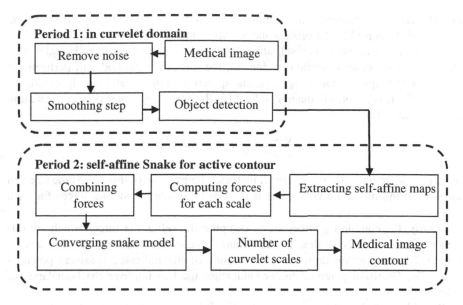

Fig. 1. Process flow of the proposed method.

$$T = \frac{1}{2^{j-1}} \left(\frac{\sigma}{\mu} \right) M \tag{13}$$

where j is number of level at which the shrinkage is applied, σ is the standard deviation, M is the median and μ is the mean of absolute wavelet coefficients. In here, we use the number of decomposition levels is 5 and 32 directions. After this step, the input medical images had become medical images denoising.

The proposed method continues with smoothing step by the B-spline curves. The below Eq. (14) is the other cases of (8), as follows:

$$N_{i,p} = \frac{u - u_i}{u_{i+p} - u_i} N_{i,p-1}(u) + \frac{u_{i+p+1} - u_i}{u_{i+p+1} - u_{i+1}} N_{i+1,p-1}(u) \tag{14}$$

The distance measure is calculated to base on the 8-connected neighborhood. Then, the smooth curves look like straight in sub-images. In each sub-image, a local ridgelet transform applies in its with multiple scales. The result is the medical images denoising. We call this images as I and with c_J is a coarse or smooth of the image I, w_j is the scale details at 2^{-j}. We have Eq. (15) for spatial partitioning of each block:

$$I(x,y) = c_J(x,y) + \sum_{j=1}^{J} w_j(x,y) \tag{15}$$

Based on the coefficients value which calculates in curvelet domain to locate the around edges and in the right directional of blocks. At the end of period 1, the output of this process is the medical image which is detected the location, size of objects.

Objects have the boundaries and continue to be improved by self-affine Snake in the next period. In period 2, the process include five steps:

Firstly, the extracting the self-affine maps. The extracting step includes two sub-steps. From some M section of domain, the allocation method will perform the parameters of maps include: r_i, s_i, t_i, p_i, and q_i using a block matching algorithm.

Secondly, r_i is to form domain, $r_i = [s_i, t_i]$ is the vector of center point. A matching cose is evaluated by:

$$C = \sum\nolimits_{x \in M_i} |g(x) = g(m_i(x))| \tag{16}$$

where $g(x)$ is the intensity values for all images. The purpose of this step is the selected values from the minimum cost – this is the results of the computing forces for each scale.

Thirdly, the combining forces are to compute the sefl-affine forces which are difference between wavelet scales. The self-affine force is calculated in each pixel a = (x, y) in the decomposition domain by the values of the indicated Gaussian potential forces. The Gaussian potential forces values are used to improve the boundaries of period 1.

Fourthly, self-affine forces are applied for all image pixels that finished all forces. The boundary is moved by the sum of Eqs. (10) and (11). It means that the intensity values can be decreased or increased by this case. Equation (12) is calculated in here by the boundaries values which are given by self-affine forces.

Finally, the Gaussian potential force is given from the combining forces is the key for the increasing of capture range. This is the number of coefficient scales which uses in reconstruction steps of curvelet transform. If we call n is the number of curvelet scales and L is the distance which is calculated to base on the 8-connected neighborhood, we will the number of curvelet scales be:

$$2^n x R > L \text{ and } n > \log_2(L/R) \tag{17}$$

At the end of period 2, the output is the boundaries which have improved by the self-affine snake. And the continued step is the reconstruction the output images from curvelet domain.

4   Experiments and Results

Medical images have not many objects in each image because of the direction from the doctors. The boundary around each object is very necessarily clear. As mentioned in the previous section, we propose a method for object detection and improve the quality of boundaries from medical images. In the proposed method, we use the features of curvelet transform for denoising medical images and B-spline for smoothing images. That is the prepared step for the object detection in curvelet domain. In this paper, we use 5 levels for decomposition of the input medical images into curvelet domain. Then, we apply threshold to remove noise details. This is the improvement process for medical images which have weak objects. In other methods of object detection, the removing noise uses Gaussian filter to remove. However, we herely propose cur-velet because it is the best choice of the represented curves. B-spline is used for smoothing steps to prepare for the detection in curvelet domain. This is the end of period 1 in our algorithm. In period 2, the boundaries given from period 1 are improved by the self-affine snake.

The results of our proposed method are compared with the other methods such as: Otsu method [14] and *curvelet-based geodesic snake method* [21]. We have many edges and clear contour more than other methods. Our dataset is the medical images collected in many hospitals. There are more than 1000 medical images, and in many sizes: 256 × 256, 512 × 512, 1024 × 1024. We test many medical images from this dataset. In here, we show some cases when we test and compare them. In Fig. 2, we test the medical image which has a strong object.

In this case, Fig. 2(a) is the original medical image. The result of Otsu method is

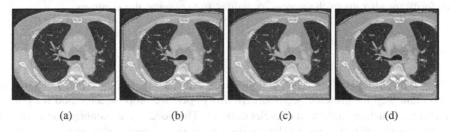

(a)   (b)   (c)   (d)

Fig. 2. The results of boundaries detection by other methods with strong object. (a) The strong object in the original medical image. (b) Boundaries detection by Otsu method [14]. (c) Boundaries detection by *curvelet-based geodesic snake method* [21]. (d) Boundaries detection by the proposed method.

Fig. 2(b), the result of *curvelet-based geodesic snake method* is Fig. 2(c) and (d) is the result of our proposed method. We can see that the boundaries detected by the pro-posed method is better than the result in Fig. 2(b) and (c).

In Fig. 3, we test the medical image which has a weak object. A weak object is an object of which boundaries are blurred and noised. In this case, we use Gaussian noise and Gaussian blur added to medical images with the variance noise is 0.00005 and the values of point spread function of Gaussian blur. The reason of our selection is Gaussian is the plus noise and blur into pixels of medical images. The plus noise and blur is popular in medical images.

The result of Otsu is Fig. 3(b), *curvelet-based geodesic snakes method* is Fig. 3(c). We see that there are clearer boundaries by our method, Fig. 3(d), than by other methods.

From the results from Figs. 2, 3 and many other test cases, we conclude that the results of the proposed method are better than Otsu method [14] and *curvelet-based geodesic snake method* [21] in two cases: strong object and weak object. Our exper-iment is the combination between transform and active contour model for presenting the boundaries. Especially with medical images, the transform is useful for object

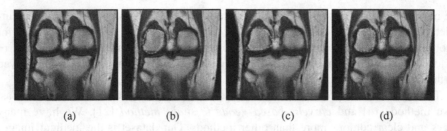

| (a) | (b) | (c) | (d) |

Fig. 3. The results of boundaries detection by other methods with weak object. (a) The weak object in a noised and blurred medical image. (b) Boundaries detection by Otsu method [14]. (c) Boundaries detection by *curvelet-based geodesic snake method* [21]. (d) Boundaries detection by the proposed method.

detection and active contour model. The coefficient values of decomposition step of transform are also given the neccesary values for showing the contours.

5 Conclusions

Active contour model is used widely in boundaries detection. So, the object detection is a important step for presented contours. In this paper, we propose a method for object detection and active contour in curvelet domain. This idea is the combination between the transform and self-affine Snake. In decomposition domain, although each object will be strong or weak the object will also be detected and improved the quality of boundaries. The proposed method includes two periods: object detection in curvelet domain by denoising with curvelet and smoothing with B-spline, self-affine Snake for active contour model. The results of our algorithm have tested in medical images and compared with other methods such as: Otsu method [14], and *curvelet-based geodesic snake method* [21]. The compared results make known that the proposed method is better than the other ones.

References

1. Chan, T.F., Vese, L.A.: Active contours without edges. IEEE Trans. Image Process. **10**(2), 266–277 (2001)
2. Canny, J.: A computational approach to edge detection. IEEE Trans. Pattern Anal. Mach. Intell. PAMI **8**(6), 679–698 (1986)
3. Vincent, O.R., Folorunso, O.: A descriptive algorithm for sobel image edge detection. In: Proceedings of Informing Science & IT Education Conference (InSITE) (2009)
4. Wang, Y., Cai, Y.: Multiscale B-spline wavelet for edge detection. Sci. China (Series A) **38**(4), 499–512 (1995)
5. Brigger, P., Unser, M.: Multi-scale B-spline snakes for general contour detection. In: Wavelet Applications in Signal and Image Processing VI, SPIE, vol. 3458 (1998)
6. Brigger, P., Hoeg, J., Unser, M.: B-Spline snakes: a flexible tool for parametric contour detection. IEEE Trans. Image Process. **9**(9), 1484–1496 (2000)

7. Zhang, L., Bao, P.: Edge detection by scale multiplication in wavelet domain. Pattern Recogn. Lett. **23**, 1771–1784 (2002). Elsevier
8. Binh, N.T.: Image contour based on context aware in complex wavelet domain. Hum. Centric Comput. Inf. Sci. **5**, 14 (2015). Springer Open Journal
9. Gonzalez, C.I., Castro, J.R., Melin, P., Castillo, O.: Cuckoo search algorithm for the optimization of type-2 fuzzy image edge detection systems. In: IEEE Congress on Evolutionary Computation (CEC), pp. 449–455(2015)
10. Binh, N.T., Khare, A.: Image Denoising, Deblurring and Object Tracking, A New Generation Wavelet Based Approach. LAP LAMBERT Academic Publishing (2013)
11. Candes, J.: Ridgelets. Theory and Applications. Stanford University (1998)
12. Zhang, J.M.F., Starck, J.L.: Wavelets, ridgelets and curvelets for poisson noise removal. IEEE Trans. Image Process. **17**, 1093–1108 (2008)
13. Starck, J.L., Candès, E.J., Donoho, D.L.: The curvelet transform for image denoising. IEEE Trans. Image Process. **11**, 670–684 (2002)
14. Otsu, N.: A threshold selection method from gray-level histograms. IEEE Trans. Syst. Man. Cyber. **9**(1), 62–66 (1979)
15. Kass, M., Witkin, A., Terzopoulos, D.: Snakes: Active Contour Models. Schlumberger Palo Alto Research (1988)
16. Xu, C., Prince, J.L.: Gradient Vector Flow: A New External Force For Snakes, pp. 66—71. IEEE Computer Society (1997)
17. Gupta, R., Elamvazuthi, I., Dass, S.C., Faye, I., Vasant, P., George, J., Izza, F.: Curvelet based automatic segmentation of supraspinatus tendon from ultrasound image: a focused assistive diagnostic method. BioMedical Engineering Online (2014)
18. Binh, N.T., Thanh, N.C.: Object detection of speckle image base on curvelet domain. Asian Res. Publish. Netw. (ARPN) **2**(3), 14–16 (2007)
19. Saadatmand-Tarzjan, M., Ghassemian, H.: Self-affine Snake: A New Parametric Active Contour, pp. 492–495. IEEE (2007)
20. Saadatmand-Tarzjan, M., Ghassemian, H.: Self-affine snake for medical image segmentation. Elsevier Journal (2015)
21. Shan, H., Ma, J.: Curvelet-based geodesic snakes for image segmentation with multiple objects. J. Pattern Recogn. Lett. **31**, 355–360 (2010)

Computational and Comparative Study on Multiple Kernel Learning Approaches for the Classification Problem of Alzheimer's Disease

Ahlam Mallak[1,2], Jeonghwan Gwak[1,3], Jong-In Song[1,3],
and Sang-Woong Lee[1,2(✉)]
for the Alzheimer's Disease Neuroimaging initiative

[1] National Research Center for Dementia, Gwangju 61452, Republic of Korea
ahlam.mallak@ymail.com, james.han.gwak@gmail.com,
jisong@gist.ac.kr, swlee@chosun.ac.kr
[2] Department of Computer Engineering, Chosun University, Gwangju 61996,
South Korea
[3] School of Information and Communications, Gwangju Institute of Science and
Technology, Gwangju 61005, South Korea

Abstract. Several classification methods have been proposed for assisting computer-aided diagnosis of Alzheimer's disease (AD). Among them, classification methods including (i) support vector machines (SVM), and (ii) generalized multiple kernel learning (GMKL) are getting increasing attention in recent studies. Nevertheless, there is little research on the comparison among these methods to find a better classification framework and further analysis of brain imaging features in the study of AD. To deal with this issue, we carry out exhaustive comparative study in this work to evaluate efficiency of these different classification methods. For the experiments, we used FreeSurfer mean cortical thickness dataset downloaded from the ADNI database (adni.loni.usc.edu) baseline data. The classification accuracy (in classifying the three classes CN, LMCI, AD) of comparative methods has been evaluated using 3-fold cross validation. From the comparative study, we could observe that GMKL is the most promising framework if the sufficient training data can be provided.

Keywords: Alzheimer's disease · Support vector machines · Multiple kernel learning · Generalized multiple kernel learning

Data used in preparation of this article were obtained from the Alzheimer's disease Neuroimaging Initiative (ADNI) database (adni.loni.usc.edu). As such, the investigators within the ADNI contributed to the design and implementation of ADNI and/or provided data but did not participate in analysis or writing of this report. A complete listing of ADNI investigators can be found at: http://adni.loni.usc.edu/wpcontent/uploads/how_to_apply/ADNI_Aknowledgement_List.pdf

P.C. Vinh et al. (Eds.): ICTCC 2016, LNICST 168, pp. 334–341, 2016.
DOI: 10.1007/978-3-319-46909-6_30

1   Introduction

Alzheimer's disease (AD) is a neurodegenerative disease that causes degenerative changes in the neurons, which results in progressive loss of memory and several other cognitive functions. Alzheimer's disease is the most common form of dementia [1]. Currently, AD is generally detected at a late stage at which treatment can only slow the progression of cognitive decline. This is especially important for individuals with late mild cognitive impairment (LMCI), who are at high risk to develop AD in the near future comparing to cognitively normal (CN) or the other mild cognitive impairment (MCI) groups.

The main goal of this study is to elucidate different classification approaches based on kernel machines in differentiating the groups of AD, LMCI, and CN subjects given mean FreeSurfer cortical thickness data for 365 subjects of age range between 70 and 80 years old, which include 107 CN subjects, 76 AD patients and 182 LMCI subjects.

Data used in the preparation of this article were obtained from the Alzheimer's disease Neuroimaging Initiative (ADNI) database (adni.loni.usc.edu). The ADNI was launched in 2003 as a public-private partnership, led by Principal Investigator Michael W. Weiner, MD. The primary goal of ADNI has been to test whether serial magnetic resonance imaging (MRI), positron emission tomography (PET), other biological markers, and clinical and neuropsychological assessment can be combined to measure the progression of mild cognitive impairment (MCI) and early Alzheimer's disease (AD). For up-to-date information, see www.adni-info.org.

The organization of the paper is as follows: Sect. 2 introduces the kernel machines including SVM, multiple kernel learning (MKL), and generalized MKL (GMKL). In Sect. 3, we briefly mention the data used in this work. Section 4 describes the experimental results and comparative study. Finally, the conclusions and future work are discussed in Sect. 5.

2   Kernel Machine Algorithms

2.1   Support Vector Machines (SVM)

In this section we briefly sketch the SVM algorithm and its motivation. A more detailed description on SVM can be found in [2, 3].

Let us start things off with a fairly simple case of two linearly separable classes. Given a two-class, separable data set $D = \{(x_i, y_i)\}_{i=1}^{l}$ of labeled examples, where $y_i \in \{-1, 1\}$ we want to determine which one, among infinitely many linear classifiers separating the data, will have the smallest generalization error. One good choice is the hyperplane (i.e., the decision boundary) that makes the maximum margin between the two classes in which margin is defined as the sum of the distances of the hyperplane from the closest point (i.e., the support vector) of the two classes.

For non-separable two-class problems, we can still consider the hyperplane that maximizes the margin and minimizes misclassification error. The tradeoff between the margin and misclassification error is controlled by a positive constant chosen in advance. It can be shown that the solution to this problem is a linear classifier given as

$$f(x) = sign\left(\sum\nolimits_{i+1}^{i} \alpha_i y_i x^T x_i + b\right) \tag{1}$$

When the data is not linearly separable, slack variables $\xi_1, \ldots, \xi_N$ with $\xi_i \geq 0$ are introduced as

$$y_i(w.x_i + b) \geq 1 - \xi_i, \quad i = 1, \ldots, N \tag{2}$$

The purpose of the variables ξ_i is to allow misclassified points, which have their corresponding $\xi_i > 1$ Therefore, $\sum \xi_i$ has an upper bound on the number of training errors. While the first term is minimized to control learning capacity as in the separable case, the second term is added to control the number of misclassified points.

The input data is mapped into a high-dimensional feature space through some nonlinear mapping chosen a priori [4].

Given a kernel $K(x_i, y_i) = \varphi(x_i).\varphi(x_j)$ where $\varphi(x)$ is the mapping function of x in the feature space, only K is needed in the training algorithm and φ is never used explicitly. Conversely, given a symmetric positive kernel $K(x, y)$, Mercer's theorem [2] indicates that there exists a mapping φ such that $K(x, y) = \varphi(x) \cdot \varphi(y)$. Then, the decision function becomes

$$f(x) = sign\left(\sum\nolimits_{i=1}^{N} \alpha_i y_i K(x_i, x) + b\right) \tag{3}$$

SVMs are originally designed for binary classification. Since three classes are available in the classification process, we need an appropriate multiclass-based classification method such as multiclass SVMs [4]. There are two possible ways for such purpose by combining several binary classifiers (i.e., SVMs): (1) "one against one" [5] that applies pairwise comparisons between classes by combining two binary classifiers, and (2) "one against the others" [6] that compares a given class with all the others putting together. According to the comparison study [7], it is known that the accuracies of these methods are almost the same. As a consequence, most researches have been chosen the one with the lowest complexity and thus "one against the others." is the commonly adopted approach in many practical applications. In this work, we also used the approach.

2.2 Multiple Kernel SVM (MK-SVM)

As discussed in Sect. 2.1, SVMs are one of the kernel approaches that can be used efficiently to solve classification or regression problems [12]. For solving non-linear separable problems using SVMs, we need to create a function called the kernel function $K(x, x')$. Let us assume that $\{x_i, y_i\}_{i=1}^{l}$ is the used learning set, where x_i is a subject with some feature(s) belongs to some feature space X and y_i is the intended label for some pattern of subjects x_i. Then, the learning problem that the kernel learning needs to solve is formulated as

$$f(x) = \sum_{i=1}^{l} \alpha_i^* K(x_i, x) + b^*, \tag{4}$$

where α_i^* and b^* are the coefficients to be learned from the training process, while $K(\cdot, \cdot)$ is a given positive definite kernel.

Many recent studies have proven that using multiple kernels can enhance the performance of the learning process, when compared to single kernel solutions [8, 9]. Thus, a new approach has been developed as a convex combination of basis kernels $K(x, x')$

$$K(x, x') = \sum_{m=1}^{M} d_m K_m(x, x'), \text{ with } d_m \geq 0, \sum_{m=1}^{M} d_m = 1, \tag{5}$$

where M shows the number of kernels used, while K_m is the basis kernel which can be any classical kernel (such as Gaussian kernels) with different parameter values. Thus, the main idea for multiple kernel learning is finding the suitable kernel parameters (i.e., weights) d_m that gives the optimal solution of the problem as well as finding the optimal classification coefficients α_i^*.

2.3   Generalized Multiple Kernel Learning (GMKL)

GMKL is an optimized algorithm of MKL aims to learn the optimal parameters of the SVM. Specifically, it estimates the kernel parameters d as the MKL (in Sect. 2.2) does, which enables it finds more optimal solutions for this function $(x) = w^t \varphi_d(x) + b$.

The GMKL process is summarized as follows [10]:

(1) Choose a non-convex formulation that is because the kernel combinations $w_k^t w_k$ and the weights for each kernel should not approach to zero.
(2) The regularizer $r(d)$ should be placed in the objective and given a scalar parameter within it.
(3) We can relax the constraint $d \geq 0$ by making it more generalized. As a result, the learned kernel parameters are required to be positive and definite values.
(4) We need to check whether the gradient descent algorithm whether it is still applicable or not, by checking the gradient of the regularizer $\nabla_d r$ if it exists or not.

The optimization problem $f(x) = \sum_{i=1}^{n} \alpha_i \sum_{m=1}^{M} d_m k_m(x, x_i) + b$ can be divided into two nested loops; inner and outer. The outer loop $\sum_{i=1}^{n} \alpha_i k(x, x_i) + b$ is used to learn SVM parameters. While, the inner loop $k(x, x_i) = \sum_{m=1}^{M} d_m k_m(x, x_i)$ is used to learn the kernel parameters (weights) d.

From the above operations, compared to MKL, GMKL can learn general kernel combinations which is subject to general regularizations on the kernel operations.

3   Classification Study Data

All source imaging data used in this paper consist of 1.5 T T1-weighted MRI volumes in the NIfTI format downloaded from the ADNI1: Complete 1Yr 1.5T Data Collection. All images were processed using three neuroimaging software pipelines: (1) Free-Surfer, (2) Advanced Normalization Tools (ANTs), and (3) Mindboggle the result of this process are tables consist of many features from many different regions of the brain.

FreeSurfer (https://surfer.nmr.mgh.harvard.edu/) is an open source software suite that is used for human brain MRI processing and analysis. Many processes can be done using FreeSurfer, such as skull stripping, image registration, subcortical segmentation, cortical surface reconstruction, fMRI analysis and much more.

In this work, FreeSurfer mean cortical thickness data were used for AD, LMCI and CN subjects of age range between 70 and 80 years old. Table 1 lists the results of (clinical) diagnosis and demographics of the dataset.

4   Experimental Results

We tackle the multiclass classification problem of the baseline FreeSurfer mean thickness data to find the best framework to study Alzheimer's disease. The classification framework adopts the different kernel methods: (1) multi-class SVM using one vs all multiclass classification and the Gaussian radial basis function (rbf) kernel with a quadratic programming method to separate the hyperplane, (2) the standard MKL algorithm, and (3) the GMKL algorithm. Both MKL and GMKL used 15 rbf kernels to measure the efficiency in terms of accuracy and computational time for the comparison purpose. Tables 2 and 3 show the experimental results for each group of different number of training samples. Note that for each method, the highest accuracy in Table 2 and the lowest execution time in Table 3 are highlighted in boldface.

Table 2 lists the classification accuracy results. From the experimental reults, we could see that multi-class SVM tended to perform the worst with the accuracy of only 60 % when almost all the data is used for training and the rest for testing. The relatively poor performance was due to the fact that multi-class SVM uses only one kernel comparing to the other techniques which combine many kernels in different scenarios. In contrast, the highest accuracy was obtained for GMKL when only ten training samples were used and the rest fo testing with the accuracy up to 80 %. In addition, there is a very tight coupling between the two in MKL and GMKL in terms of the accuracy.

The comparison between the previous methods was also done for computational time (in terms of elapsed time) as well. Although GMKL achieved the highest

Table 1. Statistics of the dataset used for training and testing.

	No. of subjects	Diagnosis results (CN/LMCI/AD)	Gender	
			Male	Female
ADNI1 data	365	107/182/76	222	143

Table 2. Comparison results of accuracy

No. of training samples	Multi-class SVM (%)	MKL (%)	GMKL (%)
10	49.57	49.80	**80**
20	49.56	49.85	**80**
30	49.85	**53.01**	80
50	**50.47**	51.79	68
100	50.18	49.33	65
200	50.90	–	66.5
360	60	–	–

Table 3. Comparison results of execution time for both the training and testing phases

No of training samples	Multi-class SVM (sec.)	MKL (sec.)	GMKL (sec.)
10	1.308	**0.349**	540.60
20	0.557	0.358	490.20
30	0.552	0.446	453.60
50	0.510	0.771	431.46
100	0.464	1.711	290.90
200	0.361	–	**174.32**
360	**0.300**		
		–	–

classification accuracy, it consumed the largest time of roughly 540 s. However, both multi-class SVM and the standard MKL achieved the accuracy of almost 60 % and 54 % in only 0.3 and 0.446 s, respectively. As shown in Table 3.

Finally, the performance of the three methods multi-class SVM, MKL and GMKL in terms of classification accuracy was also validated using the 3-fold cross-validation technique. In 3-fold cross-validation, the overall dataset is divided randomly into 3 equal sized partitions. Each time a single partition is used for testing and the remaining two partitions (i.e., 2/3 from the total dataset) are used for the training process. This process is repeated three times (i.e., same as the number of partitions or folds), so that each time one different partition is used for testing. Finally, the accuracy is measured in each time and the overall accuracy is the averaged accuracy from the three trials. As a result, as shown in Table 4, the accuracy of each method after the validation using 3-fold cross validation was 49.58 % for multi-class SVM, 52.61 % for MKL and 75.75 % for GMKL. Similar to the previous results, we observed that GMKL has the highest accuracy among all these kernel methods when we validate using 3-fold cross validation method.

Table 4. Comparison results of accuracy using 3 cross-validation

No of training samples	Multi-class SVM (%)	MKL (%)	GMKL (%)
	49.58	52.61	75.75

5 Conclusions and Future Work

Several classification methods have been studied for the computer-aided diagnosis of Alzheimer's disease. Classification methods such SVM, MKL and GMKL have been widely used in recent studies. However, there is lack of comparisons for these methods to find a better framework for classification and analysis of brain imaging features in the study of Alzheimer's disease. In this paper, the efficiency of the classification methods including SVM, the standard MKL, and GMKL were compared in terms of accuracy and execution time. From the experimental results, we could verify that GMKL achieved the highest accuracy among all the others although it requires more computational time. To extend this work, we can include other methods such as generalized and/or adaptive multiple kernel learning approaches. Also, other different multimodal features (such as PET imaging and other clinical facts) can be incorporated in the framework to build more robust framework, which is also one of our research agendas.

Acknowledgments. This paper was supported by the National Research Foundation (NRF) grant funded by the Korean government (NRF-2013R1A1A2012543,NRF-2014M3C7A 1046050).

Data collection and sharing for this project was funded by the Alzheimer's Disease Neuroimaging Initiative (ADNI) (National Institutes of Health Grant U01 AG024904) and DOD ADNI (Department of Defense award number W81XWH-12-2-0012). ADNI is funded by the National Institute on Aging, the National Institute of Biomedical Imaging and Bioengineering, and through Data collection and sharing for this project was funded by the Alzheimer's Disease Neuroimaging Initiative (ADNI) (National Institutes of Health Grant U01 AG024904) and DOD ADNI (Department of Defense award number W81XWH-12-2-0012). ADNI is funded by the National Institute on Aging, the National Institute of Biomedical Imaging and Bioengineering, and through generous contributions from the following: AbbVie, Alzheimer's Association; Alzheimer's Drug Discovery Foundation; Araclon Biotech; BioClinica, Inc.; Biogen; Bristol-Myers Squibb Company; CereSpir, Inc.; Eisai Inc.; Elan Pharmaceuticals, Inc.; Eli Lilly and Company; EuroImmun; F. Hoffmann-La Roche Ltd and its affiliated company Genentech, Inc.; Fujirebio; GE Healthcare; IXICO Ltd.; Janssen Alzheimer Immunotherapy Research & Development, LLC.; Johnson & Johnson Pharmaceutical Research & Development LLC.; Lumosity; Lundbeck; Merck & Co., Inc.; Meso Scale Diagnostics, LLC.; NeuroRx Research; Neurotrack Technologies; Novartis Pharmaceuticals Corporation; Pfizer Inc.; Piramal Imaging; Servier; Takeda Pharmaceutical Company; and Transition Therapeutics. The Canadian Institutes of Health Research is providing funds to support ADNI clinical sites in Canada. Private sector contributions are facilitated by the Foundation for the National Institutes of Health (www.fnih. org). The grantee organization is the Northern California Institute for Research and Education, and the study is coordinated by the Alzheimer's disease Cooperative Study at the University of California, San Diego. ADNI data are disseminated by the Laboratory for Neuro Imaging at the University of Southern California.

References

1. Hebert, L.E., Beckett, L.A., Scherr, P.A., Evans, D.A.: Annual incidence of Alzheimer disease in the United States projected to the years 2000 through 2050. Alzheimer Dis. Assoc. Disord. **15**(4), 169–173 (2001)
2. Vapnik, V.: The Nature of Statistical Learning Theory. Springer, New York (1995)
3. Cortes, C., Vapnik, V.: Support vector networks. Mach. Learn. **20**, 1–25 (1995)
4. Chapelle, O., Haffner, P., Vapnik, V.: Support vector machines for histogram-based image classification. IEEE Trans. Neural Netw. **10**(5), 1055–1064 (1999)
5. Boser, B. E., Guyon, I. M., Vapnik, V. N.: A training algorithm for optimal margin classifier. In: Proceeding of 5th ACM Workshop on Computational Learning Theory, Pittsburgh, PA, pp. 144–152 (1992)
6. Pontil, M., Verri, A.: Support vector machines for 3-D object recognition. IEEE Trans. Pattern Anal. Mach. Intell. **20**, 637–646 (1998)
7. Blanz, V., Schölkopf, B., Bülthoff, H., Burges, C., Vapnik, V., Vetter, T.: Comparison of view-based object recognition algorithms using realistic 3D models. In: Malsburg, C., Seelen, W., Vorbrüggen, J.C., Sendhoff, B. (eds.) ICANN 1996. LNCS, vol. 1112, pp. 251–256. Springer, Heidelberg (1996). doi:10.1007/3-540-61510-5_45
8. Lanckriet, G.R.G., Deng, M., Cristianini, N., Jordan, M.I., Noble, W.S.: Kernel-based data fusion and its application to protein function prediction in yeast. In: Pacific symposium on Biocomputing, p. 300 (2004)
9. Rakotomamonjy, A., Bach, F., Canu, S., Grandvalet, Y.: SimpleMKL. J. Mach. Learn. Res. **9**, 2491–2521 (2008)
10. Varma, M., Babu, B.R.: More generality in efficient multiple kernel learning. In: Proceedings of the International Conference on Machine Learning, Montreal, Canada, pp. 1065–1072 (2009)

Improving Salient Object via Global Contrast Combined with Color Distribution

Nguyen Duy Dat[1] and Nguyen Thanh Binh[2(✉)]

[1] Faculty of Information Technology, Ly Tu Trong Technical College,
Ho Chi Minh City, Vietnam
duydatspk@gmail.com
[2] Faculty of Computer Science and Engineering, Ho Chi Minh City University of Technology,
VNU-HCM, Ho Chi Minh City, Vietnam
ntbinh@hcmut.edu.vn

Abstract. Salient object detection has many applications for computer vision field. In this paper, we have proposed a method for improving salient object detection which is a combination of global contrast and color distribution. The proposed method has three main steps: to reduce color space, to create salient map and to increase the object quality. The main problems of previous research consist of the consumption of time and the quality of salient map. The proposed method solves two above problems. We used a large dataset to test the proposed method. The proposed method's result is better than other methods in two points: the running time and the quality of salient map.

Keywords: Global contrast · Hard threshold · Saliency map · Derivative operator · Color distribution

1 Introduction

In real scenes, computer vision is useful in control roads, airports, offices, etc. Those tasks need to process inputted images in order to detect the contrasting areas, which contain interesting objects. Detecting and segmenting are the most important tasks in computer vision applications. In the past, many researches had to enhance the quality of objects. The previous methods show good results in many datasets but it still needs improving.

To extract an object in an image, the researchers usually use the salient map technique because it bases on the global contrast, which is easy to point out the region of salient object. In order to imply that technique, there is many an approach, which is global contrast, local contrast or blurring. Each of them has private advantages and disadvantages but global contrast has showed its benefits for instance, it is likely to easily identify the region of interesting object in images. Specifically, the global contrast approach needs to use a necessary component, the color reduction. One of the most recent researches applies the soft threshold implement.

In this paper, we have proposed a method for improving salient object detection using the combination of global contrast and color distribution, a variation of method

© ICST Institute for Computer Sciences, Social Informatics and Telecommunications Engineering 2016
P.C. Vinh et al. (Eds.): ICTCC 2016, LNICST 168, pp. 342–350, 2016.
DOI: 10.1007/978-3-319-46909-6_31

which was published by Dat et al. [1]. To reduce color space, we used hard thresholds instead of soft thresholds. The main problems of our previous research [10] are the executing time and the complex structure of the first step (the reducing color space). We have focus to improve this structure. Our experiment used a public dataset from Cheng [11]. The result of proposed method is better than that of [1] in two points: the running time and the quality of salient map. The rest of the paper is organized as follows: in Sect. 2, we describe related works; details of the proposed method are given in Sect. 3; the results of the proposed method are presented in Sect. 4 and our conclusions are made in Sect. 5.

2 Related Works

Recently, many researches proposed the methods for contrast as deblurring method, combination between colors, edges and calculation. Their main purpose is to identify the interesting area but it takes so much time to solve an image. However, they have to focus on different aspects such as concentrating on key information, cutting-off unnecessary operators or creating a new computation model. Those methods are divided into two main groups: global approach and local direction. Each of them has advantageous and disadvantageous points.

The global contrast approach sets the salient value to a color basing on its distance and frequency to other colors in a specific image.

Achanta [3] used frequency of colors combined with color distance in order to measure the saliency value faster; however, there is still a large number of calculations because the possible color is 256^3. Paper [2, 3] gave an important upgrade to Achanta's method. Zhai [4] measured the saliency of each pixel, using its contrast to all other pixels. The advantage is the quality of salient map, yet main problems in which only the light dimension is used and its running time is so slow.

The local contrast aims to find out the salient value of a region by using its contrast and its salient value of neighbor areas. The quality of salient map in this method is better than the former instance because it carefully calculates the salient value for all regions. Rahtu [6] used conditional random field (CRF) to measure and to estimate the salient map. Walther [7] used attends to proto-object (APO), which would create the map. Murray [8] implied spatial pooling mechanism (SPM) in his research.

Most of them focus on color reduction by blurring the inputted image in hope of removing the small details and keeping the main features. Achanta [8] applied the color luminance measure (CLM) to all regions in the hope that we can generate a better salient picture. His research received good results but the remained problems such as: boundaries of interesting object are not well kept in all cases.

Other researchers combine some of these above methods. Tie [10] used center surround histogram (CSD) method combining global contrast and local contrast to use all advantages from both approaches. Additional, important ideas in [12, 13], analyzing the context and background, give us more solution to improve our method. Papers [14–16] suggest new approaches to us in order to reduce errors in current researches, which are used to improve the quality of objects. All the above methods have their own advantages and disadvantages. However, the salient object detection must continuously be improved.

3 Salient Object Detection Based on Combination Global Contrast and Color Distribution

Salient object detection is a hard work. In this section, we present a method for salient object detection, a variation of method which was published by Dat et al. [1].

In this paper, we improve the algorithm in [1] in two steps: to reduce color space and to increase the object quality. The remaining steps are the algorithm which was presented in [1]. The steps of the proposed method are described below:

Firstly, all inputted images are going to be deducted its color space. We replace the soft threshold method in [1] by using hard threshold method. All inputted images will be moved to LAB color space, and then 256 color values in each dimension will be split into twelve-distinct hard thresholds. After that all remained colors should be compressed by replacing low frequency colors by high frequency colors. We use hard threshold technique instead of soft threshold method because of following reasons:

(i) Decrement of executing time. In the soft threshold, the minimum and maximum values must be extracted from each channel, we have three color channels so the total operations should be $O(N)$, in which N is the total number of pixels in an image. Furthermore, the range between maximum and minimum value is going to be split into twelve parts. In fact, researchers usually use some detail methods to refine these values because they have to deal with special cases, for instance, the range has less than 24 values and we have to split them into 12 parts. That is the reason why researchers have to think over a solution for such cases. In contrast, our method automatically splits 256 values into hard twelve parts; its complexity is constant progress, $O(1)$. As a result of this solution, we do not need to apply any refining method inside this stage.

(ii) All mediated results between steps are images so the better result of the former step is, the faster the latter step will be. It means the results of these steps are affected by its previous step.

(iii) We have chosen the best coefficient for the color-reduction step. That number must be adapted to two conditions: shortening the running time and retaining the image quality as much as possible.

The distinction between these methods is the distribution of values in a color channel. The dynamic thresholds, soft thresholds are based on the maximum and minimum values in each dimension of a specific image while the hard thresholds do not care about this trouble so it eliminates time from spending for this stage.

Secondly, salient map will be created. This step includes three small parts such as to evaluate salient value of each color, to smooth the salient value of neighboring colors and lastly, a salient map for respective images will be generated.

To get the interesting object, we extract the main object in the highest contrast area. Following it, the images are going to be wiped out all wrong pixels which belong to the background or their colors are similar to the environment. After that, we reuse the HC-map algorithm and then apply the derivative operator on the distances between colors in order to remove failed pixels as [1].

Finally, increase the object quality by sharpening without the median filter as in [1]. The object will be improved its quality by the sharpening method. We choose that method because one of the criteria for evaluating the quality of an image is sharpness.

One additional improvement in this paper is to enhance the quality of extracted objects. This time, we choose sharpening technique because it satisfies conditions:

– To rise up the quality of object.
– To limit noisy troubles.

In fact, there still exist noisy pixels. The extracted objects need to be improved not only sharpen, color contrast but also eliminate small blurring areas. We have decided to use the sharpening algorithm in order to solve those problems because sharpness is one of main conditions for evaluating the good quality of images. The Fig. 1 shows some outputs of this stage.

(a) Original image

(b) Sharpening object of proposed method

Fig. 1. Result of enhancing object quality by filter.

4   Experimental Results

In this section, we have applied the procedure described in Sect. 3 and achieved superior performance in our experiments as demonstrated in this section. We evaluate the results on the public available MSRA10K database [11]. This dataset has more than 10,000 images. Our Matlab program will be executed on this dataset.

Figure 2 presents colors in a reduced image. In Fig. 2, the deduced photo remains 58 colors at the top right corner and the bar chart presents the frequency of being kept ones at the bottom. The total colors have been reduced, which is an important condition for continuing steps. For instance, the generating salient map, this stage receives the most benefits from the former step because its calculation is based on the number of colors and the quality of image. In all cases, the color range in hard threshold method is always equal or bigger than the color range in soft threshold method so that it is surely to keep high frequent colors and widen the distances between distinct colors. These are the reasons why the salient map creates better in common images. Other continuing steps are similar to our previous research. Visually, the reduced image and the original image changed only a little, presented in Fig. 2a and b. The soft threshold method takes about 0.5459 s to reduce total colors in an image while the hard threshold method costs 0.1465 s for the same task.

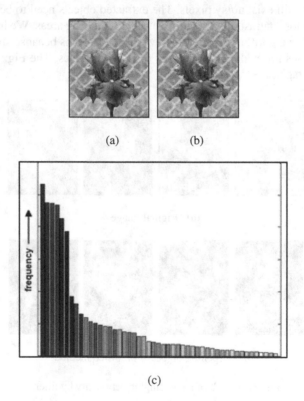

(a)   (b)

(c)

Fig. 2. Colors in a reduced image. (a) Original image, (b) Reduced image, (c) Frequency of remained colors

The Fig. 3 shows some outputs of enhancing object quality by filter in [1] and the proposed method. In Fig. 3, we see that: the result of sharpening object of the proposed method is better than that of [1].

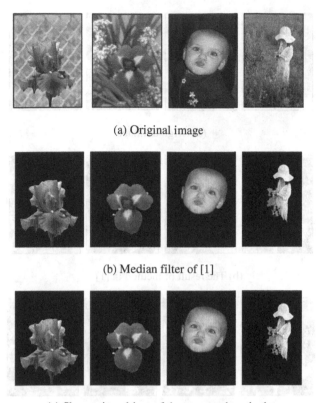

(a) Original image

(b) Median filter of [1]

(c) Sharpening object of the proposed method.

Fig. 3. Result of enhancing object quality by filter.

Now, we compare the proposed method results with the method in [1]. These methods will be compared in the executing time and the quality of saliency maps. They are computed in 20 % of images in dataset which fit our requirements.

In Fig. 4, we can visually see that the results of the proposed method which have a rather better quality of salient map than that of [1]. The difference is at the top-line pictures, the purple areas have the same contrast value in our approach while the method in [1] does not solve this problem as well as the latter method. The experiment has pointed out the advantages in the current method. Our current method needs requirements:

- Using global contrast technique.
- Background has similar colors.
- Object and background colors must be high contrast colors.
- Clear contours surround the interesting object.

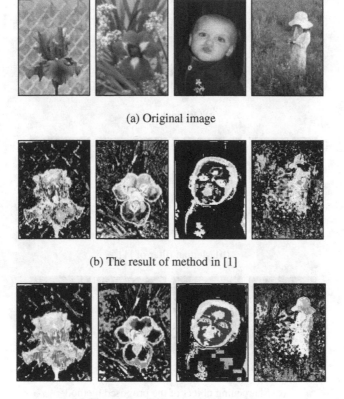

(a) Original image

(b) The result of method in [1]

(c) The result of the proposed method

Fig. 4. Salient maps.

Results are displayed in Table 1 and Table 2. This table shows the running time of all recommended methods in this paper. These algorithms are executed in Matlab 2013a environment. The hardware is Core i5-4200U 1.6 GHz (4 CPUs), 4 GB RAM, 500 HDD drive.

Table 1. The running time belongs to color-reduction stage in those methods.

Experimental	The time of method in [1] (s)	The time of the proposed method (s)
1	0.5459	0.1466
2	0.5461	0.1472
3	0.5467	0.1485
4	0.5439	0.1442
5	0.5467	0.1458
Average	0.5459	0.1465

Table 2. The running time of other stages in those methods.

Experimental	The time of method in [1] (s)	The time of the proposed method (s)
1	3.7277	2.9531
2	3.7237	2.9571
3	3.7273	2.9770
4	3.7128	2.9169
5	3.7242	2.9462
Average	3.7231	2.9500

In Table 1, the running time is measured by second and the improvement uses percentage unit. It has showed a big increase, furthermore, the color-reduction step is also increased the performance of other steps, which are presented in Table 2.

Table 2 gives us a detailed look at the effect of the development in stage one on following stages. The inputted results are better but its effect is beyond the expected, 20.76 %. To sum up, the total time of the proposed method is faster than the method in [1] by 27.4671 %, which is a good number for an improvement in the color reduction step.

5   Conclusions

Saliency has been an important problem in neuroscience, neural systems, computer vision, etc. Salient object detection is a hard task. In this paper, we have proposed a method for salient object detection using the combination of global contrast and color distribution, a variation of method which was published by Dat et al. [1]. We have successfully improved method [1] in two main points: the running time and the quality of extracted objects. Especially, time in step one is the most significant point. It has improved the efficiency of algorithm and cut off the redundant time. The usage of hard threshold has removed unnecessary operators in order to boost up the speed and results of the proposed method.

References

1. Duy Dat, N., Thanh Binh, N.: Enhancing object quality based on saliency map and derivatives on color distances. In: IEEE International Conference on Computing & Communication Technologies - Research, Innovation, and Vision for the Future, pp. 106–111 (2015)
2. Cheng, M.-M., Zhang, G.-X., Mitra, N.J., Huang, X., Shi-Min, H.: Global contrast based salient region detection. IEEE Pattern Anal. Mach. Intell. **37**, 569–582 (2014)
3. Achanta, R., Estrada, F., Wils, P., Süsstrunk, S.: Salient region detection and segmentation. In: Gasteratos, A., Vincze, M., Tsotsos, J.K. (eds.) ICVS 2008. LNCS, vol. 5008, pp. 66–75. Springer, Heidelberg (2008)
4. Zhai, Y., Shah, M.: Visual attention detection in video sequences using spatiotemporal cues. In: Annual Conference Association for Computing Machinery on Multimedia, pp. 815–824 (2006)

5. Itti, L., Koch, C., Niebur, E.: A model of saliency-based visual attention for rapid scene analysis. IEEE Trans. Pattern Anal. Mach. Intell. **20**, 1254–1259 (1998)
6. Rahtu, E., Kannala, J., Salo, M., Heikkilä, J.: Segmenting salient objects from images and videos. In: Daniilidis, K., Maragos, P., Paragios, N. (eds.) ECCV 2010, Part V. LNCS, vol. 6315, pp. 366–379. Springer, Heidelberg (2010)
7. Walther, D., Koch, C.: Modeling attention to salient proto-objects. Neural Netw. **19**, 1395–1407 (2006)
8. Murray, N., Vanrell, M., Otazu, X., Alejandro Parraga, C.: Saliency estimation using a nonparametric low-level vision model. In: IEEE International Conference on Computer Vision and Pattern Recognition, pp. 433–440 (2011)
9. Achanta, R., Hemami, S., Estrada, F., Susstrunk, S.: Frequency-tuned salient region detection. In: IEEE International Conference on Computer Vision and Pattern Recognition, pp. 1597–1604 (2009)
10. Liu, T., Sun, J., Zheng, N.-N., Tang, X., Shum, H.-Y.: Learning to detect a salient object. IEEE Pattern Anal. Mach. Intell. **33**, 353–367 (2011)
11. Cheng, M.: MSRA10K database. http://mftp.mmcheng.net/Data/MSRA10K_Imgs_GT.zip. Accessed 09/10/2015
12. Goferman, S., Tal, A: Context aware saliency detection. In: IEEE Computer Vision and Pattern Recognition, pp. 2376–2383 (2010)
13. Rahtu, E., Heikkila, J.: A simple and efficient saliency detector for background subtraction. In: Computer Vision Workshops, pp. 1137–1144 (2009)
14. Thanh Binh, N., Hong Tuyet, V.T., Cong Vinh, P.: Increasing the quality of medical images based on the combination of filters in ridgelet domain. In: Vinh, P.C., Vassev, E., Hinchey, M. (eds.) ICTCC 2014. LNICST, vol. 144, pp. 320–331. Springer, Heidelberg (2015)
15. Thanh Binh, N.: Medical image contour based context-aware in contourlet domain. In: Toi, V.V. (ed.) 5th International Conference on Biomedical Engineering in Vietnam. IFMBE Proceedings, vol. 46, pp. 405–408. Springer, Heidelberg (2015)
16. Thanh Binh, N.: Enhancing the quality of medical image database based on kernels in bandelet domain. In: Dang, T.K., et al. (eds.) FDSE 2015. LNCS, vol. 9446, pp. 226–241. Springer, Heidelberg (2015). doi:10.1007/978-3-319-26135-5_17

Edge Detection in Low Quality Medical Images

Vo Thi Hong Tuyet[1,2(✉)] and Nguyen Thanh Binh[2]

[1] Faculty of Information Technology, Ho Chi Minh City Open University,
Ho Chi Minh City, Vietnam
vothihongtuyet.dhbk@gmail.com
[2] Faculty of Computer Science and Engineering,
Ho Chi Minh City University of Technology, VNU-HCM, Ho Chi Minh City, Vietnam
ntbinh@hcmut.edu.vn

Abstract. The edge detection is very useful for contour and segmentation. But with weak objects, this is very difficult, especially for medical images which store the information of patients. In this paper, we propose an algorithm to detect the edges of object in medical images. Our method uses Bayesian thresholding for medical images denoising and B-spline curve for smoothing. The proposed method is compared with the recent methods. The results of our method are better than the other methods.

Keywords: Edge detection · Canny · B-spline · Bayesian thresholding

1 Introduction

In the field of health, images become a useful tool. Many diseases are detected based on the medical images. Medical images provide full details inside the human body, where the naked eye cannot see. Every detail becomes highly valuable if anomalies in the images are able to be detected as soon as possible. For serious diseases, if we detect as early symptoms or abnormalities, it will be more likely to maintain the life. So, the required visible pixels are extremely important. Based on the advice from health professionals, patients will be target of methods to acquire the information of their body by the stored images. In stored medical images, the combined pixels together create the contours of an object around a specific body (eg bone, liver, blood vessels, etc...). If there are any unusual locations in the details such as size, location can be shifted as initial manifestation of the diseases, helping the diagnosis and treatment of specialists. Therefore, the detecting of edges is very necessary for contour or segmentation. If we detect many edges, we will have more information about objects and will be more comfortable for detecting contour or segmentation [3].

In the past, there are many algorithms which are proposed for edge detection such as: Sobel [9], Canny [6–8], B-spline [11–15] or in the generation types of wavelet transform as [4, 11, 16, 17]. Specially, B-spline curve is the most popular in many algorithms. The authors propose multi-scale B-spline wavelet for edge detection in [11] by multi-scale for smoothing steps. In [12], the algorithm is proposed to be B-spline Snakes by multi-scale to apply for contour detection. This idea is continued with

© ICST Institute for Computer Sciences, Social Informatics and Telecommunications Engineering 2016
P.C. Vinh et al. (Eds.): ICTCC 2016, LNICST 168, pp. 351–362, 2016.
DOI: 10.1007/978-3-319-46909-6_32

Brigger [15]. The reason of applying is because of the value from the smoothing spline. On the other hand, many previous methods for edge detection are done in transforms which we must mention in wavelet of Wang [11] and scale multiplication in wavelet domain of Lei [16]. The new generation is used as discrete shearlet transform in [4]. A concept of strong and weak objects in contour is defined by Binh [17]. In [17], the contour detection based on the context aware combination in complex wavelet domain. The quality of these algorithms continues to improve. The scientists use single or double threshold, filter to show the pixels.

Most of the edge detection methods always include the removing noise steps [1, 6]. There are many causes for medical images of which quality is reduced. In case medical images have blur or noise, their sharpness will be affected. When the quality of medical images is bad, the edge detection is reduced and it is very hard to see it. This case is the weak object, and this is the hard problem for edge detection because of the gray of different levels. Although both of the blur and noise appear in the reasons of reducing the quality of medical images, the blur is not popular in medical images. Because the blur is the movement or migration, this problem is overcome by the breakdown or the quality of machinery. In [6], Canny proposes a method for edge detection. In his method, the first step is the removed noise by Gaussian filter, and all steps do not include deblurring images to prepare for edge detection. It does demonstrate that the denoising is very important to edge detection.

In this paper, we propose an algorithm for edge detection of objects in medical images. We concentrate on low-quality medical images. We present the basis of edge detection and denoising images in Sect. 2. The proposed method is presented in Sect. 3. In this section, we use Bayesian thresholding for denoising of the input medical images. Then we change the smoothing steps of Canny by using the B-spline to improve the number of edges detected. The results of experiments are compared with the recent methods in Sect. 4. And in Sect. 4, we add the concept of the weak object of [17]. Conclusions are shown in Sect. 5.

2 Background

In this section, we will present the background of edge detection and denoising images and the results of other previous methods in these fields.

2.1 Edge Detection

Edges occur on the boundary between two different regions in an image. The task of edge detection is to the important features from the edges of images, such as: lines, corners, curves, etc. This process is affected by intensity changes. And the reasons of changes are: shadows, depth, texture, or surface color. The four steps of edge detection [1] as follows:

- Smoothing: remove noise from the input images but must keep the features of edges.
- Enhancement: using the filters to improve the quality of edges.
- Detection: the thresholding is the basis of the detection.

– Localization: based on the location of each edge.

Many algorithms are proposed to detect the edges, such as: Sobel [9], Canny [6], etc but their results sometimes have no enough edges. The Fig. 1 is the results of edge detection based on the Sobel and Canny.

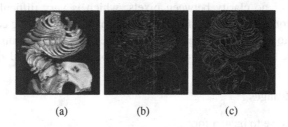

(a)   (b)   (c)

Fig. 1. The results of edge detection by Sobel and Canny method. (a) The normal image. (b) The result of edge detection by Sobel method. (c) The result of edge detection by Canny method.

Then, many methods detected in transform: wavelet transform [11, 16, 17], shearlet transform [4], etc... With transform, the authours proposed the detection based on the combination between pixels. Edge detection bases on estimating the gradient: strength, gradient direction by −90 degrees. The gradient is the two-dimensional equivalent of the first derivate and is defined as the vector:

$$G[f(x,y)] = \begin{bmatrix} G_x \\ G_y \end{bmatrix} = \begin{bmatrix} \dfrac{\partial f}{\partial x} \\ \dfrac{\partial f}{\partial y} \end{bmatrix} \tag{1}$$

where vector G[f(x, y)] points in the direction of the maximum rate of increase of the function f(x, y). And the direction of the gradient is defined as:

$$\alpha(x,y) = \tan^{-1}\left(\frac{G_y}{G_x}\right) \tag{2}$$

where α is measured with respect to the x axis.

The Sobel [9] use operator:

$$M_x = \begin{bmatrix} -1 & 0 & 1 \\ -2 & 0 & 2 \\ -1 & 0 & 1 \end{bmatrix} \tag{3}$$

and

$$M_y = \begin{bmatrix} -1 & -2 & -1 \\ 0 & 0 & 0 \\ 1 & 2 & 1 \end{bmatrix} \tag{4}$$

where M_x and M_y are approximations at (i, j).

The Canny method improved the results from Sobel method, the quality of edge detection was clearer. With the previous methods, the results of edge detection are good for strong objects. The strong objects are the objects which have the high quality and which are easy for detection by color. However, the weak objects are the objects which have noise, blur or no clarity between pixels, which is very difficult for detection. Recently, using context awareness for edge detection and smoothing contour has been proposed in [17] to give the good results. In the other methods, the authors use interval type-2 fuzzy logic to improve the quality of the Sobel technique in [19].

2.2 Denoising Images

Each image has noise to have a form:

$$g = x + n \tag{5}$$

where x is normal image, n is the noise value and g is the noisy image. The noise has many types, such as: Gaussian, speckle, salt & pepper. Most of the medical images have noising and blur because of many reasons such as environment, capture devices, technician's skills, etc [33, 34]. These reasons have reduced the quality of medical images. Consequently, enhancing medical image process is useful and necessary. However, this is very difficult for image processing.

The goal of denoising is to extrude noise details from the low quality medical images, but keep edge features. Many researches are proposed to solve this problem. The results from denoising by wavelet transform [20, 31] are very positive. In there, the authors used the threshold in decomposition domain. Calculating the threshold depends on the noise variance. Then, they based on the threshold to show or not to show the pixel details. They continued with the wavelet coefficients to reconstruct the image. The denoising results are continued to improve by discrete wavelet transform (DWT) [21, 22]. But DWT has three serious disadvantages [23]: shift sensitivity, poor directionality and lack of phase information. To overcome these disadvantages, the scientists used filters in transform such as contourlet transform [24], nonsubsampled contourlet transform (NSCT) [25, 26], ridgelet transform [27, 28], curvelet transform [29]. In contourlet domain, they used laplacian pyramid (LP) and directional filter bank (DFB) to remove the bad pixels and perform the reconstruction by discrete LP and discrete DFB. Contourlet transform is only to use 8 or 16 directions in pyramid and filter in each direction. NSCT [25, 26] includes nonsubsampled laplacian pyramid (NSLP) and nonsubsampled directional filter bank (NSDFB). In NSCT domain, the authours used multi-directional and filter in each direction. In other words, NSCT is the improvement from contourlet transform. The ridgelet transform [27, 28] is continued to improve by curves. Ridgelet transform is the first generation of curvelet transform [29] ... Most domains of transforms are denoised by threshold. At first, they used hard threshold (T_{hard}) and soft threshold (T_{soft}) which are given in equations:

$$T_{hard}\left(\hat{\partial}_{jk}, \lambda\right) = \hat{\partial}_{jk} I\left(\left|\hat{\partial}_{jk}\right| > \lambda\right) \tag{6}$$

and

$$T_{\text{soft}}\left(\hat{d}_{jk}, \lambda\right) = \text{sign}(\hat{d}_{jk})\max\left(0, \left|\hat{d}_{jk}\right| - \lambda\right) \tag{7}$$

where $\lambda \geq 0$ is parameter wavelet, I is normal parameter value.

After that, they used stationary, cycle-spinning, shiftable, steerable wavelet, Bayesian thresholding, etc. and combined between transform and threshold in [30, 32–34]. Although the results of previous methods are spectacular, the time processing is slow and the complicacy is very high. Medical images lacking information is the big problem because they must adapt to many filters or thresholds.

3   Improved the Quality of Edge Detection by Canny Combined with B-Spline in Bayesian Thresholding

In this section, we propose a method to improve the Canny technique by consolidating the quality of objects and making the smoothing. We increase the sharpness of objects

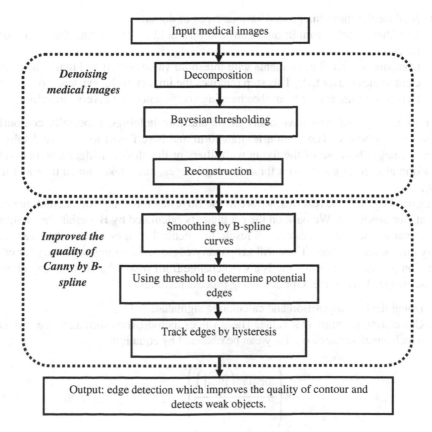

Fig. 2. The proposed method

in medical images based on the denoising image. In here, our idea uses Bayesian thresholding to remove the noise out of the medical images. Our method includes: after decomposition, we remove noise details from input images by Bayesian thresholding. The output of denoising is the medical image which has strong objects. The objects have strong edges, clear and comfortable for edge detection. If we have the good results from edge detection process, we will give more contour for medical images. These results will also help segmentation process. Then, we apply B-spline for the smoothing step. Our method is given clearly in Fig. 2.

3.1 Denoising in Wavelet Domain

In medical images, if we use many thresholdings or threshold without fixing, the results of denoising will be "too smooth". If medical images are "too smooth", they will lose several pixels. Although medical images have the high quality, the doctors will not see the details of bone or blood vessels clearly. Hence, we must propose an algorithm which is not only to denoise but also to keep features.

As presented in Sect. 2.2, there are many transforms for denoising images. The process for denoising in the above methods is similar to:

(i)   Analyze the input image into various types of domain.
(ii) Use filter (single or multi direction) and threshold by calculating the detail coefficients.
(iii) Compare the detail coefficients with threshold values given and make the coefficient values closer to 0. This step removes the impact of the existence of images.
(iv) Reconstruct the image from the changing coefficients (the inverse transform).

Therefore, the transforms have many filters and thresholdings, especially contourlet transform and NSCT. The contourlet transform and NSCT will lose many details of medical images because of the fixing with filters or thresholds. Ridgelet and curvelet transform also gives good result for denoising images; but it takes much time and it is slow.

Depending on these features, we are to use Bayesian threshold for calculating coefficients for denoising. We base on the coefficients calculated by Bayesian thresholding to reconstruct the result image. As a result, the medical images will not be fixed with many thresholds or filters. They will keep many edges and features necessary for edge detection process. The denoising is also to change from weak objects to strong objects in case images have noise. Our denoising process includes:

(i)   Doing the decomposition and calculating sigmahat.
(ii) Calculating the sigmahat value. These values include: the estimate noise variance σ and signal variance σ_s. They can be obtained by equation:

$$\sigma = \left(\frac{\text{median}\left(\left| w_{i,j} \right| \right)}{0.6745} \right)^2 \tag{8}$$

$$\sigma_s = \sqrt{\max(\sigma_w^2 - \sigma^2, 0)} \tag{9}$$

with

$$\sigma_w^2 = \frac{1}{n^2} \sum_{i,j=1}^{n} w^2(i,j) \tag{10}$$

where $w_{i,j}$ is the lowest frequency coefficient after performing transformations.

(iii) The calculation of the thresholds by equation:

$$\text{Threshold}_{\text{Bayes}} = \begin{cases} \dfrac{\sigma^2}{\sigma_s}, \sigma^2 < \sigma_s^2 \\ \max\{|A_m|\}, \sigma^2 \geq \sigma_s^2 \end{cases} \tag{11}$$

(iv) When reconstructing the image based on the Bayesian thresholded coefficients. If the value of pixel detail coefficients is less than thresholding then the result is 0. Else the result is array Y, where each element of Y is 1 if the corresponding element of pixel is greater than zero, 0 if the corresponding element of pixel equals zero, −1 if the corresponding element of pixel is less than zero.

After this process, the quality of the medical images are improved. From the results, the strength of pixels is increased and the edges are also more powerful. After denoising, our algorithm continues to do smoothing by B-spline which is presented in the next section.

3.2 Improved the Quality of Edge Detection by Canny Based on the Combination with B-Spline Curve

Many methods based on the masks such as Sobel and the proposed method takes advantage of the structure in local images. However, with the previous methods, the weak objects also cause difficulty. The Canny edge detection algorithm gives the good results in weak objects [7]. This method includes 5 steps:

(i)   Apply Gaussian filter to smooth the image in order to remove the noise.
(ii) Find the intensity gradients of the image.
(iii) Apply non-maximum suppression to get rid of spurious response to edge detection.
(iv) Apply double threshold to determine potential edges.
(v)   Track edge by hysteresis. Finalize the detection of edges by suppressing all the other edges that are weak and not connected to strong edges.

Our idea is to remove noise by the Bayesian thresholding in the previous section. We do not use Gaussian filter because the noise types in medical images are complex. When we use threshold in this step, the quality of different levels is improved. After denoising medical images, we use a B-spline curve to smooth the image. A B-spline curve is similar to Bézier curve, but B-spline curve gives more information. A Bézier curve is a parametric curve. In graphics, Bézier curves are used to model smooth curves. From the set of n + 1 control points, knot vector of m + 1 knots and a degree p. But must satisfy: m = n + p + 1. The B-spline curve of degree p ($N_{i,u}(u)$) defined by these control points and knot vector U is:

$$C(u) = \sum_{i=0}^{n} N_{i,p}(u)P_i \tag{12}$$

where n + 1 control points $P_0, P_1, ..., P_n$ and a knot vector U = $\{u_0, u_1, ..., u_m\}$.

$N_{i,u}(u)$ looks like $B_{n,i}(u)$. The basis function of Bézier bases on the number of control points, but the degree of a B-spline basis function is an input the degree of a B-spline basis function is an input.

B-spline with the smoothing function $\beta_{2^{-1}}^{n+1}$ and $\beta_{2^{-1}}^{n+2}$ uses 2^{-1} level.

$$\psi^n(x) = \frac{d}{dx}\beta_{2^{-1}}^{n+1}(x) = 4(\beta^{n+1})^{(1)}(2x) \tag{13}$$

or

$$\psi^n(x) = \frac{d^2}{dx^2}\beta_{2^{-1}}^{n+2}(x) = 8(\beta^{n+2})^{(2)}(2x) \tag{14}$$

where n is the order of wavelet transform.

We define the desirable geometric characteristics of B-Spline curves and surfaces of degree p is defined as:

$$N_{i,0}(u) = \begin{cases} 0 \ if \ u_i \leq u \leq u_{i+1} \\ 1, \ otherwise \end{cases} \tag{15}$$

$$N_{i,p} = \frac{u - u_i}{u_{i+p} - u_i}N_{i,p-1}(u) + \frac{u_{i+p+1} - u_i}{u_{i+p+1} - u_{i+1}}N_{i+1,p-1}(u) \tag{16}$$

After the smoothing step, the Kernel is applied for determining gradients of the medical images. The value of gradients is also known as the edge strengths. This value is calculated by Euclidean distance measure, and it will be used to define edges to be shown. Nonetheless, these edges will be converted to "sharp" edges in the non-maximum suppression step. In each pixel of the gradient image, we focus on the gradient direction < 45^0 and 8-connected neighborhood. The direction of edges is shown by equation:

$$\theta = \arctan\left(\frac{|G_y|}{|G_x|}\right) \tag{17}$$

where G_x and G_y are the gradients in the x and y directions respectively.

If the edge strength between neighborhood and pixel in the positive is not the largest, the algorithm will be removed. From the shown edges, the weak objects are improved by denoising and non-maximum suppression step. Thus, the number of strong objects is higher.

4 Experiments and Results

As mentioned in Sect. 3, we improve the quality of Canny algorithm by Bayesian thresholding to remove noise and B-spline at the smoothing step. This idea remove the usage of double threshold and filter of the previous Canny method. Specially, we also change the Gaussian filter used at the smoothing step of Canny. We choose B-spline for smoothing after removing noise by Bayesian thresholding because this threshold is based on wavelet coefficients. B-spline also makes the curves very clear. This is necessary for edge detection in medical images.

The proposed method uses Bayesian thresholding to remove noise of which medical images have weak objects to be improved. Doctors who apply our idea into the edge detection more have more basic information about their patients. We test in medical images which have strong objects and weak objects. The strong and weak object are defined in [17] as: "the strong object is an object of which boundaries are clear and the weak object is defined as an object of which boundaries are blurred". In here, we base on the concept from [35]: "the blur details include noise details". Consequently, we add the concept of the weak object as: the weak object is an object of which boundaries are blurred and noised.

The results of our proposed method are compared with the other methods such as: Sobel [9], Canny [8], Cuckoo Search [18]. We have many edges more than other methods. Our dataset is the medical images collected in many hospitals. There are more than 1000 medical images, and in many sizes: 256×256, 512×512, 1024×1024. We test many medical images from this dataset. In here, we show some cases when we test and compare them. In Fig. 3, we test the medical image which has a strong object.

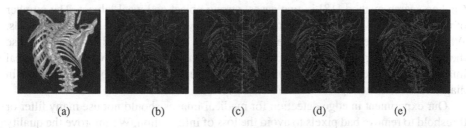

(a)   (b)   (c)   (d)   (e)

Fig. 3. The results of edge detection by other methods with strong object. (a) The strong object in the original medical image. (b) Edge detection by Sobel method [9]. (c) Edge detection by Canny method [8]. (d) Edge detection by Cuckoo search method [18]. (e) Edge detection by the proposed method.

In this case, Fig. 3(a) is the original medical image. The result of Sobel for edge detection is Fig. 3(b), the result of Canny for edge detection is Fig. 3(c) and of Cuckoo search is Fig. 3(d). In Fig. 3(e) is the result of our proposed method. We can see that the number of edge detection by the proposed method is better than the result in Fig. 3(b), (c) and (d).

In Fig. 4, we test the medical image which has a weak object. Although we state that a weak object is an object of which boundaries are blurred and noised; the blur is a problem easily overcome by the technician skill or the quality of machine. In case noise is added to medical images to create a weak object, noise details is more popular than blur details. In this case, we use Gaussian noise and Gaussian blur added to medical images with the variance noise is 0.00005 and the values of point spread function of Gaussian blur. The reason of our selection is Gaussian is the plus noise and blur into pixels of medical images. The plus noise and blur is popular in medical images.

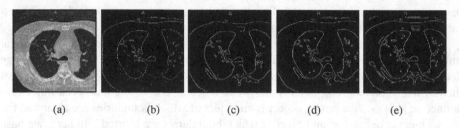

         (a)   (b)   (c)   (d)   (e)

Fig. 4. The results of edge detection by other methods with weak object. (a) The weak object in a noised medical image. (b) Edge detection by Sobel method [9]. (c) Edge detection by Canny method [8]. (d) Edge detection by Cuckoo search method [18]. (e) Edge detection by the proposed method.

The result of Sobel is Fig. 4(b), Canny and Cuckoo search alternate to be Fig. 4(c) and (d). We see that there are more edges detected by our method, Fig. 4(e), than by other methods.

From the results from Figs. 3, 4 and many other test cases, we conclude that the results of the proposed method are better than Sobel method [9], Canny method [8] and Cuckoo search method [18] in two cases: strong object and weak object. The number of edge detection which can be seen by the naked eye is higher than by other methods. Why we choose the number of edge detection. This is an unaccepted problem, because the number of edge detection is expected to be much higher. However, in medical images, they can be the foretoken of serious diseases. We try to help for the doctors in diagnosis or treatment process as much as possible.

Our experiment in edge detection for medical images should not use many filter or threshold to remove bad pixels to avoid the loss of information. We improve the quality of boundaries by threshold in the first steps of Canny, make them smoothier and give more information by B-spline or other curves. If the relationship between neighborhood and pixel, the edge strength, is not the largest, the algorithm can be removed. However, we can consider it if the strength is larger than more eight connected to the neighborhood.

5   Conclusions

Edge detection is the key for contour and segmentation. If the number of edges detection is higher, the result of contour or segmentation is better. In the previous edge detection algorithms, weak objects are a challenge. In this paper, we propose a method to strengthen the quality of weak objects in order to improve the results of edge detection. Our idea is to reconstruct the medical images which have noise. Each pixel is reconstructed by Bayesian thresholding, then we make them smoothier by B-spline curves and improve them with Canny technique. The results of the proposed method are compared with other methods such as: Sobel [9], Canny [8] and Cuckoo Search [18] method. We test with the dataset which is collected from many hospitals. The comparison of the results shows that the proposed method detects more edges than other methods.

References

1. Marr, D., Hildreth, E.: Theory of edge detection. Proc. Roy. Soc. Lond. **207**, 187–217 (1980)
2. Mumford, D., Shah, J.: Optimal approximation by piecewise smooth functions and associated variational problems. Comm. Pure Appl. Math. **42**, 557–685 (1989)
3. Chan, T.F., Vese, L.A.: Active contours without edges. IEEE Trans. Image Process. **10**(2), 266–277 (2001)
4. Easley, G., Labate, D., Lim, W.Q.: Sparse directional image representations using the discrete shearlet transform. Appl. Comput. Harmon. Anal. **25**, 25–46 (2008)
5. Zhai, L., Dong, S., Ma, H.: Recent methods and applications on image edge detection. In: International Workshop on Geoscience and Remote Sensing, pp. 332–335 (2008)
6. Canny, John: A computational approach to edge detection. IEEE Trans. Pattern Anal. Mach. Intell., PAMI **8**(6), 679–698 (1986)
7. Deriche, R.: Using Canny's criteria to derive a recursively implemented optimal edge detector. Int. J. Comput. Vis. **1**, 167–187 (1987)
8. Moeslund. Canny Edge Detection (2009). http://www.cse.iitd.ernet.in/~pkalra/csl783/canny.pdf. (last access: 15 Nov 2015)
9. Vincent, O.R., Folorunso, O.: A descriptive algorithm for sobel image edge detection. In: Proceedings of Informing Science & IT Education Conference (InSITE) (2009)
10. Morse, B.S.: Edge Detection. Brigham Young University (2000)
11. Wang, Y., Cai, Y.: Multiscale B-spline wavelet for edge detection. Sci. China (Ser. A) **38**(4) (1995)
12. Brigger, P., Unser, M.: Multi-scale B-spline snakes for general contour detection. In: Wavelet Applications in Signal and Image Processing VI, SPIE, vol. 3458 (1998)
13. Bhatt, A.D., Warkhedkar, R.V.: Reverse engineering of human body: a B-Spline based heterogeneous modeling approach. Comput.-Aided Des. Appl. **5**(1–4), 194–208 (2008)
14. Bhatt, A.D., Warkhedkar, R.V.: Material-solid modeling of human body: a heterogeneous B-Spline based approach. Comput.-Aided Des. **41**, 586–597 (2009)
15. Brigger, P., Hoeg, J., Unser, M.: B-Spline snakes: a flexible tool for parametric contour detection. IEEE Trans. Image Process. **9**(9), 1484–1496 (2000)
16. Zhang, L., Bao, P.: Edge detection by scale multiplication in wavelet domain. Pattern Recogn. Lett. **23**, 1771–1784 (2002)

17. Binh, N.H.: Image contour based on context aware in complex wavelet domain. Hum.-Centric Comput. Inf. Sci., Springer Open Journal (2015)
18. Srishti, : Technique based on Cuckoo's search algorithm for exudates detection in Diabetic Retinopathy. Ophthalmol. Res.: Int. J. SCIENCEDOMAIN Int. 2(1), 43–54 (2014)
19. Gonzalez, C.I., Castro, J.R., Melin, P., Castillo, O.: Cuckoo search algorithm for the optimization of type-2 fuzzy image edge detection systems. In: IEEE Congress on Evolutionary Computation (CEC), pp. 449–455 (2015)
20. Strang, G.: Wavelets and dilation equations. A brief introduction. SIAM Rev. 31(4), 614–627 (1989)
21. Edwards, T.: Discrete Wavelet Transforms: Theory and Implementation (1992)
22. Kociolek, M., Materka, A., Strzelecki, M., Szczypínski, P.: Discrete wavelet transform – derived features for digital image texture analysis. In: Proceedings of International Conference on Signals and Electronic Systems, pp. 163–168 (2001)
23. Binh, N.T., Khare, A.: Image Denoising, Deblurring and Object Tracking, A New Generation Wavelet Based Approach. LAP LAMBERT Academic Publishing (2013)
24. Do, M.N., Vetterli, M.: The contourlet transform: an efficient directional multiresolution image representation. IEEE Trans. Img. Process., 2091–2106 (2005)
25. da Cunha, A.L., Zhou, J., Do, M.N.: Nonsubsampled contourlet transform: theory, design, and applications. IEEE Trans. Img. Proc., 3089–3101 (2005)
26. da Cunha, A.L., Zhou, J., Do, M.N.: Nonsubsampled Contourlet Transform: Filter Design and Applications in Denoising (2006)
27. Candes, J.: Ridgelets. Theory and Applications. Stanford University (1998)
28. Zhang, Fadili, J.M., Starck, J.L.: Wavelets, ridgelets and curvelets for poisson noise removal. IEEE Trans. Image Process. 1093–1108 (2008)
29. Starck, J.L., Candès, E.J., Donoho, D.L.: The curvelet transform for image denoising. IEEE Trans. Image Process., 670–684 (2002)
30. Binh, N.T., Khare, A.: Multilevel threshold based image denoising in curvelet domain. J. Comput. Sci. Technol. 25(3), 632–640 (2010)
31. Abramovich, Sapatinas, T., Silverman, B.W.: Wavelet thresholding via a Bayesian approach. J. R. Statist. Soc. B, 725–749 (1998)
32. Chui, M., Feng, Y., Wang, W., Li, Z., Xu, X.: Image Denoising Method with Adaptive Bayes threshold in Nonsubsampled Contourlet Domain. American Applied Science Research Institute (2012)
33. Binh, N.T., Tuyet, V.T.H., Vinh, P.C.: Increasing the quality of medical images based on the combination of filters in ridgelet domain. Nat. Comput. Commun. 144, 320–331 (2015). ISSN 1867-8211
34. Tuyet, V.T.H., Binh, N.T.: Reducing impurities in medical images based on curvelet domain. Nat. Comput. Commun. 144, 306–319 (2015). ISSN 1867-8211
35. Binh, N.T., Tuyet, V.T.H.: Enhancing the quality of medical images containing blur combined with noise pair. Int. J. Image, Graph. Sig. Process., Mesc J., 7(11) (2015)

People Counting in Conference Scenes
in Shearlet Domain

Nguyen Thanh Binh[✉]

Faculty of Computer Science and Engineering,
Ho Chi Minh City University of Technology, VNU-HCM, Ho Chi Minh City, Vietnam
ntbinh@hcmut.edu.vn

Abstract. People counting is an important task in visual-based surveillance system. The task of people counting is not easy to solve problems. In this paper, the author has proposed a method for people counting which identify the objects present in a scene of conference into two classes: empty seat and non-empty seat. The proposed method based on saliency map and color smoothing in shearlet domain. The author uses shearlet transform and combine of adaboost with support vector machine for classifiers and people counting. The proposed method is simple but the accuracy of people counting is high.

Keywords: People counting · Shearlet transform · Saliency map · Color smoothing

1 Introduction

Today, computer vision is one of the important senses which helps people to receive information from the real world. Computer vision processing provides the methods and analyses images from the real world similar to the way people perform, to draw information to make the appropriate decision. Detecting the number of people in crowded scenes is an important task in visual-based surveillance system. Smart surveillance systems by image have been developed and proven effective in some specific areas such as human activity monitoring, traffic monitoring, etc. From the images obtained from various observations, the author can detect the movement of objects in the frame and identify the object that is people, vehicles, etc. Many systems have been researched and developed. For example, the problem of traffic monitoring can tell us the number of vehicles circulating through the ramp which is monitored and gives information on the speed of movement, and the path of the object to be tracked. However, the system still encountered some existences as the effectiveness of the observer always depend on the environmental conditions of observation, types of object motion or other objective reasons.

Estimating the number of people moving in crowded scenes used commonly techniques such as: detection the head information [1, 4], expectation maximization [2], low-level features and Bayesian regression [3], HOG features [5] and background subtraction [6]. Algorithm based on background subtraction utilizes the current image to compare it with the background image and detect the moving scene. Most of methods of

© ICST Institute for Computer Sciences, Social Informatics and Telecommunications Engineering 2016
P.C. Vinh et al. (Eds.): ICTCC 2016, LNICST 168, pp. 363–372, 2016.
DOI: 10.1007/978-3-319-46909-6_33

background subtraction are median filter, mean filter, temporal median filter, Kalman filter, sequential kernel density approximation and eigen backgrounds. It is hard to model the background when the environment is complex. The optical flow method was used to solve this problem. However, the drawback of the optical flow is that it has high computational complexity and it is sensitive to noise.

Teixeira [7] used custom-built camera installed on the ceiling for localizing and counting people in indoor spaces. Chan [8] mapped feature statistics extracted from the blob to the count of people. Wang [9] built a spatio-temporal group context model to model the spatio-temporal relationships between groups to people counting. Zhang [10] proposed group tracking to compensate the weakness of multiple human segmentation which completes occlusion. Jun [11] designed a block-updating way to update the background model and used an improved k-means clustering for locating the position of each person. Wu [12] proposed to learn by boosting edgelet feature based weak classifiers for body part detectors. Kong [13] proposed a viewpoint invariant learning–based on the method from a single camera for people counting in crowds. However, most of these methods are complex as the object is occluded.

In this paper, the author proposes a method to implement for estimating the number of people in conference scenes based on people features in shearlet domain. The author uses shearlet transform and apply the combine of adaboost with support vector machine for classifiers to estimate the people counting. The proposed method was tested on the dataset which is picked up in conference scene. The rest of this paper is organized as follows: in Sect. 2, the author described the basic of shearlet transform, feature and its advantages for people counting. Also details of the propose method for people counting are presented in Sect. 3. In Sect. 4, results of the proposed method are given and conclusions are made in Sect. 5.

2   Shearlet Domain and Features Selection

2.1   Shearlet Transform

Shearlet is similar to curvelet in that both perform a multi-scale and multi-directional analysis. There are two different types of shearlet systems: band-limited shearlet systems and compactly supported shearlet systems [14]. The band-limited shearlet transform have higher computational complexity in frequency domain.

The digitization of discrete shearlet transform performed in the frequency domain. The discrete shearlet transform is the form [15]:

$$f \mapsto \langle f, \psi_n \rangle = \left\langle \hat{f}, \hat{\psi}_n \right\rangle = \left\langle \hat{f}, 2^{-j\frac{3}{2}} \hat{\psi}\left(s_k^T A_{4^{-j}}\right) e^{2\Pi i < A_{4^{-j} S_{k m_{\cdots}}>}} \right\rangle \tag{1}$$

where n = (j, k, m, i) indexes scale j, orientation k, position m, and cone i.

Shearlets perform a multiscale and multidirectional analysis. For images f(x) are C^2 everywhere, where f(x) is piecewise C^2, the approximation error of a reconstruction with the N-largest coefficients $(f_N(x))$ in the shearlet expansion is given by [16]:

$$\|f - f_N\|_2^2 \leq B.N^{-2}(\log N)^3, \quad N \to \infty \tag{2}$$

The author has chosen shearlet transform because it not only has high directionality but also represents salient features (edges, curves and contours) of image in a better way compared with wavelet transform. Shearlet transform is useful for people counting due to its following properties [17]:

(i)   Frame property: It is helpful to a stable reconstruction of an image.
(ii) Localization: Each of shearlet frame elements needs to be localized in both the space and the frequency domain.
(iii) Efficient implementation.
(iv) Sparse approximation: to provide sparse approximation comparable to the band-limited shearlets.

The shearlet transform will produce a highly redundant decomposition when implemented in an undecimated form [18]. Like the curvelet transform, the most essential information in the image is compressed into a few relatively large coefficients, which coincides with the area of major spatial activity in shearlet domain. On the other hand, noise is spread over all coefficients and at a typical noise level the important coefficients can be well recognized [19]. Thus setting the small coefficients to zero will not affect the major spatial activity of the image.

2.2   The Combine of Adaboost with Support Vector Machine for Classifiers

For a given feature set and a training set of positive and negative images, adaboost can be used in both of them to select a small set of features and to train the classifier. Viola [20] firstly used binary adaboost for their face detection system. Boosting is a method to improve the performance of any learning algorithm, generally consisting of sequential learning classifier [21]. Adaboost itself trains an ensemble to weak-learners to form a strong classifier which perform at least as well as an individual weak learner [22]. Adaboost ensembles a particular feature, where each feature represents observable quantity associated with target. In this proposed work, the author has used adaboost algorithm which is described by Viola [20].

Support vector machines (SVM) include associated learning algorithms that analyze data and recognize patterns, used for classification and regression analysis in machine learning. SVM can efficiently perform a non-linear classification, implicitly mapping their inputs into high-dimensional feature spaces.

The idea of the combine of AdaBoost and SVM is that for the sequence of trained RBFSVM (SVM with the RBF kernel) component classifiers. The author starts with large s values. The s values reduce progressively as the Boosting iteration proceeds.

The steps of the combine of AdaBoost with Support Vector Machine for classifiers as below [23]:

(i) Consider a set of training samples with $\{(x_1,y_1), \ldots, (x_n,y_n)\}$. The initial value of σ is set to σ_{ini}; the minimal σ is set to σ_{min} and each step is set to σ_{step}.

(ii) The weights of training samples as:

$$w_i^1 = 1/N \text{ for all } i = 1, \ldots, n \tag{3}$$

(iii) While $(\sigma > \sigma_{\text{min}})$, the author trains a RBFSVM component classifiers, h_t, on the weighted training set. The training error of h_t calculate as: $\varepsilon_t = \sum_{i=1}^{N} wi_i^t$ and $y_i \neq h_t(x_i)$

(iv) If $\varepsilon_t < 0.5$, decrease σ value by σ step and goto (iii).
Set the weight of component classifier h_t as

$$\alpha_t = \frac{1}{2} \ln \left(\frac{1 - \varepsilon_t}{\varepsilon_t} \right) \tag{4}$$

(v) Update the weights of training samples:

$$w_i^{t+1} = \frac{w_i^t exp\{-\alpha_t y_i h_t(x_i)\}}{C_t} \tag{5}$$

where C_t is a normalization constant, and

$$\sum_{i-1}^{N} w_i^{t+1} = 1 \tag{6}$$

(vi) This process continues until σ decrease to the given minimal value. The output of classifier is [24]:

$$f(x) = \text{sign}\left(\sum_{t=1}^{T} \alpha_t h_t(x) \right) \tag{7}$$

2.3 Feature Selection

Among most classification problems, it is not easy to learn good classifiers before removing these unwanted features due to the huge size of the data. The author can reduce the running time of the learning algorithms and a more general classifier by reducing the number of irrelevant features.

A general feature selection for classification is presented as Fig. 1:

In Fig. 1, the step of feature selection affects the training phase of classification. The features selection for classification will select a subset of features. The process data with the selected features will be sent to the learning algorithm. Any object classification algorithm is commonly divided into three important components:

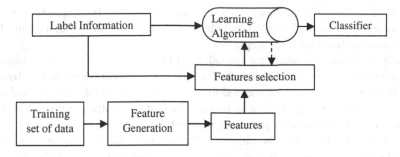

Fig. 1. Framework of feature selection for classification

extraction of features, selection of features and classification. Therefore, feature extraction and selection play an important role in object classification.

3 The Method for People Counting in Conference Scenes

In this section, the author describes a method for people counting in conference scenes in shearlet domain. People counting is hard work. In the past, there are many methods for this work. Every method has particular strengths and drawbacks depending on the scenes. The proposed method uses shearlet transform for feature evaluation and the combine of adaboost with support vector machine for identification. For experimentation, the author has considered two classes: empty seat and non-empty seat class. The empty seat class contains only objects of which seat and non-empty seat class contain people. The overall of the proposed method for object detection is described as Fig. 2.

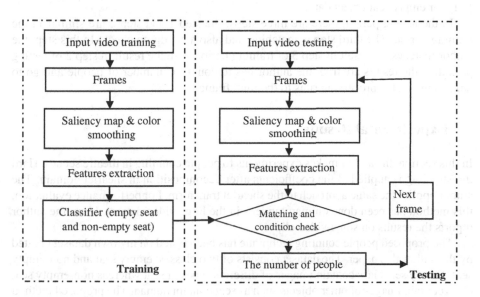

Fig. 2. The overall of the proposed method for people count.

In Fig. 2, a video sequence contains a series of frames. Each frame can be considered as an image. The proposed method includes two periods: Training and Testing. In the training periods, there are three steps:

Firstly, saliency map and color smoothing. In this step, the author uses histogram base contrast to generate the salient map. The salient map has noise problem. Therefore, the author uses color smoothing method to remove them. The histogram is used to find the saliency value for each color in an image based on the contrast method. The author uses the idea of linearly-varying smoothing weight to create the saliency map from the saliency value of each color. The saliency value of each color becomes more similar to neighbor colors and it helps grouping colors. The author also creates a binary mask to extract the object and binary the saliency maps. Defining threshold value k as average value of saliency values in the saliency map. If (the saliency value > k) then assign value = 255 and 0 otherwise.

Secondly, feature extraction and create map. The author measures a threshold value from salient map to create a mask. In here, the author uses shearlet filter for computing searched area and detecting objects. These objects are saved as the blob. The feature regression-based method will be used to describe the relationship between the low-level features together. The author defines it as: the area is total number of pixels in the blob. The perimeter is the total number of pixels on the perimeter of the blob and the total edge pixels is the total number of edge pixels in the blob.

Thirdly, the author combines adaboost with support vector machine for identification. After feature extraction for positive and negative datasets, the author will train using the combine of adaboost with support vector machine for classifiers as presented in Subsect. 2.2. The author collects sample images for training and testing the classifier. The author has collected images for two classes: empty seat and non-empty seat from conference scenes. The author has assigned value '1' for non-empty seat data and value '−1' for empty seat object data.

In the testing period, there are three steps: the step 1 and step 2 are similar in the training period. The third step is matching and also a condition check. In this step, the author matches the result in step 3 of training period with the result in step 2 of testing period. If the results are true, the author has to count the number of people and go to next frames. This processing runs to the final frame.

4 Experimental Results

In this section, the author makes experiments to people counting in theatre scenes. Hard thresholding is applied to the coefficients after decomposition in shearlet domain. The author applies the same approach to the shearlet transform. For performance evaluation, this method has been done on many videos in the large video dataset. Here, the author reports the results on some video clips.

The proposed people counting technique has been tested on my own dataset created by the author this paper. The dataset consists of two classes: empty seat and non-empty seat. Empty seat class contain images of different types of seat whereas non-empty seat class contain images of other objects such as seat contain human. The proposed method has been tested on this dataset. Some example images of both classes have been shown in Fig. 3. Some example images of conference scenes have been shown in Fig. 4.

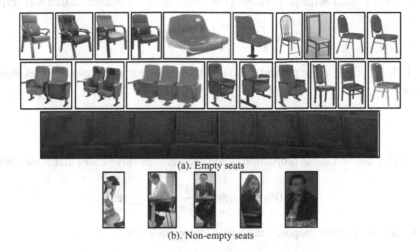

(a). Empty seats

(b). Non-empty seats

Fig. 3. Sample images of empty seat and non-empty seats objects of my own dataset

Fig. 4. Sample conference scenes in my own dataset

My experiments are scene video clips with the frame size 288 by 352. The proposed method processes this video clips at 24 frames/second. In here, the author defines as:

The different performance metrics, such as Average Classification Accuracy (ACA), True Positive Rate (TPR) (Recall) and Predicted Positive Rate (PPR) (Precision), are depended on four values: True Positive (TP), True Negative (TN), False Positive (FP) and False Negative (FN), where [25, 26]:

+ TP is the number of images, which are originally positive images and classified as positive images.

+ TN is the number of images, which are originally negative images and classified as negative images.

+ FP is the number of images, which are originally negative images and classified as positive images.

+ FN is the number of images, which are originally positive images and classified as negative images.

All above three performance metrics are defined in [25, 26]. In here, the author reviews parameters following:

+ ACA is defined as the proportion of the total number of prediction that was correct:

$$ACA = \frac{TP + TN}{TP + TN + FP + FN} \tag{8}$$

+ TPR is defined as the proportion of positive cases that were correctly classified as positive:

$$TPR \ (Recall) = \frac{TP}{FP + FN} \tag{9}$$

+ PPR is defined as the proportion of the predicted positive cases that were correct:

$$PPR \ (Precision) = \frac{TP}{FP + TP} \tag{10}$$

The accuracy of the proposed method is shown in Table 1.

Table 1. Values of performance measures of the proposed method

Video test	Time (second)	TPR (Recall) (%)	TNR (%)	FPR (%)	FNR (%)	PPR (Precision) (%)	Average accuracy (%)
Conference room 1	250	98	96	4	2	96.08	97
Conference room 2	300	98	98	2	2	98	98
Conference room 3	350	99	94	1	1	99	99
Conference room 4	400	100	100	0	0	100	100
Conference room 5	450	98	97	3	2	97	97.5

From Table 1, one can observe that the proposed method gives better performance results.

Besides, my experiments are also scene video clips with the frame size 288 by 352. The proposed method processes this video clips at 24 frames/second. In here, the author defines it as:

+ Real number presents the number of people who's sitting in conference room to scenarios.

+ Counting Number presents the number of people which the system counted.

The accuracy of the proposed method is shown in Table 2.

Table 2. The accuracy of people counting

Video test	Time (second)	Real people number in scenarios	People counting number in scenarios which the system counted	Accuracy (%)
Conference room 6	400	121	120	99.1
Conference room 7	450	59	58	98.3
Conference room 8	500	39	39	100.0
Conference room 9	550	102	101	99.0
Conference room 10	600	52	51	98.0

From Table 2, the proposed method also gives better performance results.

5   Conclusions and Future Works

People counting is an important task in visual-based surveillance system. In conference scenes, the objects are usually occlusion, blurring and noising because of low light, light changing, many color light, etc. The task of people counting is not easy to solve problems. In this paper, the author proposes a method to implement for people counting in conference scenes based on shearlet domain. The author uses shearlet transform and combine of adaboost with support vector machine for classification. The accuracy of people counting is high. However, if the conference scene is not clear the proposed method will be affected. The step of the proposed method is salient map and color smoothing. As mentioned above, the saliency value of each color becomes more similar to neighbor colors and it helps grouping colors. In the future work, the author will improve the color smoothing steps to reduce the impact of light change.

Acknowledgment. This research is funded by Vietnam National University Ho Chi Minh City (VNU-HCM) under grant number C2015-20-08.

References

1. Cai, Z., Yu, Z.L., Liu, H., Zhang, K.: Counting people in crowded scenes by video analyzing. In: IEEE Conference on Industrial Electronics and Applications (ICIEA), pp. 1841–1845 (2014)
2. Hou, Y.-L., Pang, G.K.: People counting and human detection in a challenging situation. IEEE Trans. Syst. Man Cybern. Part A Syst. Hum. **41**(1), 24–33 (2011)
3. Chan, A.B., Vasconcelos, N.: Counting people with low-level features and Bayesian regression. IEEE Trans. Image Process. **21**, 2160–2177 (2012)
4. Xu, H., Lv, P., Meng, L.: A people counting system based on head-shoulder detection and tracking in surveillance video. In: IEEE International Conference on Computer Design and Applications (ICCDA), vol. 1, pp. V1–V394 (2010)
5. Chen, L., Wu, H., Zhao, S., Gu, J.: Head-shoulder detection using joint hog features for people counting and video surveillance in library. In: IEEE Workshop on Electronics, Computer and Applications, pp. 429–432 (2014)
6. Bala Subburaman, V., Descamps, A., Carincotte, C.: Counting people in the crowd using a generic head detector. In: IEEE International Workshop on Performance Evaluation of Tracking and Surveillance (2012)

7. Teixeira, T., Savvides, A.: Lightweight people counting and localizing in indoor spaces using camera sensor nodes. In: First ACM/IEEE International Conference on Distributed Smart Cameras, ICDSC 2007, pp. 36–43 (2007)

8. Chan, A.B., Vasconcelos, N.: Privacy preserving crowd monitoring: counting people without people models or tracking. In: IEEE Conference on Computer Vision and Pattern Recognition, pp. 1–7 (2008)

9. Wang, J., Fu, W., Liu, J., Lu, H.: Spatio-temporal group context for pedestrian counting. IEEE Trans. Circuits Syst. Video Technol., 1–11 (2014)

10. Zhang, E., Chen, F.: A fast and robust people counting method in video surveillance. In: International Conference on Computational Intelligence and Security, pp. 339–343. IEEE (2007)

11. Luo, J., Wang, J., Xu, H., Lu, H.: A real-time people counting approach in indoor environment. In: He, X., Luo, S., Tao, D., Xu, C., Yang, J., Hasan, M.A. (eds.) MMM 2015. LNCS, vol. 8935, pp. 214–223. Springer, Heidelberg (2015). doi:10.1007/978-3-319-14445-0_19

12. Wu, B., Nevatia, R.: Detection and tracking of multiple, partially occluded humans by bayesian combination of edgelet based part detectors. Int. J. Comput. Vis. 75(2), 247–266 (2007)

13. Kong, D., Gray, D., Hat, T.: A viewpoint invariant approach for crowd counting. In: Proceedings of the International Conference on Pattern Recognition, pp. 1187–1190 (2006)

14. Kutyniok, G., Labate, D.: Shearlets: Multiscale Analysis for Multivariate Data. Applied and Numerical Harmonic Analysis. Birkhauser (2012)

15. Lim, W.-Q.: The discrete shearlet transform: a new directional transform and compactly supported shearlet frames. IEEE Trans. Image Process. 19(5), 1166–1180 (2010)

16. Guo, K., Labate, D.: Optimally sparse multidimensional representation using shearlets. SIAM J. Math. Anal. 39, 298–318 (2007)

17. Comaniciu, D., Meer, P.: Mean shift: a robust approach toward feature space analysis. IEEE Trans. Pattern Anal. Mach. Intell. 24(5), 603–619 (2002)

18. Patel, V.M., Easley, G.R., Healy Jr., D.M.: Shearlet-based deconvolution. IEEE Trans. Image Process. 18(12), 2673–2685 (2009)

19. Thanh Binh, N., Khare, A.: Object tracking of video sequences in curvelet domain. Int. J. Image Graph. 11(1), 1–20 (2011)

20. Zivkovic, Z., Krose, B.: An EM-like algorithm for color histogram-based object tracking. In: Proceedings of the IEEE Computer Society Conference on Computer Vision and Pattern Recognition (CVPR 2004), Washington, DC, USA, vol. 1, pp. 798–803 (2004)

21. Yilmaz, A., Javed, O., Shah, M.: Object tracking: a survey. ACM Comput. Surv. 38(4) (2006)

22. Wang, D.: Unsupervised video segmentation based on watersheds and temporal tracking. IEEE Trans. Circuits Syst. Video Technol. 8(5), 539–546 (1998)

23. Li, X., Wang, L., Sung, E.: AdaBoost with SVM-based component classifiers. Eng. Appl. Artif. Intell. 21, 785–795 (2008)

24. Morra, J.H., Tu, Z., Apostolova, L.G., Green, A.E., Toga, A.W., Thompson, P.M.: Comparison of AdaBoost and support vector machines for detecting Alzheimer's disease through automated hippocampal segmentation. IEEE Trans. Med. Imaging 29(1), 30–43 (2010)

25. Khare, M., Thanh Binh, N., Srivastava, R.K.: Dual tree complex wavelet transform based human object classification using support vector machine. J. Sci. Technol. 51(4B), 134–142 (2013)

26. Thanh Binh, N.: Object classification based on contourlet transform in outdoor environment. Nat. Comput. Commun. 144, 341–349 (2015)

Developing Database of Vietnamese Abbreviations and Some Applications

Nguyen Nho Tuy[1(✉)] and Phan Huy Khanh[2]

[1] VNPT Da Nang, Danang, Vietnam
nhotuy68@gmail.com
[2] University of Science and Technology – The University of Danang, Danang, Vietnam
khanhph29@gmail.com

Abstract. Abbreviations (CVT) in documents are widely used in various fields and in many languages including Vietnamese. In fact, currently, abbreviations are often repeatedly and unclearly used, demand for abbreviation use is increasing that requests a database of plentiful abbreviations which is saved and used conveniently, is easy to update and consistently exploited. In this article, we propose an opening solution in order to develop a database of Vietnamese abbreviations for many purposes of use during processing language and exploiting database.

Keywords: Abbreviation · Acronym · Database · Index abbreviation

1 Introdution

Abbreviations have been often used in daily life and widely used in almost all of languages in the world so far, including Vietnamese. In newspapers, magazines, we often see common abbreviations such as TƯ (Trung ương), UBND (Uỷ ban nhân dân), and also English abbreviations such as WTO (World Trade Organization, etc. Owing to abbreviations, all texts are shorter and simpler but express more capacity of information. The fact that abbreviations are often used makes the abbreviation system increasingly diversified and abundant. On the one hand, users (NSD) have many abbreviations to choose and use, on the other hand the users also run into a lot of difficulty in finding, searching its meanings and proper using of such abbreviations.

With regard to abbreviations, there are some dictionaries today such as "Từ điển giải nghĩa thuật ngữ Viễn thông" (Dictionary of telecommunication), "Thuật ngữ viết tắt Viễn thông" [8] (Dictionary of abbreviations in telecommunication; websites of CVT [16], but mainly in foreign languages. The need of abbreviations is higher and higher, wider and wider and indispensable, especially brands, trademarks, etc.

Contents of this article include: Firstly, we present information about abbreviations, history of abbreviation development, principle to create abbreviations, classification of abbreviations and influential factors in abbreviation generation. Next, we present a solution to developing database of abbreviations, statistically assess results and give solution of abbreviations. The final is conclusions.

© ICST Institute for Computer Sciences, Social Informatics and Telecommunications Engineering 2016
P.C. Vinh et al. (Eds.): ICTCC 2016, LNICST 168, pp. 373–383, 2016.
DOI: 10.1007/978-3-319-46909-6_34

2 Information About Abbreviations

2.1 Definition and Terms

The term "chữ viết tắt" (In English: abbreviation) has not been appeared in Common Vietnamese dictionary in current market[1] including in "Từ điển Bách khoa Việt Nam" Vol. 1 (Letters A-Đ[2]), but is very familiar in daily life.

We often see abbreviations or acronyms. They are used for generating abbreviations that are different from common written languages; abbreviations are used when we have to repeatedly write a word, phrase, sentence or paragraph for convenience [8]. For a long time ago, people used abbreviations to inscribe on stone, wood, etc. in order to save time, force and material. According to Manuel Zahariev [14], abbreviations are originated in Ancient Greek, *acronym* includes *akron* (the last or first one) and *onoma* (name or voice). According to some English dictionaries, abbreviations are the way to form new shorter words by using initial letters, or last letters or any letters of a word. For example, UNESCO stands for "United Nations Educational, Scientific and Cultural Organization", etc.

We also see abbreviations in short form, it means that a phrase or a paragraph is abridged in some characters, is extracted, chose or replaced any part to form a set of new characters, in order to writing and saying are more convenient. For example, abbreviations are used for geographical areas, for example, Thanh Land, Nghe Land, Quang Land, etc.

In the progress of Internet explosion, general written languages have been developed towards a new direction owing to the use of various abbreviations and conventional signs. For example, in English, email, messages, IMHO stands for "in my humble opinion", comic signs ☺, ☻, U (you)… The use of abbreviations in fields of information technology and communication today on one hand makes users beneficial, on the other hand, such diversity of abbreviations also troubles the users.

2.2 History of Abbreviations

Abbreviations have been widely used for a long time ago in foreign countries. For example, SPQR stands for "Senatus Populusque Romæ" and have been appeared for nearly 2000 years [14], QED stands for "Quod Erat Demonstrandum" in "Ethica More Geometrico Demonstrata" of a philosopher, Benedictus de Spinoza (1632–1677).

In Vietnam, today, there are some researches into Vietnamese abbreviations [4, 12], but such researches are not complete and systematic, although Vietnamese abbreviations have been early formed. The formation of "chữ Nôm" (an ancient ideographic vernacular script of the Vietnamese language) since the 18th century has been other way to write "chữ Hán" (Chinese writing), replacing "chữ Hán" after nearly one thousand years of occupation and colonization by the Han [2, 3]. In the "chữ Nôm", each "chữ Nôm" is

---

[1] Vietnamese-English dictionary, Bui Phung, published by global publishing house in 1998.
[2] Vietnam encyclopedia compilation steering council compiled. Vietnam encyclopedia compilation center published in 1995.

square, is formed by putting "chữ Hán" together in the form of onomatopoeia, picto-graphic or reducing characters, abbreviation. For example, the Chinese writing 共 (total) is reduced its characters into "chữ Nôm" 圡 (khạng), "chữ Hán" 爲 is reduced its characters into "chữ Nôm" 𡈽 (làm).

When Vietnamese national language (Current Vietnamese language) had been widely used, abbreviations have been used. The pen name C.D. standing for Chương Dân is official name of Phan Khôi in "Đông Pháp Thời Báo" in 1928. Today, Vietnamese abbreviations are being used increasingly widely in many fields.

Many authors think that Vietnamese abbreviations refer to a grammar [1, 9, 10]. According to Prof. Nguyen Tai Can, we "*use abbreviation in form of one syllable rather than in form of initial letters. The acronyms such as DT (danh từ), VN (Việt Nam), HTX (hợp tác xã), etc. only are used in writing documents*". Although there are many views of the use of abbreviations, abbreviations are existing as an internal part of Vietnamese language, and there are many abbreviation applications in communication, text processing, data exploitation [5], etc.

2.3 Principles of Abbreviation Generation

Based on the results of analysis, the demand and current status of the abbreviation use in daily life, we proposed 07 Principles of abbreviation generation as detailed [4], and now, we supplement 2 new Principles of abbreviation generation (Principles 8 and 9).

1. 7 Principles of abbreviation generation that have been developed: Principle of abbreviation; principle of word connection; principle of short connection by meaningful words; principle of sub-letters; principle of connection of foreign languages; principle of borrowing of abbreviations in foreign languages; principle of random abbreviation.

2. 2 new principles include:
   (1) Principle of encrypted abbreviations:
      In many fields and sections, reminiscent abbreviations are used in conformity with a predefined rule to encrypt the phrase. All encrypted abbreviations often must satisfy:
      i. Encrypted abbreviations often are issued by an organization with scope of use and application.
      ii. Encrypted abbreviations are unique and unduplicated to avoid ambiguity.
      iii. Encrypted abbreviations are often used new characters according to a predefined rule.
      For example, lists and tables in database, list of national codes, regional codes, sectional codes, and codes of telecom fiber optic cables, etc.
   (2) Principle of abbreviations in database:
      According to studying in theories of searching problems, relevant practical results and the efficient use of abbreviations, we propose some principles applying index abbreviations in order to search data in large database:
      i. Abbreviations only are used English letters (not Vietnamese words) and digits 0...9

    ii. Don't use special characters: punctuation marks, space (SP)

   iii. Abbreviations are reminiscent, short, not unduplicated, and not unclear: Users immediately image abbreviations after determining request for information searching.

   iv. Implement index of database on the established fields of abbreviations.

The Fig. 4 shows the results of developing database by applying abbreviations for index (called *index abbreviations)* and phone subscriber lookup in the Switchboard 108 VNPT Da Nang [5].

2.4   Influential Factors in the New Abbreviation Generation

According to the field survey, we propose 4 influential factors in the generation of new abbreviations, particularly:

Number of characters: Abbreviations shall not be too long. In general, common number of characters of an abbreviation should not more than 18 characters.

Marks in Vietnamese language: Avoid vowel with mark such as *â, ă, ơ, ê…*, don't use grave, acute, question mark and dot below in abbreviations in order to avoid misunderstanding, difficult to speak.

Spiritual factors for East Asians: Select number of characters of an abbreviation. Avoid number 2, number 4 or avoid number of characters of an abbreviation according to the conception of *birth, old age, illness, death*. In order to generate the word "*birth*", the number of characters of an abbreviation shall be 5, 9, 13, etc., and in to generate the word "*old age*", the number of characters of an abbreviation shall be 2, 6, 14, etc.

Syllable: Select abbreviations so that when being read, such abbreviations are formed opening and deep hollow notes. People often choose *a, ô, i,* or *ex, ec,* rather than *ê, ơ.*

Two last factors often are specially considered when finding abbreviated name of enterprises, companies, brands, trademarks, organizations, projects, etc.

2.5   The Use of Abbreviations

Generally, users shall define or explain all abbreviations in documents. There are two cases as below:

Using available abbreviations: Abbreviations are defined and explained previously, or commonly used, not unclear.

Using new abbreviations: Defining and using abbreviations right after initial appearance in documents in the form of:

<Complete phrase > (< Abbreviation >)

The above principles of abbreviation generation allow us to refer 05 signs of abbreviations in a Vietnamese document, particularly:

(1) Abbreviations are placed in brackets (…), or placed after the phrases: "viết tắt là", "viết tắt", "gọi tắt là"…(hereinafter referred to as…, hereinafter called, etc.) when the abbreviations are defined initially.
(2) Abbreviations are capital letters (lowercase in normal letters)
(3) Abbreviations include special letters or marks: *and (&), cross mark (/), dash (-), dot (.), space*, and letters and digits, etc.
(4) Abbreviations are words whose number of characters may be 18.
(5) Vietnamese abbreviations shall not include vowels *â, ă, ơ, ê, ô…* don't use marks such as *grave, acute, question mark and dot below*.

2.6 Ambiguity of Abbreviations

Ambiguity of abbreviations is not rare, the ambiguity is formed by natures: difficult to understand abbreviations, arbitrary abbreviations, not complying with rules, difficult to define meaning of abbreviations:

For example: VH: Văn hóa, Văn học; Abbreviations are local, uncommon: Cao Xà Lá: Cao su, Xà phòng, Thuốc lá; Phối kết hợp: Phối hợp, kết hợp; not complying with rules: SKZ: s̲úng k̲hông giật/z̲…

The principles of abbreviation generation 1–8 often cause Ambiguity. The principles 8, 9 do not cause Ambiguity within scope and application of abbreviations. However, Vietnamese abbreviations in general have the following characteristics:

(1) Difficult to define meaning of abbreviations due to the way of writing
(2) Abbreviations often are formed for easy to speak, to remember and convenient, thus abbreviations are often concise and polysemous.
(3) Abbreviations continuously change; the formation of language @ and use of foreign language abbreviations make abbreviations increasingly plentiful and diversified;

2.7 Classification of Abbreviations

There are many methods in classifications of abbreviations, basing on field of use, site, or alphabet, etc. In article published in 2006 [4], we recognized 9 fields; and by now, with classifications of abbreviations up on field of use, we recognized the 12 main fields (Table 1).

Table 1. Statistics of database of abbreviations.

Cate-gory	Fields of abbreviations	Manual update	Automatic update	Total	% of auto-update
1	Information technology and communication	754	350	1104	32 %
2	Government, political and social organizations	301	120	421	29 %
3	Science, technology and engineering	273	253	526	48 %
4	Military	202	120	322	37 %
5	Medicine	253	255	508	50 %
6	Education	301	2378	2679	89 %
7	Finance, trade	403	140	543	26 %
8	Environmental resources	163	130	293	44 %
9	Community communication	121	125	246	51 %
10	Religion	0	150	150	100 %
11	Proper name	0	75	75	100 %
12	Other	0	120	120	100 %
	Total	**2771**	**4216**	**6987**	**60 %**

3   Developing Database of Vietnamese Abbreviations and Some Applications

3.1   Model of Database

We develop database (database) for abbreviations, including 3 tables of DULIEUCVT (data of abbreviation), PHANLOPCVT (classification of abbreviation) and NGUOICNCVT (editor of abbreviation) with relations as figure below (Fig. 1).

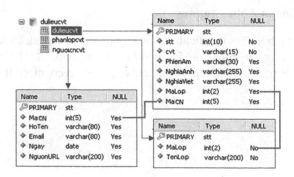

Fig. 1. Relations of database of abbreviations.

Table DULIEUCVT contains information including: order of abbreviations, field of abbreviations, phonetic field to easily read the fields, field of meanings (explanations) in English and fields in Vietnamese, fields of layer codes and fields of updated codes which are outer locks connecting to two databases accordingly. Table DULIEUCVT contains all possible abbreviations for exploit and continuous update. Table PHAN-LOPCVT enlists layers of abbreviations including code and name of layer.

3.2 Update of Abbreviations

We use different sources of abbreviations to update the database. The update process is conducted in the two main steps:

Step 1: Manually update
    Directly update into WinWord documents from different sources like books, newspapers, magazine, legal documents, scientific reports or practicality, etc.

Step 2: Auto-update from internet
    Base on the result of step 1, continue to automatically enrich database of abbreviations from Internet environment. Base on the aware signals of abbreviations in a document, we draw new abbreviations to supplement the database. We also develop a search engine for abbreviations as the introduced principles in [13]. Algorithm describes the operations of search engine for abbreviations [4] in the Internet environment is shown as below:

```
Algorithm :
Input : Address URL
Output: Data of abbreviations in table TUDONGCVT
Open intermediary database
Define operative URL
Save URL in intermediary database
Activate abbreviation counter
Repeat
   Open a file HTML
   Read content respectively HTML
   Dissect data (remove space and tags HTML)
   Find abbreviations basing on aware signals
   If found abbreviations Then
      Check whether abbreviations exist or not?
      If abbreviations exist CVT Then
         Increase abbreviation counter
      Else
         Save  abbreviations  and  put  the  corresponding
         value by 1
         Extract sentences containing abbreviations
      End If
   End If
Until no more HTML
```

After collecting abbreviations from files HTML, continue to classify abbreviations to add in database.

Step 3: Compile data for abbreviations

This phase needs the involvement of experts to retrieve, refine and edit data. The updating process will include test and warnings for repeat of abbreviations or repeat in meanings.

Interface of Admin website for update and edit of abbreviations will be developed as the Fig. 2.

Fig. 2.   Interface of Admin website for edit and update of database of abbreviations.

3.3   Statistics of the Result

Formerly, we focused on the update of abbreviations in English. By now, we have enlisted the number of existing English and Vietnamese abbreviations in database as follows:

According to the statistics result, much data of abbreviations is barely updated; abbreviations continuously change. Particularly, education field owns lots of abbreviations, mainly relating to code of colleges, professionals and specialties.

Fig. 3.   Interface of website for abbreviation exploitation.

3.4   Website for Management and Use of Abbreviations

We build a website www.chuviettat.com (Fig. 3) containing database of abbreviations and managing online searching of abbreviations in Vietnamese and English to serve users intensively.

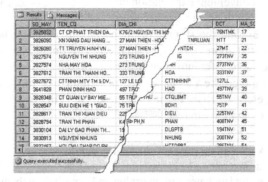

Fig. 4. Result of building database for phone subscriber lookup through Switchboard 108 VNPT-Da Nang

3.5   Abbreviation Transfer in Database

Beforehand, we transfer abbreviations from Vietnamese into English for storage which helps the online searching of foreigners, users, comparison, and definitions and avoids the repeat of abbreviations. Subsequently, the fully edition will be published in book.

3.6   Abbreviation Use in Database Exploitation

Capacity of the information search depends not only on the resource capacity of the system or searching algorithm but also operative and processing time on users' computer (users).

From the access, study and formation of abbreviation database, we use abbreviations in practical works. We informed a measure by developing a generation function for abbreviations (abbreviations) to apply into the rebuilding of database (database) upon the customer information at Switchboard 108 VNPT Da Nang. We also apply the practicality of the measure like abbreviations indicating sections, and the short insert of the word abbreviation at abbreviation search does bring practical benefits for Switchboard 108 VNPT in information search among customers [5].

4   Conclusion

Approach and study abbreviations, aggregate the principles of abbreviation generation, build database of abbreviations to serve users in exploitation, storage, statistics and use; especially the abbreviation use in the formation of indicating sections for better search of specialized database would be beneficial in enhancing productivity and practical use of data.

Besides, use abbreviations coherently and universally to standardize the system of abbreviations for users, gradually enlarge the system of vocabulary, contribute to the development of language. The proposal of rules, methods in management, building of an abundant storage, convenient exploitation and use, easy update, formation of forum, new addition of abbreviations, etc. are necessary and beneficial.

We continue to expand the storage of abbreviations in many fields, increase the number of auto-updated abbreviations, evaluation of frequent occurrences and abbreviation use; enhance the transfer into many different languages; and expand the searching capacity in multi-language like Vietnamese-Kinh, language of ethnic minorities (Cham, Ede, Thai, Kh'me, etc.), English, French, Chinese, etc. This is a righteously oriented pathway to satisfy a common interest.

Acknowledgment. Author group sincerely send our gratefulness to staffs of Switchboard 1080 VNPT Da Nang to create favorable conditions during the process of approach, building of database of abbreviations and abbreviation use, also to exploit and contribute actively for the completion of database.

References

1. Can, N.T.: Vietnamese Grammar. Publishing House of University and Professional Secondary School, Hanoi (1981)
2. Hang, L.M.: Nom in context of regional culture. In: International Conference About Nom, Between 12–13 November 2004, National Library of Vietnam (2004)
3. Nhan, N.T., Viet, N.T., Nom Na group: Nom Na process. In: Summer Conference 2002 at Maine University (2002)
4. Khanh, P.H., Tuy, N.N.: Study to build up database of abbreviations in service 1080 of Da Nang Post office. In: Summary Record of National Scientific Conference "Some selected issues of information technology and media" (2006)
5. Tuy, N.N., Khanh, P.H.: Abbreviation use in service exploitation of switchboard 108 VNPT Da Nang City. IJISET Int. J. Innovative Sci Eng. Technol. 3(1), 222–227 (2016)
6. Khanh, P.H.: Build database of multi-language vocabulary in form of document RTF Winword. In: Summary Record of National Scientific Conference ICT, rda 2003, pp. 103–110 (2003)
7. Khanh, P.H.: Use programming tools macro VBA, build up text processing facilities. In: Summary Record of the Third Scientific Conference, Da Nang University, pp. 255–261, November 2004
8. Viet, N.T., Bang, D.K.: Terms in Telecommunication abbreviations. Publisher of post office (1999)
9. Thuy, N.T.T.: Vietnamese vocabulary. Remote training curriculum of Can Tho University
10. Van Be, C.: Vietnamese grammar. Remote training curriculum of Can Tho University
11. Thuy, N.T.T., Chinh, N.H.: Overview of language and linguistics. Remote training curriculum of Can Tho University
12. Phap, H.C., Van Hue, N.: Study, collect and build up database of abbreviations in Vietnamese. J. Sci. Technol. Da Nang Univ. 7(80) (2014)

13. Hiep, H.: Build up searching tools by PHP and MySQL. J. Posts Telecommun. Inf. Technol., series 2, September 2004
14. Zahariev, M.: Acronyms. Simon Fraser University, June 2004
15. http://chuvietnhanh.sourceforge.net/
16. http://www.acronymfinder.com

Architectural Pattern for Inter-Organizational Middleware Systems

Radhouane B.N. Jrad[1](✉) and David Sundaram[2]

[1] OJI Fibre Solutions, Auckland, New Zealand
Rad.Jrad@OJIFS.co.nz
[2] University of Auckland, Auckland, New Zealand
D.Sundaram@Auckland.ac.nz

Abstract. Effective Business-to-Business (B2B) relationships typically rely on seamless integration of partner's processes. Inter-Organizational Information Systems (IOIS) have largely been endorsed as B2B enablers. They are defined as automated Information Systems crossing organizational frontiers and aiming to synergize partners' efforts in increasing competitiveness and cost management (Eom 2005). The components in IOIS responsible for the actual bridging between partners' heterogonous systems are referred to as Inter-Organizational Middleware Systems (IOMS). While IOMS critically hold business information, they lack both research and standardization. Instead, chaotic and costly efforts to architect and manage IOMS have dominated the market. As a remedy, we propose an IOMS-specific architectural pattern that could be used to develop its architecture(s). First, the notions of frameworks and architectures are presented. Then, approaches to IOIS architecture and process management are discussed, before IOMS's need for its specific architectures is presented. The MAPIS architectural design is then proposed and its merits and limitations are discussed.

Keywords:: MAPIS · IOMS · IOIS · IOS · Framework · EA · SOA · EDA · Adaptive · Middleware · Architecture · Pattern · IADR · Action Research · Design Science

1 Introduction

Humans have been architecting their assets since the beginnings (Jarzombek 2013). Classically, architecture is regarded as the art and the practice of carefully designing and constructing buildings in a manner that typically reflects the style of a specific period, place, and/or culture (Oxford 2014). Over the last decades, however, the scale of the definition has been widened to embrace other human artifacts including Information Systems (IS). The aim of this paper is to look at architectures in IS, and to put forward arguments about the need for a specific architecture to Inter-Organizational middleware Systems (IOMS), and then to actually propose and validate an architectural pattern towards answering such a need.

The ever-increasing complexity of IT created a need for order and structure in a similar way to the construction field. IEEE presents architecture in IT as "fundamental concepts or properties of a system in its environment embodied in its elements,

© ICST Institute for Computer Sciences, Social Informatics and Telecommunications Engineering 2016
P.C. Vinh et al. (Eds.): ICTCC 2016, LNICST 168, pp. 384–390, 2016.
DOI: 10.1007/978-3-319-46909-6_35

relationships, and in the principles of its design and evolution" (Drews and Schirmer 2014). Since Zachman identified the need for architecture in IS (Zachman 1987), multitudes of subgenres emerged to specifically focus on various aspects of the enterprise and its IT assets. Enterprise Architecture (EA) could be defined as a precise and unambiguous future-oriented practice for conducting fundamental analysis, design, planning, implementation, and governance of an enterprise's present and target IT landscapes; and optimizing and integrating its processes, while specifically accounting for fragmented and legacy processes (Federation of Enterprise Architecture Professional Organizations 2013; Kotusev and Storey 2015; Niemann 2006; Winter and Fischer 2006). However the development of EAs in a multi-organizational environment or for the inter-organizational use remains scarcely researched (Drews and Schirmer 2014). In today's turbulent business conjuncture where alliances are true needs in the business spectrum, the lack of integrative architectures at various levels represents a business risk (He et al. 2015). It has therefore become important that organizations promote the integration of B2B partners into their EA analysis and planning (Drews and Schirmer 2014). In that line, a clear and adaptive architecture for processes that spread beyond the organization's frontier has become a must.

2   IOIS Architecture and Processes

B2B can be achieved by different means. One particular concept that gained an explosive interest from the business world over the last decades is the Inter-Organizational Information System (IOIS). IOISs are shared automated ISs spanning over multiple organizations, with every partner managing their part of the IOIS within their own organization's structural, strategic, technological and commercial context (Jrad and Sundaram 2015a). Despite the IOIS as a phenomena has links with virtually every major area of IS research it still fails to attract enough research interest (Haki and Forte 2010; Jrad 2014). In particular, handling IOIS diffusion over multiple organizations, locations, countries, legal systems, cultures, and time zones remains feebly investigated (Jrad and Sundaram 2015b). It is therefore only fair to say that there has been no real or strong effort standardizing the approach to architect IOIS.

From an architectural perspective, Event-Driven Architecture (EDA) has been present in IOISs because it is business-logic friendly. In effect, EDA allows the development of processes that react to event-driven change of statuses (Maréchaux 2006; McGovern et al. 2006), e.g. when stock status changes to "critical". However, the arrival of Service-Oriented Architecture (SOA) has allowed IOIS to become better and more agile at integrating processes because of SOA's emphasis on loosely coupling as well as reusing systems, components, and processes through common standards and protocols (Haki and Forte 2010). Through SOA, IOIS permits otherwise independent organizations, to share common functionalities instead of each cumbersomely developing their own version of the same functionality or to develop too-complex mechanisms for sharing information (He et al. 2015; Maréchaux 2006). While the reliance of SOA on web services as front-ends permits IOIS to be efficient in including and excluding partners, the architecture allows for a lower level of trust amongst partners in the same IOIS. Indeed, since web services are the first point of contact for partners, disabling or enabling their access usually equates to adding or deleting an organization from the IOIS process.

The key feature associated with B2B and IOIS is "Integration". In order to enable business adaptivity, it is undeniably important that the integration aspect of inter-organizational business processes is designed, architected, governed, and managed on its own specifities and merits, independently from other IOIS layers. From industrial view, the authors have noted that a lack of explicit isolation of the integration layer has been an important element in the stories of failed IOIS and ERP implementations.

3 MAPIS: An IOMS Architectural Pattern

The integrator component in IOIS allowing the actual bridging between partnering organizations is referred to as the Inter-Organizational Middleware System (IOMS) (Fig. 1). IOMS is defined as an "inter-organizational collection of Enterprise Application Integration (EAI) and Enterprise Messaging Systems (EMS) policies, procedures, methods, and services that work together to allow heterogeneous applications from different organizations to communicate, exchange information and validate each other's input and output" (Jrad 2014). If it is SOA-based, IOMS can be regarded as an advanced inter-organizational Enterprise Service Bus (ESB).

IOMS goes beyond merely establishing technological channels between otherwise architecturally heterogeneous computer systems from different partners. It in fact is a true part of the business process spectrum and as such holds business logic. However, because of its invisibility to most stakeholders, and because it is not a business generating instrument, it is common to ignore IOMS requirements in terms of lifecycle management and governance or to include them as part of IOIS or ERP processes (Jrad et al. 2013; Jrad 2014). IOMSs have in reality their own unique characteristics and particular risks and impact associated with their governance and projects. Accordingly, they need to be managed in a specific and significantly different way from other ISs. IOMS has resolutely become an expert domain requiring a strong combination of general IT knowledge with specific domain knowledge as well as business knowledge (Jrad and Sundaram 2015b). Subsequently, the importance of engaging the organization's IOMS teams in projects has increased in importance. As opposed to other ISs, IOMS projects are indeed better managed and run by the organization's employees while being supported by external resources, not the other way around

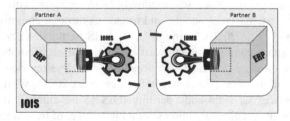

Fig. 1. Placement of IOMS inside IOIS

(Jrad and Sundaram 2015b). As such, researching IOMS would be most suitable using methodologies that allow the researcher to be knowledgeable of the subject and involved in the project, even part of the organization itself.

Architecting IOMS cannot be fully achieved using existing IOIS and ERP upgrade methodologies (Jrad 2014). Oddly, not only there is a lack of research into the subject, but market observation has highlighted a clear lack of managerial acknowledgement of the need to architect IOMS. Instead, organizations tend to resort to ad-hoc, "quick-and-dirty" solutions to fulfill integration requirements. The culmination of reliance on quick fixes is often a serious problem of legacy processes that has developed even though IOMS as a concept is relatively new (Jrad and Sundaram 2015c). One of the reasons for the absence of standardized IOMS architectures is the shortage of IOMS frameworks. Applying partly or completely irrelevant frameworks has been identified as a common cause for failed IOMS upgrades (Jrad and Sundaram 2015c). In this work, we are proposing a high-level IOMS-specific architectural pattern that could be applied to create actual adaptive architectures for IOMS. We label this architectural pattern as the Middleware Architecture Pattern for Inter-organizational Systems (MAPIS) (Fig. 2). MAPIS was constructed based on the Framework for Upgrading IOMS (FUI) which is an IOMS-specific framework (Jrad and Sundaram 2015c). MAPIS accounts for both SOA and EDA designs. While SOA lacks reactivity to events, EDA suffers from processes dependency. The ED-SOA combination (Levina and Stantchev 2009) allows for event and service based processes to coexist while ensuring services decoupling.

Looking at Fig. 2, MAPIS divides transactions handling into 2 tiers: At first Front-End processes receive details and content of transactions and transform them into canonical/standardized formats. Then, Back-End processes perform the required tasks associated with these transactions. The separation of the processes into 2 tiers ensures that regardless of what is being received all data of same nature is processed in a similar (standard) way. For instance, while various partners would send invoices in different formats, these invoices are converted into the organization's standard invoice format before being processed. When a new partner joins the IOIS, the effort is put into transforming their invoices into the standard format without affecting other partners'

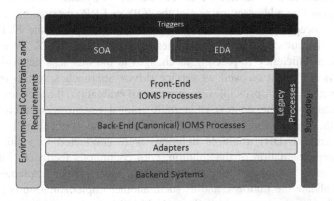

Fig. 2. Middleware Architecture Pattern for Inter-organizational Systems (MAPIS)

invoices. In the eventuality that the canonical format requires modification, the change would be in one place for all partners. Such maneuver enables the flexibility required in managing partnerships. Importantly however, MAPIS acknowledges that not all processes can be easily subjected to the 2-tier process. Legacy processes can be a challenge to reengineer or even impossible to modify. These types of legacy processes are referred to as unupgradable legacy processes (Jrad et al. 2013).

The triggers in the MAPIS refer to internal and external start points for the process (e.g. user passing an order), while the environmental constrains and requirements represent legal, project, security and other environmental aspects. The MAPIS architectural pattern has been constructed based on a combined 20 years of the authors' experience in IOIS and IOMS projects. As such, it has gone through multitude of iterations from concept to refinement, to application and validation. To test its implementability, an IOMS project in an international company with advanced e-business capabilities and cross-continental IOIS and IOMS systems was used. Guided by the concepts and principles of Insider Action Design Research (IADR), we embarked on a project to upgrade the IOMS infrastructure to the latest available technology (if/where possible). IADR methodology uses the researcher's interaction with the observed phenomenon and the feedback loops to create and implement a system as an outcome of the research (Jrad et al. 2014; Jrad and Sundaram 2015c). IADR consists of Design Science iterations aiming at building and refining the solution, backed by iterations of Action Research cycles to implement and analyze the said solution (Jrad et al. 2014). After agreeing on the FUI framework as a basis for developing the architecture, and leaning on IADR, Design Science cycles were used to design and collect feedback about the architecture, while the actual implementations were performed using Action Research rounds. Every loop returned feedback that was used to enhance subsequent cycles. Multiple iterations were executed until the final and agreed architecture was reached.

4 Discussion and Conclusion

In this paper we proposed a tailored architectural pattern for IOMS that we labeled Middleware Architecture Pattern for Inter-organizational Systems (MAPIS). We argued that IOMS cannot be addressed as part of the IOIS or ERP systems, but instead as an independent concept. MAPIS architectural pattern was based on the FUI framework supported by the authors' extensive experience in IOIS and IOMS. To ensure adaptivity as well as efficiency in reacting to changes in the business network, the architecture allows for event as well as service driven approaches, while remaining in compliance with the SOA principles. As a means of evaluation, the architecture was put to implementation in the context of a multinational organization taking part of a complex IOIS. Driving the implementation based on the concept of Insider Action Design Research (IADR), multiple iterations were conducted to validate both the design and implementation of the solution, with continuous feedback. The merits of MAPIS, however, should not hide its limitations. First, further implementations are required to validate the findings, and as such, another implementation is planned in a second multinational organization. Second, MAPIS does not account for simpler business scenarios. Indeed, it might be regarded as too complex for basic business contexts. MAPIS is therefore restricted to the context of mid to large organizations subscribing to complex IOISs. Further research is critically needed to offer different options when it comes to IOMS architecture.

References

Drews, P., Schirmer, I.: From enterprise architecture to business ecosystem architecture. In: 2014 IEEE 18th International Enterprise Distributed Object Computing Conference Workshops and Demonstrations, pp. 13–22. IEEE Comput. Soc. (2014)

Eom, S.B.: Inter-Organizational Information Systems in the Internet Age. IGI Global, Missouri (2005). Eom, S.B. (ed.)

Federation of Enterprise Architecture Professional Organizations: A common perspective on enterprise architecture. Archit. Gov. Mag. 9, 1–12 (2013)

Haki, M.K., Forte, M.W.: Inter-organizational information system architecture: a service-oriented approach. In: Camarinha-Matos, L.M., Boucher, X., Afsarmanesh, H. (eds.) PRO-VE 2010. IFIP AICT, vol. 336, pp. 642–652. Springer, Heidelberg (2010)

He, J.J., Jrad, R.B.N., Sundaram, D.: Adaptive business network systems. In: Proceedings of the Sixth International Conference on Information, Intelligence, Systems and Applications (IISA 2015) (2015)

Jarzombek, M.M.: Architecture of First Societies: A Global Perspective. John Wiley & Sons Inc., New Jersey (2013)

Jrad, R.B.N.: A roadmap for upgrading unupgradable legacy processes in inter-organizational middleware systems. In: 2014 IEEE Eighth International Conference on Research Challenges in Information Science (RCIS), pp. 1–6 (2014)

Jrad, R.B.N., Ahmed, M.D., Sundaram, D.: Upgrading unupgradable middleware legacy processes: misconceptions, challenges, and a roadmap. In: Proceedings of SEM 2013: 1st International Workshop in Software Evolution and Modernization, vol. 1(1), p. 8 (2013)

Jrad, R.B.N., Ahmed, M.D., Sundaram, D.: Insider action design research: a multi-methodological information systems research approach. In: Research Challenges in Information Science (RCIS), pp. 28–30. IEEE Comput. Soc., Marrakech (2014)

Jrad, R.B.N., Sundaram, D.: Challenges of inter-organizational information and middleware system projects: agility, complexity, success, and failure. In: Proceedings of the Sixth International Conference on Information, Intelligence, Systems and Applications (IISA 2015) (2015a)

Jrad, R.B.N., Sundaram, D.: Inter-organizational information and middleware system projects: success, failure, complexity, and challenges. In: Americas Conference on Information Systems (AMCIS), p. 12. Communications of the AIS, Puerto Rico (2015b)

Jrad, R.B.N., Sundaram, D.: Inter-organizational middleware systems: a framework for managing change. In: Proceedings of the Sixth International Conference on Information, Intelligence, Systems and Applications (IISA 2015) (2015c)

Kotusev, S., Storey, I.: Consolidating enterprise architecture management research. In: Bui, T.X., Sprague Jr., R.H. (eds.) 48th Hawaii International Conference on System Sciences (HICSS), pp. 4069–4078 (2015)

Levina, O., Stantchev, V.: Realizing event-driven SOA. In: Proceedings of the 2009 4th International Conference on Internet and Web Applications and Services, ICIW 2009, pp. 37–42 (2009)

Maréchaux, J.-L.: Combining Service-Oriented Architecture and Event-Driven Architecture Using an Enterprise Service Bus. IBM Developer Works, pp. 1–8, March 2006

McGovern, J., Sims, O., Jain, A., Little, M.: Enterprise Service Oriented Architectures: Concepts, Challenges, Recommendations (2006)

Niemann, K.D.: Enterprise Architecture at Work: Modelling, Communication, and Analysis. Springer, Heidelberg (2006)

Oxford. Oxford Dictionaries (2014)

Winter, R., Fischer, R.: Essential layers, artifacts, and dependencies of enterprise architecture. In: Proceedings - 2006 10th IEEE International Enterprise Distributed Object Computing Conference Workshops, EDOCW2006, pp. 1–12, May 2006

Zachman, J.: A framework for information systems architecture. IBM Syst. J. **26**(3), 276–292 (1987)

Twitter Sentiment Analysis Using Binary Classification Technique

B.N. Supriya[1], Vish Kallimani[2(✉)], S. Prakash[3], and C.B. Akki[1]

[1] Department of ISE, SJBIT, Bangalore 560060, India
[2] UTP, Seri Iskandar, Malaysia
knowvp@gmail.com
[3] Department of CSE, Dayanand Sagar University, Bangalore 560078, India

Abstract. The popularity of World Wide Web has brought a latest way of expressing the sentiments of individuals. Millions of users express their sentiments on Twitter, making it a precious platform for analyzing the public sentiment. This paper proposes a 3-step algorithm for sentiment analysis. Cleaning, Entity identification, and Classification are the 3 steps. Finally we measure the performance of the classifier using recall, precision and accuracy.

Keywords: Sentiment analysis · Recall · Precision · Heterogeneous Architecture Research Platform (HARP)

1 Introduction

During the previous years, the web has become a huge source of user-generated content. When we searched for keyword "social network" on Google, we get a hit of about 617000000 in just 0.37 s as on 09/06/2015 at 12:15 pm which speaks about its popularity.

A social network is a structure, made up of a specific group of individuals or organizations, that allow users to come closer, communicate and share information. Jacob Moreno is credited with developing the first sociograms in 1930 s to study interpersonal relationships. SixDegrees launched in 1997 was the first recognizable social network site [1]. Further, many sites like Asian Avenue, Black Planet, Ryze, Friendster, MySpace, Hi5, YouTube, Facebook, supporting various combinations of profiles publicly articulated friends were launched [1].

In contemporary, explosive growth of online social media microblogs have become a quick and easy online information sharing platform. These platforms generate rich and timely information (reviews, comments, ratings, feedbacks etc.) that requires informational filtering down to successful relevant topics and events. Twitter launched in 2009, is one such extremely popular micro blogging site where millions of users express themselves, give opinion and gets feedback via a short text message called tweets. Over 240 million tweets are being generated by the tweeter per day. This available voluminous data is being used for making decisions for enhancing profitability or for purpose. Processing of such large amount of heterogeneous data in an

© ICST Institute for Computer Sciences, Social Informatics and Telecommunications Engineering 2016
P.C. Vinh et al. (Eds.): ICTCC 2016, LNICST 168, pp. 391–396, 2016.
DOI: 10.1007/978-3-319-46909-6_36

effort to uncover hidden pattern, unknown correlations gave birth to a field called as sentiment analysis.

Sentiment analysis is one of the newest research areas in computer science. Sentiment analysis is a natural language processing technique to extract polarity and subjectivity from semantic orientation which refers to the strength of words and polarity text or phrases [2]. The sentiments can be categorized into positive and negative words [7, 8]. There are two main approaches for extracting sentiment automatically which are the lexicon-based approach and machine-learning based approach [2–6].

2 Related Work

Contemporary Sarlan et al. [9] describes the design of a sentiment analysis, extracting a vast amount of tweets. This paper explains the different approaches, techniques available for sentiment analysis and also focuses on the application requirements, functionalities of developing the twitter sentiment analysis application.

Alec Go et al. [10] introduces a novel approach for classifying the sentiments of twitter message using distant supervision. In this approach the data which consists of tweets with emotions are used as noisy labels. This paper also describes the accuracy of the different machine learning algorithms.

Jiguang Liang et al. [11] introduces a sentiment classification method called AS_LDA which assumes that words in subjective documents are of two parts sentiment element words and auxiliary words. These words are further sampled according to the topics. Gibbs sampling is used to verify the performance of this model.

Harshil T. Kanakia et al. [12] proposes a method called as Twitilizer to perform the classification of tweets into positive and negative tweets using Naive Bayes classifier. This method collects the tweets from the twitter and stores it into the persistent medium. The tweets are further pre-processed to the required format. The features are then extracted by removing the stop words and punctuations from the tweet. The sentiment property returns the polarity and subjectivity of the tweets. The displays of top positive and negative sentiments are obtained by the ranking algorithm. The results are tabulated and shown statistically.

Vadim kagsn et al. [13] uses the sentiment analysis technique for forecasting the 2013 Pakistan and 2014 Indian elections. This technique was used to predict who the prime minister would be. They considered 3 leading candidates from the politics in the dataset. The datasets were collected from Resselaer Polytechnic Institute and a Twitter Indian Election Network tool was built. Later the data was analyzed using the diffusion estimation model. The estimated results were found to be correct when compared with the actual election results. This paper also concludes that twitter can be a good measure for public sentiment on election related issues.

Li Bing et al. [14] analyzed that lot of work still needs to be done on summarization and analysis techniques for social data. Motivated by this problem the authors proposed a matrix-based fuzzy algorithm called FMM system, to mine the twitter data. The paper concludes that the problem of Li Bing et al. [14] analyzed that lot of work still needs to be done on summarization and analysis techniques for social data. Motivated by this problem the authors proposed a matrix-based fuzzy algorithm called FMM system, to mine the twitter data. The paper concludes that the problem of handling big data for data mining can be solved using FMM algorithm that adapts map reduce framework and also the speed of the execution can be increased significantly. The author has intensively worked on stock price movement through FMM system and his results are with high prediction accuracy.

Farhan Hassan khan et al. [15] presents a novel algorithm which classifies twits into positive, negative and neutral feelings. This paper gives us a distinct method for pre-processing when compared with [12]. In this algorithm the collected twitter streaming APIs are refined using different pre-processing task that removes slangs and abbreviations. The classification of the tweets is done by using the techniques such as emoticon analysis, Bag of words and SentiWordNet. The result of the algorithm shows the increase in the accuracy, precision, recall, f-measure when compared with other techniques. The framework is also further enhanced by using visual analysis of classified tweets location that is drawn on the map.

Many researchers have proposed different algorithm in recent years in order to classify the sentiments in the tweets. These researchers focused on the text mining in order to determine the sentiments. The study of existing research shows that the sentiment analysis results are not convincing.

3 Sentiment Analysis on Social Media Text

With the exponential growth of many social media such as Facebook, Flickr, Google+ etc., twitter has emerged as one of the most influential online social media service. These multiple media social networks generate a variety of data like text, video or visual etc. Our research mainly concentrates on the sentiment analysis of text only. For analysing textual sentiments, the following 3-step algorithm is being discussed here

The proposed 3-step algorithm consists of following steps:

Step 1: Input the tweet into HARP.

Step 2: Data Cleaning

The raw data that has been collected from the source will be cleaned as below:

- Check for the terms and their frequencies: The tweets may contain a single word or word n-grams. Their frequencies or presence are checked.
- Retweets and Duplicated tweets are removed
- Usernames if included should be integrated with the symbol @ before the name. Further Hash-tags and user names must be identified.
- Users often include the URL's in their tweets. This URL's must be converted to equivalent classes.
- All the text present in the tweets must be converted to a single format (Higher to lower case or vice versa).
- Spell check must be done and must be corrected if there is any.
- Stop words are deleted from the tweets.
- Slangs and abbreviations are corrected.

Step 3: Entity Identification

The cleaned data obtained from step 2 can contain a lot of distinctive properties like actors, target objects, nouns, adjectives, kinds of sentences etc. These properties are termed as entities. The identification of these entities is the task of step 3. This can be achieved as given below:

- The actors, target objects can be identified by named entity recognition and relation extraction method. The emotions can be identified by the database created manually.
- A speech tagger can be applied to a tweet which identifies the kinds of sentences.
- A part of speech tagging must be applied to a tweet that identifies the noun, verb, adjectives, adverb, interjection, conjunction, pronoun, pre-position.

Step 4: Classification

This step takes the input from the entity identification and classifies the words as positive or negative. Once the topic classification has been done, we can apply the binary classification for given data, where positive word (pw) can be initialized to 1, and negative words (nw) can be initialized to 0.

Step 5: Calculate the sentiments

Once the words are classified, the number of positive and the negative words are counted. We then check the result set (rs) by using

Rs = (tpw – tnw) / total no of words (tw).

Where tpw = total positive words,

tnw = total negative words.

$$rs = \begin{cases} Positive\ tweet,\ rs \geq 0 \\ Negative\ tweet,\ rs < 0 \end{cases}$$

The Fig. 1 shows the flow chart for the proposed algorithm

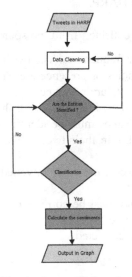

Fig. 1. Proposed flowchart

The performance of the proposed algorithm can be evaluated using accuracy, precision, recall measures.

Accuracy is defined as the ratio between correctly classified tweets from proposed classifier and manually labelled tweets. The formula for the same is

$$\text{Accuracy} = (\text{tn} + \text{tp}) / (\text{tn} + \text{fp} + \text{fn} + \text{tp})$$

Where tn = true negative, tp = true positive, fp = false positive, fn = false negative.

Precision is defined as the ratio between true positive (tp) and both true positive (tp) and false positive (fp). The formula for the same is

$$\text{Precision} = \text{tp} / (\text{tp} + \text{fp})$$

Recall is defined as the ratio between true positive and both true positive and false negative (fn). The formula for the same is

$$\text{Recall} = \text{tp} / (\text{tp} + \text{fn}).$$

4 Conclusion

In this paper, we propose a 3-step algorithm for efficient sentiment analysis. The first step cleans the data, the second step identifies the different entities and the last step uses the binary classifier to classify the tweets as positive or negative. The result can be shown through the graphs and the performance can be calculated using recall, precision and accuracy. The proposed method is simple and we expect to get better performance when compared to the other methods available in the literature however the experiment is yet to be performed.

References

1. Boyd, D.M., Ellison, N.B.: Social network sites: definition, history, and scholarship. J. Comput.-Mediat. Commun. **13**, 210–230 (2008)
2. Taboada, M., Brooke, J., Tofiloski, M., Voll, K., Stede, M.: Lexicon-Based Methods for Sentiment Analysis. Association for Computational Linguistics (2011)
3. Annett, M., Kondrak, G.: A comparison of sentiment analysis techniques: polarizing movie blogs. In: Conference on Web Search and Web Data Mining (WSDM). Department of Computing Science, University of Alberia (2009)
4. Goncalves, P., Benevenuto, F., Araujo, M., Cha, M.: Comparing and Combining Sentiment Analysis Methods (2013)
5. Kouloumpis, E., Wilson, T., Moore, J.: Twitter sentiment analysis: the good the bad and the OMG!. In: International AAAI, vol. 5 (2011)
6. Sharma, S.: Application of support vector machines for damage detection in structure. J. Mach. Learn. Res. (2008)

7. Saif, H., He, Y., Alani, H.: Semantic sentiment analysis of twitter. In: Proceeding of the Workshop on Information Extraction and Entity Analytics on Social Media Data. Knowledge Media Institute, United Kingdom (2011)
8. Prabowo, R., Thelwall, M.: Sentiment analysis: a combined approach. In: International World Wide Web Conference Committee (IW3C2). University of Wolverhampton, United Kingdom (2009)
9. Sarlan, A., Nadam, C., Basri, S.: Twitter sentiment analysis. In: International Conference on Information Technology and Multimedia (ICIMU), 18–20 November 2014
10. Go, A., Bhayani, R., Huang, L.: Twitter Sentiment Classification using distant Supervision (2009)
11. Liang, J., Liu, P., Tan, J., Bai, S.: Sentiment classification based on AS-LDA model. Inf. Technol. Quant. Manag., Proc. Comput. Sci. **31**, 511–551 (2014). doi:10.1016/j.procs.2014.05.296
12. Kanakia, H.T., Kalbande, D.R.: Twitilyzer: designing an approach for ad-hoc search engine. In: International Conference on Communication, Information & Computing Technology (ICCICT), 16–17 January 2015
13. Kagan, V., Stevens, A., Subrahmanian, V.S.: Using twitter sentiment to forecast the 2013 Pakistani Election and the 2014 Indian Election. IEEE Intell. Syst. (2015)
14. Li, B., Chan, K.C.C.: A fuzzy logic approach for opinion mining on large scale twitter data. In: IEEE/ACM 7th International Conference on Utility and Cloud Computing (2014). doi:978-1-4799-7881-6/14
15. Khan, F.H., Qamar, U., Javed, M.Y.: SentiView: a visual sentiment analysis framework. In: 2014 IEEE International Conference on Information Society (i-Society 2014). doi:978-1-908320-38/4

Author Index

Printed in the United States
By Bookmasters